D1195539

Writing/Disciplinarity

A Sociohistoric Account of Literate Activity in the Academy

Rhetoric, Knowledge, and Society

A Series of Monographs Edited by
Charles Bazerman

Writing/Disciplinarity

A Sociohistoric Account of Literate Activity in the Academy

Paul A. Prior
University of Illinois at Urbana-Champaign

LEA LAWRENCE ERLBAUM ASSOCIATES, PUBLISHERS
1998   Mahwah, New Jersey   London

Lawrence Erlbaum Associates, Inc., Publishers
10 Industrial Avenue
Mahwah, NJ 07430

Cover design by Kathryn Houghtaling Lacey

Library of Congress Cataloging-in-Publication Data

Writing/disciplinarity : a sociohistoric account of literate activity in the academy / Paul A. Prior
    p. cm.
    Includes bibliographical references and indexes.
    ISBN 0–8058–2296–8 (alk. paper)
    1. English language—Rhetoric—Study and teaching—Social Aspects.   2. Interdisciplinary approach in education—Social aspects. 3. Academic writing—Study and teaching—Social Aspects. 4. Communication in the social sciences—Social aspects. 5. Communication in the humanities—Social aspects. 6. Communication in science—Social aspects. 7. Written communication—Social Aspects. I. Title
    PE1404.P655   1998
    808' .042' 07—dc21   97–50354
                                         CIP

Books published by Lawrence Erlbaum Associates are printed on acid-free paper, and their bindings are chosen for strength and durability.

Printed in the United States of America

10 9 8 7 6 5 4 3 2 1

Contents

Editor's Introduction

Charles Bazerman
University of California, Santa Barbara

Writing is a constant struggle, as we project a text by considering multiple resources, memories, and experiences; conversations with colleagues and mentors; perceived restrictions imposed by genre, audience, and occasion; our attitudes and desires; and a thousand other considerations that bear on the moment of articulating our thought. Some of these forces consciously weigh, whereas others appear without our reflecting. Some we manage to harmonize and coordinate with each other, whereas others are just there, almost by happenstance within proximity of the others. In the end, if we are lucky and persistent, we have something neatened up enough to put into an envelope and give the appearance of a completed product. When I was in college more than a few years ago, a friend of mine (whose name I no longer remember) wrote a poem on the elegant symmetry of a paper clip, ending with the line, "our words do not deserve such grace."

Paul Prior perceives the apparent coherence of a completed text as the result of a mangle of practice and the lamination of experience—terms borrowed from Andrew Pickering and Erving Goffman. Prior, through his ethnography, reveals the complexity of experience of writing we always struggle with, as we try to press too much together with the hope that somehow the cloth will hold. This represents the first half of his compound title *Writing/Disciplinarity*.

However, in the writing is also the creation of *Disciplinarity*, the second half of Prior's language. As these graduate students write, they socialize themselves into a discipline. They inscribe themselves and are inscribed as disciplined scholars and, in interaction with their professors and peers, they influence the disciplinarity of each other. At sufficient distance, disciplines appear to be coherent, bounded, ordered wholes, made up of well-focused individuals engaged in distinctive practices and the distinctive texts they produce. However, Paul Prior reminds us that up close all those people are struggling with the mangle of practice and the lamination of experience, trying to produce something that will represent their contribution to an ever-changing disciplinary space constantly being recreated by the utterances of people just like them. Despite the institutional force of disciplines that impress on us their solidarity, they are liquid; if you look closely with Prior, what you see is a process of disciplinarity as people write themselves into authorship.

This sophisticated and precise study reveals people in the process of becoming—within the context of their chosen fields, their mentors, their peers, and their research experiences. Paul Prior reveals graduate education is nothing so neat as the training of individuals in a fixed and disciplined practice. It is rather the messy production of persons in situations, a process as much determined by the persons who inhabit the situation of graduate students as by the professors who may mistakenly believe they control more than a small (although influential) part of the situation.

However, Prior shows us something more than why graduate students may feel wrung out after they are put through the mangle of practice. Writing is draining to all of us, and we are all constantly being produced as authors by the situations we find ourselves in and put ourselves into—situations we only understand in their complex laminations and contingency as we come to live through and try to address them within the mangle of our writing. By constantly engaging in the process of disciplinarity through writing ourselves into disciplinary being, we rewrite ourselves and rewrite those around us who share the disciplines we believe we subscribe to.

Paul Prior, by disciplined research, provides as rich a picture of the writing experience of graduate students he studies as we experience within ourselves. In doing so, he helps us articulate why writing is so hard—and so rewarding. This is a remarkable book.

Preface

Writing/Disciplinarity represents the culmination of more than a decade of observation, thinking, research, reading, discussion, and writing. Its roots stretch back to the mid-1980s, when I taught academic reading, writing, and conversation in an English as a second language (ESL) program at the University of Wisconsin–Madison. Working with a very multicultural, multilingual, and multidisciplinary group of undergraduate and graduate students, I became increasingly interested in the question of what kinds of communicative competence, particularly in relation to writing, these students needed to be successful in their academic work. At that time, the literature in applied linguistics and the rhetoric of the disciplines typically analyzed published professional writing (e.g., Bazerman, 1988; Swales & Najjar, 1987) or indirect accounts of the types of writing (e.g., long research papers or lab reports) that students did for classes (e.g., Bridgeman & Carlson, 1983; Horowitz, 1986b; Johns, 1981). As exciting and provocative as those analyses were, what I did not find at first were situated studies of the writing students actually did in courses, of how expectations for the form and content of that writing were communicated, and of how that writing was assessed by faculty. Eventually, I did locate a few studies (e.g., Herrington, 1985, 1988; McCarthy, 1987) from that period that had begun to investigate writing tasks situated in particular university classes. Taking up that line of research, I began in 1989 a series of situated studies of writing in graduate seminars.

Although my research began with practical questions about how writing tasks were communicated, negotiated, performed, and assessed, I soon found myself asking basic questions about classroom communication, writing, learning, disciplinary socialization, and disciplines themselves. As I examined situated writing processes and the relationship of that writing to students' socialization into disciplinary communities, I turned increasingly to sociohistoric and practice theories (e.g., Bakhtin, 1981, 1986; Lave & Wenger, 1991; Vygotsky, 1978, 1987; Wertsch, 1991). I also altered the methodological designs of my studies as I moved to address new questions.

In analyzing the four seminars on which I report in this book (seminars in language education, geography, American studies, and sociology), I have pursued three interconnected lines of inquiry: Developing situated case studies of writing and disciplinary practices; working reflexively to refine methodology (ways of collecting, analyzing, and writing up data); and exploring theoretical frameworks, asking both how sociohistoric theories could illuminate the case studies and how the case studies might in turn inform sociohistoric theories.

Given the confluence of social, developmental, epistemological, and rhetorical issues that can intersect in any study of writing and disciplines in the academy, scholarship in this field has been predictably diverse, with a wide array of objects of study, empirical tools, theoretical perspectives, and disciplinary positionings. The field includes rhetorical interpretations of historical texts in the sciences; close ethnographic examination of how students talk, write, and learn in undergraduate classrooms; context-sensitive analysis of publication processes in the disciplines; genre analysis of non-native speakers of English writing research papers; and protocol studies of students and professionals reading and writing in quasi-naturalistic settings.

To locate my work in this multifaceted field, I would situate it in several ongoing conversations. First, *Writing/Disciplinarity* covers topics of traditional interest to researchers, theorists, and practitioners in writing, composition, and rhetorical studies. The case studies and theory examine writing processes (particularly response and revision), task representation, genre, authorship, and the linkages of individual discourse to social contexts. Because this research is centered in graduate seminars in the disciplines and analyzes the writing of both native and non-native speakers of English, it is particularly linked to work in Writing Across the Curriculum, English for Academic Purposes, and the Rhetoric of the Disciplines. Finally, this book takes up a practice-oriented approach to language, knowledge, and social life. It draws on and is intended to contribute to the cross-disciplinary field of practice theories that includes inquiry in cultural psychology, activity theory, and socially distributed cognition; the microsociologies of science, technology, and face-to-face interaction; contextualized rhetorics of disciplines and professions; anthropological studies of cultural practices; and the ethnography of communication.

CLOSE ENCOUNTERS WITH WRITING AND DISCIPLINARITY

This book presents a series of case studies—thick descriptions of the contexts and processes of graduate students' writing. This kind of close attention to histories of textual production is usually reserved, if given at all, for prominent works and authors (literary, political, scientific). Some readers may wonder if it is worthwhile to delve into the detailed motives, contexts, and activities of graduate student writers and their professors. I have found this kind of attention critical, not only because it produces a baseline description of what happens in these contexts, but also because that description poses a challenge to both everyday and specialized accounts of writing, learning, and knowledge construction. In other words, these close encounters with situated practices suggest the need to rethink conventional concepts and narratives of writing and disciplinarity.

From Writing to Literate Activity

Usual representations of writing collapse time, isolate persons, and filter activity (e.g., "I wrote the paper over the weekend"). Actually, writing happens in moments that are richly equipped with tools (material and semiotic) and populated with others (past, present, and future). When seen as situated activity, writing does not stand alone as the discrete act of a *elaboration* writer, but emerges as a confluence of many streams of activity: reading, talking, observing, acting, making, thinking, and feeling as well as transcribing words on paper. Close encounters of this kind with writing also challenge conventional notions of authorship, captured so well in that impossible but often repeated formula for avoiding plagiarism,"put it in your own words." Even given my agreement with the Bakhtinian view that our words and ideas are borrowed (or rented or stolen) from others' mouths and texts, I was surprised to see how thoroughly individual authorship is compromised and distributed in practice, how many voices and moments of activity buoy and flow through the apparently fixed, one-dimensional words of a page. Tracing processes of writing situated within multiple streams of historical activity led to one of the central contentions of this book: "Writing" is too partial, too contextually thin, a unit of analysis. Drawing on sociohistoric theories as well as situated research into writing, I argue explicitly in theory and implicitly in the content of the case studies for an alternative unit, *literate activity*.

From Entering a Discourse Community
to Participating in Communities of Practice

Our usual notions of learning a discipline are grounded in metaphors of entering a discourse community. Everyday references to "going into" a field, metonymic expressions like "psychology has explored," and more specialized analyses of disciplinary discourse communities have been grounded in images of disciplines as unified social territories or abstract systems of codified knowledge. Such accounts, however, become difficult to sustain under situated examination. Even in advanced seminars, academic writing tasks (typically glossed as "the assignment") appear not as a single shared task with definite criteria of assessment, but as a collage of task representations and actions, at best roughly coordinated by selective points of resemblance. At this level of analysis, disciplines appear as very human moments, in which hybrid actions and understandings weave together personal, interpersonal, artifactual, institutional, and sociocultural as well as disciplinary histories.[1] In this view, graduate students are not entering the autonomous social and cognitive spaces of discourse communities, but engaging in active relations with dynamic, open, interpenetrated communities of practice (to use Lave & Wenger's, 1991, terms). Disciplinary enculturation then refers not to novices being initiated, but to the continual processes whereby an ambiguous cast of relative newcomers and relative old-timers (re)produce themselves, their practices, and their communities.[2] These images of participation in disciplinary practices point to doing things rather than having something or being someplace; they suggest a process view of disciplines; hence, a second key term in this analysis is *disciplinarity*.

The Sociogenesis of Disciplinarity

Disciplinary communities of practice are critical sites of sociohistoric development and should be critical sites of inquiry. Over the past century, disciplines, subdisciplines, and interdisciplines have proliferated, producing a dense jungle of texts, technical objects, practices, and encultured persons. They have co-evolved with thick institutional networks, including university departments and programs; government, corporate, and academic think-tanks, laboratories, and institutes; local, regional, national, and international associations and agencies; and government and private

---

[1]By sociocultural, I am thinking of Giddens' (1984) representation of the macrosocial in terms of what is widely dispersed and influential in time and space (e.g., general and specialized symbolic codes, bodies of knowledge/practice, material and technological structures and resources, social and economic structures and practices, and demographic and ecological trends and states).

[2]Use of the parenthetic prefix *(re)* with produce, and other terms, is a shorthand way to signal the simultaneous blend of continuity and change, in this case, of reproduction and production.

grantors. Scientific, technological, and cultural disciplines have been linked to radical and global changes in our daily lives. However, sociology, anthropology, and education have historically directed their attention away from such privileged Western sites and practices. Respectively, they have focused instead on the social practices of marginalized groups at home, exotic cultures globally, and early education in schools. As one reflection of this orientation, extensive research on situated talk and literacy in the early years at home as well as in elementary and secondary classrooms has been active since the 1970s (e.g., in the work of scholars such as Courtney Cazden, Anne Dyson, Sarah Freedman, Shirley Brice Heath, Hugh Mehan, and Sarah Michaels). However, only in the last decade has a relative scattering of situated studies of discourse and graduate education appeared (e.g., Berkenkotter, Huckin, & Ackerman, 1988, 1991; Blakeslee, 1997; Casanave, 1992, 1995; Chin, 1994; Jacoby & Gonzales, 1991; Ochs, Jacoby, & Gonzales, 1994; Prior, 1991, 1994).[3]

The most sustained and developed inquiry into disciplines has focused on science and technology studies (e.g., Bazerman, 1988, in press; Collins, 1985; Knorr-Cetina, 1981; Latour 1987, 1996; Myers, 1990; Pickering, 1995); however, these studies have generally taken professional practice as the starting point, asking, for example, how physicists do their work rather than how they become physicists. A basic methodological principle of sociohistoric research (see Luria, 1932; Vygotsky, 1987, 1997; Wertsch, 1991) is that mature practices are heavily abbreviated, presuppositional, and tacit. To make such practices visible, it is necessary to examine them in non-routine use, in development as relative newcomers are learning them, or when routine functional systems are disrupted. To study the sociogenesis of disciplinarity, that is, to understand both its mature practices and how those practices are developed, graduate education is a strategic site, and writing, a strategic domain of practice. In graduate schools, writing is a focal activity, providing opportunity spaces for (re)socialization of discursive practices and mediating the (re)production of disciplinary communities of practice (e.g., as students attain relative levels of success through course writing, institutional examination, and disciplinary publication).

OVERVIEW OF *WRITING/DISCIPLINARITY*

The core of this book features case studies offering thick descriptions of

---

[3]Becker, Greer, Hughes, and Strauss' (1961) study of medical school is an important exception to this trend, but paid limited attention to discourse.

graduate work, of talk in seminars, of students' representations and processes of writing, of their draft and final texts, of professors' representations
of tasks, and of their responses to students. These case studies are presented
in terms that remain close to the participants' perspectives. They include
samples of participants' texts and transcripts of seminar and interview talk.
The overall sociohistoric framework that has informed, and been elaborated
in, this research is concentrated in chapters 1 and 5. However, the case studies
also develop and illustrate specific theoretical notions (e.g., semiotic genres
in chap. 3, authoritative and internally persuasive discourse in chap. 8).
Finally, methodological reflections on research are woven throughout all of
the chapters, whether it is in considering how structuralist theories of
discourse communities have shaped research into academic writing in chapter 1, or the detailed display of method and analysis presented as part of the
case study offered in chapter 8. Particularly intense methodological reflections appear at the end of the book, in the final section (chap. 9 and 10), and
in Appendix A. These three lines of inquiry (case studies, theory, and
methodological reflexivity) interanimate one another throughout this book.

Chapter 1 introduces the basic theoretical framework of the book. It
begins with a critical analysis of the structuralist assumptions embedded in
the notion of discourse communities, a notion that has shaped theory and
research on writing in the disciplines. It then presents the alternative
premises of sociohistoric theories. Finally, it constructs a framework for
exploring writing and disciplinarity as functional systems of activity.

The next section of the book offers thick descriptions of academic writing
tasks. With data drawn from studies of three seminars (in education,
geography, and American studies), it explores relations among classroom
interactions, writing, response, and disciplinary enculturation. Chapter 2
reports on my first full study of academic writing tasks in a seminar.
Analysis of the ways representations and practices varied across times,
contexts, and participants led to a recognition that the students and the
professor were coordinating what amounted to multiple writing tasks, not
doing a single task. As I traced the microhistory of these writing tasks, how
they were cued, interpreted, negotiated, undertaken, read, and responded
to, I ended up with the question of how to reconcile the complexity made
visible in the analysis with the basically routine character of the seminar
from participants' perspectives. Chapter 3 takes up that question in terms of
the central notion of typification, the way people orient and are oriented to
the routine and recognizable in their own and other's actions. Typification
has been the cornerstone of recent theories of genre. Working from Bakhtin's

notion of typified utterances (speech genres), I propose a notion of semiotic genres, constituted by situated, mediated activity and involving signifying practices in the broadest sense, not only intentional communication. Focusing on the ways topics contextualized students' texts and activities, the chapter analyzes how graduate students and the professor co-produced the semiotic genres of the seminar assignments.

The case studies of chapters 2 and 3 display a marked diversity of tasks and texts in each seminar and suggest the tenuous nature of intersubjectivity. This heterogeneity raises the question of how experiences in seminars are linked to form a trajectory of disciplinary enculturation. Chapter 4 then takes up the question of longer-term trajectories of participation in communities of practice. After characterizing three modes of participation in graduate study (passing, procedural display, and deep participation), I compare the work of two international students from the production of research proposals in the language education seminar (analyzed in chap. 2) to the completion of their master's theses. Although each student is awarded the master's degree, their trajectories of participation appear to be radically different. Finding that one student used source texts in her master's thesis in a way that would almost certainly be labeled plagiarism, the analysis raises the question of how different forms of appropriation should be understood from a developmental and dialogic perspective.

The third section of the book (chaps. 5–8) explores ways to link literate activity, the social distribution of authorship, and disciplinary enculturation. Chapter 5 analyzes conventional images of writing and authorship and considers theoretical resources for rethinking those notions. After describing five prototypical scenes that have powerfully shaped research on writing in the academy and disciplines, the chapter turns to theories that disrupt conventional representations, particularly taking up Goffman's (1981) discussion of footings, LeFevre's (1987) delineation of the social bases for invention, and Wertsch's (1991) notions of mediated action and mediated agency. This chapter elaborates the notions of literate activity and mediated authorship, which are then explored in chapters 6–8 with case studies of textual production and representation in a sociology seminar/research team that straddled the boundaries of school and discipline.

Chapter 6 provides vignettes of the complex processes involved as participants in the sociology seminar/research team talked about, wrote, and responded to texts while also negotiating representations of authorship. The analyses illustrate the complex and sometimes problematic relations between histories of textual production and the representation of both authorship and non-authorship (exclusion or plagiarism). Where chapter 6 examines the situated complexities of collaborative authorship, chapter 7 takes up the difficulty of moving beyond individuals, even acting collaboratively, to a notion of mediated authorship that incorporates the agency sedimented in mediational tools. Sociohistoric research and science studies alike have addressed this kind of challenge by tracing the histories of tools to see what presuppositions and affordances have been built in along the way. Chapter 7 pursues this strategy to explore ways that one student's authorship in the sociology seminar was mediated by a blend of artifacts, practices, people, and institutions.

Chapter 8 continues to focus on the notion of mediated authorship, asking not only how texts get produced and their authorship represented, but how these processes constitute situated learning, in this case, disciplinary enculturation. It presents a microhistory of a series of response–revision rounds between a sociology graduate student and her professor as the student works on a conference paper and related preliminary examination. Initial analyses of the texts revealed that the professor's responses often involved rewriting as well as commentary and that the student routinely incorporated that rewritten text into subsequent drafts. This chapter then narrates how a mix of theoretical concepts (Bakhtin's notions of authoritative and internally persuasive discourse) and methodological strategies (intertextual analysis and parallel discourse-based interviewing) was employed to explore what these texts meant to the student and the professor, how they indexed and constituted situated negotiations over knowledge, identity, and community. Finally, it draws together the analyses and discussions of the preceding chapters by connecting literate activity and mediated authorship to disciplinary enculturation.

The final section of the book is more reflexive, working to both summarize this research and forecast future directions. Chapter 9 takes up Bakhtin's notion of chronotopes (the subjectified and interpenetrated time–place worlds of embodied and representational activity) to uncover problematic assumptions embedded in research designs (including this one), particularly noting how privileged institutional perspectives define objects and sites of study. The value of this notion of chronotopes, for developing substantive accounts of literate activity as well as for methodological reflexivity, is illustrated through a detailed case study of a master's student in American studies and her writing across three seminars. The chapter concludes by suggesting ways to redraw the maps of research on writing in the disciplines.

Chapter 10 briefly summarizes the central findings that emerge from these studies and sketches a framework for future investigations of literate activity and disciplinarity. It then concludes with a reflexive exploration of some of the diverse streams of literate activity that shaped my analysis. Appendix A, in effect, extends this reflexivity, as it provides multiple images of the origins of the research and details some of the situated practices of data collection, analysis, and writing.

ACKNOWLEDGMENTS

Having argued that authorship is radically mediated and distributed, I turn to acknowledgments with a sense of how partially I can account for all the ways that my research and writing have been scaffolded. It would be reasonable to acknowledge, as I analyze in chapter 7, the many artifactual, practical, and institutional resources (everything from disciplinary discourses, microcomputers, and modern universities, to the English language and the counterculture movement of the 1960s) that contributed to the research and writing of this book. However, I will violate Latour's principle of symmetry here in the hope that things will not, yet at least, either expect or appreciate my acknowledgments.

First, I thank the anonymous students and professors of the four seminars, whose generous cooperation and openness made this research not only possible, but rewarding.

Second, I must acknowledge some of the many people who have contributed to my thinking and writing virtually through the older technologies of books and articles or the newer ones of e-mail and internet discussions (particularly XMCA sponsored by the Laboratory of Comparative Human Cognition at the University of California–San Diego). Included in this list are such historical figures such as Mikhail Bakhtin, Erving Goffman, A. N. Leont'ev, V. N. Voloshinov, and Lev Vygotsky, as well as a long list of contemporaries, including, but certainly not limited to, Jerome Bruner, Michael Cole, Yrjo Engestrom, Anne Herrington, William Hanks, Edwin Hutchins, Jean Lave, Bruno Latour, Karen Burke LeFevre, Elinor Ochs, Louise Phelps, Ragnar Rommetveit, Etienne Wenger, James Wertsch, and Stephen Witte.

Third, I wish to acknowledge at least some of that smaller circle of my contemporaries who I know personally and who have contributed directly and indirectly to the ideas and texts of this research. With apologies to any I have failed to include, I thank Chris Anson, Dennis Baron, Diane Belcher,

Carol Berkenkotter, Deborah Brandt, Lillian Bridwell-Bowles, Christine Pearson Casanave, Elaine Chin, Kathryn Evans, Gregory Colomb, Gail Hawisher, George Kamberelis, Dale Lange, Greg Myers, William Perry, John Swales, Constance Walker, and Patricia Webb. In the late stages of this project, I particularly appreciated the responses of Andrew Pickering to chapter 7 and the detailed reading and constructive critique David Russell provided to the penultimate manuscript. I owe a particular debt to Charles Bazerman, for blazing disciplinary trails, establishing the communicative forum of this series, and providing exceptional support and insightful response throughout the writing process.

In the closest circles of my life, I have been blessed with supportive and stimulating in-laws, Herbert and Jane Hengst and Randy and Joan Hengst. All of this book is predicated on the inestimable support of my mother, Marlys Prior, and grandmother, Mabel Hahlweg, who together nurtured me through thick and thin. Over the last ten years, Nora and Anna have illuminated my days (and often my nights) with their love, joys and sorrows, and insights that continue to teach me much about life. Finally, for 22 years, Julie Hengst has been my full partner in all spheres of activity. In addition to remarkable moral and material support, she has contributed to my thinking in general and to this specific text in innumerable substantive ways, only hinted at by the discussion in chapter 10 of the influence of her research. I dedicate this book with love and gratitude to P.J., Nora, Anna, and Julie.

—*Paul A. Prior*

PART I

Introduction

1

Resituating the Discourse Community: A Sociohistoric Perspective

(critique of structuralism)

The Ethnography of Communication, the Rhetoric of the Disciplines and Professions, English for Academic Purposes (EAP), and Writing Across the Curriculum (WAC) are loosely associated fields that have emerged over the past four decades and that have substantive interests in communicative practices of disciplinary and professional communities. From Toulmin's (1958) identification of field-specific forms of reasoning and argumentation to Hymes' (1971) notion that competence must be seen as communicative rather than linguistic and as grounded in diverse speech communities rather than national languages, these fields have been formed in opposition to the structuralist search for, or indeed assumption of, universal systems of rules that govern communication, thought, and action. However, rather than questioning the basic structuralist trope that abstract rule systems govern performance, these fields have generally challenged structuralist traditions on two other fronts. They have expanded the range of phenomena to be explained (e.g., rules of language use as well as language form), and they have multiplied the number and shrunk the jurisdictions of those abstract systemic governors. This balkanization of national and global systems of logic and language into speech and discourse communities has prompted close attention to, and real progress in, studies of communication, discourse, and rhetoric. However, it has also left intact a number of structuralist ways of doing business. Located on the borders of these fields, I began research on academic writing to explore the complex intersections of writing, response, classroom discourse, and disciplinary enculturation that arise as texts are imagined, produced, read, and deployed within graduate programs in the academy.

Initially, I accepted the basic notion that writing, reading, and knowledge are situated and learned within *discourse communities*, a central tenet of research into writing in disciplines and professions since the early 1980s. Over time, I became more and more aware of tensions and disjunctions between the ways I had framed my research and what I was finding. I traced a number of these tensions to structuralist tropes common in discussion of speech and discourse communities. An example of how structuralist tropes are reflected in research on discourse communities can be seen in the following excerpt from Walvoord and McCarthy's (1990) study of writing and thinking in four college classrooms:

> In this view, writing, like speaking is a social activity *that takes place within* speech communities and accomplishes meaningful social functions. In their characteristic "ways of speaking," community members *share accepted intellectual, linguistic and social conventions* which have developed over time and *govern spoken and written interaction.* ... *Newcomers to a community learn the rules for appropriate speaking and writing* gradually as they interact with competent members, and as they read and write texts deemed *acceptable* there. We chose to see the classroom within this theoretical frame.
>
> In our view, *when students enter a classroom, they are entering a discourse community in which they must master the ways of thinking and writing considered appropriate* in that setting and by their teacher. We also understand their writing to be at the heart of *their initiation into new academic communities*: it is both the means of discipline-based socialization and the eventual mark of competence. (p. 21 [italics added])

The spatial metaphors that equate disciplinary enculturation with *entering into a place*, the emphasis on the *shared* nature of *rules and conventions,* the trope that rules and conventions *govern* interaction, and normative allusions to "appropriate" behavior and "initiation," all mark a reliance on structuralist approaches to language, knowledge, and society, a basically territorial image that figures the discipline as both authoritative and unified. Walvoord and McCarthy do acknowledge conflicts, but the conflicts are only *between* ways of thinking and communicating appropriate to one community and ways appropriate to another.

As I began an initial pilot research project, this portrayal of discrete, consensual, rule-ordered discourse communities and their associated codes was being questioned theoretically. Harris (1989) and Cooper (1989) noted that notions of *community* tend to evoke an image of shared cozy unity (or perhaps oppressive authoritative unity). The issue, they argued, is not whether writing is a social activity, whether classrooms and the writing undertaken within them are involved in socialization processes, or whether social formations of some sort exist. The issue is how we conceptualize the social. Notions of complexly differentiated and conflictful societies also exist. Situated research into academic and disciplinary writing began to produce empirical findings that also complicated or questioned notions of discourse communities (Casanave, 1992, 1995; Chin, 1994; Chiseri-Strater, 1991; Myers, 1990; Prior, 1991, 1994).

This chapter presents a critical analysis of, and an alternative to, received structuralist notions of communication, knowledge, learning, and the person that are at the heart of the notion of discourse communities. First, I contrast structuralism to a sociohistoric approach and analyze structuralist influences in the formation of sociolinguistic notions of speech and discourse communities. I then examine how those influences have played out in the methods and findings of research on academic writing in the disciplines, looking specifically at Walvoord and McCarthy's (1990) research. Finally, I sketch a sociohistoric framework in which writing and disciplinarity are studied as situated, distributed, and mediated activity. This theoretical framework undergirds the close analyses in subsequent chapters of writing, response, classroom discourse, and disciplinary enculturation in four different graduate seminars.[1]

DUELING DICTIONARIES: SAUSSURE, RICOUER, AND BAKHTIN ON STRUCTURALISM

Language exists in the form of a sum of impressions deposited in the brain of each member of a community, almost like a dictionary of which identical copies have been distributed to each individual. ... Language exists in the individual, yet is common to all. Nor is it affected by the will of the depositaries. Its mode of existence is expressed by the formula: 1 + 1 + 1 + 1 ... = I (collective pattern).

—Saussure, 1959, p. 19

The work of Saussure has played a foundational role in 20th-century linguistics and semiotics. His image of language as an external dictionary impressed in the minds of its speakers is quintessentially structuralist. By structuralism, I do not mean the specific schools of linguistics and anthropology that have taken that name (although I would certainly label those schools as structuralist), nor am I referring to a general philosophy, some body of beliefs (although I certainly see structuralism as related to beliefs). Instead, I see structuralism as a confluence of a set of interpretive practices

---

[1]I should stress that this theoretical framework, both the critique of structuralism and the argument for a sociohistoric perspective, is very much a result of the research rather than part of its origins. Appendix A provides more detail on the history of the research.

for understanding the world with a set of rhetorical practices for constructing authority.

Structuralism, in this sense, involves three basic practices. The first is the development of an observational perspective, the constituting of a privileged research space that transcends the everyday and the common (de Certeau, 1984). Attaining this higher ground is a fundamental rhetorical move in constructing authority; it places the researcher and the research context outside of and above the phenomenon and its context (now figuratively "under study"). The second practice involves several forms of decontextualization and abstraction. The historical particularities of persons, places, and events are reduced to a simpler set of abstract typifications. Thus, for example, particular historic individuals may be recoded into types (male or female, expert or novice, an instance of one of a dozen income categories). In more radical forms of decontextualization, whole human actors are synecdochically displaced by algebraic formulae, black box cognitive graphics, and branching diagrams. Time and history are also backgrounded or removed in the linked processes of detemporalization and spatialization. Finally, as phenomena are abstracted and spatialized, projected onto the surface of a flat plane, certain elements or features are located in superordinate or causal (typically higher) positions, whereas other elements or features are deprivileged by being located in contingent (typically lower) positions. In Chomsky's tree diagrams (e.g., Chomsky, 1965), these practices can be seen in the decontextualized representation of language (as sentences without speakers or contexts), in the synoptic spatialization of temporal speech, in the visual and notational privileging of the sentence node as the prime mover of language, and in the trivialization of words as a kind of superficial epiphenomenon. The final practice involves government. Abstracted, spatialized, and hierarchicalized, a now closed and unified system of discrete and ordered elements is brought under the control of a set of rules that allow prediction and explanation. This final move closes the rhetorical circle of structuralism: The optical authority claimed in the first move is legitimated by the demonstrated authority of the final move.

Ricouer (1974) offers a careful analysis of the assumptions of structuralist theory in linguistics. He recalls Saussure's separation of the abstract system of language (*langue*), from situated historical speech (*parole*). Taking *langue* as the essence of language and *parole* as its disordered and distorted reflection, Saussure simultaneously constituted the system of language as an object and linguistics as a science. Ricouer describes how

Saussure defined synchrony as a state of language, diachrony as simply a change of states, and language as a closed system of signs, with significance only coming from difference, either between signs or internally within the sign. Ricouer (1974) argues that much was excluded in this construction of linguistics:

> The act of speaking is excluded not only as exterior execution, as individual performance, but as free combination, as producing new utterances. Now this is the essential aspect of language—properly speaking its goal. At the same time, history is excluded, and not simply the change from one state of system to another but the production of culture and of man in the production of his language. What Humboldt called production and what he opposed to the finished work is not solely diachrony, but rather the generation, in its profound dynamism, of the work of speech in each and every case. The structural point of view also excludes, along with free combination and generation, the primary intention of language, which is to say something about something. (pp. 83–84)

Finally, Ricouer notes that the speaking subject herself is excluded. Summing up the effects of these exclusions, he argues that structuralism's epistemological decision "to remain inside the closure of the universe of signs" creates an autonomous system that "does violence to linguistic experience" (pp. 84–85).

Voloshinov's (1973) Bakhtinian analysis of "abstract objectivism" provides a complementary summary and critique of structural linguistics.[2] Pointing to the historical development of linguistics as a science of dead languages, Voloshinov argues that linguistic systematization makes living languages dead, turning dynamic streams of polysemous language dispersed through time and space and across persons and social formations into a static system. In this systematization, word/signs full of social, ideological, and affective meaning, words spoken in concrete and particular situations, are turned into word/signals, emptied of all but a marginal, fixed denotative sense, uttered by no one, nowhere, no time. Voloshinov (1973) concludes:

> This system leads us away from the living dynamic reality of language and its social functions.... Underlying the theory of abstract objectivism are presuppositions of a rationalistic and mechanistic world outlook. These presuppositions are least capable of furnishing the grounds for a proper understanding of history—and language, after all, is a purely historical phenomena. (p. 83)

---

[2]Voloshinov (1973) also critically analyzes individual subjectivism (e.g., Humboldt) for its account of generation as individual expression without reference to sociohistoric forces.

Bakhtin and Ricouer are both critical of the structuralist assumptions and strategies of linguistics. Both argue against its abstraction, its conception of language as a closed system, its exclusion of the concrete historical utterances of speaking subjects. In seeking an alternative, both reverse Saussure's privileging of the system of language over the actuality of speech:

> For speech can exist in reality only in the form of concrete utterances of individual speaking people, speech subjects. Speech is always cast in the form of an utterance belonging to a particular speaking subject, and outside this form it cannot exist. (Bakhtin, 1986, p. 71)

> Someone speaks to someone—that is the essence of the act of communication. By this trait, the act of speech is opposed to the anonymity of the system. (Ricouer, 1974, p. 88)

Both also come to see the word as a critical site in reimagining language. Bakhtin sees the word as a contested space filled with multiple and conflicting senses, uses, indexical and intertextual connections, expressive and evaluative accents. The word is a field where socially and biographically positioned people struggle to produce meaning and identity. Ricouer notes that although the word, like the uttered sentence, is part of the transitory, actuality of speech, unlike the sentence, the word survives the utterance. Thus, he argues, the word travels between system and event, bringing structure to the event and contingency and change to the system.

In their accounts of the word, we can see that Bakhtin and Ricouer differ on one essential point: the status of the system. For Ricouer, the system remains an object to be accounted for. He is interested in bringing system and event together into a unified frame, mediated by a third force, the word. For Bakhtin, the system is an ephemeral social force, a posited system designed to exert centripetal (centralizing, unifying) pressures on language in use. In place of the system, Bakhtin offers historical chains of utterance, chains that simultaneously trace trajectories of individual lives and sociocultural histories. This divergence is expressed clearly in the two following quotes as Ricouer and Bakhtin construct very different roles for their metaphorical dictionaries (although both roles differ radically from the one suggested by Saussure in the quote that opens this section):

> In the dictionary, there is only the endless round of terms which are defined circularly, which revolve in the closure of the lexicon. But then someone speaks, someone says something. The word leaves the dictionary; it becomes word at the moment when man becomes speech, when speech becomes discourse and discourse a sentence. (Ricouer, 1974, p. 92)

> The word in language is half someone else's. It becomes "one's own" only when the speaker populates it with his own intentions, his own accent, when he appropriates the word, adapting it to his own semantic and expressive intention. Prior to this moment of appropriation, the word does not exist in a neutral and impersonal language (it is not, after all, out of a dictionary that the speaker gets his words!), but rather it exists in other people's mouths, in other people's contexts, serving other people's intentions: it is from there that one must take the word, and make it one's own. (Bakhtin, 1981, pp. 293–294)

Saussure's, Ricouer's, and Bakhtin's metaphorical dictionaries represent three positions on a continuum from structuralism to historicism.[3] What is definitive here is neither where the abstract system rests (whether the dictionary is at the level of local speech communities, national languages, or the species), nor the domain of knowledge—the metaphorical dictionary is supplemented by mental grammar books, pronunciation guides, manuals of rhetorical style, guides to etiquette, encyclopedias, and, as Clark (1992) notes, personal diaries. What defines these positions is the relationship each sets up between the historical activity of persons and abstract systems of knowledge and language. Saussure's view fully privileges an abstract, unified, almost Platonic realm of knowledge. Ricouer gives precedence to history, to the event, but sees an evolving system as an important source of tradition and structure for events. Bakhtin takes up a fully historical perspective, one in which situated historical activity has no outside.[4] Different positions on this continuum of system and history presuppose different theoretical, research, and practical orientations to communication, knowledge, and community.

SPEECH COMMUNITIES, DISCOURSE COMMUNITIES, AND RESEARCH DESIGNS

The history of the notion of discourse communities in writing studies is relatively clear. The focus on community emerged as part of a general reaction against cognitive accounts of writing processes based on laboratory research. In 1982, Bizzell, Heath, and Nystrand separately published arti-

---

[3]Coming from another tradition, experimental psycholinguistics, Clark (1992) criticizes theories of meaning built around metaphorical dictionaries in the brain: "I have argued against the traditional view of word meanings as fixed entities in a mental lexicon. I have suggested instead that word meanings are the result of a process. This process assesses the lexical and conceptual possibilities readily accessible in common ground at the moment and selects the most salient one" (p. 380).

[4]In this perspective, "decontextualized" knowledge and "literal" meaning are seen as products of specific sociocultural practices (see e.g., Linell, 1992; Minick, 1993; Rommetveit, 1988)

cles that related interest in the social contexts of writing/literacy to notions of community (see also Beach & Bridwell, 1984; Gere, 1980). Although Bizzell (1982) apparently coined the term *discourse community*, she never explicitly defined it. She talked about discourse communities in terms of conventions, habits of language use, "traditional, shared ways of understanding experience" (p. 217), shared expectations, and patterns of interaction with the world. Graphically, she represented discourse communities as partially overlapping circles beginning with the native discourse community of the home and extending to those formed in school, the workplace, and other (unnamed) sites. She referred to the university as the academic discourse community. Bizzell noted that discourse communities change over time and suggested that they always have internal fuzzy areas for personal initiative. Nystrand (1982) provided an extended analysis juxtaposing the notion of audience in rhetoric with the sociolinguistic notion of speech community, emphasizing particularly how we need to study both the ways that writers address audiences and the ways they acquire the resources (a community's accepted and understood ways of "speaking") to do so. Examining the diverse ways that oral and written varieties of language were socially organized in three micro-communities, Heath (1982) traced how patterns of home literacy played out in school literacy and success. Since the early 1980s, much has been written about social contexts of writing in general and discourse communities in particular. Instead of attempting to review this broad literature, I will reexamine the work of a critical link in the intellectual chain, Dell Hymes, a central source for Bizzell, Nystrand, and particularly Heath.

In the late 1960s and early 1970s, Hymes worked to channel the interest in and excitement about language that Chomsky (1957, 1965) had ignited beyond Chomsky's narrow interest in generative grammars and the abstract linguistic competence of ideal and perfect speaker-listeners in "completely homogeneous" language communities (Chomsky, 1965, p. 3). In challenging Chomsky, Hymes had to critique a foundational notion of linguistics, Saussure's *langue–parole* distinction, rearticulated by Chomsky in terms of competence and performance. For Saussure and most linguists of the 20th century, *parole* (performance) was essentially a disordered domain, a tangle of idiosyncratic choices and errors about which little of interest could be said. Hymes acknowledged the need for linguistic competence, but sought to broaden the notion of competence (and the object of language study) by arguing that people employed other kinds of tacit ordered knowledge in actually using language. One way of achieving his goal was to argue for the rule-governed nature of actual speech: "There are rules of use without which the rules of grammar would be useless" (Hymes, 1971, p. 10). Specifically, Hymes (1971) argued that language users need to employ tacit knowledge of whether and to what extent something is formally possible (linguistic competence), feasible, appropriate, and probable. The third term, the notion of social appropriateness, is probably the component of his approach to communicative competence that has been taken up the most: "Sentences will be seen as judged for acceptability in terms of their appropriateness under rules governing relations between scenes, participants, genres, channel, and the like—who can say what, in what way, where and when, by what means and to whom?" (p. 15). However, Hymes also emphasized knowledge of situated probability, knowing how likely certain language forms or ways of speaking (including silence) are in particular contexts, knowing how likely it is that certain people (and this includes people in social and institutional roles) will employ some language form in a situation. This knowledge of probable occurrence relates to current notions of intertextuality and indexicality (see Ochs, 1988, for a discussion of indexical socialization).

Although communicative competence is generally seen just as tacit knowledge, Hymes's (1971) definition actually went beyond knowledge to include factors such as affect, motivation, and social identity. He identified these factors as part of a non-cognitive *ability for use* (a somewhat confusing label, I believe): "Competence is understood to be dependent upon two things: (tacit) *knowledge* and (ability for) *use*" (p. 16). This definition further shifts the locus of communicative competence from the anonymous (collective) domain toward the individual language user and her interlocutors in specific situations. It also reflects Hymes's concern with language use in schools and, more generally, with the ways social identities influence change and resistance to change within and between speech communities, producing socially significant patterns of differential competence.

Finally, Hymes (1974) grounded the individual language user's communicative competence in socially mediated experiences, particularly through the idea of speech communities (however, here again he emphasized shared rules, the structuralist formulation): "A speech community is defined, then, tautologically but radically as a community sharing knowledge of rules for the conduct and interpretation of speech. Such sharing comprises knowledge of at least one form of speech, and knowledge also of its patterns of use" (p. 51). Because speech communities are defined by actual interaction, Hymes argued that language researchers should engage in more contextualized, ethnographic inquiry, studying situated language performance. The notions Hymes developed or articulated of speech communities, communicative competence, and ethnography of communication have played important roles in a wide range of applied and theoretical language disciplines, including sociolinguistics, anthropology, applied linguistics, discourse analysis, language education, and literacy studies (reading and writing).[5]

As was noted in the introduction of this chapter, Hymes's arguments carried a strong structuralist subtext, a subtext that has usually been amplified in the reception of his ideas. The research that has emerged in the wake of Hymes's work is a hybrid practice that carefully and insightfully attends to the particularities of situated language in use, but ends up seeking an abstract system—the rules and conventions of the community that govern performance and are passed on like family heirlooms to new members.

Structuralist metaphors and perspectives could be a superficial discursive trait in this research. However, I would argue that they have deeply influenced methodological and interpretive practices. To illustrate the consequences of structuralist perspectives in this hybrid, I will examine a recent and well-known study of academic writing and response in disciplinary classrooms, Walvoord and McCarthy's (1990) *Thinking and Writing in the Disciplines*. As seen at the beginning of this chapter, Walvoord and McCarthy framed their research in a structuralist idiom as a study of student *initiation* into the *shared conventions* of discourse communities that *govern* how *members* speak and write. To illustrate how this structuralist notion of discourse communities played out in their research, it is necessary to closely examine their methodological and analytic decisions and their final representations.

Interested in how students were inducted into the ways of thinking and writing in classes of four disciplines (business, history, psychology, and biology), Walvoord and McCarthy (1990) sought to identify what factors led to successful enculturation of students and what factors blocked that process. To determine whether students' texts were successful, they supplemented class grades with a research assessment. After the courses had

---

ended, they worked with the professors to develop primary trait scales that would "articulate" their expectations for writing assignments. Students' papers were then rated on these scales. The development of a primary-trait scale to explore a professor's tacit and explicit evaluation seems quite innovative and justified as a research activity. However, instead of using the scale and the ratings for triangulation, as an analytic tool to search in the original response for evidence and counter-evidence of those expectations, Walvoord and McCarthy purified evaluation by operationalizing success in a single construct that collapsed both classroom and research evaluations:

> Our definition of *high success* and *low success* in each class is based upon the tacit and explicit values and assumptions of the teacher for whom the student wrote the paper. A high-success or low success paper in this study is a paper that received a high or low grade during the course and *also* a corresponding score on the post-course primary trait analysis. (p. 36)

Although details of the actual rating of texts were not clearly reported, it appears that the primary trait rating for the four courses was often done by Walvoord alone rather than by the professors, adding another level of purification. In at least one case, they further purified their representation of expectations. Rating the experimental reports of students from two different years of a biology course, they first removed the abstracts because they appeared to have a halo effect on the scores.[6]

In another basic analytic framework of their research, Walvoord and McCarthy (1990) developed a common construct of roles to identify ways that students in all four disciplines took up writing tasks. Assuming enculturation into the discipline as the goal of instruction, they constructed three possible roles for the students: professionals in training (the good role), text processors (a bad student role), and laypersons (another bad student role). However, they constructed no explicit roles for the professors except the tacit one of a professional training professionals-to-be.

Walvoord and McCarthy's procedures do not work to uncover the professors' socializing practices and do not consider the possibility that professors' evaluations of students' papers might be unstable or subject to multiple influences. What unifies these procedures is a tacit acceptance of the professors as pure purveyors of their disciplines. Because Walvoord and

---

[6]Avoiding halo effects on an institutional exam or in an experimental study may be routine (though see Charney's, 1984, questions about the effects on validity of pursuing reliability in writing assessment); however, it is difficult to understand this procedure in a naturalistic study of writing and evaluation in a course where the abstract was part of the assigned task.

McCarthy assume that an underlying shared core of disciplinary values exists and that students are being socialized into that core, they can justify analytic practices such as reifying a stable response or elaborating only student roles.

In their narrative accounts of how professors and students negotiated specific academic writing tasks in classrooms, these same structuralist assumptions are visible. Walvoord and McCarthy (1990) documented considerable complexity in how the students and teachers acted in these classrooms. For example, a business professor, Sherman, had asked his students to assess the layout and work design of two fast-food restaurants and to evaluate them. His assignment handout concluded: "Chapters 7 and 8 in the Stevenson text can provide guidance, and a visit to each site may be unavoidable" (p. 62). After tracing the processes students engaged in, Walvoord and Sherman[7] identified three factors associated with the professor's grading: whether the students actually *visited both restaurants*, whether they *took notes at* the restaurants or just ate there, and whether they *read the textbook before* they went to the restaurants. This analysis of situated task execution and professor evaluation is quite interesting. However, rather than going on to ask why some students did and some did not engage in some or all of these processes, they simply concluded that Sherman's assignment should have explicitly and unambiguously told the students to read the chapters before going on the visit, to go to both restaurants, and to take notes at both about the layout and work design. In fact, in their 45-page report on this undergraduate business class, Walvoord and Sherman suggested at least nine times that the professor (Sherman) was not explicit enough in telling students what he wanted them to do. Their summation of research in this classroom singled out this issue: "After our analysis of the data, we believed that the most important thing Sherman might do to help his students was to expand and clarify his assignment sheet, to institute better guidance for students at the beginning of the writing and thinking processes, and to help them use procedural knowledge" (Walvoord & McCarthy, 1990, p. 95). In short, working from the assumption that the professors were experts engaged in a one-way process of initiating passive and cooperative novices into their discourse communities, they ended up interpreting any gaps or anomalies as essentially transmission problems.

Their analysis of another of Sherman's assignments also illustrates the structuralist assumptions embedded in their view of discourse communities.

---

[7]Walvoord and McCarthy are the listed authors of the book, but each professor co-authored the report on his or her class and is listed under "with" on the title page.

In one assignment, Sherman asked students to use what they had heard in the past year to propose and justify a new site for a major-league baseball stadium. He indicated that the paper should be "directed to the members of your class rather than to the decision makers" (p. 57). One of the students (called Harrington) took the cue "what you have heard" to think of street corner conversations of baseball fans and then took the cues to write to the class and justify her choice as calling for an argument that would "win over" her fellow students. She ended up arguing for a site in terms of fan concerns, particularly pricing. Sherman, however, found this paper weak (although we are not told how he actually graded it), because justifying a site only in terms of fan concerns is not a professional way to approach such business decisions. Summing up this case, Walvoord and Sherman said:

> Our chosen view of the classroom—as a place where students, under the guidance of their teachers, are learning to be competent communicators—lets us construct Harrington's story as the story of a student trying to learn an appropriate role and ethos acceptable to her teacher, and, in this case, missing the mark in certain ways. In this perspective, Sherman's language on the assignment sheet miscued the student, evoking her view of herself and her classmates as baseball fans. Certainly she and other students seemed eager to learn to be business decision makers and to adopt the roles and strategies that would meet Sherman's expectations. It would be possible, however, with the use of other perspectives, to explore Harrington's story as a conflict of gender and power or as her struggle to reconcile various roles or selves. Each interpretation, we recognize, would allow a different insight into this very complex difficulty that occurred as Harrington and others tried to construct an audience and a self. (Walvoord & McCarthy, 1990, p. 71)

It is difficult to recover the insights into gender and power conflicts that the authors obliquely refer to. They do note that lack of assumed background knowledge emerged as a serious problem. They might be suggesting that baseball is still a fairly gendered topic, that Harrington seemed to lack the assumed background knowledge, and that such a disadvantage was more likely because of her gender. However, the data provided on Harrington's case also suggests other interpretations. For example, she may have taken on another basic role you might predict in a business environment, salesperson or marketer. Told to justify a site to a specific audience, Harrington asks herself what would win over her assigned target audience and develops the argument for her paper in accordance with that goal. If this interpretation is reasonable, interference arising from competing professional roles could, in fact, have extended Walvoord and McCarthy's argument that students' assumed roles shaped their writing and learning. However, active strategizing and competing professional roles would have conflicted with their

assumptions of a passive compliant novice and an unproblematically unified community.

Obviously, researchers must take up certain perspectives and ignore
others, and Walvoord and McCarthy (1990) repeatedly allude, as in the last
quote, to their reflexive awareness of their perspective and the possibility
that other perspectives would produce other stories. Nevertheless, these
examples lead me to conclude that framing their study in terms of discourse
communities limited and constrained the way they collected and analyzed
data in problematic ways.[8]

Recent research and theory on disciplinarity (e.g., Bazerman, 1988;
Becher, 1989; Foucault, 1972; Klein, 1990; Messer-Davidow, Shumway,
& Sylvan, 1993; Pickering, 1995) has pointed to the complex configurations possible as practitioners are situated within multiple heterogeneous networks shaped by factors such as the objects of study,
methodologies (including use of instruments), theories, nested institutional sites and roles, audiences, researcher biographies, and personal
relationships. In addition, disciplinary activities and discourses do not
appear to be closed, autonomous systems: disciplinarity is embroidered

---

[8]Berkenkotter, Huckin, and Ackerman have published three reports (1988, 1991; also Berkenkotter
& Huckin, 1995) of an ethnographic case study of a graduate student's ("Nate," eventually revealed to
be Ackerman) socialization into the rhetoric program at Carnegie Melon University (CMU). Theirs was
the first close study of writing and disciplinary enculturation in graduate education. Their argument that
research methodology and language encoded a shared model of disciplinary knowing, their location of
the discipline in institutional communicative forums, and their intertextual comparison of Nate's texts
to those of his professors and other rhetoricians represent valuable steps toward a sociohistoric study of
writing and disciplinary enculturation. However, as with Walvoord and McCarthy, their collection and
interpretation of data were filtered through the structuralist lens of the discourse community with several
problematic consequences.

One of the consequences is their representation of Ackerman/Nate as having limited literacy—signaled, for example, by references to his "writer-based prose" and "oral strategies," terms typically
encountered in discussions of emergent literacy or "basic writers." These representations of Acker-
man/Nate appear problematic given his background before entering CMU: B.A. in English, M.Ed. in
Curriculum and Instruction, composition instructor at an open-admissions university, and Fellow in a
NEH Summer Seminar for College Teachers. Assuming, like Walvoord and McCarthy, that faculty were
stable instantiations of unified discourse communities with shared models of knowing, they also paid
little or no attention to professor's responses to Nate's papers, to differences in discourse and knowledge
values among professors, to peer interactions, or to possible effects of Nate on his professors' models
of knowing and discourse. Finally, as with Walvood and McCarthy, the structuralist assumptions of
discourse communities were visible in measures. For one intertextual measure, they asked three
rhetoricians to identify words or phrases "that strike you as being off-register, i.e., either too casual or
too formal or too belletristic for social science research writing" (Berkenkotter, Huckin, & Ackerman,
1988, p. 16). They then calculated an off-register index for each text by simply averaging these scores,
in spite of the fact that agreement was questionable (e.g., on one of Nate's texts, the three raters identified,
25, 35, and 45 register flaws) and that disciplinary texts appeared to display different registers (e.g., an
average of 15 "flaws" in a sample from James Kinneavy's (1971) *Theory of Discourse* compared to only
1 in an article by Richard Young, a faculty member at CMU).

in history and in sociocultural values, beliefs, narratives, tropes, and ways of life (e.g., Foucault, 1972; Geertz, 1983; Gusfield, 1992; Harding, 1991; Landau, 1991). As Myers's (1990) longitudinal research into the professional writing of established biologists documents, even the experts in a discipline do not find themselves operating in a predictable arena of shared values and conventions. Given this kind of counter-evidence, it is worth asking why structuralist notions of abstract, unified discourse communities have held such a sway over situated research into writing in the disciplines.

FROM CONDUITS TO COMMUNITIES TO PERSONS:
A STRUCTURALIST NETWORK

(add) centripetal; directed or moving toward a center

Structuralism has been a dominant discourse for a number of reasons. By design, structuralist analyses are quite effective at foregrounding patterns, and language and knowledge are certainly phenomena rich in patterns. Structuralism also developed in close association with sociopolitical projects of centralization (i.e., nation and empire building), and, thus, has both reflected and served these kinds of centripetal interests (e.g., Voloshinov, 1973). And, of course, structuralist practices bear close relations to, and are often modeled explicitly on, canonical images of scientific work. Structuralism in the social and psychological disciplines has, thus, traded heavily on the borrowed authority of natural science. However, I would also argue that a major attraction to structuralist accounts is that they are powerfully grounded in a dominant folk model of communication, a model that implicates particular views of knowledge, learning, communities, and the person.

Reddy (1979) identified the prevalence in English of a large family of metaphors and expressions for communication that appear to be traceable to an underlying trope, the conduit metaphor. The conduit metaphor depicts speech as a three-step process. The speaker puts thoughts into word-containers. These word-thought objects are then transferred from the speaker's mind through a conduit (the air) to the mind of the listener. Finally, the listener extracts the thoughts from the words. Technological analogues of this model exist in a host of modern communication devices (everything from telephones and televisions to networked computers and sophisticated encryption machines). All work because sending and receiving devices share a system of coding (or at least complementary systems for encoding and decoding). The conduit model also seems to invoke a shared contextual framework for commu-nication.[9]

The conduit metaphor implicates an ensemble of structuralist notions. If a sender and a receiver can communicate (i.e., achieve shared understanding or intersubjectivity) only because they possess the shared language and shared knowledge that ensure the message encoded will be the message decoded, then language and knowledge must be highly sharable, that is, they must be abstract and uniform systems, not plural, particular, and personal. Structuralist theory has, thus, been primarily interested in uncovering the formal properties of such abstract systematic knowledge (whether it is the syntactic structures of a language or schematic scripts for cultural events like eating at a restaurant). Following these models of communication and knowledge, language communities (at whatever level) must be spatialized, figured as discrete, autonomous territories with core regions constructed from common language, knowledge, values, and rules. As novices enter the community and travel from the periphery to the center, they move toward expert status (or full membership). In other words, social progress in ap-proaching this shared space is paralleled by cognitive progress in internaliz-ing the core language, knowledge, values, and rules of the community.

Structuralism offers two basic accounts for how people get the necessary abstract knowledge. The first mechanism is maturational, what Vygotsky (1978) identified as the botanical model, where knowledge simply blossoms given appropriate conditions and nutrients. A strong version of this mecha-nism is seen in nativist accounts of language acquisition (e.g., Chomsky, 1965; Pinker, 1994). The second is a simple extension of the conduit model of communication to the special case of learning as transmission. Knowl-edge must be transmitted to the person and deposited there—what Freire (1970) referred to as the banking model of education. Specific accounts of the mechanisms of transmission and of storage in the brain are, of course, quite varied. In practice, innate maturation and social transmission may be blended in diverse mixtures.

The intersection of an abstract, unified model of communities (the social) and equally abstract representations of knowledge structures (the cognitive) leaves little room for multiplicity and agency. From this structuralist per-

---

[9]Tracy (1991) points out that studies of discourse routinely assume that goals are simple, visible, and shared elements of communication. She questions this assumption, illustrating how problematic it is by exploring participants' goals in one setting, a departmental colloquium. She found that participants in the colloquium had multiple, often paradoxical goals: emphasizing personal intellectual display, but also community membership, displaying non-defensive distance from ideas, but also investment and involvement.

spective, the person appears as little more than a specialized container within which language can be encoded and decoded and schemata can be structured and restructured. By separating the person from what is communicated and learned, transmission models create a kind of teflon subject—an a priori, asocial self not really altered by communication or learning.

The conduit metaphor's account for how meanings are transmitted offers a very persuasive image of mutual understanding (intersubjectivity). Indeed, it seems like common sense. How else could we account for communication? It provides a powerful ground for structuralist theories such as Saussure's, making many of their claims and entailments appear natural. In this view then, a novice graduate student's task is essentially to make a cognitive journey to the center of a discipline, to internalize the discipline's language, rules, and knowledge. That image fits well with dominant cultural representations of academic work as rational, asocial, impersonal, and disembodied. Working from different communicative premises, sociohistoric theories point to a different conceptual ensemble.

SOCIOHISTORIC PERSPECTIVES:
INTERSUBJECTIVITY AS DIALOGIC

In contrast with the structuralist penchant for abstraction, uniformity, and spatialization, sociohistoric theories offer accounts of communication, knowledge, learning, community, and the person as concretely situated, plural, and historical phenomena. Where structuralist theories begin with a strong account of communication as shared understanding made possible by shared language and knowledge, sociohistoric theories propose a weaker model of intersubjectivity. As Rommetveit (1985) argues,

> Human discourse takes place in and deals with a pluralistic, only fragmentarily known, and only partially shared social world. Vagueness, ambiguity, and incompleteness—but hence also versatility, flexibility, and negotiability—must for that reason be dealt with as inherent and theoretically essential characteristics of ordinary language. (p. 183)

Rommetveit (1992) represents communication/intersubjectivity as complex processes of mutual attunement, in which interlocutors are dynamically negotiating drafts of contracts for categorizations of and attributions for the world. This weaker account of intersubjectivity assumes that communication, even when successful and unproblematic from the perspective of participants, always involves some elements of mis- and non-communication as well (cf. Coupland, Wiemann, & Giles, 1991; Taylor, 1992).

Bakhtin (1986) criticizes the graphic depiction of the conduit metaphor (the common picture of talking heads, or brains) because it alienates language from the streams of situated activity within which it occurs and particularly because it represents the listener as a passive recipient (nothing more than a decoder). For Bakhtin (Bakhtin, 1981, 1986; Voloshinov, 1973), language is fundamentally dialogic. As noted earlier in the chapter, he sees the word not as a solid meaning object, but as a dynamic social field saturated with multiple meanings and accents. His basic unit of analysis is not the sentence or proposition of abstract systems, but the *utterance*, language in its concrete situated use. Utterances (spoken and written) are not dialogic because they involve conversation-like exchanges, much less because such exchanges are conducted in an open and egalitarian fashion. Instead, utterances are rendered dialogic because they are sedimented with traces of their sociohistoric use, indexed in the immediate situation, addressed to anticipated responses, imbued to varying degrees with individuals' situated intentions and accents, and actively and reactively constructed by recipients. Within this theory, all discursive phenomena, from national languages to a single, situated utterance, are not simply dialogic, but also dynamic, forged in evolving local interactions of centripetal (centralizing) and centrifugal (decentralizing) forces. For Bakhtin then, what people acquire in the course of their communicative development is not knowledge of the rules and terms of abstract systems (not the metaphorical library of dictionaries, grammar books, encyclopedias, and so on). Instead, he sees communicative development as the accretion and active appropriation of concrete historical knowledge of practices-in-use, knowledge that traces the trajectory of an actively orienting person through a complexly differentiated sociohistoric landscape.

Communication is, therefore, understood not as the transmission of fixed meaning objects, but as a complex, sociohistorically situated working out of dynamic meanings, the end result of which is some imperfect approximation of mutual understanding or, more radically, simply some approximate coordination or alignment of activity. This account of communication carries directly over into views of learning and community. For example, Lave and Wenger (1991) have proposed defining learning as *legitimate peripheral participation* in *communities of practice*. By emphasizing participation in practices, they are pointing to the centrality of situated activity, activity that is partially improvised by individual participants, but is also strongly shaped by situational contexts and tools that embody a collective history of pursuing certain goals with certain resources within particular forms of social interaction. Directly countering the trope of territoriality, Lave and Wenger reject homogeneous accounts of community, emphasizing the plurality and heterogeneity of communities of practice:

> Given the complex, differentiated nature of communities, it seems important not to reduce the end point of centripetal participation in a community of practice to a uniform or univocal "center," or to a linear notion of skill acquisition. There is no place in a community of practice designated "the periphery," and, most emphatically, it has no single core or center. (p. 36)

Instead of a single fixed goal for learning—the ideal member of an idealized community, Lave and Wenger (1991) argue that "there are multiple, varied, more- or less-engaged and inclusive ways of being located in the fields of participation defined by a community" (p. 36). In their view, a community is not defined by a discrete shared core of abstract knowledge and language that people internalize to become expert members; instead, a community is an open, dynamic body, "a set of relations among persons, activity, and world, over time and in relation with other tangential and overlapping communities of practice" (p. 98). A key corollary of such views is that changes in the participation structure of a community of practice always work to shape and reshape the community as well as the person.

With this concrete, historical perspective, sociohistoric theories are able to assert a notion of the person with particularity and agency without resorting to an a priori, asocial self. Lave and Wenger (1991) contrast the "nonpersonal view of knowledge, skills, tasks, activities, and learning" promoted by cognitive (structuralist) models with a sociohistoric "focus on the person, but as person-in-the-world, as member of a sociocultural community" (p. 52). Bakhtin (1981) describes development as the evolving interaction of authoritative and internally persuasive discourses that arises as a person actively assimilates and resists others' voices, words, values, affective and evaluative stances, and so on. In contrast with the teflon subject, the image of the person as a container, Leont'ev (1981a) argues that "the process of internalization is not the *transferal* of an external activity to a preexisting, internal 'plane of consciousness': it is the process in which this internal plane is *formed*" (p. 57).

Shifting from views that privilege disembodied knowledge fixed in abstract centralized systems to views that privilege embodied action dispersed across places, times, and persons, sociohistoric theory challenges a number of deeply entrenched categories, particularly the dichotomy of the individual and society. In sociohistoric accounts, the individual and social are interpenetrated. Vygotsky (1978, 1987) argued for an understanding of human learning and development, particularly the higher psychological functions like memory, thinking, attention, and speech, as a process of sociogenesis (whereby social interactions and resources are progressively, constructively internalized). His often repeated formula states that every function appears twice, first between people on the interpsychological plane and then within the person on the intrapsychological plane (see, e.g., Vygotsky, 1978, p. 57).[10] Central to this view is the notion of mediated action. Vygotsky emphasized the way that individual activity is mediated by socially developed tools and practices (e.g., language, technologies of writing, practices of classification). For Vygotsky, it is this sociohistoric legacy of mediational means, external and internal, material and semiotic, that makes humans human.

Critiquing translations of Vygotsky's work that represent learning as the dyadic scaffolding an anonymous expert provides an anonymous novice in a zone of proximal development, an interaction whose sole function is transmission of conceptual knowledge, Minick, Stone, and Forman (1993) argue for the need to move beyond "decontextualized universalistic representations of social interaction, language, and cognition ... toward a theory that highlights the rich interconnections between cultural institutions, social practices, semiotic mediation, interpersonal relationships, and the developing mind" (p. 6). Emblematic of this reconceptualization is the following observation: "Educationally significant human interactions do not involve abstract bearers of cognitive structures but real people who develop a variety of interpersonal relationships with one another in the course of their shared activity in a given institutional context" (1993, p. 6). Thus, current sociohistoric theories have begun to converge on a theory of learning as the formation of a person's consciousness through participation in social practices, a theory that stresses affect, motivation, perspective, embodied ways of being in the world, and identity as well as conceptual development.

Because mediated action blurs the boundaries between the individual, society, and the world, sociohistoric theories have sought a holistic, integrated unit of analysis. Activity theories (e.g., Engestrom, 1987; Leont'ev, 1981a, 1981b; Wertsch, 1985, 1991; Zinchenko, 1985) have proposed

---

[10]Vygotsky also stressed that internalization was reconstruction and transformation of external activity, not simply transferal, for example," the central tendency of the child's development is not a gradual socialization introduced from the outside, but a gradual individualization that emerges on the foundation of the child's internal socialization" (Vygotsky, 1987, p. 259).

motivated, mediated activity-in-the-world as that unit. Vygotsky (1987) argues that any adequate account of human consciousness and action must be based ultimately in an account of affect and motivation: "Thought has its origins in the motivating sphere of consciousness, a sphere that includes our inclinations and needs, our interests and impulses, and our affect and emotion" (p. 282). He also argues that thought, motivation, and affect are co-evolving, not independent systems. Taking up that argument, Leont'ev (1978, 1981a, b) describes concrete activity as a composite of three fused planes: activity, action, and operation. Activity is linked to the basic motive, whereas actions are oriented to specific goals. This distinction is meant to capture the point that different actions may have similar motives, whereas similar actions may have different motives. If we take hunting a deer as an example of an action, it could be part of different activity systems—in one case, the provision of food, in another, the social competition of a recreational sport.[11] To address the motive of food, paid work and grocery shopping might represent alternative actions. Leont'ev's third level, operations, is related to the situated conditions of action. Hunting a deer may be accomplished in various ways depending on available or chosen tools, skills, and contexts. Leont'ev (1978) stresses that all concrete activity will be infused with a situated hierarchy of multiple motives (e.g., work activity has social as well as productive motives). The central point then is that activity is socially and historically organized and learning to participate in such activity involves appropriating packages of motives, goals, social relations, and contexts as well as mediational means.

Cole and Engestrom (1993) and Engestrom (1993) emphasize the way "cognitive" functions and actions are socially distributed in activity and the ways activity involves multiple perspectives, motives, means, and forms of social organization, which may or may not be aligned toward some convergent end(s). Working from the basic mediational triangle that connects a subject (an actor), an object (the goal or problem space of the activity), and mediational means (material and psychological), Cole and Engestrom (1993) generate a fascinating series of models of mediation, applying them to three situations (teaching reading, providing outpatient medical care, and engendering newborns). One model is Engestrom's extension of the mediational triangle, which adds community, rules, and division of labor. Although this model places activity explicitly in social contexts, Engestrom

---

[11]This example also illustrates that the relations between activity, action, and operation are historically flexible. For some, the action of hunting has been elevated to an activity.

(1993) rejects a homogeneous reading of such contexts: "An activity system is not a homogeneous entity. To the contrary, it is composed of a multitude of often disparate elements, voices, and viewpoints. This multiplicity can be understood in terms of historical layers. An activity system always contains sediments of earlier historical modes, as well as buds or shoots of its possible future" (p. 68). Engestrom (1987, 1993) emphasizes the contradictions (internal and external) as well as the heterogeneity of activity systems. Studying doctor–patient consultations in Finnish clinics, Engestrom (1993) identified contradictions and heterogeneity in the multiple voices/perspectives of the interactants, the layered presence of medical ideologies from different historical periods, and the ways consultations were structured by specific institutional legacies and linked to competing historical models of work.

How to handle such heterogeneity is an issue. Consider a classroom as an example. The complex intersections of social, pedagogical, and institutional forces, the striking asymmetries in motives and actions between teachers and students and among students, and the varied configurations of interpersonal and intergroup relations that exist in classrooms can reasonably be seen as a durable holistic pattern that defines a distinct system of activity. However, subsuming all of the heterogeneity in the image of one activity system could lead to a kind of creeping spatialization, a view in which activity systems become the kind of autonomous, discrete territories that discourse communities have been. An alternative way of conceptualizing this heterogeneity is suggested by Goffman's (1981) notion of face-to-face interaction as laminated and Goodwin and Duranti's (1992) notion of context as mutable, dynamic configurations of foregrounded and backgrounded elements. In other words, I am suggesting that activity is laminated, that multiple activities co-exist, are immanent, in any situation. Whereas one or more of these activity footings (e.g., school learning) may be relatively foregrounded at any one time, the backgrounded activities (e.g., of home, neighborhood, work) do not disappear. Moreover, activity is perspectival as well as laminated, with co-participants holding differently configured activity footings (see, e.g., Gutierrez, Rymes, & Larson, 1995; Holland & Reeves, 1994; Newman, Griffin, & Cole, 1989; Rommetveit, 1992). Viewing activity as laminated and perspectival makes it clear that neither situated activity nor systems of activity can occur in autonomous spaces. In any case, these kinds of complex dialogic models of activity systems offer alternative ways of envisioning discourse communities and disciplinary enculturation.

RESITUATING DISCIPLINARITY

Where the combined legacy of everyday tropes for, and structuralist theories of, discourse and society has encouraged us to imagine disciplines as autonomous objects existing in a detemporalized space, as territories to be mapped or systems to be diagrammed, sociohistoric theories point toward an image of disciplines as open networks, forged through relational activity that intermingles personal, interpersonal, institutional, and sociocultural histories (Minick, Stone, & Forman, 1993).

This kind of account of disciplinary communities has been suggested by some empirical studies of the sociology of knowledge. For example, to investigate the social organization of scientific fields, Crane (1972) asked scientists whom they asked for advice, who had influenced their research, whom they worked collaboratively with, who had been their teachers, and who had sat on their thesis committees. She also examined patterns of publication and citation. Crane found that fields (in fact subfields, like rural sociology) had complex historical patterns of development and were highly differentiated into subgroups, pairs, and isolated individuals. The following segment of her analysis provides a sense of her basic findings:

> One of the large groups of collaborators in the mathematics area … was dominated by a highly productive mathematician who had trained or collaborated with half of the other members of the group. In turn, a few of his students and collaborators (one of whom was highly productive) had acquired students and collaborators of their own, producing smaller subgroups within the group. The other group of collaborators was based principally upon collaboration rather than student-teacher ties. Three highly productive members had collaborated with each other and with several others. These three men provided some focus for the group that grew by adding collaborators instead of students. This was surprising since all three men were located in universities where graduate students were available. (pp. 60-61)

Crane's research portrayed not a unified anonymous structure of linguistic, rhetorical, and epistemic conventions, but instead a very human world of prominent professors and their students, of professional collaborations, of large and small groups and isolated individuals, of long-term relationships and interpersonal influences. Not assuming that disciplinary communities were abstract, unified structures, Crane's "invisible colleges" emerge as something more like the visible colleges I have experienced, as hierarchical, complexly differentiated, sociohistoric worlds full of particular individuals and institutions and shaped by complex interactions with a wide range of internal and external forces.

Bazerman's (1988, 1991) accounts of the rhetorical situations that scientists write in have also portrayed discourse communities as highly differentiated and open. Following the histories of particular scientists and institutions, he describes complex negotiations over roles, tasks, and outcomes in social fields with diverse actors, including "employers, funders, editors, referees, critics, and audiences who grant the researcher various powers to continue, publicize, and gain acceptance for their work" (1988, p. 184). Discussing sources of change in science, he maps a multivalent social-material ecology:

> Some sources can be from outside the scientific community such as political ideological movements (state Marxism has served as both a stimulus and a constraint within Soviet sciences), changes in other forms of communication (such as the rise of a periodical press), new means of communication (whether printing press or modem), or idiosyncratic individuals with complex personal histories that import foreign styles (as when physicists went into biochemistry, or Newton perceived physics as mathematics). Or the sources of change may come more directly from within the activity of a science—as when phenomena refuse to fit formulations or when a new idea developed for a narrow problem is seen to have much broader power, or when an individual, whose work is rejected, discovers new and compelling means to assert his position. (Bazerman, 1988, p. 308)

Bazerman develops an image of disciplines not as abstract, autonomous spaces, but as open historical systems buffeted by, absorbing, and emitting multiple sociohistoric currents. This kind of portrayal of disciplines, which has emerged particularly clearly in science studies (see also Latour, 1987; Latour & Woolgar, 1986; Myers, 1990), offers us a way to usefully reconceptualize disciplines and disciplinary enculturation as open and heterogeneous processes rather than closed and homogeneous structures. In this sense, I find it useful to talk more of *disciplinarity* than disciplines, because disciplinarity evokes a process rather than a place or object.

Disciplinarity can be seen as one domain of the general process by which people jointly constitute social worlds and identities in activity (see Kamberelis & Scott, 1992). Because disciplinarity is a relatively modern and extensively institutionalized social formation, I have found the analogy of U.S. political parties useful. When I invoke political parties as analogies, I am not thinking of structuralist images of such parties, like the formal organization of the Democratic Party displayed in a complex diagram (as an autonomous unified object) with membership as an easily determined category. Instead, I am thinking of the extremely complex interactions of evolving alliance, influence, conflict, and context that mark practical everyday work in the dispersed and quite varied sites of the "Democratic Party," everyday work that occurs at a confluence of multiple histories (personal, interpersonal, local, institutional, national, and international). In this sense, the party is a dispersed network, formed by "internal" interactions among a complex, loosely organized set of institutions that are often dominated at particular points in time by individuals with strong personalities or by particular cliques, and by "external" interactions with other persons, institutions, and sociocultural forces. Membership is uncertain and contestable. Is Lyndon LaRouche a Democrat? How many registered Democrats do reside in Chicago? This network is interactively stabilized (Pickering, 1995) by the co-evolution of aligned people, institutions, artifacts, and practices and exists in reciprocal relations to other sociohistoric spheres of activity (workplaces, national government, the international system, the family, public media, religious organizations). While the Democratic Party is not a definite object, not an autonomous space, it is certainly a social fact of some consequence. It does not evaporate into a deconstructivist free play of significations. It is a fact not just as a durable social representation that shapes people's perceptions and actions, but also as a sedimented, productive subsystem in the ecology of society. I believe that disciplines are comparable social formations.

In disciplinarity, much of the work of alignment is centered around texts, around the literate activities of reading and writing. However, it is important again to note the structuralist assumptions that have typically been embedded in discussions of literacy. Brandt (1990) analyzes theories of literacy (e.g., Goody, 1986; Ong, 1982; Olson, 1977) that present it as asocial and decontextualized. She suggests that these theories have defined literacy not in terms of the practices of readers and writers but of features of material texts (e.g., transportability generating decontextualization and impersonality). As Scribner and Cole (1981) documented so thoroughly, the consequences of literacy are less linked to generic textual technologies than to particular cultural practices. In place of these "strong-text views," Brandt (1990) argues that literacy must be seen as the situated moment-to-moment work of writers and readers making meaning. In this sense, literacy is not only always contextualized, it actually requires enhanced intersubjectivity. Texts must provide cues not only to what they say (propositional meaning), but also to how they are to be taken (the joint intersubjective work of reading and writing). For example, Brandt (1990) notes that strong-text theorists have seen textual cohesion as exemplifying "the capacities of language-on-its own in its sheerest glory," but she argues:

> This reputation has been derived primarily from analysis of finished texts, searches for patterns in static artifacts. One can take a pencil and trace lexical reiteration, pronoun reference, and other devices by which texts point back and forth and usually in at themselves. But tracing such structural patterns in language-on-its-own is like coming upon the scene of a party after it is over and everybody has gone home, being left to imagine from the remnants what the party must have been like. I have been arguing in this chapter for a view of texts that is based on how they are coming over the horizon for writer and reader. (p. 76)

Analyzing how texts come over the horizon, Brandt concludes that cohesion relates to the unfolding shared histories of the writer and reader, that it is about social involvement rather than alienation, about rapport as much as propositionality. Brandt's account of literacy as joint, moment-to-moment intersubjective work mediated by texts points to the need for a broader unit of analysis than writing, a unit such as literate activity (see Preface and chap. 5).

Reflecting on intersubjectivity from a developmental perspective, Bruner (1994) points to the importance of joint attention. He notes that babies' early joint visual attention with caregivers, a phenomenon that originally seemed relatively simple and trivial, came to be recognized as profound and complex as researchers realized that joint attention entails mutual knowledge and, thus, a theory of other minds. Bruner presents a developmental account of joint attention that stretches from that early joint visual attention to the shared presuppositional attention established among people in specialized interpretive communities (e.g., intertextual references between law professors in the space of constitutional jurisprudence). These varied forms of alignment, Bruner argues, are not simply questions of procedural knowledge because "joint attention is not just joint attention, but joint participation in a common culture" (p. 11). To understand joint participation in disciplinary communities of practice and the ways literate activity mediates that participation, we must pursue closely situated studies of the activity in which heterogeneous elements of the networks, including the participants, are (re)produced. Such research must be perspectival, sensitive to the multiple positions and developmental trajectories from which participants orient to literate and disciplinary practices. In terms of Brandt's party metaphor, this approach suggests studying not only the unfolding scene of the party, but the multiple streams of activity that converge on that scene and flow from it.

WRITING AND DISCIPLINARITY IN FUNCTIONAL SYSTEMS OF ACTIVITY

Because of his strategic interest in sign mediation of higher psychological functions (e.g., memory, conceptualization, speech) and his practical interests in regular and special education, Vygotsky's theory (e.g., 1978, 1987) and much subsequent work in this tradition have focused heavily on the notion of internalization (sociogenesis of higher psychological functions, inner speech, the zone of proximal development as a shift from assisted to independent performance). However, an exclusive focus on internalization can sustain a dichotomized view of the individual and society, and can lead away from embodied aspects of activity (see Packer, 1993). As Lave and Wenger (1991) noted, "given a relational understanding of person, world, and activity, participation, at the core of our theory of learning, can neither be fully internalized as knowledge structures nor fully externalized as instrumental artifacts or overarching activity structures" (p. 51). Leont'ev (1978) stressed that it is important to recognize the centrality in activity of externalization (speech, writing, drawing, the manipulation and construction of objects and devices). Learning is not a one-way flow from external to internal, nor is action a one-way flow from internal to external. Activity is always an interpenetrated confluence of internal and external. Internalized practices are constantly being externalized, to be distributed among people, embedded in fleeting or durable artifacts, and (re)internalized. Moreover, as Vygotsky (1987) argued for inner speech, the situated processes of internalization and externalization are always formative and, thus, transformative (not movements of fixed objects across boundaries).[12]

Activity implicates co-action with other people, artifacts, and elements of the social–material environment. In research on distributed cognition in modern U.S. naval navigation, Hutchins (1995) describes the way that the computation of a position, the cyclic action of taking a fix, involves the propagation of representational states across representational media in functional systems, a process that links things happening within and between artifacts, people, and the world. For Hutchins (1995), functional systems are constituted through "processes of entrainment, coordination, and resonance among elements" of such systems (p. 288). Hutchins (1995) concludes:

> The real power of human cognition lies in our ability to flexibly construct functional systems that accomplish our goals by bringing bits of structure into coordination. That

---

[12]For this reason, Leont'ev prefers appropriation to internalization.

culturally constituted settings for activity are rich in precisely the kinds of artifactual
and social interactional resources that can be appropriated by such functional systems
is a central truth about human cognition. (p. 316)

He also proposes that learning be seen as "the propagation of some kinds
of organization from one part of a complex system to another" (p. 290).
From a sociohistoric perspective, learning is ubiquitous, woven into all
human activity, not limited to those peculiar arenas or events that are
culturally designated as learning. It is in this sense that Lave and Wenger
(1991) describe learning as "the historical production, transformation, and
change of persons" (p. 51). This formulation raises a key issue in light of
the notion of functional systems. If we view situated, historical activity
rather than abstract decontextualized systems as the locus of social and
individual development, then what are the productive forces and what are
the products of that historical activity?

Hutchins (1995) offers one answer in his model of a moment in human
practice. He depicts the moment as an open cube with three arrows moving
through it. Each arrow traces a line of development. In the most immediate
sense, the moment of practice traces the conduct of activity, the ongoing
flow of a situated functional system. A second line represents the development of persons, their learning through participation in practice. The third
line represents the development of the practice itself, of its material and
conceptual tools and forms of social organization. Although all these lines
of development happen simultaneously in situated activity, Hutchins notes
their distinctive heterochronicity (e.g., the conduct of activity is brief and
quickly changing, the development of persons occurs over longer stretches
of time, and the development of a practice may span decades, centuries,
even millennia of history).

If historical activity is constituted by and lays down sediments in
functional systems that coordinate various media with different properties,
then a finer grained model of those media could be useful. Figure 1.1
represents an attempt at such a model, elaborating on the media that
Hutchins represents as practice. The pentagon identifies five kinds of
media for functional systems: persons, artifacts (semiotic and material),
institutions, practices, and communities. The central pentagon within the
pentagon represents the flow of activity, where the media are fully integrated in situated functional systems.

I assume references to persons in this diagram are clear, but the other
terms need some explanation. *Artifacts* refer to material objects fashioned
by people (e.g., written texts, furniture, instruments, and built environ-

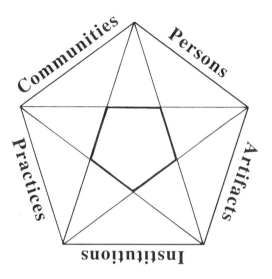

FIG. 1.1. The constitution of functional systems in activity.

ments) or taken up by people (e.g., ocean currents for travel, the night sky as a navigational aid, animals as domesticated food stock, a stone as a weapon). Artifacts are also durable symbolic forms, like natural languages, mathematics, and specialized disciplinary discourses that may be inscribed in material objects, but that are also internalized by and distributed across persons. By *practices*, I refer to ways of acting-with and interacting in worlds that include artifacts and persons. *Institutions* refer to stabilizations of activity around formal and informal social groupings (workplaces, organizations, families, recreational groups, gangs, etc.). *Communities* refer to potentials for alignment that emerge from any "common" experiences. In this sense, communities are realized as interactive accomplishments, constructed along a continuum of commonalties from the thinnest and most trivial to the thickest and most profound. These various media do not stand alone and are not mutually exclusive categories by any means; in fact, they mutually constitute one another in evolving histories of functional systems, that central pentagon. In this sense, the course of human activity can be seen as the fluid, dynamic weaving and reweaving of functional systems composed of such heterogeneous elements.

    In sociohistoric perspectives, activity (although somewhat variously defined) is the fundamental unit of analysis. It is a holistic unit, fusing the often separated categories of culture, biology, and the physical world; of thinking, communication, individual development (learning), and social reproduction; of production, consumption, and exchange. Activity may be conceptualized as the situated and distributed weaving (Cole, 1996) together of histories into functional systems that are open and perspectival, durable and fleeting. Functional systems of activity involve the co-genesis of persons, practices, artifacts, institutions, and communities. The basic theoretical argument of this book then is simply that writing and disciplinarity must be understood as activity in this sense.

From this perspective, writing is a fully dialogic process, literate activity that is situated, mediated, and dispersed (see chap. 5 for fuller discussion of this notion). Disciplinarity is a sociocultural sphere of activity, a set of what del Rio and Alvarez (1995) refer to as cultural architectures for mind and agency. In graduate education, literate activity points to the laminated processes by which students come to represent tasks and produce texts as well as the way those texts are received and used by professors, peers, and others. This literate activity is central to disciplinary enculturation, providing opportunity spaces for (re)socialization of discursive practices, for foregrounding representations of disciplinarity, and for negotiating trajectories of participation in communities of practice. In the chapters that follow, I explore these notions of disciplinarity and literate activity by closely analyzing the way students and professors produce texts, knowledge, identities, and institutions within the confluence of situated and durable functional systems in graduate programs.

PART II

Situated Explorations
of Academic Writing Tasks

2

Multiple Exposures: Tracing a Microhistory of Academic Writing Tasks

To study situated academic writing tasks, I first conducted research in a graduate seminar in second language education at Midwestern University, a major public research university in the United States.[1] The seminar, *Language Research*, was one of five courses designed to prepare students for advanced research and scholarship in second or foreign language education. Institutionally, it was particularly addressed to the need for students to produce doctoral dissertations and master's theses. The instructor for the class, Jay Mead, was a senior professor in second languages education, active and well published in his field, and with many years of experience at the university. A total of 15 students, 12 female and three male, were enrolled in the class. Of the 15, eight were international students: four from the People's Republic of China (PRC), three from the Republic of China (ROC), and one from Spain.[2] Seven of the 15 students were pursuing master's degrees; the remaining eight, PhD's. Although all the students were degree candidates in second languages education, they were a fairly diverse, multilingual, and multicultural group.

The seminar met late in the afternoon twice a week in a windowless room in the basement of one of the education buildings. The students and the professor sat in chairs arranged around three rectangular tables. On the days I observed, I joined them. The seminar was organized in a fashion typical of many seminars. Mead led several of the early sessions; then, students

---

[1] Names of participating students, professors, and institutions are pseudonyms.

[2] In this seminar, nationality (U.S. vs. international) coincided with English-language status (i.e., English as a native or non-native language). For simplicity, I refer to international and U.S. students with the understanding that these terms simultaneously distinguish native speakers of English (NSE) from non-native speakers of English (NNSE).

began to take responsibility for presenting information. As I examined the writing tasks in this seminar, I came to understand them historically, as a discursive cycle triggered by the assignment and culminating in a final graded paper. I also identified multiple perspectives on those tasks. Combining the cycles of activity with the perspectives, I mapped the microhistory of writing tasks in this seminar around five questions: How the professor communicated his expectations for form and content, how the students interpreted those expectations, how the assignments were negotiated, how the students undertook the assignments, and how the professor evaluated and responded to students' final written texts.[3]

Examining the ways a group of students responded to a summary writing task, Flower et al. (1990) found that students not only produced quite different texts, but that those texts in effect represented different underlying representations of the task. In addition to uncovering this multiplicity in students' task representations, they also found that those representations were powerfully tacit (i.e., students assumed they were doing the task their neighbors were, and instructors would presumably see the task variation as variation in text quality, how well the summary was written, rather than what task was done). Although Flower and her colleagues suggested that task representation should be an object of instruction, which presumes the potential for contexts to influence such representations, they did not examine how the history of the course, the instructor's actions, or the particular histories of the students shaped their representations. Instead, they attributed the variation in task representations entirely to the students, emphasizing the cognitive repertoire of writing strategies they were likely to have developed in previous school writing. Seen from the particular, evolving

---

[3]Information on the students and the professor was gathered from class observations and collection of class documents, semi-structured interviews with students and the professor, questionnaires, the students' final texts with comments and grades on them, and text-based interviews with the professor. The text-based interviews with Mead were conducted in two ways. The first was a stimulated elicitation, in which I asked him to look quickly at each student's papers and say whatever seemed most salient about the content of the paper, its history, or the student. The second was a modified version of the discourse-based interview procedure outlined by Odell, Goswami, and Herrington (1983). In discourse-based interviews, the researcher brackets selected passages of a text, writes in possible alternatives, and asks a writer (or reader) whether she would accept the alternatives and why or why not (see chap. 8 for detailed examples of data from this technique). For this seminar, I conducted discourse-based interviews with Mead on a sample of eight papers, with prompts directed at his own written responses as well as passages of the students' texts. I took extensive fieldnotes of the classes I attended (about 70% of the total). Ten of the 15 students in the class agreed to interviews (20-40 minutes in length). I conducted about five hours of interviews with Mead two months after the semester ended, approximately one month after he had graded and responded to the papers. Twelve of the 15 students released all their papers for the research. The three students who did not were all master's students (two U.S., one international).

perspectives of participants, the synoptic image of a writing task multiplies and fragments along many dimensions, not just representations of the task, and for many reasons, not just students' prior experience of school writing.

In this chapter, I explore that multiplicity. I first present eight, overlain exposures of the writing tasks in this seminar. The real writing task, I argue, is not in any one exposure or any privileged perspective on them, but in their densely textured totality. To integrate these multiple images, I then trace a finer grained history of one student's work on one writing task for the seminar. Analysis of the writing tasks in *Language Research* and of the diverse forces that produced their multiplicity was what initially pushed me to explore the kinds of theoretical framework I introduce in chapter 1. However, this case study makes little explicit use of that framework, remaining closer to participants' perspectives. In addition to my belief that a richer image of writing in the academy emerges when participants' discourses and the theoretical frameworks interanimate one another, I especially want to produce a less theoretical account in this chapter, to, in a sense, re-pose the problem as I first encountered it. As my study of this seminar set the stage for my subsequent research, this chapter is intended to set the stage for the somewhat more theoretically oriented analyses of the case studies that follow.

EXPOSURE 1: THE WRITING TASKS AS TEXTS

Figure 2.1 presents part of the syllabus, describing the work students would be expected to do in *Language Research*: reading three to five articles or chapters from textbooks for each class, presenting oral critiques of at least three articles over the semester, writing up two of their article critiques (later amended to one), writing a critique of a dissertation (for PhD students) or a master's thesis (for MA students), and writing a research proposal (4–6 pages) appropriate for MA or PhD research (see Appendix B for informa-tion on the reproduction of textual data). A section headed "Responsibili-ties" described the writing tasks (see Fig. 2.1). Point 1 lists the sections expected for the research proposal. Point 4 gives the outline for the article and dissertation or thesis critiques, specifying four major sections: an abstract, the critique, what was learned, and important next steps. Beyond providing a structure for students' final texts, the assignments represented heuristics for thinking about, reading, and writing research in the field. Part b of the critique assignment, for example, is a skeletal echo of the research

Responsibilities

1. A proposal for a study, with bibliography. The proposal should contain a tentative title, statement of the problem, background to the study, statement of research questions or hypotheses, method (to include procedures for data collection and data analysis), and significance of the study as major headings. The details will get worked out as the proposal is adapted to the individual problem. The proposal should be no longer than four to six pages, exclusive of bibliography.

2. A written critique of a PhD dissertation (or an MA Paper), preferably one in second language education, against the outline in Borg and Gall, pp 71–106 or the outline of Baker and Schutz, pp. 277–279 which I will provide.

3. Formal, written critiques of two of the studies you examined in class based on the discussion in Borg and Gall, pp. 192–233 or the criteria of Baker and Schutz, pp. 277–279 which I will provide and/or McMillan and Schumacher, pp. 46–54 for quantitative research and pp. 54–68 for qualitative research.

4. The critiques, based on the guidelines stated in 2 and 3 above, should consist of the following sections:
   a. An abstract;
   b. Critique
      1) Design
      2) Data Gathering and Analysis
      3) Conclusions
   c. What Have We Learned?
   d. Important Next Steps.

5. An ERIC (MA students) and a DATRIX search on the proposal topic.

6. There is no final examination.

FIG. 2.1. Writing assignments extracted from the seminar syllabus.

proposal. The textbooks on educational research cited under points 2 and 3 in the syllabus provide further guidelines, sets of heuristic questions, and models for evaluating and writing up research reports and proposals.

All of the written assignments would be due on the last day of the quarter, and there would be no tests. The syllabus calendar also represented the process of writing. Weekly readings began with a line to write in the name of the student who would orally critique the reading (and oral critiques preceded and echoed the structure of written critiques). In addition, the calendar noted the days when students were scheduled to present and discuss drafts of sections of the research proposals, beginning with the presentation of tentative titles in the second week of the seminar. In short, the syllabus provided a fairly elaborated textual representation of the expected products and processes for the writing tasks.

EXPOSURE 2: THE PROFESSOR'S TASK
REPRESENTATIONS

Studies of classroom writing have suggested that an instructor's ideology, goals, and ways of structuring the class have important effects on students' writing (e.g., Casanave, 1995; Herrington, 1985, 1988; Michaels, 1987). Given that the professor chose the readings, designed the assignments, and led classroom activities, it was important to examine his perspectives on the seminar and its writing tasks. At the end of the first interview, Mead summed up his goals for the individual assignments and the class:[4] "Maybe, Paul, the whole thing comes down to one large goal, whether it's writing or critiquing or giving presentations or whatever, [the goal] is simply to think–to get people to think about what they are–what they're doing, what it is they're engaged in, what the results are, what they contribute, and to be aware of that." As with many of his classroom interactions, this comment reflected Mead's concern that students understand the choices they make in personal, professional, and ethical as well as intellectual terms, suggesting that Mead saw disciplines much as Geertz (1983) discussed them, not just as conventions and content, but as ways of being in the world. This interest in ways of being in the world was reflected in the seminar in his attention to questions of career paths, lifestyles, collegial relationships, and ethical choices.

Earlier in the interview, Mead had identified two major goals for the course: first, that students "have an opportunity to read across the research literature in language education," and second, that they "read critically what is there." Regarding this second goal, he noted that students often found critique difficult:

> People seem to feel that what's on the printed page is truth, and I think what I was trying to do was to suggest, in getting people to read critically, that as human beings we make mistakes, we make mistakes in doing research as well, and that truth is, in a sense, kind of relative in that regard, and one has to be able to take something from what one reads and be able to apply it to different situations.

Critical evaluation and taking something from the work being critiqued

---

[4]Interviews from this seminar have been slightly edited. False starts and repetitions have been removed; punctuation and capitalization have been added. See Appendix B for further details.

were recurrent themes in Mead's comments in class and were embodied in the critique assignment itself (see Fig. 2.1), the last two sections of which were: "What have we learned?" and "Next steps?" Mead was asking students to read constructively as researchers and not just as students learning the content. I originally saw the oral critiques as ways of engaging students with the content and, given my interest in writing processes, as drafts for the written critiques. Thus, I was surprised that, when asked about his goals, Mead replied that the oral critique forced "people into recognition that, as academics in their future careers, they are going to have to present papers at conferences." Mead's repeated reference to students' future careers pointed to the broader contexts of disciplinary enculturation, but also to potentially conflicting contextualizations for the writing tasks in *Language Research.*

Discussing goals for the research proposal both in class and in the interviews, Mead emphasized process, what he referred to as "shaping and molding." He explained that the discussion of draft sections of the proposal in class was designed not only for task-oriented goals (e.g., focusing on the pieces to avoid getting overwhelmed, clarifying content expectations for each section), but also to get students "to recognize that more eyes on a piece of work is better than none, and that you can get feedback from your colleagues, and that that's important information that you can use." He indicated that the goal for the final draft of the research proposal was to "put it all together," to use the information and feedback from the seminar to generate "an initial draft" of a research proposal for a dissertation or thesis. Overall, Mead's goals for the class and for the specific assignments appear to reflect the three contexts Anson (1988) identified for academic writing: the curricular (writing as part of a program of instruction occurring within a particular institutional context), the professional (writing as part of a disciplinary or professional discourse community), and the developmental (writing as part of an intellectual process into which students are being enculturated).

EXPOSURE 3: MAKING AND REMAKING THE ASSIGNMENTS

The static images of the writing tasks presented in the syllabus were not the final word. They were supplemented by oral restatements of the writing tasks in and out of class. For example, in the fifth session of the seminar, Mead outlined on the blackboard the assignment for the research proposal. In some cases, his outline elaborated on that given in the syllabus (see Fig.

2.1). Where the syllabus presented a section on "method (to include procedures for data collection and data analysis)," the blackboard representation
of this section read:

5. Methodology
— population
— instruments
— procedures
— data analysis

As Mead went over the organization of the research proposal, he also talked
more about the content and goals of each section. An example of this kind
of elaboration came in discussions of the section represented simply as
"background to the study" in the syllabus. Mead spent considerable time in
this session representing the content and goals of that section, stressing the
need to define crucial terms clearly and to review the relevant literature that
would eventually lead to specific research questions. He also characterized
common problems with literature reviews, such as simply dumping the
content of notecards. In these elaborations, he presupposed connections
between the seminar research proposal and institutional and disciplinary
genres (institutional research proposals, dissertations, theses, and journal
articles). For example, to illustrate problems with literature reviews, he
talked not of previous student papers in *Language Research,* but of dissertation proposals and dissertations themselves. He evoked a generic disser-
tator becoming terribly upset with the need to revise a literature review and
noted the need for patience and understanding on both sides, student and
advisor (not student and teacher). To stress that the literature review must
be selective, he told a story of his negotiations with a former student, an
Arab (now a Dean of Education in his home country), who wanted to include
every study ever published on a certain form of language testing in his
dissertation review of the literature. He recounted that the student argued
that his colleagues at home would expect a comprehensive review, that he
(Mead) reminded the student that he was writing his dissertation in the
United States, and that they had finally compromised on what to include.
In other words, Mead mixed paradigmatic and narrative modes to define
and contextualize the research proposal's rhetorical situation, its underlying
goals and values, and its content.

Throughout the quarter, Mead emphasized social-scientific research
(statistics, experimental design, rational argumentation, and the philosophy
of science). In relation to the critiques and research proposals, he stressed

research values of care, attention to detail, full public disclosure of methods, skeptical testing of assumptions, and careful reasoning. For example, during oral critiques, Mead repeatedly nominated or ratified social-scientific research issues, such as the importance of randomization in experimental studies and of providing reliability measures for tests used. As critiques were given, he often raised the issue of replicability explicitly or implicitly (by criticizing missing information). Discussing students' drafts of sections of the research proposal, Mead repeatedly rehearsed social-scientific research topics as well as the generic structure of the research proposal.

Mead also linked the writing tasks to other spheres of activity. He introduced public, political, and cultural issues in the seminar, particularly in relation to the critiques. He also stressed institutional contexts of the tasks, relating them to the departmental program, particularly the dissertation, and to disciplinary publications. With his discussions of "shaping and molding," Mead was referring to general processes of writing and research. In addition, Mead often foregrounded the personal in relation to the disciplinary, telling tales of his experiences of life in the discipline.

Mead also had opportunities to explicitly and implicitly restate or elaborate on his expectations for the writing tasks when students presented their oral critiques of articles or discussed drafts of research proposals. The first day that students passed around drafts of their problem statements, several were fairly long, including one that ran two pages. Mead took this opportunity to remind students of the length of the entire proposal (4–6 pages) and to suggest that the problem statement should be concise, probably no longer than a paragraph. In the next class, five students presented problem statements and all were one paragraph. In a number of oral critiques, students did not provide the last two sections of the critique (perhaps because discussion had interrupted their delivery or time had run out). In these cases, Mead would reinforce the syllabus outline, asking them to briefly address "What have we learned?" and "Next steps."

Other opportunities to restate the task arose from student-initiated interactions. Students asked questions or presented their interpretations of the task or their plans for their texts in class, in the office, and during breaks. In some cases, Mead filled in the students on interactions that happened outside the seminar. For example, although the writing assignments were not due until the last day of the semester, four students turned in their critiques early, asking him to check over their work. When Mead read these critiques, he was very dissatisfied with them because they did not strictly follow the syllabus outlines and did not use the outline headings. He returned the critiques to the students, offering them the opportunity to revise. However, he also informed all the students at the opening of a seminar session about the problems he had seen in these critiques and that he had returned them to the four students with a recommendation that they revise. Thus, these students' critiques became, in effect, the first written drafts of the critiques on which the class as a whole received feedback and an opportunity for Mead to stress that he wanted the students to follow and display the task outlines on the syllabus.

Classroom observation made it clear that writing assignments were not a one-time event made early in the semester and expressed primarily in a syllabus statement of the task. The writing assignments were made and re-made within the history of the seminar, in a complex, ongoing stream of events. In these dispersed and situated processes, multiple, sometimes conflicting, representations of the tasks were conveyed and constructed.

EXPOSURE 4: STUDENTS' REPRESENTATIONS
OF MEAD'S TASK

To understand Mead's assignments, students seemed to use, to varying degrees, all of the explicit and implicit sources of information about form and content noted earlier. When asked in the interviews to describe the assignments and Mead's expectations, most referred to the outline or guidelines given in the syllabus (and embodied in the presentations of draft sections). Debra, for example, described the research proposal by saying, "I know I have to state the purpose of the research, the problem statement, provide some sort of bibliography in order to establish a background for the study, formulate some research questions, and I think that's where we stop." The omission of any reference to methodology in her case is interesting. Drafts of the methodology sections were not presented until late in the quarter (after this interview), and then only about half of the students had the opportunity to discuss them. Moreover, Mead identified methodology as a weakness in Debra's final research proposal.

Tang, a PhD student from the PRC, began describing the critique assignment by commenting, "Well, first of all, to give a brief summary of the paper and then look at it critically. That means that you have to look at first of all the research question, and then look at a little bit about the literature review, the theoretical background, to see if it really leads to the research question." Tang continued in this fashion through each point of the outline, displaying elaborate representations of explicit and implicit expectations for the content and form of the assignment. Mead's positive response to his final critiques suggested that he had indeed understood and executed this assignment well.

Mai, a master's student from the ROC, described the critique in this way: "I think I just follow the outline he listed in the syllabus, the abstract, critique, including design, data gathering and analysis, conclusions, what I've learned, and next important steps.... I think his expectations will be mainly on the what have we learned and the important next steps. He requires our personal judgment and interest, I think." Mai's recalled representation of the critique is almost an exact quote from the syllabus (see Fig. 2.1), but offers no elaboration on the content of sections. It also appeared to echo seminar presentations, where Mead repeatedly asked "What have we learned?" and "Next steps." Once again, Mai's representations of the assignments may have been reflected in her final written texts, which carefully followed the form, but provided minimal content (chap. 4 looks at Mai's work in detail).

Students' ways of taking the tasks were also shaped by their representations of Mead's personality. For example, in his interview, Wang said he was looking for unique points on which to critique articles rather than commonplace ones, indicating that he expected Mead to "use creativity as a very important criteria" for grading because he felt Mead was "an original thinker," who had "a lot of unique views on many issues in this field." Steve, a U.S. master's student, when asked how Mead would respond to the critiques, wondered if he would tell students if they were "way off track." When asked why, he responded, "He's kind of Freirian, I think, he would be more likely to nudge you rather than say this is what you haven't done, this is what you have done, that's just his style from what I've picked up in the course." Thus, students were constructing task representations by interpreting not only the writing assignments, but also the person who had made and would ultimately judge them. The uncertainty of such situated judgments was seen clearly in this case: Steve was one of the four students whose critiques were returned for revision at the end of the quarter. Students' representations of the writing assignments clearly reflected both the written and oral statements made by Mead as well as the implicit communication of expectations in the seminar sessions. The diverse backgrounds of the students and the wealth of potential cues for the writing tasks embedded in the history of the course provided ample resources for students to construct heterogeneous representations of both the writing tasks and their communicative and social contexts.

EXPOSURE 5: A DRAFT BY ANY OTHER NAME?

Sternglass (1989) noted that her subjects/students, many of whom were composition teachers themselves, found the language of assignments (e.g., Write a summary of _____) to be quite ambiguous (see Flower et al., 1990). For the students in *Language Research*, the multiple sources of information about the assignments arising from classroom discussion worked both centripetally to reduce ambiguities, such as the appropriate length for the problem statement, and centrifugally, sustaining or even intensifying ambiguities, as in the case of the research proposal's representation as "a draft."

Most of the students interviewed echoed Mead's statement that the research proposal was "just a draft." However, varied senses of "a draft" led to a visible breakdown in the communication of expectations. The notion of draft seemed to lower students' concerns. For example, on Wang's two critiques combined (eight pages of text), Mead made 17 responses related to problems with form (i.e., language, mechanics, manuscript form); however, on Wang's research proposal (six pages of text), he noted 43 problems with form. That a breakdown in the communication of expectations occurred was also reflected in Mead's response to the research proposals, which was qualitatively more negative than his response to the critiques in both his comments and his grades ("Exposure 8" offers more details on Mead's response). How did this miscommunication occur?

One factor that facilitated the breakdown seemed to be public discussions of the assignment that were addressed to individuals. For example, in a session near the end of the quarter, Lin, a doctoral student from the PRC, passed out her research questions, expressing uncertainty about them. After a number of serious problems with her methodology had been identified, Mead moved to put the research proposal into perspective, emphasizing that writing is a process and suggesting that some people might not even be able to give him an initial draft, but that what was important was that they had gone through the process. In a text-based interview, Mead said that Lin "had a tendency to put herself down in very subtle ways," although he felt she was quite competent. In an interview shortly after that class, Lin described the class discussion of her research questions, saying that the problems raised led her to conclude that she had been "turned down." Her representation of the seminar response suggests that Mead's concerns about her confidence were reasonable. Lin changed topics in the last two weeks of the quarter and ended up with a paper that impressed Mead. It seems likely that Mead's comments on Lin's proposal were designed to take the pressure off and encourage her. However, other students, who in a sense overheard this dialogue, could easily construe his comments as addressed to them and as implying that their drafts could be quite rough indeed.

How the draft was imaginatively contextualized also seemed to contribute to the breakdown. When asked in the interview what he meant by an initial draft, Mead described ideal goals, only occasionally qualifying them in terms of their "initial" character. Later in one discourse-based interview, I asked Mead if he would change a grade on a research proposal from a B to a B+ or A-:

> Oh the grade, I would not change it, I would not change it because I don't feel that it is a moldable, malleable draft, because I don't know what is to be done, from my perspective I don't see- I think she and I would have to sit and do some talking before- and she might even have to go back and think about what it is that she really wants to do.... I get something in the form of a proposal, but it's not specific enough to be able to say, "Yeah, ok, now let's take and work this over." It's just not there, it's just not there.

From these interviews, it is clear that Mead not only had high expectations of what an initial draft would look like (that it would meet the basic genre requirements and be carefully thought out and executed), but that he contextualized it as a text an advisee would bring into his office, one that they could begin to refine together. In other words, Mead was thinking of it not simply as a draft for the seminar, but as a draft for an actual dissertation or thesis. In the students' interviews, "just a draft," sounded much different, conjuring up images of a rough draft, an easy assignment. In calling the research proposal a draft and in emphasizing the importance of process, Mead may have been invoking the wider institutional and disciplinary contexts that he often invoked in class, whereas many of the students seemed to be hearing these comments in the narrower contexts of the class and grading or through the intertextual echoes of writing process pedagogy.

EXPOSURE 6: NEGOTIATING THE TASK

Students explicitly negotiated several aspects of the assignments. Negotiation generally started and sometimes ended with a student asking a question or presenting a problem. For example, in a session late in the quarter, several students questioned whether it made sense for the length of the dissertation and thesis critiques to be the same as that of the article critiques, given that those texts were so much longer than the articles. When Mead said the limits were the same and would be strictly kept, the students briefly argued, but to no avail. Several international students told Mead (outside of seminar sessions) that they were having trouble keeping up with the extensive reading and writing requirements. This finally led him, reluctantly, to reduce the reading assignments and drop one of the written article critiques. In an interview after the quarter, Mead explained that he made this decision, in part, on the grounds that some of the international students he perceived as strongest were vocally expressing their concerns, leading him to conclude that those he perceived as weaker were probably just lost. It is important to recall here as well that this issue affected over half of the class.

The presence of implicit negotiation, although not as open and perhaps not even fully intentional, could also be inferred. Students generally followed the letter of the written assignments as stated on the syllabus; however, their texts provided evidence of some significant, implicit negotiation, particularly on the critiques. All 12 students whose papers I received followed the outline of the research proposal, using headings identical or nearly identical to those given in the syllabus or written on the board in the second week of class. However, none of the four students who turned in their critiques early followed the syllabus outline so closely. Most either had no headings or simply "Abstract" and "Critique." The third and fourth sections of the outline, "What have we learned?" and "Important Next Steps," were either entirely missing or deemphasized and not clearly marked. In spite of the strong signal Mead sent when he returned the four students' critiques and explained to the class why he had, two students (not from the original four) still failed to follow the outlines in either of their critiques, and two others deviated significantly in one of the two critiques. Moreover, only four of the twelve used the subheadings (design, data gathering and analysis, and conclusions) listed in the syllabus outline (Fig. 2.1) under "b) The critique."

Why did students align their research proposals so tightly to Mead's assigned organization, but their critiques, so inconsistently? The different modes of presentation for "drafts" may have affected alignment. Whereas the students presented drafts of the research proposals in isolated sections and in writing, the critiques were presented orally in their entirety, mixing prepared and spontaneous remarks with not infrequent interruptions for questions and discussion. Mead's responses in class to critiques might have been less comprehensive, less precise, or less recognizable than his in-class responses to the written drafts of sections of the research proposals. However, the question of authority also seemed important. The research proposal represented a clear disciplinary and institutional genre. When Mead asked students to follow this form, he was asking them to follow a form they would have to use, minimally, for their thesis or dissertation proposal. It was also a form that might be used again for grant proposals. Finally, parts of the proposal (e.g., the literature review, research questions, methodology) strongly resembled parts of research reports in the journal articles, theses, and dissertations they were reading intensively in this seminar (and probably others). The critique assignment, on the other hand, bore a more distant resemblance to any disciplinary genre, the closest being reviews of research within literature reviews or perhaps book reviews.[5] In effect, I am suggesting that students were implicitly negotiating the critique task by resisting it. Or perhaps, more than the form itself, what was being negotiated was the authority of the students as writers to take the spirit rather than the letter of the assignment.[6]

Students also implicitly negotiated the writing tasks in other ways. Turning the critiques in early and asking for feedback on them, as four students did, might be seen as a form of implicit negotiation, essentially renegotiating the terms of the assignment to create a kind of provisional final draft. Similarly, students negotiated the length of papers. Although Mead had threatened at one point to return without a grade any paper that exceeded the length limits, some students went slightly over the limits in their final papers. Somewhat more subtly, others adjusted line spacings, which the syllabus had specified as double spaced, or font sizes in order to "meet" the limits. Mead accepted these small deviations, apparently another example of successful negotiation by the students.

EXPOSURE 7: SITUATING THE WRITING TASKS IN STUDENTS' PROJECTS

All of the students I interviewed reported that factors beyond Mead's assignments and the seminar shaped the way they undertook seminar writing tasks. Most reported that the topics they selected for their research

---

[5]Based on my interviews with Mead, I believe he saw the critique assignment in the developmental context (Anson, 1988), as an exercise that recapitulated important thought processes (summation, critical analysis, integration with personal knowledge, creative adaptation) students would need as professionals, and not in the professional context, as a disciplinary genre to master. However, nothing in my fieldnotes or the student interviews indicates that he explained the assignment in these terms to the students.

[6]Mead's comments in the seminar often invited students to see themselves in professional roles. Herrington (1985) found that the roles professors took in class influenced how students construed their roles and their authority in writing.

proposals were related to personal interests arising from their life experiences, particularly from work and study experiences. Many indicated emotional attachments to or political or ethical concerns with issues related to the research. Some noted that their research was shaped by practical concerns, particularly access to potential subjects. Many related their research proposals for *Language Research* to other classes they had taken, often ones outside the department. In their critiques of theses and dissertations, at least five of the students chose texts to critique that were closely related to their research proposals, and several had volunteered to critique articles that related as well. Looking ahead, all the students saw the research proposals as at least probable candidates for their actual theses or dissertations. Several were actively preparing to carry out the research or to pilot it. Although classroom discussion, course readings, and the structure of the writing assignments implicitly and explicitly emphasized experimental and quantitative research traditions, half of the research proposals were qualitative or ethnographic. In short, students' research proposals and critiques were embedded in and infused with motives, contexts, and resources that extended well beyond the seminar.

One of the most striking examples of the ways that students' own projects influenced their writing involved the research proposal developed by Teresa, a master's student from Spain whose work I examine in greater depth in chapter 4. Teresa reported that the idea for her research had arisen a year earlier in a course dealing with Limited-English-Proficient students in U.S. schools. Coming from a Castilian-speaking family in a Catalan-speaking province, she had connected her experience of being a language minority, although she spoke the national prestige dialect, to the experience of language-minority students in the United States. She decided to research use of Catalan, which had in post-Franco Spain been officially recognized and become the primary language of the school curriculum in the province of Catalonia. Pursuing her interest, she took a course in sociolinguistics offered by the Spanish Department and then *Language Research* to help her finalize the details of the research. Teresa planned to begin her MA research in Spain the last week of the quarter. Anxious to complete her real proposal and plans, she actively bid to have draft sections of her proposal discussed in the seminar, approached Mead during breaks on several occasions to ask his advice, and also visited his office at least once to discuss her research and emphasize her need to be ready by the end of the quarter. In her interview, Teresa mentioned that she had been invited to and had attended a meeting of ABD (all-but-dissertation) doctoral students, where she presented her research and got useful feedback on it. She also noted that she had asked Mead for a master's thesis to critique that dealt with sociolinguistics, in effect, making the critique contribute to her work on the research proposal.

In the seminar, Teresa heard for the first time that she should submit her research proposal to the university's Human Subjects Review (HSR). Going through HSR was a requirement of the actual research, not the seminar. Her final research proposal for the seminar provided detailed consideration of procedures, especially concerning confidentiality, that was rare in other students' research proposals:

> *Procedure:* Before administering the questionnaire the researcher will explain to the participants what the research consists of. Participants will be volunteers. During the administration of the questionnaire the researcher will not be present. It will be administered by a teacher who will be provided with directions. Once the questionnaires will be finished, these will be sealed in an envelope and given to the researcher. From now on, noone except the researcher will have access to them. Filling in the questionnaire will occur during a regular class period.

As the final seminar sessions were held, Teresa was in Spain collecting her data. In short, because of the project she brought to the seminar, Teresa's research proposal was not just a seminar assignment; it was laminated literate activity in which several contexts were foregrounded. Interpreting her writing of this research proposal only from the perspective of the seminar would be like judging a movie still in production on the basis of a few disconnected frames.

EXPOSURE 8: RESPONDING TO STUDENTS' FINAL WRITTEN TEXTS

Earlier sections of this chapter have indicated ways that Mead responded in class to students' oral critiques and drafts of the research proposal. This section focuses on the written response he gave to students' final papers. His expectations for the initial draft of the research proposal have already been discussed. Concerning criteria for response to the critique assignments, he indicated that he was looking at whether students understood the work and could evaluate it critically and whether the critique hung together in relation to the outline. Asked what he wanted to achieve through his response, Mead stressed that he wanted to be supportive, to be appreciative of the time, effort, and thought students put into the writing. When he had things to say that were not supportive, he indicated he would offer comments and questions "to generate the person's thinking further about the issues."

Displayed on students' papers, Mead's response was complex and difficult to describe. In bare descriptive terms, he edited the language and form of texts; underlined or circled key words, phrases, even sentences, often with no related comment; wrote marginal comments and questions relating to a variety of issues (both form and content); and made a final summary comment at the end of each paper coupled with the grade. His responses ranged from editing symbols indicating need for a space to single words (e.g., *good, really?*) to multisentence remarks that filled the margins. Mead's responses were primarily to content, with response to form mostly limited to international students' papers.

He clearly responded to research proposals differently from the critiques. On research proposals, Mead asked for missing information or more specificity, questioned assumptions or the relationship between different elements of the proposal (e.g., the research questions and the methodology), and raised institutional or disciplinary issues. The following examples give the flavor of much of the response:[7]

- How do you document a lack of research?
- How often? Each time they meet? How many? Who will do the interviews? Of what will they consist?
- I wouldn't trust your memory—I would record each conference and transcribe soon afterwards so as not to lose anything.
- Are Flower and Hayes the major resource here or are there others who support their perceptions and research?
- We need to talk about this study if you intend to go about actually doing it!

His responses were typically oriented to revision of the proposal or to actually conducting the research. They also reflected his familiarity with the proposals, each of which had been discussed to some degree in the seminar on several occasions.

Mead's response to the critiques was more complexly situated and varied. In general, it was more summative than formative, more evaluative, and less oriented toward revision. He focused particularly on students' reading of the articles and their execution of the form. The following examples are indicative:

---

[7]Mead's written comments are reproduced here without editing. Authors cited are not pseudonyms.

- Outstanding abstract! This is a very complicated study to capture in so few words!
- What makes them <u>too</u> general? Some elaboration on your part would have helped.
- Was the "natural order" taught? Why would one do that?
- True! Good comment!
- I think you have an excellent point here—The terms are much more precise today! For example, the Swain and Canale article in <u>Applied Linguistics</u>, volume one, didn't appear until 1980.
- <u>What have we learned</u>? <u>What next steps</u>? These two sections are left untouched!

However, in response to the dissertation and thesis critiques, many of which he had been involved with, Mead often introduced his personal knowledge:

- No, I would argue that there was a distinct block against such critique. I tried the heavy hand on this matter, but with no success and a temporary freeze on the dissertation—I backed off.
- The [language] tests [at this university] are not set up for the purpose of examining variability.

Moreover, when a student critiqued an article or dissertation related to his or her research proposal, Mead often responded more to the disciplinary and methodological issues raised, sometimes referring directly to the student's own research proposal.

Mead clearly responded to the papers of international students somewhat differently from those of U.S. students. He noted in an interview that he read their papers three times (rather than his usual two) because he wanted to ensure that he understood them clearly before he began to respond to them. All of the international students' papers exhibited lexical, syntactic, and mechanical problems. Mead's response to them was much more directed at form than his response to U.S. students, reflected in more editing of language and in marginal comments that often stated rules for writing. However, content clearly remained the major focus of his response and evaluation. When his final comments indicated that language problems, sometimes euphemistically referred to as "mechanical problems," had affected the grade, it was either because the problems compromised meaning or because he believed they reflected a lack of care rather than ability.

One of the most important forms of feedback a professor gives a student is the grade. The distribution of grades displayed some interesting patterns.

First, at least for the 12 students who released their papers for the research, no one received a grade in the C range on any of their assignments. Second, some students' grades were consistent across assignments, but others' were not. Five students were in the A range on all three assignments, whereas two, both international students, were in the B range on all three. Five students were mixed, and, in each of their cases, A's on both critiques were coupled with B's on the research proposals. Interestingly, four of these five were doctoral students (three of them U.S. students). This distribution shows that grades on the research proposals were markedly lower than grades on the critiques, and that U.S. doctoral students, as a group, displayed the greatest drop (three out of four receiving B grades).

In spite of Mead's relatively strict enforcement of some elements of his task representation (e.g., the organizational schemes), his responses also revealed considerable flexibility in other areas. Figures 2.2. and 2.3 display excerpts from two critiques with Mead's comments. In both excerpts, his responses are positive, and both critiques received good grades (A- and A).[8] However, the two critiques appear quite distinct in content and disciplinary orientation. Figure 2.2 displays Mead's response to Barbara, a U.S. doctoral

There were several problems with the research design. The sample was small and not randomly selected, there was no control group, subjects were not randomly assigned to experimental groups, the sample (from an intensive, non-credit program) was not representative of many ESL classrooms, and not enough information was given about the subjects (e.g., gender, first language). In addition, Nash did not mention possible effects of the pretest, who administered the tests or observed the classes, the reliability or validity of the tests, how some of the tests were adapted, or by whom they were adapted. Her three criteria for communicative competence did not include communication of meaning, and thus the reader could not be sure that the proficiency tests used tapped this aspect of communication at all. The observation period of five hours per day, once a week, for four weeks was short, but Nash notes this as a limitation of her study.

These are most if not all of the design problems which by the way are considered. And you are really C aware of them.

FIG. 2.2. An excerpt from Barbara's article critique.

[8]Mead's end comment on Barbara's paper excerpted in Fig. 2.2 suggests that the minus on the A was related to problems with the section on next steps, not to the critique of research displayed in the figure.

A clock, rather than a human observer, determines when the students will be observed. The implication is that the methodology will be more scientific if it is run by an impartial machine rather than a biased human being.

Critique

The reasoning behind this methodology disturbs me for several reasons. Quark and Zane describe categories for "engaged behavior" as writing, speaking, listening and thinking (Reading is not included, but that may be just an oversight.). I do not think it is possible for any observer to accurately assess whether a person is thinking or listening to the material being presented, as many students are masters at appearing to be engaged when they are actually busy thinking about something else. At the same time, I think that it is very important to allow students a proper amount of time to digest material by listening and thinking. Since I am familiar with the authors' teaching style, I suspect they do not address this issue precisely because they are not concerned with giving students much time to think. Their classes consist of a blitz of input and active engagement which allows very little time for reflection. In short, I do not think it is fair to assess student engagement using very limited observations driven by the clock. I suspect it will not give a good overall picture of what is happening during that 50 minute class period, and makes absolutely no assessment over a longer period of time. To get a broader picture we really need a movie rather than *YES!* a snapshot.

FIG. 2.3. Excerpt from Pat's article critique.

student, who has critiqued an article by Susan Nash (a pseudonym). Mead's marginal comments and especially his underlining of phrases in her text strongly ratify Barbara's references to topics such as control groups, random assignment, sampling, representativeness, and sufficient information. Barbara's critique and Mead's response are tightly aligned, following the deeply etched grooves of the privileged topics of social-scientific research that Mead rehearsed intensely in the seminar. Figure 2.3 displays Mead's response to Pat, another U.S. doctoral student, who critiqued an article by Quark and Zane (again pseudonyms). (The excerpt from Pat's critique begins with the final two sentences of the abstract.) Compared to Barbara's critique, Pat's is clearly more personal and political. In the nine sentences of the critique, Pat has seven first-person pronouns, six of which begin clauses (i.e., "I think," "I don't think," "I suspect," and "I am familiar with"). Moreover, Pat invokes personal knowledge of Quark and Zane to critique their research and teaching. Problems in the research are tied to questions of what amounts to the bad faith of the researchers and the subjects. Tropes are also foregrounded in Pat's text. Learning is represented metaphorically as a digestive process. Images of clocks and tropes of film index modern political critiques of the technocratic nature of society and the decontextualized nature of social sciences. Mead does not question or even mention Pat's style and content (either in his written response or in text- and discourse-based interviews on her papers). In fact, his marginal comments and underlining ratify Pat's text as a commendable analysis of the research methodology. Overall, Mead's written responses on students' papers suggest that his reception of students' texts was as complexly laminated and situated an activity as the students' production of those texts.

A MICROHISTORY OF A RESEARCH PROPOSAL:
THE CASE OF HAN

To illustrate how these multiple exposures of the academic writing tasks were integrated in particular trajectories of activity, I will explore the microhistory of one student's research proposal. Han, a female PhD student from the PRC, presented a tentative title for her research proposal in the seminar the second week of the quarter: "Effects of cross-cultural experience on teaching." She related this title to her work as an English as a second language (ESL) instructor in China, where she had felt that Chinese scholars preparing to visit the U.S. needed some kind of cultural orientation to help them communicate with Americans.

A week later, Han passed out the following draft of her "Statement of the Problem" to the class (italics have been added for reasons explained below):

The Effects of Cross-Cultural Experience on
The Comprehensibility of Native Speech

There are now increasing numbers of Chinese researchers and scholars who come to
the United States to study and work in various academic fields, their daily interaction

with their native colleagues has revealed basic problems covering a wide range of linguistic, cultural and academic adjustment to the new environment. My interest in this study is drawn prticularly to the problems of how those visiting scholars, as language learners, could make full use of their cross-cultural experience to create for themselves advantageous opportunities to develop their communicative skills with respect to transmitting and interpreting the native speech.

The purpose of this study is to compare and analyse the different results with respect to levels of comprehensibility of native speech between learners with different attitudes toward the daily cultural bumps and conflicts they encounter. Namely between learners who actively involve themselves in their daily interactions with native speakers and learners who behave like passive vessels into which culture is poured.

The study also indicates a pedagogic need for designing a special training program to prepare scholars or students going abroad with a positive attitude and effective skills to develop their language proficiency in a cross-cultural situation.

Han presented her draft late in the first session in which drafts of problem statements were discussed. Early in this session, one student had presented a two-page problem statement for what was to be a research proposal no longer than six pages. In responding to that and other drafts, Mead had been stressing the need for a concise and precise statement. Turning to Han's draft, Mead continued that focus. He pointed to the first sentence and the middle paragraph (italicized in the previous extract) as elements essential to a "statement of the problem." These selections discarded Han's discussion of her interests in the research and her sense of its pedagogical goals, leaving a problem statement that was more abstract and theoretical.[9] Mead closed discussion of Han's research that day by noting that she was addressing a "very difficult" issue.

Two weeks later in the quarter, Han presented a draft of her research questions to the class. However, as sometimes happened, discussion focused less on her text than on broader issues triggered by the text. In this case, emphasis shifted from the questions, which Mead suggested might be unanswerable and were the work of a lifetime, to issues of methodology, particularly practicality, and to the subject domain of the research, problems with cross-cultural communication. My fieldnotes indicate that Han was interested in qualitative case studies. However, Mead was concerned about the wide scope and undefined nature of one of her constructs, "cultural

---

[9]This kind of selective foregrounding and backgrounding of contexts for texts has been reported in other studies of disciplinary writing (e.g., Knorr-Cetina, 1981; Latour & Woolgar, 1986) and was found repeatedly in this research. In chapters 7 and 9, it is discussed as a key strategy for constructing disciplinarity.

interference."[10] He proposed a more experimental design, using simulated situations. Going to the board, he sketched out a sequence of boxes and arrows to illustrate how Han could set up scenarios that would be likely to trigger cross-cultural miscommunication, get some kind of response from the Chinese subjects, and then ask native speakers to respond to the same situation or to respond to the Chinese subject's response. Han expressed a concern that the design Mead proposed would not be "natural." Mead suggested several other faculty members she might talk to about her research and then focused on the difficulty of capturing and recognizing examples of cross-cultural miscommunication in everyday interactions.

In an interview with me several weeks later (about three weeks before the final proposal was due), Han discussed her interest in the proposal, but expressed continuing uncertainty about it. She reported that she had chosen to critique a dissertation on native speakers' reactions to Japanese speech samples, hoping it would discuss cultural issues, but had been disappointed. She said her "temporary" title for the proposal was now "Mother Culture Interference and Comprehensibility of Native Speakers." Although Han's new title did not mention teaching, in the interview she still emphasized that her underlying motive was that Chinese visiting scholars in the U.S. faced serious problems with communication and cultural adjustment and that she wanted to research those problems so that she could develop a training program to help reduce them.

Later in the interview, as I asked more about the research proposal, she discussed Mead's responses to her draft sections. She recalled that Mead had been interested in the title, but thought it would be difficult to do. As she talked, other influences on her topic choice began to emerge. She noted that Mead, her advisor for her MA as well as her PhD work, was very knowledgeable on culture and that this had attracted her to cultural issues in ESL. She mentioned the needs of her country and the visiting scholars who came to the United States. She reported that the idea for this research had germinated in a course on English for Special Purposes that she had taken earlier in the year. For that course, she had taped interactions in a science laboratory between a Chinese visiting scholar and an American colleague and done an informal needs assessment. She concluded that she was facing a difficult dilemma: Should she choose some easy topic for her

---

[10] Features and patterns of a first language are known to interfere with the learning of a second language. This linguistic interference has prompted applied linguists to do contrastive analyses of languages to predict probable areas of trouble. Han's notion of cultural interference was an extension of that notion to questions of cross-cultural communication.

research proposal, one she could handle well, or should she pursue the topic she was actually interested in for her dissertation? When I asked how Mead would grade and respond to the research proposals, she emphasized his many references to writing and research as processes:

> Since he has emphasized so much "shaping and molding", now I am not really worried, I don't think I worry a lot about the grades, because anyway he thinks you just handing in a kind of rough drafts, at first I was worried because I don't think I could finish this within one quarter and in every class he said, "That's just shaping and molding" and "I don't expect a really complete proposal".... I say, "Why don't I just write down something and I have one or two years to write on a dissertation?" So I have kind of a dilemma, I thought maybe I just write a kind of tentative title for this course, not really my dissertation title, or I try to find the real topic for my dissertation starting from this point, finally I decided I would write to find a title for my dissertation—even it's not very logical and the design is not very good, that's ok, Dr. Mead will understand about that, if I can't get a good grade, that's ok.

In Han's final research proposal, the influence of the draft presentations could be seen in her problem statement, which referred to Chinese students' problems, but did not talk about pedagogical solutions. Han also appeared to narrow the scope of the research, from all "cultural differences" to the issue of differences in cultural values. Figure 2.4 presents the research question, methodology, and significance sections of her final proposal with Mead's written responses. Discussion in class of her research questions had focused on what she wanted to study and methodology. She never did present draft methodology and significance sections in class. All of these sections display a very hybrid discourse. For example, Han suggests that she will select six to eight subjects for case studies, but adds that they will *randomly* vary on five separate background factors (e.g., gender, age, length of stay in United States). "Randomness" here seems to represent Han's attempt to align with the topics and values of social-scientific research that Mead foregrounded in the course. However, she uses the word in a way that could not be meaningful within the discourse of experimental design. The section on procedures displays a tension between her desire to do a natural-istic study like the one she had done in the previous course and Mead's suggestion that she consider a more controlled study. Han states that she could record Chinese visiting scholars talking with American volunteers in a conversation-partner class at a church, but then says she will try to collect data in situations that are as natural as possible.

The tension that arose around her original problem statement between Mead's foregrounding of theory and research and Han's practical motiva-tions and interests reemerges at several points. The second "hypothesis" in her research questions section seems to imply that she will test the effectiveness of a particular pedagogical solution, increased awareness. Likewise, in her final section on significance, she returns to her earlier framing, as she talks about how cultural factors (not cultural values) influence comprehension and about the need for special training programs.

The roughness of this proposal is visible in the lack of detail in the methodology section, which draws a series of marginal questions from Mead, and in the presence of very obvious language errors (e.g., "sppeces" for "speeches"). It is also reflected in Mead's final comments at the end of the paper: "The proposal tackles a difficult problem in a difficult way. It is clear that you have a draft of a proposal, but there are some things that could have been included even in this draft—see question for you on page 4. Also there are many mechanical writing issues that you need to examine. B+." This roughness, however, needs to be read in light of Han's perception that Mead had invited "rough drafts" and "incomplete proposals" and of her decision to pursue the topic she was actually interested in for her dissertation rather than to seek to optimize her performance in this seminar by selecting an easier problem.

Having contextualized the production of this paper, I now turn to its reception and evaluation. A central point here is that Mead was responding to Han as well as to Han's paper. When asked in the general interview if he responded differently to NNSE, Mead indicated that he responded to them more as individuals than as members of a group and then discussed several examples, one of them Han:

> ...and then there were some people who didn't say very much at all, Han for example, although I would have to say I was dumbfounded by her oral report, I was just literally blown away by it, it was so good, and I was concerned when she was going to give it because this was a study—and again I don't remember the exact study, but it was one that I didn't think she could handle—but she did handle it very very well, better in oral form than in written form, that's my impression.

Mead's comments on Han's proposal revolve around notions of what a workable, malleable draft is; of what the text says about the student's effort, insight, and commitment; and finally of how his response can or should contribute. In the text-based interviews, Mead's general response to Han's proposal was:

> I know if I recall this correctly that I did not think it was very well thought through and therefore didn't feel that it had the wherewithal to be considered really solid as an initial proposal to be worked on, although, there is certainly the germ of an idea here, and I think that I did say something about a difficult idea to deal with, I just

IV.   Research Questions

What are the major factors relating to Chinese value concepts that affect visiting scholars' comprehensibility of native speech in their daily face-to-face interactions with American people? This question could be expanded into the following two hypotheses:

1)   The problem of Chinese scholars' inappropriate response in ✓✓ conversations could be caused by their culturally misinterpretation of the native speech.

2)   A self-awareness of mother culture interference in comprehending the native speeches could reduce the opportunities of the the breakdown of the conversation.

[handwritten: These two could be subbing questions of your major question. they are not proper hypotheses to be tested and might be better framed as questions.]

V.   Methodology

* Subjects

The subjects of this study would be 6-8 Chinese visiting scholars whose age, language proficiency, acadamic field, time of stay in this culture and *[handwritten: OK]* geographical origion in China vary in random. The obsevation also include American native speakers participating in the conversations with the visiting scholars.

* Procedures

✓ The proposed reserach would be designed as a case study *[handwritten: ies]* using qualitative ✓ methodology. The whole procedure of research would be conducted ✓ through observation and interviews. Questionnaires addressing a larger size of sample might be added when necessary for reference. *[handwritten: Will this actually be done? Of what will the questionnaire consist?]*

Cassette tapes and recorders would be used as instruments to collect conversational data. Observation *[handwritten: s]* could be carried out in churches where

FIG. 2.4. Excerpt from Han's final research proposal.

conversational pairs of Chinese learners and American volunteers have their

weekly language teaching and learning activities. The process of

observation and data collection would cover several weeks to three months,

depending on how frequent the subjects have their conversational activities.

each subject would at least contribute three conversations. The

conversations would be tape recorded in situations as natural as possible.

Two interviews for each subject would be given to provide additional data

for analysis.

Recording of each conversation would be carefully listened, and attention

would be particularly drawn to finding out any factor relating to Chinese

value concept that influence the learners' comprehending the native speeces.

Data would be analysed and discussed under the assumption that factors like

age, gender, personality, academic field, geographical origions in China

would not be considered as effective variables.

A pilot study is suggested to evaluate the method and to measure the

instrument. The pilot study differs from major study mainly in its scales.

VI.   Significance of the Study

Chinese visiting scholars, as a special group of adult EFL learners, is

confronting with the comprehension problems in their daily conversations

with American friends and colleagues. To find out the factors in their own

culture that influence their comprehensibility is an issue of importance from

a practical standpoint in developing their communicative skills. A need for

such information become more and more apparent to Chinese language

teachers in designing and developing special training programs for

preparing people who are going abroad.

FIG. 2.4. (continued).

61

don't think that she had enough opportunity or took enough time or worked or even talked about it with other people, other than me, to think about how she could carry this out, there seems to be some ideas here that could be workable, but she just doesn't have it, it doesn't hold together, and then there are a wide variety of proofreading problems that she just didn't deal with.

In a later discourse-based interview, when asked whether he would be willing to delete a comment he had made in the margins of the background section ("I'm not sure of what more literature there is on the subject but it seems to me a little skimpy"), Mead responded:

> I would not want to drop that simply because I want to keep some pressure on this individual to continue to look broader, what she did at the very beginning of the quarter, in beginning to talk about this, was, from my perspective, to want to narrow down right exactly to her topic, and I was surprised I will have to say at what she did give me with the background and that there's more here that's related to her study than she really realized, and my note is intended to say, "I'm happy to see what you have here, but don't stop here." Ok, that's the intent and I would not want to change that.

Asked if he would drop the four sets of questions that appear in the right margin questioning Han's procedures (see Fig. 2.4), Mead replied:

> I would not wish to give up any of those because these, I think, are the kinds of issues that—when you asked me yesterday, "What are you talking about as a proposal that can be accepted, as meeting the basic criteria?" Here I think are issues that have not been significantly addressed, each one of them would give me a feeling that the individual has thought through the process with some degree of specificity, has an idea, and it's solid enough to be able to say, "Ok, from here, let's really get into the nitty-gritty and how does it, how does what you're talking about here then fit into everything?" And, therefore, those are really I think good examples of the kinds of issues that people need to address in order to have a malleable proposal that we can then take and work on.

Mead's interview comments suggest he was not simply comparing Han's proposal to an ideal proposal, as any student's work, but was reading and responding to it as Han's work and using his understanding of Han from the seminar and other contexts as well as what he inferred about her from this proposal in seeking to have an impact on her future work. His comments also express his sense of disappointment with Han's work, his uncertainty about its quality, and his desire to push her to develop her ideas more carefully.

PICTURING THE ACADEMIC WRITING TASK

Han's final research proposal for this seminar and Mead's response to it are complex events. Han decides to treat the proposal as groundwork for her actual dissertation (something that Mead explicitly and implicitly urged students to do) rather than to optimize her performance in the seminar. Paradoxically, however, Mead's dominant image of an initial draft is of the kind of document an *advisee* would bring in to him, a text that has been carefully thought through, is presented with care, and, most importantly, signals the student's commitment to pursue a line of inquiry, a research plan that they could together shape and mold. Thus, Han proceeds along a course that she perceives Mead invited her to take, but Mead shows little or no recognition of her uptake of his goals. For him, problems with the proposal suggest that she has not taken up the task he intended.

Han's writing for the seminar traces a history of literate activity involving talk, reading, and observation as well as writing. Her research proposal emerges as a complex, highly indexical document pointing to private and public histories, to the seminar and other contexts. As we see here, Han revised the sections that were discussed in class, following Mead's suggestion. However, in the sections that were not discussed in class, her original representation of the problem reemerges. In a sense, although her texts were coming to conform to Mead's expectations, it is not clear that her thinking was changing. (For a clearer exploration of this kind of process, see chap. 8.) Her final text is a particularly heteroglossic mixture of discourses. Her use of notions like "randomization" and "hypotheses" signals attempts at alignment; they may mark out a space for joint attention, but the meanings moving in that space appear to be wildly divergent. From Han's perspective, the research proposal is only weakly bounded to the occasion of the seminar; as a trajectory of activity, it is strongly linked to other contexts (past, present, and future).

Han's "task" in this analysis emerges as a densely textured collage where conflicting notions of academic work collide in tangled knots of interpretation and misinterpretation almost below anyone's awareness—resolved, if at all, by power. However, nothing suggests that Han or Mead found this a particularly extraordinary or complex event. The gap between the complexity I am claiming in this analysis and the participants' experience of it as fairly routine raises the obvious question. Whose perspective best represents *the academic writing task?* I would argue that our understanding of academic writing tasks needs to embody *both* the kind of complex microhistories of situated action, perception, and evaluation that I have only thinly sketched here *and* the strategic interpretive work that renders such histories typical, unexceptional, practically invisible to participants. In the next chapter, I explore this kind of complex working out of academic writing tasks on both levels, considering the microhistories of writing tasks in two seminars as the situated work of typification, of making genres.

3

Making Semiotic Genres: Topics, Contextualizations, and Literate Activity in Two Seminars

As I analyzed situated literate activity in *Language Research* (chap. 2), I became increasingly aware of the need for analytic and theoretical tools that would respect the complexities arising as the event structure of academic work (how writing tasks are cued, produced, and evaluated) interacts with participants' perspectives (their evolving interpretations and goals) and with the lamination of activity (the multiple trajectories of personal, interpersonal, institutional, and sociocultural histories being relatively foregrounded or backgrounded by participants). In addition, those tools would need to account for the ways participants normally manage those complexities, often finding them, as Han and Mead did, routine and unremarkable.

One likely tool seemed to be the notion of typification (see Schutz & Luckmann, 1973; Hanks, 1996b) and specifically of genres as typified communicative practices that arise under the demands of recurrent sociorhetorical situations (e.g., Bazerman, 1988, 1994b; Berkenkotter & Huckin, 1995; Miller, 1984; Swales, 1990). Genres in these accounts are based on similarities of situations and communicative activity, not on their identity, with each generic act involving some degree of judgment and innovation. Generic typification is seen as not only offering the individual resources to manage complexity, but contributing to the stabilization and, thus, (re)production of social institutions and communities. These notions of typification and genre have obvious applications to the seminar writing tasks I was analyzing. Classrooms and school writing assignments are almost tediously recurring sociorhetorical situations. Yet, as chapter 2 suggests, specific writing tasks are rarely routine, involving complexly situated and novel features. Moreover, the writing tasks graduate students are being asked to do are expected to promote advanced enculturation into disciplinary knowledge and discourse (including genres). Thus, examining how students and professors undertake such writing tasks in seminars becomes a strategic site to trace the co-genesis of genres and disciplinary communities of practice.

In this chapter, I first develop a sociohistoric account of genre as semiotic activity. I then turn to analysis of writing in two seminars taught by the same professor (Arthur Kohl), but in fairly different institutional and disciplinary contexts. One seminar, in Kohl's home department of Geography, was small (four enrolled students) and involved a vaguely articulated writing task. The second, in American Studies, was larger (18 students) with a foregrounded task involving field research as well as writing. In the microcosm of these two seminars, I want to explore genre in the making, the ways the students and Kohl co-produced recognizable versions of the writing tasks, the ways they aligned their literate activity around these tasks, and the resources they used to do so.

BAKHTIN'S SPEECH GENRES

Bakhtin's (1986) notion of speech genres has provided a particularly useful framework for exploring the situated co-construction of academic writing tasks. Bakhtin also treats genre as communicative typifications centered on typified social activity; however, his approach to genre is specifically grounded in a dialogic unit of analysis, the utterance (see also chap. 1). Bakhtin describes utterances as dialogic because they are multiply linked and aligned. Utterances build on prior utterances, forming chains in which "each utterance refutes, affirms, supplements, and relies on the others, presupposes them to be known, and somehow takes them into account" (p. 91). Because these chains are utterances, not sentences, not linguistic abstractions, but the situated talk or text of particular persons, they index personal, interpersonal, institutional, sociocultural, and material histories and are charged with affective overtones and motivational trajectories as well as semantic meanings. Utterances are also dialogically addressed, anticipating the responsive understanding of recipients, future utterances by others or the speaker herself, and future actions or events in the world. Finally, utterances are dialogic because they are not the solo acts of speakers and writers, but joint constructions, co-constituted through the active understanding and response of recipients. In all these senses, utterances are dialogic because they represent particular fusions of heterogeneous centripetal and centrifugal forces.[1]

For Bakhtin, utterances are deeply historical, not History as a kind of bird's-eye anonymous abstraction, but histories, the situated trajectories of persons acting in the world. Speech genres then are genres of dialogic utterance:

> Language is realized in the form of individual concrete utterances (oral and written) by participants in the various areas of human activity. These utterances reflect the specific conditions and goals of each such area not only through their content (thematic) and linguistic style, that is the selection of lexical, phraseological, and grammatical resources of the language, but above all through their compositional structure. All three of these aspects—thematic content, style, and compositional structure—are inseparably linked to the *whole* of the utterance and are equally determined by the specific nature of the particular sphere of communication. Each separate utterance is individual, of course, but each sphere in which language is used develops its own *relatively stable types* of these utterances. These we may call *speech genres*. The wealth and diversity of speech genres are boundless because the various possibilities of human activity are inexhaustible, and because each sphere of activity contains an entire repertoire of speech genres that differentiate and grow as the particular sphere develops and becomes more complex. Special emphasis should be placed on the extreme *heterogeneity* of speech genres (oral and written). (Bakhtin, 1986, p. 60)

When Bakhtin (1986) emphasizes compositional structure as a force constituting genre, he is not referring to linguistic or textual features alone. He elaborates the notion of compositional unities as "particular types of construction of the whole, types of its completion, and types of relations between the speaker and other participants in speech communication (listeners or readers, partners, the other's speech, and so forth)" (p. 64). Typified addressivity, an element of completion, is one key to the compositional structure of speech genres: "Varieties and conceptions of the addressee are determined by that area of human activity and everyday life to which the given utterance is related" (p. 95). Bakhtin's construction of the whole implicates human activity in material as well as social worlds: "Genres correspond to typical situations of speech communication, typical themes, and, consequently, also to particular contacts between the *meanings* of words and actual concrete reality under certain typical circumstances" (p. 87). As Kamberelis (1995) summarizes this view, genres and systems of

---

[1]Centripetal and centrifugal forces are often figured as categorical (e.g., dictionaries and public schooling are centripetal; differences in gender, occupation, biography, and recreation are centrifugal). However, the directionality of these forces is profoundly protean in practice. It depends on perspective and on actual as well as intended consequences. Every communicative act reflects and exerts a multivalent and layered blend of centripetal and centrifugal forces.

genre arise and are embedded in typified, but dynamic and open configurations of the socially and materially situated production, reception, and distribution of utterances.

Speech genres are "boundless" and display "extreme heterogeneity" because they are multiply determined, formed in the confluence of some specific dialogic content, situated processes of production (reading and writing, talking and listening, sensing and acting), linguistic and discursive forms (their construction and style), laminated activity footings (personal, interpersonal, institutional, and sociocultural trajectories), and the kinds of receptions and consequences anticipated and actually occurring. Changes in any of these textual or contextual elements alter the generic quality of a text to some extent. Writing an experimental report for a professor to grade is different from submitting an experimental report to a journal. A term paper on history is different from one on optical memories for computers. An article about primate behavior based on field research is different from an article on primate behavior based on laboratory study. This kind of contextual sensitivity helps to explain why Bakhtin emphasized the plasticity and boundless heterogeneity of speech genres. It also points to boundless possibilities for significant commonalties across speech genres, to the dialogic interpenetration of genres themselves.

In many ways, Bakhtin's approach to genre shares considerable common ground with current genre theories (e.g., Freedman & Medway, 1994; Miller, 1984; Swales, 1990), which argue that genres are constituted not simply through textual forms, but, more fundamentally, through the relatively stable goals and resources of social actors in typically recurring social situations. However, these theories have tended to conceptualize recurring sociorhetorical situations through the structuralist lens of the discourse community (see chap. 1). Although Bakhtin also invokes typification in relatively stable spheres of social activity, he sees activity as historically situated, heterogeneous, and perspectival rather than as abstract, unified, shared elements inhering in a situation. Another way to state the difference is to note that Bakhtin argues that we can only produce utterances (never genres), although those utterances dialogically resonate with other utterances and are oriented toward the typified, holistic forms of communication in particular spheres of activity. From the perspective of utterance, typification must involve practices sufficiently flexible to address the deep uncertainties and asymmetries of communicative action—the recurrent (and hence normal) challenges people face in managing multiple activity footings and in coordinating meanings, social relations, and actions within fields of partial and even conflicting intersubjectivity. In fact, speech genres are partially constituted by the very ways such complexities are managed, the ways a particular balance of centripetal and centrifugal forces is configured.

Hanks (1996b) argues that genres are modes of practice that are deeply dispositional, which helps to explain why, as in the history of Han's research proposal, participants normally perceive interactions as routine and manageable. In fact, a fundamental disposition that facilitates coordinated activity and communication is a generalized trust, a belief in and presupposition of intersubjectivity in an objectively shared world (see Bruner, 1990, Rommetveit, 1985, Schutz & Luckmann, 1973). In any case, a Bakhtinian perspective portrays genres, even in their typification, as wildly complex and profoundly particular, suggesting the need to pay careful attention to the way co-participants compose and coordinate their activity under such conditions.

GENERATING GENRES

As I began to apply the notion of speech genres to analyzing the complex literate activity I found in seminars, I encountered an obstacle. Tracing the ways content, contextual and textual construction, and style were being linked and negotiated proved to be a productive analytic framework. However, when I sought to identify *the* speech genre (or even genres) at play in each seminar, it seemed to freeze the dynamics and flatten out the diversity of that situated activity. I eventually realized that I was still assuming that an analysis of genre must produce some kind of template, a fixed structure that stood behind the texts and action. In Bakhtin's terms, I was mistakenly thinking that people produce genres instead of utterances. I began to see that a different concept of the relationship between genre knowledge and generic activity was needed.

A useful analogy can be seen in the notion of scripts in cognitive psychology. Schank and Ableson (1977) initially viewed scripts as abstract knowledge structures that governed interpretation and action for situational events like eating at restaurants. However, Schank (1982) soon radically reworked this view:

> Part of the justification for this modification of our old view of scripts is that it really is not possible to say *exactly* what is and what is not part of any script. Particular experiences invade our attempts to make generalizations. To put this another way, we do not believe in the script as a kind of semantic memory data structure, apart from living breathing episodic memories. What we know of restaurants is compiled from

a multitude of experiences with them and these experiences are stored with what we have compiled. (p. 23)

Like several other schema theorists in the early 1980s (e.g., van Dijk & Kintsch, 1983), Schank came to emphasize the centrality of episodic memory and the need for cognitive processes that would apply open and variable strategies to complex worlds rather than mechanical rules to closed, well-structured systems. Noting the inadequacy of theories of scripts as stable mental structures, Kintsch and Mannes (1987) argue that scripts are "generated from an unorganized associative net in response to a specific task demand in a specific context" (p. 62). They suggest that this situated script generation (as opposed to instantiation of stored scripts) is needed to account for the flexibility and context sensitivity people demonstrate in their cognitive functioning. While Kintsch and Mannes locate the resources for script generation in cognitive structures (with context playing a triggering role), a sociohistoric perspective would also direct attention to joint activity and the distributed resources of historically constituted functional systems.

In a closely parallel development, Bauman (1992) argues for the need to move from static, taxonomic classifications of folk stories as texts to a dynamic performance-oriented analysis of tellings. For example, instead of asking whether a folk story is traditional or not, Bauman analyzes traditionalization, the practices the storyteller and listeners employ in a particular telling of a tale to represent it as traditional. This shift in perspective—from discourse as a fixed object to discourse as doing—is characteristic of much recent discourse theory (see Hanks, 1996b, for a recent discussion). Of course, genre itself has often been one of those discourse objects. In this sense, it makes more sense to speak of genre generation, genrification, or generic activity.

Whatever the terminology, the question arises of what it is people are generating when they generate genre. Bazerman (1988) suggests:

> Genre is a sociopsychological category which we use to recognize and construct typified actions within typified situations. It is a way of creating order in the ever-fluid symbolic world.... The formal features are only ways more fundamental relations and interactions are realized in the act of communication. In recognizing and using genre, we are mobilizing multidimensional clusters of our understanding of the situation, our goals, and our activity. (p. 317)

Thus, locating a text in a genre is a multidimensional and socially distributed act of classification. As Wittgenstein (1958) argued in his discussion of games, classifications are matters of family resemblance rather than formal logic. To generate a genre then, people have to align their words and actions recognizably to the genre, which also means aligning to others who will receive it as that genre, as a recognizable but flawed attempt at the genre, or as not the genre at all. If a genre is an open family of utterances (written and spoken) with fuzzy and contested boundaries, then the joint work of alignment, that is, of making or avoiding resemblances, must be central to the process of genrification.[2] Swales (1990) argues that family resemblance alone is too robust a process (anything can resemble anything) without some constraints. Although he notes domains of activity (like eating) as one possible constraint, he focuses particularly on the cognitive notion of prototypicality, proposing communicative purpose as a privileged feature of prototypicality for genres. A sociohistoric perspective points to another way of stabilizing family resemblance: the co-genesis of multiple elements of functional systems of activity.[3] In other words, resemblance is not only an in-situ cognitive accomplishment, but is also sociohistorically mediated and distributed. We should ask then what textual and contextual resources speakers and writers employ to produce or avoid resemblance, what resources recipients use to make or unmake it, and what kinds of practices surround this coordinated activity.

SEMIOTIC GENRES

I am proposing a change from Bakhtin's terminology (speech genres) for several reasons. First, everyday connotations of "speech" as talk make it a constant struggle to communicate that this theory applies to writing. More seriously, as Witte (1992) has argued, communicative practices are multi-modal—with talk, text, bodily stance and gesture, graphics, mathematics, and other symbolic activity woven together in threads of interactional history. Taking up Witte's view in relation to their study of a student's drawing, Smagorinsky and Coppock (1994) propose the term *communication genre*. However, considering the full range of resources implicated in

---

[2]Alignment is a powerful and pervasive communicative practice. It has been studied in terms of speech accommodation (e.g., Giles, Coupland, & Coupland, 1993), non-verbal forms of synchronization and reciprocation (e.g., Birdwhistle, 1970; Kendon, 1990), and various types of repetition (e.g., Becker, 1988; Johnstone, 1994; Tannen, 1989).

[3]Hanks (1996a) provides a wonderful illustration of this in the contrast between seeing a Mayan rain ceremony as happening at a table in a forest clearing and understanding how the table is an altar, how the clearing is significantly oriented to other spaces, how the timing of the ceremony is linked to agricultural cycles, and so on. His point here is less the value of an emic perspective than the centripetal weightiness of the ceremony as it is constituted within multiple cultural-historical axes.

generic activity, it is clear that genres are constituted by contextual associations as well as communicative intentions. This point leads me to prefer
semiotic to communicative: semiosis does not imply intentionality, whereas
communication normally does.

To articulate this notion of semiotic genres, I examine it first in a
hypothetical scenario. The question I pose in this scenario is: When is a
constitution a constitution? Say I am a professor of constitutional law and
have assigned my students the task of drafting a national constitution for a
country of their choice as a final project (worth 15% of the course grade).
Now it happens one of my students is from a small Pacific island on the verge
of independence, and she has been designated to draft the island's first
constitution and present it to the island's constitutional convention. At the
end of the semester, her text appears with 30 others in my departmental
mailbox.

On its face, this "constitution" is situated in a sequence of school activity.
It is written by a student in response to my assignment and turned in at an
institutionally appropriate time for grading. Whatever its textual verisimili-
tude, I receive it not as a constitution, but as a course assignment. This
receptive classification of the text may be made whether it looks like the
other students' constitutions or not. The text may bear visible traces of
participation in other institutionalized activity, as Teresa's research proposal displayed traces in its content and style of its submission to Human
Subjects Review (see chap. 2). Contextualizing it as an assignment however, I will take up any differences as variations in the quality of the text or
its conformity to the task (e.g., as a constitution that is perhaps unusually
thorough or that has gone beyond the set page limit). That the constitution
appears in my departmental mailbox and sits in a pile of constitutions on
my desk is not a feature of its internal communicative design, not in that
sense intentional, but these contextual associations contribute to a semiotic
signification that the constitution is a student text written for a class, and
not a charter document operating in the sphere of national and international
law and politics.[4] That part of my reception is a grade that enters into the

---

[4]That I call this text "a constitution" is interesting, but does not determine its genre. The way the
text is produced, distributed, and received in the law-school setting bears little resemblance to the way
proposed, in-force, or former constitutions are produced, distributed, and received in national political
systems. That the text may strongly resemble national constitutions is also interesting, pointing to our
ability to embed, or rekey (as in parody), activity. Bakhtin (1986) notes that genres, especially complex
cultural ones, often incorporate other genres or genre fragments, and Goffman (1981) describes the
frequent and mundane quality of highly complex embeddings (as in represented speech). What is critical

institutional record further locates the text in school activity, not incidentally foregrounding a specific identity configuration (teacher to student). When the text circulates in the sphere of school activity, it may be taken as an assignment.

However, the same text at the same time could be distributed to the island congress, where it is read as a political document, and responded to in very different ways and ultimately with quite different consequences. More subtly, the student's constitution could be recontextualized in my reception. Let's add one other event in the chain: The student stops me in the hall one day and mentions almost in passing that the assignment is particularly exciting to her because she has been chosen by her people to draft their first constitution. With this short talk inserted into the history, I might receive her text, bearing the same semiotic traces of its contextualization in the institutional sphere of the course, as, to some degree, a constitution. Minimally, I might respond to its content and form in a fashion different from that displayed in responses to other students (as Mead responded differently to critiques he perceived as related to students' research proposals and potential dissertations). Going beyond that, I might engage the student in a radically different fashion, initiating a series of meetings to talk over the constitution, asking about process issues, like her plans for consultation with various local stakeholders. I might even set up a local working group to advise the "student," now foregrounding her identity more as a representative of a foreign government than a student and mine as a political-legal consultant more than a professor.

I will not belabor the various pathways of this scenario, but I believe it does suggest that genrification must be dialogically located in sociohistoric streams of activity, that textual and contextual elements contribute to generic signification, and that alignments of texts, contexts, and identities are dynamic and mutable, not fixed frameworks inhering in situations. In this hypothetical case, contextual associations (the place of a text in an activity) and specific historical events (e.g., hallway talk) played central roles in answering the question of the extent to which the constitution was taken up as a constitution or an assignment. In less dramatic fashion, the cases in this chapter will display similar processes of semiotic alignment. Before turning to that data, I explore some key semiotic resources that facilitate this kind of generic activity.

---

from a sociohistoric perspective is that the alignments of literate activity indexed by this naming are predicated on the co-genesis of law, law school, and governmental systems and on the colonial and post-colonial internationalization of European and U.S. forms of government and education.

TOPICS, CONTEXTUALIZATIONS, AND JOINT ATTENTION

Bakhtin (1986) emphasized the power of content in determining genres. I believe that the importance of content to semiotic genres may be productively explored by relating Bakhtin's dialogics, rhetoric's notions of topics (*topoi*) and special topics (*eide*), and Bruner's (1994; see also chap. 1) account of the sociogenesis of joint attention as participation in cultural practices. Content may be particularly crucial because of its relationship to contextualizing and coordinating joint activity.

In Aristotle's (1932) rhetoric, the common and special topics were places rhetors could go to generate lines of argument and to find material for those arguments. Topics formed a fixed landscape of the culture, a topography composed of issues, concepts, propositions, and narratives. Miller and Selzer's (1985) examination of special topics among transportation engineers decentered and expanded Aristotle's notion in two key ways. First, following the modern rhetorical stance (e.g., Perelman, 1982) that rhetoric is ubiquitous, Miller and Selzer treated scientific concepts, which Aristotle had treated as arhetorical first principles, as topics. Second, they formulated a more social and multidimensional approach, suggesting that the texts they examined were shaped by the intersection and interpenetration of three topical domains:

- the generic—implicit and explicit models and expectations for the form and content of particular types of texts;
- the institutional—concepts, procedures, values, issues, and narratives connected with particular institutional bodies or forums;
- the disciplinary—concepts, procedures, values, issues, and narratives connected to specific disciplines.

Special topics may be explicitly or implicitly signaled in a text. For example, when we read the first paragraph of a newspaper story, the who-what-where-how scheme is not explicitly displayed, but can be seen to have shaped the text. On the other hand, in a research report, a scheme that elaborates methodology as subjects, instrumentation, procedures, and analysis may be explicitly signaled with subheadings. (In both cases, if we look into workplace practices or the sociogenesis of the authors' writing practices, the schemes are more likely to appear.) Topics are not simply organizational schemes or general issues; they include specific propositions, concepts, stories, tropes, images, mathematical formulas, typographic formats, and so on.[5] A sociohistoric perspective would further decenter and expand topical dimensions, as discourse is fully grounded in the concrete, situated, and laminated activities of people rather than in abstracted terrains.

While topics in rhetoric are located in metaphoric spaces (no-wheres), I am suggesting that words and other signs become topics, a kind of semiotic artifact, by being located within discourses, where discourses are fuzzy sets of semiotic artifacts and practices that have come to be associated and associable through histories of particular spheres of activity. Discourses and topics are not codified in some abstract structuralist dictionary, but are products of history. For example, words like *method* and *randomization* come to index scientific discourses through histories of use in the utterances of scientific spheres of activity. Of course, words like *method* and *randomization* remain dialogic, infused with multiple senses among different people and in different situations. Han's use of the topic randomization in her final proposal (see chap. 2) suggests how tenuous the intersubjective grounds of joint attention can be, even in the writing of graduate students. Topics are, therefore, dispersed, heterogeneous, and open, related and relatable to other discourses. There is no literal core of shared stable meaning, but at best somewhat stabilized shoals (see Linell, 1992; Minick, 1993; Rommetveit, 1988, 1992). In this sense, words and other signs are situated in a dynamic multidimensional space where they may suddenly jump from one discursive surface to another or be suspended between surfaces. Where traditional and modern notions of topics (common or special) posit relatively stable landscapes of culturally shared ideas and values, this dialogic perspective on topics evokes a fluid semiotic field, something more like the aurora borealis than a map.

From this perspective, topics emerge as artifactual resources people employ to orient to, constitute, and coordinate streams of activity. Topics, in other words, are tools of joint attention, marking, as Bruner (1994) suggests, co-participation in communities of cultural practices. They are particularly useful in doing the work of contextualization (proposing, forming, and negotiating contexts). Context often invokes dramatistic tropes (a particular place and time as a setting, participants as actors playing roles, events as plots, and some key themes to be resolved or explored). A

---

[5]For example, in their analysis of transportation engineers' texts, Miller and Selzer (1985) identified as special topics not only organizational schemes for genres (e.g., transit plans) and thematic issues (e.g., cost), but also certain graphics (e.g, land-use maps), certain tabular presentations (e.g., tables with survey responses), corporate slogans (e.g., service to clients), and disciplinary concepts (e.g., memory scheduling, productivity analysis, zone fare structure).

focus on contextualization rejects context as the schematized lens of some privileged version of the "play" in favor of context as something more like the simultaneous, layered interpenetration of the multiple streams of activity of actors, writers, stage crew, critics, audiences, non-audiences, play scripts, props, architectural designs, and the many networks of production and socialization that sustain the theatre (see Becker's 1982 discussion of art worlds). In this sense, as Goodwin and Duranti (1992) argue, contextualization is interactive praxis.

How do topics index discourses and contextualize activity? In analyses of classroom talk, Wertsch (1991) examined how teachers' and students' asymmetrical negotiation of referential content and perspective worked to privilege certain discourses (or voices or social languages) over others (see also Wertsch & Minick, 1990). For example, Wertsch analyzed how an emergent topic in a conversation (a piece of lava an elementary student brought to class for share-time) fluctuated between multiple discourses as referential content and perspective (what I am calling *topics*) were negotiated. Over the course of a 41-turn exchange, the lava appeared as a physical object connected to the personal history and experience of the child, as an object subjected to formal, scientific taxonomies like light–heavy and smooth–rough, as a sign defined in terms of other signs in a dictionary, and as a sign/object subsumed within geological narratives of volcanic activity. In this brief interaction, the teacher introduced the formal, scientific, sign type–sign type exchanges, pushing the students to reconceptualize (and recontextualize) the lava outside of the personal history of the child. Wertsch notes how such microdiscursive exchanges fit into a significant sociohistoric pattern as the teacher initiates and privileges what he calls the Western "voice of rationality" (see Wertsch, 1990).

In a more exotic example that illustrates the interaction of topics, identities, and activities, Lindstrom (1992) analyzed an oral debate on the island of Vanuatu. In the debate, the participants strategically employed what I would identify as topics to establish the truth of their positions by invoking or contesting different (sometimes contradictory) island discourses. For example, a crucial topic in the debate was whether the death of a boy was connected to his grandfather's cursing him or to his parents' early resumption of sexual relations. (This example highlights the cultural relativity of topics, which often appear so obvious and natural at home.) Participants also used topics to constitute and contest foregrounded contextualizations and identities. One thread in the debate involved whether the death was an internal family or community issue, that is, whether there should be a debate at all and, if so, who had rights to speak in it.

These examples from conversational exchanges suggest that topics have powerful functions in coordinating joint attention and action. As intersubjective spaces where affective and conceptual attention accumulates, topics range from widespread, deeply sedimented, well-worn sociocultural ruts to highly transient, local and emergent currents in a particular stream of communication. Topics index historical activity and, thus, their use by participants may nominate, sustain, and challenge emergent contextualizations, configure participants' identities and relationships, and fabricate goal-oriented actions. Finally, because topics often coordinate attention around highly indeterminate or divergent spaces (as in Han's use of *randomization* in her research proposal), they may function as the kind of proleptic or presuppositional devices that Stone (1993) and Bruner (1990) have argued are central to the semiotic mediation of learning. In the next sections of this chapter, I explore how the students of two seminars and their professor indexed, contextualized, and constituted their literate activity, especially through topical alignments, as they co-constructed the genres of seminar writing tasks.

MAKING GENRES IN TWO SEMINARS

Arthur Kohl grew up in Midwest City and studied geography at Midwest University (MU) in the late 1940s. After finishing his master's and with university enrollments skyrocketing, he was invited to join the faculty in Geography as an instructor. He never pursued a PhD, but moved into the tenure track, eventually becoming a full professor and, for a time, chair of the department. His vita displays a moderate number of professional publications and a series of prestigious positions in professional organizations, government agencies, and university administration. Early in his career, when many cultural geographers were analyzing human settlement in terms of social physics (e.g., "gravity" models), Kohl took up an ethnographic and philosophic orientation, specializing particularly in the history and philosophy of geography and in cultural and urban geography. He also had a strong interest in interdisciplinarity, expressed not only in his formal association with American Studies, but also in his support as an administrator for interdisciplinary programs and his participation in archeological research teams at sites in the eastern Mediterranean (particularly Greece and Turkey) and the United States. When I contacted Kohl about participating in my research, he invited me to propose the research to the students in either or both of the seminars (*Geography* and *American Studies*) he was teaching the next quarter. As it turned out, I stayed in both.[6] In class, Kohl seemed open and iconoclastic, a teller of academic and non-academic tales. However, his relaxed informality mixed uneasily with instruction often dominated by lecturing and with a style of responding to others (in written responses as well as in seminar talk) associationally, as triggers for recollection of his own experiences and ideas. In any case, Kohl played an important role in constituting the situated and typified functional systems of both seminars.

— one who seeks to overthrow traditional ideas or institutions

Doing Final Blue-Book Essays in Geography

Kohl's prose seminar (three of which were required for graduate degrees in the department) was in the area of geographic thought and philosophy (one of seven designated areas). *Geography* met for 2 hours one evening a week in a small classroom full of maps and globes. Six students had enrolled in it, but two dropped out after the first meeting. Three of the four who remained had completed their written work when my data collection ended about 4 months after the quarter: John, an MA student interested in cartography; Liz, an MA–PhD student interested in culture and global development; and Betty, an MA–PhD student from the Republic of China (the only NNSE in the seminar) interested in urban economics. Kohl was teaching another graduate course, an introductory survey of the history of geography. He suggested the students might want to sit in on that course, and some did, at least on occasion. Around the third week, two female PhD students who were taking the survey began sitting in on the seminar and attended regularly from there on. Kohl also invited Leo Turner, an anthropology professor, to lead discussion in two sessions that focused on the Frankfort School of critical theory. When Turner led the class, another PhD student sat in and participated actively.

Kohl asked students to read a relatively small number of articles, most of which dealt with some aspect of the philosophy of geography or the disciplinary history of the field, although many more readings were recommended. Several of the articles he provided were ones he had authored. In the seminar, Kohl tended to lecture on the readings. Participation was fairly

---

[6]See Appendix A for methodological details of the research in *Geography* and *American Studies* (as well as for *Sociology*, which is presented in chaps. 6, 7, and 8).

minimal among those enrolled in the class. In an interview, Kohl referred to John, reasonably accurately, as "the one who never spoke." The two PhD students, who were preparing for preliminary examinations, participated more actively, often initiating discussions that some enrolled students, particularly Liz, then entered. The sessions Leo Turner led were also more interactive as he passionately argued his opinions and pushed students to express and defend theirs. The Geography Department that quarter had organized a colloquium on cultural and postmodern geographies. Discussions from that departmental forum often carried over into *Geography*.

Kohl's single writing task for the quarter was described telegraphically in the syllabus:

Final: Critique
– Value of the Seminar
– Topics: as a whole
– Topic: one, in depth

In class, Kohl introduced this task as three "blue-book essays." Noting that prose seminars offered broad surveys, Kohl indicated that one essay on the final would call for a broad survey. Turning to the in-depth topical essay, Kohl advised students to consider topics that they could develop for master's or PhD work. The final essay was to be a critique of the organization of materials and issues in the seminar.

This writing task received very little attention in the seminar. In an interview before class in Week 8, I asked Liz to describe the tasks for *Geography* and she replied:

Liz: Uh, do the reading every week, um think about a topic that particularly interests you, "think about it" whatever that means, and then um write about it at the end of the quarter
Paul: How do you, what form do you have to write about it in?
Liz: Well I think he said he'll distribute a blue book, um, essay form, I think we'll just write an essay
Paul: Ok, and the topics?
Liz: And the topics, I'm not clear about the topics, I assume he means the topics on the syllabus although uh eeerr, I don't think I'm actually going to do the task that way, I mean um,
Paul: What-
Liz: I'm uh, I'm interested in the French school of geography, and that doesn't appear actually per se on the syllabus, as a- as an entity in

itself, but I'm sort of picking up strands that I think are related to it, from each of the sessions that we've had

Later that evening, at the end of the seminar, Liz asked Kohl whether the final exam would be in class (her question might well have been prompted by our interview). In response, Kohl alluded to three tasks, although the two topical essays seemed to merge:

Liz: Do we- are we going to meet and write that in class?
Kohl: No.
Liz: Oh [laughter]
Kohl: On the tenth week, the last meeting we have, I'll just say uh, by the end of finals week turn in something, and I'd like three sort of comments, one on the way in which we did this, the sequence of readings and so on, did they make sense, or how did it flow through the- should we have done something different, started with the modern and go back to the roots rather than picking up a thread, ( ), secondly, I want you to pick out some particular theme you want to comment on, that you're interested in, I suspect it has to do with the methodology of your own particular research, and I'd like some critical comment of whatever you've been reading outside, that is, common readings have led you to do more work in something else, or in some other class you're doing something for your masters papers or your PhD thesis ... ok, so next time

Kohl did not provide a definitive assignment until the last session, when he described the task as "a take-home final" with two questions rather than three. He wrote the following prompt on the board before the session began:

Take-Home Final—end of Finals Week
2 Questions—Two Blue Books maximum in length
1) Critique of seminar—Organization, Readings, Sequence, etc. (only limitation—keep in mind this was designated as a Pro-seminar by the department.)
2) Your choice—one topic in depth or a comparison of two or more readings.

In response to this prompt, Liz asked if the final had to be written in blue books:

Kohl: I'm not asking you to write in a blue book, if you have a computer or you type or something like that, that's fine with me, but I don't particularly want a long paper

Liz: About how long would you suppose a blue book is if you typed it
            double spaced, do you have any i- I mean, do I have to write the
            thing in here first and then type [laughter]
Kohl: No, just estimate how many words you've got to a page
Liz: Oh, ( )
Kohl: The point is that uh, you could write forever on any topic you choose,
            it's basically how you organize this second question that is the
            criteria I would use evaluating what you said, because I think that
            if you get the questions (straight) and see a buildup of those
            questions, and some kind of a conclusion, that's really the key to a
            good answer, I don't know that there's any right answer to any of
            this, did you all get copies of the papers?

Even in this session, Kohl's representation of the task was not particularly
elaborated. That the assignment included only two of the three essays he
had described throughout the quarter was never mentioned by Kohl or the
students in the seminar that evening.

Throughout the quarter, Kohl repeatedly introduced special topics relevant to the writing task. The overall organization of content was historical,
beginning with the roots of geography in ancient Greece and ending with a
focus on critical and post-modern theories in the 20th century. In class
discussions, the readings, and the syllabus, Kohl emphasized relations
between philosophy and geography, arguing that geography was organized
around enduring questions, the answers to which were transitory. Each
session had a somewhat playful title on the syllabus that further marked
these historical and philosophical emphases (e.g., "Old World, New Ideas:
Antipodal Utopias"; "Hettner to Hartshorne to Chance: Triple-Play";
"Critical Theory: Frankfort Geography"; and "Post-everything"). Highlighting disciplinary debates, he repeatedly modeled a critical orientation
to received opinion. He opened the seminar by rewriting the conventional
history of geography's origins in classical thought. In other sessions, he
deconstructed landscape classifications such as the Great Plains, questioned
the land claims of a local Native-American tribe by pointing to archeological evidence of their relatively recent migration into the area, and sharply
criticized the adoption of scientific concepts and quantitative methods in
human geography. In this way, Kohl evoked a broad field, the history of
geographic thought in the West over two millennia, but also projected a
definite orientation to the material (e.g., his emphasis on philosophy, on the
way social contexts shaped geographic inquiry, the permanence of questions and impermanence of answers). Institutionally, Kohl foregrounded

tasks from the graduate program (thesis, preliminary examination, dissertation) more than the seminar task. The final writing task was backgrounded, discussed rarely and inconsistently.

Tracing ways that these topical affordances were taken up in students' final texts and in Kohl's evaluation suggests much about the nature of generic activity in this seminar. John, Liz, and Betty each produced a fairly distinct version of the task. John actually did write in blue books, filling one (handwritten) with his essay and four pages of a second with his course critique. His essay, a history of cartographic representation, was composed of short paragraphs and referred to few sources. His final product resembled an in-class essay exam except for a few short quotations. Betty, on the other hand, produced her texts on a letter-quality printer, a page and a half for the course critique and five pages for the essay. Discussing Kohl's place in debates over the role of science in geography, her essay resembled a short term paper, with a 10-item bibliography, standard citation, and paragraph-length quotations. Liz struck an intermediate note, writing a little over two pages (letter-quality print) in response to each prompt. Her topical essay on French School geography referred to sources regularly, but maintained a fairly informal style. Kohl read, commented on, and graded the essays. In his written comments, he responded to the content of John and Liz's essays and to the content and language of Betty's. He used grades to differentiate student performance, A's to reward work he appreciated and B's to mildly censure work he did not. Analysis of the essays points to ways that topics aligned literate activity in making all three texts "final blue-book essays."

John, the cartographer who never spoke in the seminar, wrote a historical overview of mapmaking from ancient Greece to the modern era. The following excerpt gives a flavor of his text:

> Meanwhile, an idea fundamental to the evolution of geography (and of cartography), a spherical earth, gained widespread acceptance and led to attempts to determine the earth's circumference. Using his knowledge of geometry, Eratosthenes succeeded in calculating the size of the earth with a remarkable degree of accuracy (given the limits of geographic knowledge at the time).

> Logically, this brought about the development of globes and depictions of a spherical world on flat surfaces based upon the concept of projection. Hipparchus of Nicaea, an astronomer and follower of Eratosthenes, contributed much to modern cartography, including the Stereographic and Orthographic projections, and a refined rectangular system (or graticule) of parallels and meridians. He also insisted on the accurate location of places according to latitude and longitude, as determined by astronomical observation.

John's documentary narrative of mapmaking basically ended in the early 1800s, with one paragraph glossing different kinds of maps developed since then and no mention of recent developments related to computers or remote sensing from satellites.

John aligned his essays to Kohl's topics in several ways. He turned in his two essays on time and placed them in the blue books Kohl had referred to, aligning to the institutional topic of the final essay exam. His substantive essay aligned to two prominent themes in the seminar (representations of the world and the history of geography as a discipline). As Kohl had recommended, John chose a topic he was personally and professionally interested in and knowledgeable about, mapmaking. Explicitly and implicitly, he also contextualized his work as that of a student of cartography in alien disciplinary territory. In his critique of the seminar, John indicated that he found the early survey quite useful, but that the modern topics, particularly critical theory, raised issues that he was not really interested in and did not understand. In a rare example of grading being explicitly topicalized in writing, John concluded the critique with a plea: "I hope you can see your way clear not to fail me." Discussing John's substantive essay in an interview, Kohl acknowledged its accuracy and detail, but was not particularly impressed with it. Mapmaking is a disciplinary topic and history matched the overall organization of content in the seminar; however, John's history was a textbook history of completely unproblematized discoveries and inventions, whereas Kohl's was a highly contested affair, full of philosophical debates and critical, even skeptical, evaluation. Kohl's strongest reaction in the interview was triggered by John's seminar critique, which he felt signaled an anti-intellectual attitude and an unprofitable attempt to separate representation from its social contexts. Kohl indicated that the grade he wrote on the bluebook (a "B") expressed his dissatisfaction with both John's final essays and his lack of participation in the seminar.

Examining Kohl's place in modern geographic debates, Betty's essay opened by quoting from and discussing several articles Kohl had written criticizing the translation of concepts from the physical sciences into human geography. The following excerpt comes from near the conclusion of Betty's five-page paper:

> Geographical and historical methods are based on Kant's classification of knowledge. Although Kantian time-space limits our imagination in multi-dimensional space, yet it is basically the way we look at this phenomenal world. For example, we can study a place by knowing its location, size, shape, history and population, and so on. Then we should know the cultural groups of this place, and try to understand their behavior patterns such as their traditions, customs, heritage, preferences and habits. After

collecting these facts, we should record the data on the map, and describe the place as a whole in a well-organized form of writing.

However, one problem remains unsolved between the processes of data-collecting and description of spatial phenomena. How can we conceptualize the physical world? It seems there is no clear answer for this question. The most common way is by characters, that is, the process of conceptualization relies on good writing. However, the inconsistency and misinterpretation of terminology causes problems in communication. Also, sometime scholars use very technical and complicated word to describe the empirical world, which isolates the studies away from the public. Eventually, geographical inquiry remains distant from the reality. Thus, looking for a way to improve conceptualization of spatial phenomena is needed.

Since we talk a lot about the scientific method in social sciences, we have to ask a question: can geography become scientific? It depends. If we try very hard to quantify the studies of geography into mathematical regulations, the answer is no. Not every issue of geography can be quantified.

Kohl's written response to Betty foregrounded issues of form over content. He edited Betty's language throughout the essay, and his final summary comment read as follows:

You are on the right track, I believe, but your vocabulary and syntax aren't quite up to communicating your thoughts. I sympathize with what your ideas are—and, therefore, I think I know what you are saying—but I can't prove it by what you actually write. good straight-forward writing is difficult—and takes time, and practice.

Betty's essay aligned with several topical threads in the seminar. Again, she produced her texts on time. In length, format, and style, her essay aligns with a typical seminar task (the final paper) more than with Kohl's sketchily described take-home final. Focusing on Kohl's place in geographic debates over the role of science, Betty takes up a topic Kohl had raised directly in seminar discussions and indirectly through distribution of his own articles. She also addresses geography from a somewhat philosophical and certainly problematized perspective.

However, in an interview with Kohl, a complex interpersonal context for Betty's writing emerged as well, pointing to other possible contextualizations of Betty's text. Kohl indicated that he had been meeting with Betty regularly over the past year to work on her writing problems in relation to an unfinished, year-long independent study:

Betty's a problem, she can't write, so I've had her in every two weeks for an hour or two, and what she's trying to do outside of this particular class, and the reason she sat in the class, was essentially to figure out what my particular role in the last 30 years has been in geographic thought, I don't usually encourage students to do that, but since she's a foreigner, and she's had a very traditional geographic education in Taiwan, it seemed to me to be a good time for- to introduce this, because she'd been interested in (a) thesis topic … in what's essentially economic urban geography, in what's going to happen to urban types and sites and locations and relationships in the Far East, but she can't write, yet in exchanges with her, every two weeks for an hour or so, it's very clear that she has ideas, and she vigorously defends her ideas, I accuse her of uh trying to make geography into a mathematical science and so on, and uh she uh falls back on what to me is an excuse, that she can't express herself [he laughs], you know, in English.

Kohl's extensive comments on Betty in this interview oscillated between Betty's problems with writing in English and their conflicting theoretical orientations to geography (his cultural-philosophic and hers scientific-mathematical). He mentioned that Betty had had three advisors and, during that year, he had become her latest. He concluded with a pessimistic assessment of her prospects: "I don't think she can get a degree basically unless she has vast improvement." Kohl's comments recontextualize Betty's texts in another stream of activity, one that easily and invisibly converges with that of the seminar. Betty's focus on whether geography can be quantified and on Kohl's writings on this issue could plausibly have arisen in the seminar; however, for Betty and Kohl, it appeared to be more indexed in their biweekly debates in Kohl's office. As in my hypothetical constitution scenario or Teresa's research proposal (chap. 2), Betty's text was distinctly doubled, and its most powerful contextualization fore-grounded another history, not that of the seminar.

Liz's essay took a historical topic (French School geography) that she was interested in (see earlier interview comments) and wrote about it in ways that were personal, philosophical, and problematizing. It also happened that Kohl had distributed to the seminar an article he had written on French geography, particularly Vidal. The following edited excerpt from her essay reveals a text quite different from John's or Betty's:

As interesting as the roots of culture in nature is Durkheim's concern for social morphology: structures of society. Buttimer asserts that, with the concept of *genre de vie*, Vidal uses Durkheim's idea of the livelihood group as the unit of cultural and geographical analysis. By combining the society-milieu relationships suggested by Ratzel with the livelihood group as organizing unit, *genre de vie* offers a principle for rich evocations of culture. While description is the strength of the French School, explanation has been perceived as its weakness. Vidal's critics disparaged a lack of methodological rigor in his holistic approach to understanding cultures and places.…

In addition to the criticism that *genre de vie* lacked explanatory value, Buttimer points out that Vidal's ecological and holistic studies were viewed as helpful only when applied to "traditional" societies. They seemed inadequate to explain and describe complex "modern" societies. Today, cultural ecologists are also burdened by this charge. I think the feeling is that, the farther people stray from the land (in terms of its direct role in their subsistence), the less rooted they are in the local environment, and the less relevance the local environment has for maintaining culture, save as history.

I do not dispute these criticisms; indeed, it seems to me that such charges are applicable to all of the geographies I find most appealing. However, I think there is a place for these works which preserve the adventure of geographic discovery.

When I handed Liz's essay to Kohl in a text-based interview, he responded: "Yeah, I thought that she was the best student by far in there … and obviously I had some attachment to her particular interest in the French School, since I've been doing work on that, published papers on that, I think that um, she's probably as good a student as I've had in *that* kind of a seminar." It was a small seminar, and Kohl had found the other two students' final essays problematic, so identifying her as the best student in the seminar could be faint praise, but his final comment suggests it was not.

So far, I have emphasized ways that Kohl and the course cued topics and the ways Kohl and the students aligned students' diverse texts with those topics to make the "take-home final." However, even when such alignment appeared most successful, as in Liz's case, interviews suggested that the intersubjective representations of those texts (including the work involved in their production) were only partially "shared." When I asked Liz what she remembered about writing the essay in an interview four months after the seminar, her recollection contrasted sharply with Kohl's praise:

Um, I wrote it, I wrote it in a hurry, it's- it's difficult for me to write, and I didn't really allow very much time, maybe I allowed enough time for somebody else, but not for me, you know I did it- I think I did it, um, the day before I had to leave town, um yeah, and I do remember being very disappointed in this paper, although um, it seemed to me that I prepared all along in the class, I didn't actually know what I was going to write, but I knew what I was interested in from the very beginning of the quarter, which was the French geographers, and um, so I paid particular attention to them when we did some of that reading, and, when we had the discussion about them, I was a little more tuned in, and I did some reading on my own, just sort of over the course of the quarter, but I still, up until the very day I was supposed to write this essay, I didn't really know what I wanted to say, so it was kind of a tough one to write

When she turned in her essays, Liz had not expected the "A" she received.

The divergent representations were not limited to evaluation of the quality of the essay or inferences about how engaged a process its production was. Liz had not picked up her paper from Kohl (and indicated that she probably never would have). Thus, when I handed her the essays with

Kohl's comments on them and asked her to talk through his responses, it was her first reading of that response. One of Kohl's final summary comments read: "As you may have guessed I find the French School more original in its thinking and not a big borrower of ideas from Ratzel and Durkheim." I asked Liz if she had guessed this, and she replied:

> Um, never thought about it, I mean, I know that he loves the French school, I mean that came across in the seminar but um, "more original in its thinking and not just borrowers from Ratzel and Durkheim," hm, no, I hadn't guessed that, I mean I didn't know very much about it so uh, you know, tracing the antecedents of something like the French School of geography is a total mystery, I mean if somebody tells me that uh Ratzel and Durkheim had, you know, sort of contributed to this line of thought, then, sounds good, you know what I mean? [laughing] 'cause what do I know?

Liz also noted that Kohl's comments did not really address the ideas she was struggling with, pointing to one area where she thought the text probably signified something different to Kohl than it did to her:

> I mean, I'm sure he can't know that I was very uncertain about all of these terms I was using, *genre de vie*, you know, was I using it the right, well he knows what it is exactly, and um so he may have just glossed over reading it, whereas I had to really kind of struggle with it, and- and I'm not sure if I did get it in the end, you know? But he might have read more into it than is there, I guess.

Multiple, even conflicting, representations of texts are hardly news theoretically (e.g., Bartlett, 1932; Richards, 1929). However, they are often treated as simply the outcome of general cognitive–interpretive processes or "legacies" of prior experience or knowledge, as yet another illustration of reader-response theory or the power of cognitive schemata. By situating these representations in specific contexts, I believe that we may gain valuable insights into connections between literate activity and disciplinary enculturation.

Liz's suggestion that Kohl may have "read into" her texts accords well with current interest in ways that miscommunication, presupposition, and prolepsis may foster learning and socialization, not only by prompting joint attention, but also by sustaining participation in the activity. Topics like *genre de vie*, French geography, Vidal, Durkheim, and Ratzel marked out the intersubjective grounds for Kohl and Liz's joint attention. However, those topics were infused with divergent senses, intertextual connections, and affective colorations. What Kohl experienced as a pleasant stroll through the familiar intellectual countryside of France represented obscure and uncertain ground for Liz, who worried she might have lost her way.

Kohl's tacit practice of "reading into" Liz's texts may have helped sustain co-participation under conditions of marked asymmetry (see the Ochs, 1990, discussion of the role of miscommunication in adult–child interactions and child language socialization). In other words, seeing Kohl read more into Liz's use of terms like *genre de vie* and her citation of scholars like Durkheim and Ratzel, we might be glimpsing a practice in which not only is greater knowledge presupposed, but also greater disciplinarity, in which this joint alignment to topics proleptically propels Liz into a disciplinary role she does not yet fill, but is more likely to attain as a ratified participant. I would characterize this not as performance before competence (Cazden, 1983), but as co-participation through mutual and mediated alignment.

With diverse topical resources cued in the seminar and drawn from other streams of activity, the students in *Geography* produced diverse texts. All of the essays contextualized themselves by drawing from geographic discourses in general and particularly from the special topics of "geographic thought" that Kohl had rehearsed in the seminar. Moreover, all of the essays aligned to (relatively backgrounded) institutional topics: They were turned in as assignments at the institutionally appropriate time, and as diverse as they were, all displayed recognizable features of academic writing.

If topical alignments were quite visible, intersubjectivity seemed more obscure. Handwritten in a blue book, John's essay displayed a certain embedded addressivity that seemed to say "Read me as a one-draft, extemporaneously produced in-class exam." Around this text, John and Kohl arrived together at a space labeled "the history of geography," but their notions of that history were quite divergent. Betty's printed five-page paper on Kohl's place in geography was saturated with their history of meetings as well as the seminar task. Around this text, Betty and Kohl apparently reenacted a long history of conflicting representations not only of the role of science and mathematics in geography but of the reasons for their disagreements. Kohl and Liz came to a much more convergent space in which *genre de vie* and French geography circulated comfortably, but Kohl's space was more richly equipped than Liz's, leaving considerable divergence there as well, a divergence Liz unmistakably felt.

As a dialogic process, genrification is achieved in acts of reading as well as writing. Kohl's relatively centrifugal structuring of the final writing task was echoed in his centrifugal reading of the final texts. Kohl read these three very different texts as "the essays" he had assigned, regardless of variations in format and print, topics and language, length and citation. Their differences he read as differences in quality. In this sense, making the genre of "the blue-book essay" in *Geography* involved mutual alignments mediated by texts, topics, and discourses, forming a multidimensional space where a variety of specific trajectories were both possible and accepted.

Outlining Field Research in American Studies.

The seminar in field research that Kohl was teaching capped a three-quarter sequence. The American Studies Department had a small core faculty, supplemented by a number of associated faculty (including Kohl). The three-quarter sequence was a requirement for graduate students majoring or minoring in American Studies. The first two quarters of the sequence had been taught by one of the senior core faculty. In this final quarter, the seminar was cross-listed in Geography. Sixteen students enrolled through American Studies, and two, through Geography. (One of the geography students, Nathan, was also enrolled in Kohl's *Geography*, but did not turn in work for either seminar). Seventeen of the 18 were graduate students, most working on master's degrees. The 18th was an undergraduate from Hungary. Sixteen were NSE; two, the student from Hungary and a Chinese geography student, were NNSE. Seven were male, and 11, female. Aside from the two geography students, the 16 who had taken the whole sequence were mostly first-year majors in American Studies, although at least two were majoring in History and minoring in American Studies.

The third quarter of the seminar was designed to give students some experience of field research in areas of interest they had developed the previous two quarters. Kohl had selected a book on urban geography as a text for the seminar, but it was background reading, rarely even mentioned in class. He represented the central task for the seminar, field research, primarily in terms of investigating a neighborhood or a specific place, but also encouraged students to take advantage of the seminar to develop academic projects they could use (e.g., thesis projects, work they were doing or had done for other courses). The final written product students were to turn in was described (orally) as *an outline* for a larger work (e.g., a master's thesis, dissertation, or article), with some *discussion* (about five pages) of one section of the outline, and *an annotated bibliography* including primary (particularly interview) and secondary sources.

In class, Kohl foregrounded a number of topics related or relatable to the field research and outline writing. The seminar met seven afternoons during the quarter. The first session met in a small, basement classroom of the old building that housed American Studies; subsequent classes (except for the third) met in a large lecture room in a modern building near the Geography Department (over half a mile from the original building).[7] The third session met in a chartered bus. Microphone in hand, Kohl gave students a tour of Midwest City, sketching how its geography related to histories of its commercial and industrial districts and residential neighborhoods, particularly stressing ethnic succession in neighborhoods. The tour was a particularly clear signal of Kohl's representation of field research in terms of particular places. In seminar sessions, Kohl lectured about fieldwork, urban geography, and the history of Midwest City. He referred regularly to maps, spending over an hour in one session showing varied maps of Midwest City and its neighborhoods (topographical, demographic, economic, infrastructure; past and current). He also told personal stories based on his experiences growing up in the city. He emphasized the importance of place, the value of observation and interviewing, and the idea (as in *Geography*) that questions are crucial and enduring whereas the answers are almost always transitory. He initiated discussions of students' individual projects and, on a few occasions, of research methodologies, epistemologies, and politics. A substantial amount of class time was spent discussing the field research project and the product he wanted to receive. After the tour, Kohl canceled the next three sessions to give students time to do research and to consult with him individually if they chose. He also offered to go into the field with individual students if it would be useful. Several students did go to his office and at least one drove around the city with Kohl in an attempt to reconstruct the setting of a 1930's trucking strike. In the seventh week, Kohl asked students to turn in a draft of their outline the next week. He responded to that draft in writing, returning it to students in Week 10, the last class. The final draft of the outline–discussion–annotated bibliography was due at the very end of the quarter.

Because the seminar focused on field research, the task, both as research practice and as written product, was a frequently foregrounded topic. Kohl began the first class by asking students what their research interests were. As each student replied, Kohl worked to tie their interests into his view of field research—to local neighborhoods and people. Although planning, conducting, and writing up the field research were repeated and sustained

---

[7]This move indexed the cross-departmental contexts of the American Studies program locally, the interdisciplinarity of American Studies in general, and Kohl's position in both contexts. Chin (1994) provides a fascinating example of the way the semiotics of material-social spaces shaped the writing and disciplinary enculturation of a cohort of graduate journalism students.

topics, the students seemed fairly uncertain about Kohl's expectations. For example, in Week 7, after having not met for three weeks, Kohl announced for the first time that students should hand in a draft of their outline the following week and reviewed the outline and the bibliography in some detail. This announcement triggered a variety of questions, some, like the following, clearly negotiations over ways of doing the task:

James: Would you mind a bibliographic essay instead of an annotated bibliography?

Kohl: Yeah, handle the bibliography in any way you want

Some of these negotiations led toward more open-ended probes about the task. For example, Roger asked if Kohl wanted Roman numerals, phrases, sentences, or paragraphs in the outline. Kohl indicated that it did not have to be a formal outline, that it could include paragraphs where students said, "Chapter 1, I want to introduce this subject, these are the conceptual frameworks I'm thinking about." Roger then continued:

Roger: and how long of a paper is it roughly [some laughter]

Kohl: Two or three, I think two or three pages is certainly enough for an outline

Roger: I'm saying if we actually completed the project, the outline would represent a 10-page paper? Or a 50-page paper? Or a dissertation?

Kohl: oh, I think of something between 20 and 30, you know, what you'd do for if the topic was handed to you and you had enough time to do it,

Kohl's representation of the task in these exchanges was contradictory. He had just talked about the research and the outlines in terms of thesis or dissertation research and animated the voice of a student writing a prose outline in terms of "chapters" ("Chapter 1, I want to introduce ... "). However, he then suggests to Roger that the outline should be for a 20- to 30-page paper. In the first instance, Kohl's representations of the outline indexed his goal of making seminar tasks contribute to the larger projects of graduate work (to theses and dissertations). In the second instance, his representations seemed addressed to allaying students' anxieties by making the task seem manageable.

Other exchanges were directed to, even challenging of, the disciplinary topics Kohl was stressing. For example, Dan asked Kohl why he emphasized a geographic context, suggesting that place was not an important issue in his research on a Jewish community center. After discussing disciplinary divisions in American Studies (particularly English and History vs. the social sciences), Kohl turned to his task and Dan's research:

Kohl: So I think there is a tendency in American Studies' students to essentially emphasize narrative, emphasize literary and historic kinds of exposition, I would encourage obviously a sociological analysis, or an economic analysis, but that's up to you, I wouldn't want to impose a particular kind of construct or framework on your particular issue, so use whatever you are interested in, whatever sources (you're after), I don't mean to not explore, you may find that a geographic context, whatever that is, may be better than what you started out with, looking at the bibliographic material, or tracing the evolution of Jewish centers in Midwest City, that may be adapted to it, because Jewish centers obviously do have a geography, they are in places, ( ), they change as the center of gravity of the Jewish community changes, uh, Jewish communities tends to be clustered, as against being scattered, uh, I ( )

Dan: Are you sure about that?

Kohl: Yeah... I've had M.A. theses where they pose the question of where is the Japanese community in Midwest City, I mean there are four or five thousand Japanese, where are they? Well, there's one here, one here, one over there,

Dan: I just keep on asking Jews whether they live in West Hill and nobody answered in affirmative yet, so it's strange

female?:   Maybe they're ambivalent about it

female?:   But in general they do, I mean that's just the only way to form a Jewish community, is to stick together, I mean that's the general pattern

Kohl: Have you been to West Hill?

Dan: Yeah, I have

Kohl's responses to student questions and negotiations broadened the topical affordances of the task. For example, he authorized bibliographic essays and outlines in paragraph form as document guidelines. Animating possible student text, he evoked an informal, in-progress, and personal voice ("Chapter 1, I want to introduce"). He repeatedly referred to students' own goals and invited them to graft other institutional tasks (papers for other courses, master' theses, doctoral dissertations) onto his assignment. However, he also reinforced his emphases on the particular local (often ethnic) communities and neighborhoods that he wanted students to explore.

In his written responses to students' drafts, Kohl was positive and encouraging. He focused on specific substantive issues (e.g., what he found most interesting, possible resources to consider, questions he had about specific issues). In the final session, after he returned the outlines, he offered some general responses to them, including these:

> I found uh, them all very interesting, there's a large range and variety, they're really fascinating because I think somehow you've conveyed to me what I'm after, that is, I don't think I would perceive the problems and the issues the way you do, but that's an (attitude), my perspective, I don't know whether I've influenced you, but I think you bought the idea that it's the questions that are important and not the answers, that's one of my ( ) standard beliefs... I imposed upon you an outline, wherein you do something in some detail, and obviously including that outline, it's too big, it's too broad, and some people worried about uh, how I get this into 30 pages, thinking about 8 to 10 pages, well I don't want 30 pages, (we) have a 10-week period, I do want an outline, and I think most people can do that with 10 pages, I mean three pages typed, I think you don't need more than five or six pages to take a topic out of that, and I don't necessarily want you to spend some of that written material explaining where this is in the outline, I should be able to figure that out ... but I do want you to handle a topic, so that I can see how you're going to develop it, or how you think you're going to develop it, in many ways for me the annotated bibliographies are the most important, and some of you have done amazing things with it, in the sense of the breadth of that bibliography, and the places where you're finding–what I didn't get in the bibliography so far—I'd love to hear it—is where are the gaps, what couldn't you find or do in those 10 weeks.

Kohl presented students with complex, potentially conflicting topical cues for doing and writing up their final research. He mixed extensive descriptions of the process and product with centrifugal invitations for students to do something useful, to use whatever frameworks fit their questions, and to relate his task to other work. Importing topics (concepts, issues, methods, tasks) from other coursework, however, would often involve not field research, but theoretical or textual work. Kohl's status as a professor of geography, his frequent use of historical maps, and his constant topicalizing of local neighborhoods and ethnic succession pointed students toward geographic and historical orientations to the task. His representation of fieldwork as interviewing and observation and his sug-gestion that bibliographies should be divided into primary sources (particu-larly, interviews) and secondary sources pointed toward an ethnographic orientation to the task. His emphasis on the process of research and his repeated assertion that he was interested in the questions more than the answers suggested an informal, in-progress approach to the writing, whereas his request for an outline and a section of the outline written up might imply a more formal text. In addition, Kohl made specific suggestions to some students in class, to some in office conferences, and to many in his written responses to their draft outlines in Week 10.

Given such diverse topical resources and such a centrifugal task, students' texts were, perhaps predictably, fairly diverse. Papers ranged from five pages to more than 20. Students' selection from and use of this array of topics was quite complex, although all aligned themselves to some aspects of Kohl's topical cuing. A number of students made their questions and their research plans (rather than any findings) the focus of their discussions. Most papers included recognizable outlines; however, several used headings to invoke that structure. One outline Kohl particularly liked used questions for most of the subpoints under major headings. Another student, who turned in a full draft of a long paper in Week 8, used headings but also wrote in ink on the top of the first page: "My outline is embedded in this draft." Eleven papers aligned to Kohl's representations of field research by doing and writing about interviews, but the others did not. Students also aligned to Kohl's geographic themes: At least 10 of the papers focused on specific sites and three presented maps. Students' research often explicitly topicalized social identities relating to ethnicity, gender, religion, and sexual orientation: seven of the 17 projects included an ethnic or identity term in the title. These identity topics could be linked to Kohl's discussion of ethnicity, class, and sexual orientation in specific neighborhoods, but identity was also a topic that saturated the students' course work as well as the texts of disciplinary journals and books. In all but one case, students were topicalizing personal identities. Thus, a lesbian student planned to do research comparing Midwest City's gay community to San Francisco's. An Irish woman from a Catholic background was writing on the role of Irish Catholic nuns in a local parish around the turn of the century. Two Jewish students were writing on local Jewish communities. The Hungarian student wrote about local Hungarian immigration early in the century. One student planned a project on his family's migration from Norway to the United States in the 1800s. The Chinese student wrote on Southeast Asian businesses in a particular neighborhood. Overall, the papers ranged from those displaying limited evidence of the task or content topics Kohl had stressed to those that were tightly aligned to Kohl's dominant topics. To illustrate the variations in generic alignment in *American Studies*, I examine two extreme examples here. Chapter 9 presents a more in-depth examination of another student's work in the seminar.[8]

---

[8]A related analysis of this seminar also appears in Prior (1997).

Dwight, a history student, aligned his work to the course in the most limited fashion. In an interview, he explained that he had written a senior thesis on a 1930's strike that occurred in Midwest City, was writing on the same strike for this seminar, and planned to continue researching it. He was perhaps the only student who took Kohl up on his offer to drive around Midwest City during the three weeks when classes were cancelled. Kohl pointed out key sites connected to the strike and helped Dwight to visualize the urban landscape of the 1930s and how that landscape had shaped events of the strike. Dwight said his tour with Kohl had been very useful, but then added that he felt the drive represented "enough work" for the course. He opened his paper as follows:

> Examining the 1935 Truckers' Strike allows scholars to confront two theoretical barriers which plague working-class history: the structural Marxist model and the liberal/consensus model. I propose employing Historian David Montgomery's "shop floor/workers' control" thesis as an appropriate interpretive vehicle, thus allowing a broader historical perspective to emerge. While sacrificing a nationalist framework, a more significant regionalist context arises in which both working-class and middle-class responses to industrial capitalism may be measured. Such responses, when examined at the community or grass-roots level, allow for a more clear understanding of both class development and community social history. Contemplating the '35 Strike, then, allows me the opportunity to apply and test this thesis.

Dwight's final paper (4 1/2 pages of text plus a two-page bibliography) did not display any sign of an outline (not even the use of headings) and made no references to local geography. The introduction above was followed by 2 1/2 pages in which Dwight briefly reviewed the history of the strike and elaborated on his theoretical framework. Near the end of the paper, Dwight offered a more informal, in-progress assessment: "My field and archival research indicates a rich body of under-used resources. Clearly, this is a project rife with potential." Not incidentally, he alludes here to "field" as well as archival research, possibly in reference to the drive with Kohl. His sources in the bibliography were all textual and not annotated, although his final three paragraphs could be construed as the bibliographic essay option. In those paragraphs, he discussed his main sources on the strike and alluded, possibly aligning with Kohl's emphasis on interviews, to a local collection of oral histories he planned to study. In the two changes he made between his draft and final papers, Dwight displayed some clear accommodations to Kohl's task representations. He added one paragraph in response to a question Kohl had asked in his written comments about internal divisions in the union. He also expanded his concluding discussion of sources from one paragraph to three (recall Kohl's emphasis on bibliography in the final session). Nevertheless, Dwight's paper appeared to be off-the-shelf work, largely derived from prior texts. He aligned perceptibly, but minimally to Kohl's task, choosing a local topic he was researching for other contexts, taking the drive with Kohl, and turning in a text that displayed a few features Kohl had cued.

In the text-based interview on Dwight's paper, Kohl discussed the strike and the drive around the city that he took with Dwight, but said he was disappointed Dwight had not displayed in the paper what he had learned on the drive. Dwight's assessment that the drive around Midwest City was enough (for the seminar) was evidently accurate in that Kohl's disappointment with the product was tempered by his sense that Dwight had learned something useful in the seminar. Certainly, Dwight's grade ("A") did not suffer.

Sarah, a student majoring in American Studies, strongly aligned her texts with the special topics Kohl has stressed. Her opening paragraph densely echoes those topics: a local neighborhood, ethnicity, geographic distribution of population, interviewing, future work, and especially questions (five of the 12 sentences are syntactically questions and three others thematize questioning semantically):

> My first interview with a resident of the North Grove neighborhood led me to wonder if this area is truly a Jewish "community." Certainly a large number of Jews live there. At some time in the 1960s as much as eighty percent of Midwest City's Jews had settled there. However, this woman, who had been a resident for almost forty years said she doesn't feel that it's a particularly Jewish community. Granted, this is one person's opinion. However, her comments have led me to question the status of contemporary Jewish communities. How has the increase in social and economic standing changed the Midwest City Jewish community? Do they see themselves as tied by their common heritage, or by their geographical groupings? As overt anti-semitism has lessened, and as Jews have shed their status of "immigrant" and "other," have they lost the community bonds that they experienced as residents of the lower North Side? Is there a tightly knit community today? If there is, what is it that now ties Jews together? As I have pursued more interviews, I have discovered that the characteristics and strength of the community is more a matter of perception than a matter of fact. The main focus of my future work, therefore, would be to investigate and compare different perceptions of the community by interviewing a large cross section of the community.

Sarah's expanded section of the outline reinforced this initial orientation to Kohl's topics: It consisted of a discussion of what she had learned in each interview with a local resident of the North Grove neighborhood. This kind of informal, research-oriented approach to the task was quite common. It was an approach that Kohl generally seemed to appreciate, perhaps in part because it documented an in-progress engagement in fieldwork, his central goal. On Sarah's paper, he commented positively on her use of interviews, although he questioned her references to ethnic decline, a continuation of an argument that had been hotly debated in class.

Kohl's relatively centrifugal writing task invited students to pursue diverse tasks and produce diverse texts—which the students did—and Kohl took up those diverse texts (and the tasks they referred to) as what he was looking for. Some students, like Dwight, aligned minimally to Kohl's task. Others, like Sarah, clearly aligned to the topics he had stressed in class and to the task he had given, displaying their engagement in field research. Institutionally, Kohl equated their work: All were graded as A's and given the same number of credits.

MAKING GENRES SEMIOTICALLY

Analyzing these academic writing tasks as semiotic genres points to ways the students and Kohl aligned their literate activity in the seminars. In both seminars, Kohl mixed centrifugal representations of the writing tasks with fairly centripetal representations of disciplinarity. In both seminars, students produced very different texts, using varied resources and topics to align to "the task." In both, especially *American Studies*, those texts indexed very heterogeneous activity. In both, Kohl read these markedly different texts (implicating different work) as the task requested, with differences being treated—if at all—as issues of quality. In both, a kind of situated topical bricolage coordinated joint attention, but marked out quite partial grounds of intersubjectivity, grounds that were sometimes, as in Liz's case, opportunities for proleptic invitations to disciplinary participation, but in other cases (e.g., Betty's, John's) led to negative evaluations of students' work and potentially marginalization from the community of practice.

Kohl's two seminars embodied somewhat different blends of centripetal and centrifugal forces. In *Geography*, Kohl invoked a wide topical field indexing diverse discourses and offered centrifugal structuring of the final essay (in terms of process and product), producing a quite centrifugal task overall. In contrast, in *American Studies*, Kohl rehearsed key topics in relation to the task and the text extensively. He structured the writing process, asking students to put together a rough draft of the outline and responding to it in writing, a response that was to varying extents taken up in the final texts, even Dwight's. Although Kohl allowed considerable play in the tasks and texts students might pursue, this centripetal orientation produced visible consequences in many students' work.

It is important to note that the blend of centripetal and centrifugal forces involved alignments of functional systems of activity, not just the strength or coherence of Kohl's topical emphases. *American Studies* and *Geography* involved very different generic activity in part because of continuities structured by departmental, disciplinary, and other spheres of activity. Whereas Betty, Liz, and John arrived in *Geography* as a weakly aligned collection of people, the majority of students in *American Studies* were a cohort who had taken at least the two previous seminars together. When Kohl asked in the first class what kind of research they planned to pursue, they all had ready answers. Another factor in *American Studies* was the convergent orientation of the students and the field to using personal social identity as a disciplinary topic, an orientation with sometimes striking implications for lamination, for the activity footings on which students and others constituted disciplinarity. Liz's interest in the French School or Betty's continuation of office debates with Kohl tapped streams of activity of quite a different order from those tapped by Sarah's and Dan's involvement as Jews studying Jewish communities. If the students engaged in field research as Kohl invoked it, that alignment involved active participation in other streams of activity (e.g, spending hours interviewing people in a local community as a number of students did).

In both seminars, the students and Kohl were so centripetally oriented to the institution of schooling that those alignments were largely dispositional and tacit. When Kohl made assignments or structured seminar activities, he rarely offered any account, or was asked to account for, those actions. They were his taken-for-granted prerogatives. Kohl made assignments and students sought clarification, less for the familiarly named topic "final blue-book essay" than for the less typified task, the outline-expanded-discussion-of-a-section-annotated-bibliography-in-relation-to-field-research. Students marked their participation in school through procedural display (turning in texts and drafts at appropriate times, comporting themselves as students in the classroom) as well as by aligning their texts to Kohl's topics. The strength of these orientations is particularly suggested by the fact that in both seminars students produced and Kohl accepted a typified institutional genre (the final term paper), although Kohl's stated tasks in each case called for different types of texts.

In both seminars then, the students and Kohl coordinated their literate activity to make classroom genres, drawing on short- and long-term alignments of a laminated array of functional systems. The heterogeneity in the students' work and texts and in Kohl's reception, although it was rarely remark-able to participants, is a key finding, and one also seen in *Language Research* (chap. 2) and *Sociology* (chaps. 6–8). This analysis offers an image of how semiotic genres get made in situated activity. Topics, the discursive artifacts of spheres of activity, mediated joint attention, constructing intersubjective grounds (however partial and tenuous) that generally sustained participation (however heterogeneous). However, these situated alignments cannot stand alone. They are supposed to be linked together to produce disciplinary enculturation, not just temporary communicative accommodation. In the next chapter then, I move into a somewhat wider framework to explore this kind of heterogeneous literate activity from a developmental perspective, as trajectories of participation in communities of practice.

4

Trajectories of Participation: Two Paths to the MA

In chapter 3, examination of the writing tasks in two seminars found not only that the students produced, and were ratified in producing, markedly diverse texts, but also that the activities that surrounded those texts were highly heterogeneous. Viewed only in terms of describing the writing tasks in seminars, such variation is striking. However, academic writing tasks are not isolated events; they are intended to form links in a chain of learning, enculturation, and institutional advance. The link between situated social activity, the development of persons, and social formation has been a central tenet of sociohistoric theory.[1] Thus, a key question is raised by this variation: What are the developmental implications for these kinds of differences in activity, or, in the context of this research, what do these differences suggest about disciplinary enculturation?

Lave and Wenger (1991) offer one framework to explore writing tasks from a developmental perspective with their notion of situated learning as forms of participation in heterogeneous communities of practice (see chap. 1). In Lave and Wenger's view, learning (the historical production of a person) is not generated by abstract macrosocial and historical forces, but by a person's embodied, active, perspectival trajectory through multiple, interpenetrated, and internally stratified communities of practice in the world, communities that are themselves dynamic, open, and evolving. Seeing learning as participation suggests the value of examining the paths and modes of participation afforded to and created by participants in a

---

[1]Sociohistoric theory has generally identified four lines of development: microgenesis (specific situations), ontogenesis (persons), cultural-historical (cultures), and phylogenesis (species). Cole (1995) proposes adding another level, mesogenesis, that of local cultural systems of activity. Scribner (1985) elaborated three lines of cultural-historical development (general human history, histories of specific cultures, and histories of psychological systems). Bazerman (1988) argues for the importance of studying the genesis of cultural forms or artifacts. See also the discussion of lines of development in functional systems in chapter 1.

community's activities. Trajectories of participation in social activities are individual and particular, but also socially typified. Reflecting on data from all the seminars, I developed a general framework to talk about typified modes of student participation in graduate study. After describing that framework, I will sketch a comparative account of the trajectories of participation traced by two students as they moved from their research proposals in Mead's *Language Research*, into their actual master's (MA) research, and finally to completion of their master's degree.

Analysis of the two students' work suggests that, although they were making common institutional advances in the same program at one university, their modes of participation were radically different. In particular, the analysis focuses on their literate activity and appropriation of disciplinary texts. In the case of one student, analysis of the use of source texts in her MA thesis revealed practices that would probably be identified as plagiarism. However, as Scollon (1995) argues, modern Western conceptions of authorship and plagiarism rest on problematic theories of language, knowledge, and the self that bear little relation to current research on communicative and knowledge-making practices. Sociohistoric theories certainly emphasize what should be obvious, that none of us have "our own words" to put our thoughts into and that even our most innovative knowledge is heavily mediated by cultural tools not of our making. The analysis in this chapter then also considers practices of appropriation from a developmental and dialogic perspective, as a critical question for any theory in which, to paraphrase Bakhtin, we get our words from other people's mouths, texts, and electronic documents.

MODES OF PARTICIPATION: PASSING, PROCEDURAL DISPLAY, AND DEEP PARTICIPATION

In my research, I came to identify three general modes of participation in graduate study: passing, procedural display, and deep participation. These three modes of participation involve ascending levels of access to and engagement in disciplinary activity. I am not proposing these modes of participation as a general stage model, or, for that matter, even a comprehensive classification. Certainly they do not capture the particular and nuanced qualities of engagement that critically index sociocultural, institutional, and individual identities and practices (as seen in the case studies presented throughout this book). Although a limited heuristic, these three modes of participation do capture, I believe, some important patterns of participation in school-based disciplinary enculturation.

Passing represents a mode of participation defined purely from an institutional perspective: the institutional reductions of full, situated academic performances into textual tabulations of credit hours, grades, and programmatic requirements checked off. Silent on what performances underlie this bureaucratic accounting, passing offers a public view of education as a process of social certification. Of course, this institutional perspective is also strongly represented in participants' situated understandings, motives, and practices; passing is a matter of focal interest and concern for instructors, students, and administrators in educational contexts. In fact, ethnographic studies of schooling (e.g., Becker et al., 1961; McNeil, 1986) have routinely reported tensions for students between passing and learning, a contradiction often resolved in favor of passing. In addition, passing is of interest to external audiences (e.g., employers, government and non-governmental bodies offering professional licensure or certification). Institutional certification controls or influences access to a wide variety of workplaces and professions. Finally, as the case of at least one student in my studies suggested (see discussion of Park in chap. 6), passing can represent the dominant mode of participation. For all of these reasons, this institutional perspective on participation in schooling is important to identify.

Procedural display is a notion I have adapted from Bloome, Puro and Theodrou's (1989) analyses of classroom lessons. Bloome, Puro and Theodrou identified procedural display as "the cooperative display by teachers and students to each other of a set of interactional procedures that can be counted (interpreted) as doing a lesson by teachers, students, and members of the community" (p. 266). In this view, "doing a lesson" is not a simple procedural assembly; it is rather a cultural event that is defined relationally within a semiotic field of cultural meanings and roles. Bloome, Puro, and Theodrou define procedural display as collective and cooperative: Conflict and resistance in the classroom may disrupt "doing a lesson" and lead to a different cultural event. They suggest that procedural display represents not only a basic condition for the cultural production of "a lesson," but that this jointly coordinated activity also produces an opportunity space in which substantive learning might occur. Nevertheless, they also identify interactions in classrooms where display appears to be an end in itself. As a joint accomplishment, procedural display highlights practices of alignment and coordination that I argue are central to communication, learning, and activity.

To describe students' participation in seminars and graduate work, I am adapting their notion in two ways. First, I am extending it from its original focus on what counts as *doing a lesson* in a classroom to a broader range of cultural events relevant to graduate studies (e.g., what counts as *doing a seminar discussion*) and to literate events, often extended, that involve hybrid blends of texts and talk (e.g., what counts as *writing a research proposal*). Some, indeed most, of these activities are, thus, dispersed in time and space (another significant departure from Bloome, Puro, and Theodrou's focus on face-to-face interaction). Second, although they argue that procedural display should be seen as a strictly collective accomplishment, I would also add an individual interpretation of procedural display. In other words, I see the person's ability to participate in a particular practice (a question of appropriated tools and identities) as an issue.

Before describing deep participation, I need to recall from chapter 1 Lave and Wenger's (1991) argument that forms of participation in communities of practice are diverse, multiple, always peripheral, and that there is no core to such communities. In his discussion of genres, Kamberelis (1995) captures this complexity well. Noting that genres exist within systems of genres, that practices can be embedded in a variety of fields, that fields of practice are highly connected, and that individuals participate in "multiple, overlapping, and sometimes contradictory communities of practice, moving in and out them quite seamlessly," he concludes: "With all this overlap of fields, practices, texts, and people, the forms, functions, and practices of different genres leak into one another in a kind of metonymic or interdiscursive process of social semiosis" (p. 139). Instead of referring to a single idealized scale of disciplinary expertise, participation directs attention to specific modes of being newcomers and mature members of such interpenetrated communities of practice. In this regard, it is important not to reify and idealize developmental paths. For example, it may be instructive to compare students whose initial participation in a community occurs in schools to newcomers whose initial participation comes when they are established professionals.[2] To distinguish newcomers from mature members, Lave and Wenger (1991) refer to mature forms, still plural and diverse,

---

[2]Myers' (1990) account of Bloch, a well-established cell biologist who ventures into research on molecular genetics, is an excellent account of this phenomenon. Blakeslee's (1992) account of a physics research group seeking to publish work in biochemistry offers a view of newcomer paths in a hierarchical team (professor, post-doctoral fellow, and graduate student). Of course, students' roles are also heterogeneous. Certainly, Winsor's (1996) students moving through a co-op engineering program appear to be engaged in paths of enculturation quite different from Herrington's (1985) students in a more traditional engineering program.

as *full participation*. They also mention the notion of *centripetal participation*. Evidently, centripetal participation describes forms of participation that are likely to lead to full participation. Three other notions they discuss are related to understanding the characteristics of centripetal participation: access, sequestering, and transparency. Access is the basic ground of participation: "The key to legitimate peripherality is access by newcomers to the community of practice and all that membership entails" (p. 100). Sequestering is a partial or full denial of access to a relevant community of practice. For example, Lave and Wenger suggest that high school physics students are largely sequestered from participation in the practice of physicists, engaged instead in the quite different practices that mark students in school. Transparency refers to the degree to which an artifact or practice makes available to its users (or viewers) its operation as a tool and to the way its design and operation reflect the social practices and worlds it was designed in and for. Presumably, the transparency of tools (whether material or semiotic) is a special case of access/sequestering. For example, if I work in an automobile factory and my job consists simply of sitting in a windowless room and pressing a button whenever a red light flashes, I would be effectively sequestered from practices of automobile manufacturing. In contrast, if I cycle through alternating roles in a team that assembles cars from start to finish, I will have considerably richer access to the structure of an automobile and the processes of its manufacture.

With these notions in mind, I see a need for a term that designates a form of centripetal participation marked by rich access to, and engagement in, practices. I am suggesting *deep participation* as a way of talking about this kind of participation.[3] Deep participation not only opens paths toward full participation, that is, taking up some mature role in a community of practice, but also increases opportunities to assume privileged roles in a community. Deep participation may be displayed in the roles the person assumes, in her relations to other participants, and in qualitative aspects of her engagement in practices.

---

[3]These three modes are neither monolithic nor mutually exclusive. Each mode involves a continuum of qualitative variations as well as categorical features. Any student in an institution is involved in passing (with "failure" as one qualitative variation in this mode). Any student will be engaged in some forms of procedural display, but degrees and kinds will vary considerably. Some (perhaps relatively few) students may be engaged in deep participation, which also incorporates passing and procedural display. However, the coupling between qualities of participation is flexible. Students engaged in deep participation *could* be failing institutionally, and a wide variety of relations can exist between procedural display and deep participation. Over time or in different settings at the same time, a student may be engaged in different modes and qualities of participation. Of course, deep participation in disciplinary practices can also develop outside of school (e.g., see previous note on Myers, 1990).

MAI AND TERESA

In many ways, Mai and Teresa appeared to be tracing similar trajectories in *Language Research* and the departmental program. Both were international students and non-native speakers of English (NNSE), pursuing the MA in the Second Languages Program of a College of Education. Both planned to do a research project for their master's degree in the summer following Mead's seminar, and both anticipated PhD work after completing the master's. Both drafted their thesis research in the research proposal for Mead's seminar. Both actually began their research projects in the summer after the seminar and successfully completed their master's degrees in the next year. However, a situated analysis suggests that, however similar they appeared from an institutional perspective, Mai and Teresa were engaged in quite different modes of participation at this stage in their graduate work.[4]

Mai appeared to be working in relative isolation, to have limited access to relevant communities of practice, and to find disciplinary texts more opaque than transparent. Teresa, on the other hand, appeared to have rich and growing access to communities of practice and to find texts reasonably transparent. Their modes of appropriation (e.g., use of source texts) emerged as a particularly important gauge of their modes of participation. In this chapter, I trace their trajectories of participation over time, from the origins of their research proposals, to the development of their research proposals in the seminar, to Mead's reception of their texts, to their writing and research processes in their MA thesis, and finally to the finished texts for their MA degrees. I argue that Mai's participation in both the seminar and her master's research were dominated by passing and procedural display, whereas Teresa's activity was marked by features of deep participation.

ORIGINS OF THEIR RESEARCH

As was noted in chapter 2, I found that students' literate activity in *Language Research* was laminated, that they worked to align Mead's seminar assignments to the broader projects of their institutional programs and their lives. Interviews and texts repeatedly pointed to the continuities and connections in students' activity across time and settings. As was noted

---

[4]This case study began in *Language Research* (see chap. 2, footnote 3 for methods used there). It was resumed a year later when I obtained copies of the final theses of Mai and Teresa and conducted semi-structured and text-based interviews with each on her thesis and seminar research proposal.

in chapter 1, activity theory is grounded in the notion of motive; however, motive has often been reified through the assumption that a single motive resides in a situation. In a similar way, studies of academic writing have often assumed that students' motives coincide with the official goals embedded in the course (i.e., institutional grades, program advancement) and with the stated goals of instructors (i.e., assigned writing tasks).[5] Leont'ev (1978) suggested that action always involves a situated hierarchy of motives. One way to think about this multiplicity in motives is in terms of lamination. Here then, I explore the origins of Mai's and Teresa's research by looking to that lamination (to the relatively foregrounded streams of activity woven together around Mead's assignments). The origins Mai and Teresa pointed to in interviews and that appeared to be embodied in their texts and actions were complex and heterogeneous.

Origins of Mai's Research

When I asked Mai during the quarter of the seminar to describe how she had chosen her research project, she offered the following account:

> Oh, um, last quarter, I have uh discussed with my advisor Elizabeth and uh because she had, she has offered me a suggestion that she- she's think- because this quarter I am taking her course, testing, on Saturday, and he has- he suggest me that one of his- one of her students, a student from China, Tang Shu, and he has made, he has uh- he has- he make- he wrote his ... MA paper on the analysis of uh college entrance examination in- in China, so it gives me an idea I can write uh one, but in that case is in Taiwan, and I, because from my study, for, you know, program, for two courses, I have some idea on the ACTFL proficiency guidelines, so I- I want to combine, I want to use the guidelines to make an analysis because I think only- only item analysis is too simple.[6]

Mai's comments here suggested a rather limited personal engagement. Her choice of topic appeared to be shaped mainly by the opportunistic conjunction of her advisor's suggestion, courses she had taken, the availability of a closely related textual model (Tang Shu's MA thesis), and her knowledge of guidelines for proficiency tests. Passing (in this case completing the MA thesis) seems to be the dominant motive here.

---

[5]Chapter 9 explores these assumptions and their effects on research.

[6]ACTFL is the American Council of Teachers of Foreign Languages. ACTFL's language proficiency guidelines for speaking, listening, reading, and writing differ from conventional language tests theoretically and procedurally.

However, earlier in Mead's seminar, when she first introduced a tentative title for her research project, she began not with her advisor's assessment course, but with a personal contextualization, noting that she had taught ESL in Taiwan for 5 years and describing how teaching methods were "totally influenced by items on the tests." Likewise, in the interview after Mai had completed the thesis, her response to one question also invoked multiple contextualizations for her research as a school task and as part of wider projects directly connected to her interests, future work, and social practices:

Paul: Ok, what was the most valuable thing about it [the thesis research], do you feel like- was- was there something that you learned most from it, or- or was it mainly an obstacle to get through [I laugh, she laughs]

Mai: I think most valuable thing I got, may- maybe it's uh, the, I g-, the sense, the uh, the sense of accomplishment, yeah, uh because uh, yeah, uh when I see that, uh I have, ummm, because it is not a very easy work for me, so when I see that um, that all my efforts and time have spent and got this, got this thesis, yeah, I think that's the most valuable thing, and the- and the- moreover, uh, I think this paper, maybe because it- it talk about the language testing in Taiwan, so maybe it's- of course, it's not useful here, but when I- I think when I come to Taiwan and teaching English in university, I think this paper will be useful for them, or in, or in some- in some center or conference in Taiwan, maybe I will present this paper,

Paul: That was another question I had is, when you were writing it, what audiences were you imagining would read, obviously the committee, but any audiences besides that, were you thinking that someone in Taiwan might read it for example, or

Mai: Ah, yeah, uh, I think, yeah, … I have been an English teacher in Taiwan for five years, so when I write, when I wrote this- this paper, I- I think- I- I- I'm- I'm in- I'm informing those English teachers in Taiwan and provide, well, because uh, I'm, in fact, I know that, maybe- maybe that's the-,maybe the pressure of the examination, and maybe the- some factors, I know that the- the- some of- many the teaching methods are- are not appropriate for the students to learn English, so I think I'm informed, I'm like informing them, and uh, persuading them, and providing my my point of view, yeah, so I think my, my audi-, I think I'm- I'm talking to those English teachers.

Mai's first response here, that the value of the thesis was in a personal sense of accomplishment, suggests locating the task in the encapsulated context of school. However, her allusions to her experiences as an English teacher in Taiwan and to problems with English teaching pedagogy and English testing suggest at least the possibility that her research was linked to other activities, to problems she had experienced as both a teacher and student of English and that she hoped the research might usefully address.

Origins of Teresa's Research

As I noted in chapter 2, Teresa reported that the original idea for her research had arisen a year earlier in a course dealing with Limited English Proficient students in U.S. schools. In that course, she connected the experience of language-minority students in the U.S. to her own experience coming from a Castilian-speaking family in a Catalan-speaking province of Spain. She decided to research use of Catalan, which had recently been officially recognized and become the primary medium of instruction in her province. To pursue this idea, she had selected a sequence of courses (first a Spanish sociolinguistics course and then Mead's seminar).

In an interview after she completed her thesis, Teresa also discussed her experiences as teacher when I asked her to explain an unelaborated allusion in the conclusion of her thesis to improving school curricula. Her answer offered a richer contextualization of the kinds of connections she was making between her experiences and those of students in the United States:

Teresa: I don't mean that I'm against the curriculum that is now, but I think that there should be some attention to all these other influence, cultural influence ... if a person speaks most of the time Castilian in the house, and and feels more identified with Castilian than with Catalan, um, (if)- depending on the teacher, you know, if the teacher has, is more, put more strength on Catalan than Castilian, this person may feel bad and you know all these things, this is what I mean about that, but of course I (didn't test), difficult to test

Paul: From your, from your teaching experience and your experience in schools, does that seem to be a problem, that there's-

Teresa: Well there's no (dr-), but the thing is that I was, at that time, I was teaching lang- foreign languages, so you know I didn't- I didn't notice much of it, but um, always in the class, I always ask, "ok, if some of you don't understand Catalan," because sometimes I use the native language, "then just let me know," um, hardly ever they said they weren't, but if a guy, if a student addressed to me in Castilian, I immediately changed to Castilian, and from that time, in all the appointments I had with him and in all the meetings I had with him, I will always speak Castilian, I haven't you know, most of the teachers in Catalonia wouldn't do that, but um, I guess I'm doing it because I am a bilingual person myself and um, sometimes I feel more comfortable talking with someone in Castilian rather than in Catalan, so I'm aware of that, but um, for a Catalan teacher, you know, a teacher that, his native language is Catalan, I don't think they are very aware of that.

When I asked about potential audiences for her completed thesis, Teresa pointed to the three audiences she had explicitly addressed in the conclusions of her thesis: sociolinguists (who she might address in journal articles or conferences) and curriculum specialists and administrators in the Catalan Department of Education. Beyond imagining these audiences, Teresa mentioned that she had gone to the Catalan Department of Education and talked with an official there about her research and that he had asked for a copy of her research report.

Origins for Mai and Teresa

Through much of my analysis, I read Mai's origins as largely driven by institutional demands and at-hand resources, whereas I read Teresa's as deeply situated in long-standing, meaningful projects (particularly as a language-minority student and teacher). However, my perceptions might have been shaped by differences in expression. Mai's allusions (in the seminar, interviews, and her texts) to problems with testing and teaching in Taiwan, and to her own experiences as a student and teacher, suggest she may have aligned her research to her interests and concerns more than I had recognized. Nevertheless, clear differences in origins still do emerge. Teresa traces the genesis of her research to her own reflections, as she read sociolinguistic studies of Spanish speakers in the United States, on her experiences as a language minority in Spain. Mai, on other hand, traces her research to her advisor's suggestion. In addition, Teresa proactively selects a sequence of two courses to take in order to develop her research, whereas Mai seems to retrospectively "find" that the courses she has taken could be used for the research (although, as it turned out, she did use "only item analysis," not the ACTFL guidelines).

DRAFTING THE PROPOSAL IN *LANGUAGE RESEARCH*

As was discussed in chapter 2, I collected data from several sources on ways students represented and undertook the writing tasks in Mead's *Language Research*. Although Mai and Teresa appeared to be at similar points in the longer term process of developing their thesis research, their versions of this seminar task differed markedly.

Mai's Draft Proposal

When I asked Mai (the quarter of the seminar) about Mead's expectations for the research project, she represented it as an exercise ("It's only a draft, a draft, so I think he just want us to learn the ways to write a proposal."). Asked how he would grade or respond to the proposal, what he would be looking for, Mai said, "I think first will be the length of the proposal, he-he's emphasized that it only four to five pages, so I think too long or too short would not be good, and second, as you will have those components he give us, you will have the form he required, and in each part you cannot go away or go beyond his emphases." Mai's representation of the proposal emphasized formal requirements such as length and topical schemes (which perhaps not incidentally had been written down in the syllabus or on the board) and Mead's attitude toward compliance, but said little about content or purpose. When I asked Mai to talk about Mead's written comments on her seminar proposal in a text-based interview a year later, she refused, recalling instead that she was taking four courses that quarter and had put limited effort into the proposal: "When I write this proposal, I just think, regard- regarded it as a- an assignment for this course, that's all, yeah, I don't really think that I will use it for my real research for the [MA] paper, so I just think that's a 3 or 4 pages assignment ...since I only regard it as as class assignment, and uh, I didn't- I- I only wrote then in a short time."

In taking up Mead's assignment to critique a thesis or dissertation, a number of students chose texts related to their research. For her thesis critique, Mai chose Tang Shu's thesis, the one on language tests in the PRC that her advisor had recommended. Mai's seminar proposal (and her actual research) appear closely related to Shu's.[7] In her critique, Mai wrote that Shu had engaged in a descriptive content analysis of test items and the

---

[7] I was not able to explore intertextual connections of Mai's proposal to Shu's thesis because his thesis was lost.

overall organization of tests across several years. Her seminar proposal (and her final thesis) involved the same basic design. She also wrote that "from this study, I learn a new way to analyze English tests" (i.e., one not involving statistical analyses of validity and reliability); thus, it appears she did use Shu's thesis as a model for her research design.

When Mai presented her draft "Statement of the Problem" in the seminar, it took the (unusual) form of research questions:

Problem: 1. Are the test items able to assess what the students can do in reading and writing English according to the generic descriptions of the ACTFL Proficiency Guidelines?
2. How can the test items be improved to assess the high school graduates' English proficiency in Taiwan by consulting he ACTFL Proficiency Guidelines?

As was often the case in seminar discussions of drafts, students made some initial comments and then Mead jumped in with what was usually a move to closure and transition to the next student's text. One student suggested that Mai's second question sounded biased, as though she had already decided the tests were inadequate. Mai responded that the tests had already been criticized. Another student suggested that the first question sounded like the *research* issue, and Mai replied she was thinking of just doing the first question. Mead then jumped in. He said that there was nothing wrong with being biased, then commented briefly that a statement of the problem did not have to state research questions, and finally questioned whether the scope of the research was sufficient for a dissertation. Mai replied that she was doing the MA, and Mead said he thought she working on her PhD.

Immediately after that exchange, another student asked if it was appropriate to assess a language test according to guidelines it was not designed to address. At this point, Mead responded with a simple "sure" and moved to some general arguments about the relation of teaching to learning. This exchange becomes interesting as we will see in the next section. Responding to the final proposal, Mead sharply criticized the design because it would *not* be appropriate for Mai to use ACTFL guidelines to assess the tests in Taiwan. I am not sure how to explain the apparent contradiction between Mead's response in the seminar and his response to the text. Miscommunication is certainly a possibility. Mai's questions did not contextualize her research and her quietness in and out of the seminar meant that Mead had no other information on her work. Mead's response may have presupposed a different methodology. From my notes, it seems likely that he was imagining a standard testing design in which Mai would assess *students* using the ACTFL guidelines, relate their performance on that test to the current exam, and use that relationship to assess the exam. My fieldnotes suggest that Mai never got a chance to present the methodology of her research proposal in the seminar. In any case, a potential opportunity for Mai to anticipate and address what turned out to be a problem was missed in this exchange.

Mai did seem to take up the issue of bias. In her final research proposal for the seminar, she revised both research questions into noticeably more neutral terms:

1. What skill levels of reading and writing on the ACTFL Proficiency Guidelines are the College Entrance English Examinations presented to assess?
2. What do the results of analyzing the College Entrance English Examinations in terms of the skill levels on the ACTFL Proficiency Guidelines reflect?

However, the second question has become quite vague in this revision.

Teresa's Draft Proposal

As was noted in chapter 2, Teresa actually planned to conduct the research for her MA thesis in the last week of the quarter. In presenting her tentative title and statement of the problem to the seminar, Teresa was still groping with translating her experiences as a language minority in Spain into a researchable topic. After noting that Catalan had become the dominant language of instruction in schools since a decade earlier, her draft suggested her study would demonstrate a specific consequence of this curricular shift: "Therefore, since in most of the schools the curriculum is all in Catalan and Castilian is used as a language in a few classes per week, the study proposed here will seek to demonstrate that as the Catalan is the most used at school, it will be the most used out of school as well, Castilian being relegated to second place." Her handwritten notes on that draft point to several issues that arose in class discussion. One was that her hypothesis would only address the effect of Catalan instruction on those who did not speak Catalan at home. Another suggested looking at what happens in the school and at how Castilian speakers use Catalan in other settings and activities.

Several weeks later, Teresa presented her research questions:

1. What language, either Castilian or Catalan is spoken in different contexts?
2. What are some of the factors that influence this language choice?
3. Have changes in the curriculum affected this language choice?

In the seminar discussion of these questions, Teresa responded to another student's question about the factors that influence language choice by noting the issues of gender and context (e.g., which language do boys use on the playground?).

Teresa's final research questions display considerable elaboration and refinement:

1. What language, either Castilian or Catalan, does the population from our sample use in a set of different contexts and when doing different activities, as speaking, listening, reading, and writing?
2. What are some of the factors that adolescents perceive to this language choice?
3. Are there significant differences between males and females with regard to language use?

In her first question, she has intertextually indexed previous research by pointing to modes of language use (with a four-skill scheme) and to a specific (but unstated) scheme for contexts. The subject for this question "the population from our sample" represents a clear, if inverted, attempt to take up the voice of social scientific research. She has revised Questions 2 and 3 so that they fit with her research design (a one-time questionnaire without cross-sectional sampling). She has altered Question 2 so that it asks what subjects *perceive* to influence their language choice rather than the much more difficult and broader question of what actually influenced that selection. She has also replaced the complex historical question of how changes in the curriculum affected language choices, a question her design could not address (as it was neither longitudinal nor cross-sectional), with the question of whether gender differences exist in language use (again intertextually indexing other disciplinary discourses).

Anxious to get her actual proposal and plan ready, Teresa actively sought out opportunities to get feedback. A week after she had presented her research questions, she bid for class time to have a draft of her methodology discussed (only a little more than half of the students were able to do so). The day Teresa presented her research methodology to the seminar, my fieldnotes indicated that she commented at the beginning of the session that she needed to present her draft that day, and that she was the second person to present. During the discussion, Mead focused attention on her question-naire to elicit data on language used in different contexts (home, school, among friends) and in different activities (speaking, reading, writing, taking notes). Teresa proposed using letters (e.g., A for all Catalan, B for more Catalan than Castilian, down to E for all Castilian). Mead argued for the use of Likert or semantic differential scales, and discussion focused on the nature of these scales and their advantages and disadvantages. Several other students who were interested in development of questionnaires participated actively in this discussion. Mead also suggested that she could focus on descriptive statistics rather than the t-tests her analysis section proposed. When he called a mid-session break, Teresa immediately went up to him to continue talking over her proposal. In this discussion, Mead asked why she needed 200 students and how many different groups she planned to sample (guessing perhaps five). When she replied "13," he suggested she could cut down on the number of groups and the number of subjects. He also encouraged her to talk about these issues with her advisor; however, by Teresa's own account, her advisor was unresponsive during this whole period, much to her frustration. Teresa took up several of Mead's suggestions as she revised her research proposal. She reduced the number of students she sought to 150 and the number of groups to three. She did not change her questionnaire scales, but did switch to largely descriptive statistics.

Teresa's active solicitation of advice was not limited to the seminar. She reported she had gone to Mead's office to discuss her research and stress her need to have it ready by the end of the quarter. She had also been invited to and had attended a meeting of ABD doctoral students, where she presented her research proposal and got useful feedback on it. She also noted that she had asked Mead for a master's thesis to critique that dealt with sociolinguistics so that that critique would contribute to her work on her proposal. When Teresa discovered that she would have to submit the research proposal to the university's Human Subjects Review (HSR), a hurdle that did not exist in Spain, she was astonished. (Of course, going through HSR was only a requirement for her actual research.) Knowing that I had gone through the process, she asked me for a copy of my application and for general information about procedures. Teresa filed the HSR application and was approved the first time. The demands of this process could be seen in the procedural detail of her final research proposal (see chap. 2).

Mai and Teresa Develop Proposals

In Mead's seminar, Mai and Teresa appeared to be doing quite different tasks. Both engaged in basic forms of procedural display: producing draft sections of the proposal for seminar discussion, organizing their texts around the topical scheme Mead had provided in the syllabus (see Fig. 2.1), and turning in their proposals by the due date. However, Mai saw the task mainly as an assignment for the seminar, an exercise in form. Looking back on the process after she had completed her thesis, she felt she had not begun her "real" research until after the seminar. Teresa, on the other hand, was intensely engaged in developing not only the plan, but the materials for her research. Her audiences extended beyond Mead to her advisor, the HSR committee, teachers in Spain who would have to follow her procedures, parents who would have to sign informed consent forms, and students who would have to fill out her questionnaires. The last class of the quarter, Teresa was absent, in Spain collecting her data.

A major difference also appeared in the ways Mai and Teresa approached academic work. Teresa actively sought interaction and feedback from multiple sources. She bid for seminar time to discuss her research, pursued conversations with other students and Mead during breaks and after class, and talked with Mead during office hours. Her gregarious intellectual approach created multiple opportunity spaces to rework and refine her plan. (For example, her continuation into the break of the discussion with Mead on her methodology section led to a significant simplification of her data collection.) As an important by-product of this approach, Mead and others became aware of her research interests and her institutional contexts. In contrast, Mai was very quiet, rarely talking unless Mead called on her, and never bidding for class time.[8] Nor do I have any indication that she sought interaction and feedback from others during this time. As we see in the next section, these differences in literate activity were clearly reflected both in the texts Mai and Teresa produced and in Mead's responses.

RECEPTION IN *LANGUAGE RESEARCH*

Figure 4.1 provides one image of the research proposals Mai and Teresa produced for the seminar. In terms of overall organization, both displayed the general section headings that Mead had listed for the proposal. The first four sections of each text are also roughly comparable in length (although Mai writes a bit more in her "Statement of the Problem" and Teresa more

---

[8]My fieldnotes from the seminar only record her presenting two of the four sections of the proposal that were discussed. Although those notes do not cover all meetings, they do reflect presentation of three or four sections by all but one other student.

Teresa's final research proposal	Mai's final research proposal
Tentative Title (3 lines)	Tentative Title (2 lines)
Statement of the Problem (2 para., 15 lines)	Statement of the Problem (2 para., 21 lines)
Background to the Study (1 para., 38 lines)	Background of the Study (4 para., 29 lines)
Research Questions (3 para., 8 lines)	Research Questions (2 para., 6 lines)
Research Method (total 5 para., 42 lines)	Methodology (1 para., 10 lines)
Subjects (1 para., 8 lines)	
Materials (2 para., 20 lines)	
Procedure (1 para., 9 lines)	
Data Analysis (1 para., 5 lines)	
Significance of the Study (1 para., 22 lines)	Significance of the Study (1 para., 12 lines)
Working Bibliography (36 lines)	Bibliography (8 lines)
11 sources: 5 books (2 English, 3 Spanish/Catalan); 2 book chapters (English); 4 articles (2 English, 2 Spanish/Catalan)	3 sources: 3 books (English)

FIG. 4.1. Comparing the organization of Mai's and Teresa's proposals.

in her "Background to the Study"). However, in the methodology section, the two texts diverge sharply. Teresa provides the four subheadings that Mead had written on the board in an early discussion of the proposal (see chap. 2), and she writes over four times as much as Mai. In interviews, Mead stressed that he especially looked to the details of the methodology to determine if the student had seriously and carefully thought through the research. Another striking difference is visible in the bibliography section, where Teresa cites more, and more varied types of, sources than Mai.

Qualitative differences were also visible in the texts. Mai's and Teresa's final research questions (quoted in the previous section) displayed differences in elaboration, specificity, and disciplinary intertextuality. Whereas Mai's revision of her questions did address the issue of bias raised in the seminar discussion, her final questions remain general and somewhat vague (especially Question 2). In contrast, Teresa's revisions significantly reworked her questions, bringing them into line with her research design and incorporating disciplinary topics (schemes for contexts and modes of language, the issue of gender differences). Even without a direct comparison, it is suggestive that Teresa's detailed subsection on procedures (quoted in chap. 2) was only one line shorter than Mai's entire methodology section. Qualitative differences in disciplinary alignments were also quite visible in the background sections. In her background, Mai cites three books to construct a very global context for her research in terms of issues like classifications of language tests and the development of proficiency tests. In contrast, in her background, Teresa cites nine sources, moving from sociolinguistic research on bilingualism in the U.S. and Canada to four research studies on use of Catalan and Castilian in Spain. Her texts include disciplinary topics like effects of home language use, degree of bilingualism, differences between literate and oral language, and generational differences among immigrants. Finally, Mead's grading of the two proposals suggests his view of their qualitative difference. Of the 12 students' proposals whose grades I had access to, there was one A, four A-'s, two B+'s, four B's, and one B-. Teresa received one of the four A-'s, whereas Mai received the lone B-. I now turn to further description of Mead's reception of Mai's and Teresa's seminar texts.

Reception of Mai's Seminar Proposal

Mead's final summary comment written on Mai's research proposal read:

> I find a major difficulty with this study proposal. It is my perspective that it is inappropriate to apply the ACTFL Guidelines to a set of tests that were not designed with the guidelines in mind. Further, there is a lot of doubt about the validity of both the reading & the writing guidelines that I think would prevent your analysis from being useful. I think your proposal is an interesting exercise, but I have major and very serious doubts about its meaning. Actually, I would hope that you would not use this proposal for your MA study. It would be my hope that you would consult your advisor and think about this matter very carefully. B-

Mead's substantive response and his grade signaled his strong concerns.

When asked in an interview to look over and comment on Mai's papers, Mead examined them frowning and, taking up the proposal first, said:

> My impression is that this one really didn't hang together, that I really didn't know what she was attempting to do, and I didn't know how this could come together ... because there are basically no details here, she's done review of the literature, and then the section on methodology is only that long, one paragraph, one short, relatively short paragraph, and then significance of the study, and I guess I didn't find anything there I could do much with ... um, I don't know where she got this idea or- or why she would even want to do it.

Mead's comments display considerable doubt and uncertainty about the content of Mai's proposal and its contexts. As he turned from her research proposal to her critique of Shu's thesis, it appeared he was not aware of the relationship between the texts. He questioned whether Mai had really understood Shu's thesis, and, more generally, if she knew how to read specialized literature. In short, although she had been in his seminar, Mead did not have a distinct sense of either Mai or her research.

In text-based interviews after she had completed her MA, Mai refused to revisit Mead's written responses on her seminar proposal. She said she had not paid much attention to the comments because she generally found it hard to take advice, because she had seen the proposal as a classroom exercise, not part of her real research, and also because the grade was bad. (She compared her reaction to Mead's response with her students' reactions when she corrected their English compositions and gave them a bad grade: "usually students just throw them away.)" However, she did acknowledge that the low grade and the final comment led her to conclude that she could not use the ACTFL Guidelines to assess entrance examinations in Taiwan.

Reception of Teresa's Seminar Proposal

When asked in a text-based interview to comment on Teresa's papers for the seminar, Mead began by noting that Teresa had initially frustrated him in class with what he saw as "a supercilious attitude." However, he added, as the quarter progressed, he had perceived a change in her attitude. He recalled how he had become aware of her goals for the seminar in relation to her research: "She was relying on what was going to happen in [the seminar] to develop her final proposal for her actually doing her research because she was going to Spain to collect the data, and it- it didn't become clear to me until she came to me after class one day." Talking of her proposal, Mead indicated that she was "really attending to business" and that he was struck by its completeness and quality. Summing up, he said, "basically she did what she was asked to do and she did it very well." Asked in a discourse-based interview if he would be willing to delete his written comment ("I think you have shaped your background very well") in the margins near the end of Teresa's "Background to the Study," Mead explained why he would not delete the comment:

Because I think what it expresses is my um, um not- sort of my amazement at this um background because what I had gotten from her up to this point was, well, yeah, some attention and more seriousness and so on, but this said to me, "Hey, this gal has done her homework, she has, she has gotten into it, *really* gotten into it", which I didn't think she had, and so consequently, that was saying, you know, "You have done it."

Mead had a very precise sense of how the proposal fit into Teresa's research plans and by the end of the quarter, he was satisfied that she had not only produced an acceptable proposal for the seminar, but also an acceptable proposal for her MA research.

In text-based interviews on Mead's comments on her final proposal, Teresa indicated that his comments on her final proposal had not much affected the way she did the research or the analysis. For example, although Mead suggested she use, and she subsequently did use, non-parametric statistics (chi-squares) for some analyses, Teresa traced that decision to her husband's influence during the analysis rather than to Mead's response. However, as was noted in the previous section, Mead's in-progress responses during the quarter were taken up not only in the proposal, but in her actual research. Given that Mead responded to her proposal a month after she had conducted the research, it is not surprising that his response would have little effect on her research.

Reception of Mai's and Teresa's Proposals

Mead's reception of Mai's proposal was quite different from his reception of Teresa's. The clearest similarity was that on both texts he marked language problems (with syntax, lexicon, and mechanics). I would stress two key differences here. First, Mead clearly felt and communicated that Teresa's proposal was stronger than Mai's. The differences he identified in both his written responses and in interviews lay particularly in the content of the research questions, the literature review, and the methodology. Second, Mead was much more familiar with Teresa's research than Mai's, a result of Teresa's interactions outside as well as inside the seminar. With Mai, Mead was thrown back on the text to understand not only the design, but also where the research was coming from, what was motivating it.

DOING AND WRITING UP THE THESIS RESEARCH

In interviews after they had completed their theses, I asked Mai and Teresa to talk retrospectively about their research and writing processes. I was not able to collect drafts of their texts or to interview their professors or others they had worked with to gather their representations of process. Thus, this section is based on limited and retrospective representations of months of work. However, I believe that their representations of their work are useful for several reasons. They sketch a global overview of the process, and provide some specific images of how the research was undertaken and of who, besides themselves, became involved in it. Finally, their accounts meshed well with my own analyses of their thesis texts, which I turn to in the next section of this chapter.

Mai's Thesis Research

Mai noted that after the seminar she had gotten feedback from Mead, her advisor, and a fellow student from Taiwan who had also been in *Language Research*, all of whom told her it would not be appropriate to use ACTFL Guidelines to assess items on Taiwan's college entrance exams. She concluded that she "accepted their suggestions" and changed her topic "to make some analysis of the examination, and then provide some suggestions." Mai felt her "real" research begin that summer as she reviewed the literature, filling in notecards. For Mai, collecting the data was a simple process: "I called my sister in Taiwan and uh, and I wanted her to go to the bookstore and uh and find a book with the test items and the answers, there's a book, and he she mailed the book to me." With the tests her sister mailed her, Mai did the analysis of Taiwan's college entrance examination for English in the fall. She wrote up her thesis in the winter and turned it in to her advisor (Elizabeth Bain) in January. However, her advisor was ill, and the process did not resume until March, when Mai met with Bain to prepare for her oral examination. Mai had her oral exam in April. After the exam, Mai indicated that she made only one change to her thesis, adding a paragraph on criteria for the analysis that Bain had suggested.

When I asked how she found sources for the literature review, Mai first noted that in Mead's course she had searched the ERIC database, but had found only one useful source. Her next search procedure took a very practical, situated form:

> I went to the library, and uh, and I go ... I think it's, uh Stack 7, and uh, because I, I know where the second language books are usually in this library, so I went back that area and uh, and uh, basically my my attentions put on the- on those books deal with language- language testing, then I borrow those books.

She added that she did not have definite ideas on which books to borrow ("I just um, I think that, by chance I took uh, I take some books I think that may be useful for me and then I read the conten- I read the contents inside"). She also said that one book she cited had been a required text in her advisor's course on evaluation and assessment. Finally, she noted that most of her bibliography consisted of books, not articles, because she was not familiar with journals in her area at that time. (In fact, except for one ERIC document and one article, the bibliography of her thesis consisted entirely of books and book chapters.)

I asked Mai who she talked to, shared drafts with, or worked with during the summer, fall, and winter of her thesis work:

> Ah [laughing] no, I- maybe, I think I'm- I'm a very independent person, and uh … so I- I- I nmn uh, so I only sometimes discuss with my husband, yeah, because () this- this- this deals with the the language teaching test in Taiwan, so- so um, so he, we have the same common experience, so sometime I discuss with him, and it's convenient at home and uh, I don't remember I have- I have discussed with other, other persons, no, and only when I finish the draft, I, oh yeah, after I finish my draft, I give it to Elizabeth [Bain], and I, and I have- and Elizabeth had discuss with me, and uh, so, some of- some of the final paper, uh, are different from my draft (a lot) and Elizabeth had give me- give me some suggestion and comments, but after my- I finish my draft.

Mai later described her first meeting with Bain in March to discuss her thesis draft:

> Since my paper is not too long, so the first time we just read, page by page, and uh, so we read, she- we discuss, because I think maybe, maybe, I'm I'm a non-native speaker so sometimes uh, uh, Elizabeth did not quite understand what I mean and I explain to her, then she understood … she didn't force me to accept her comments, she- she said I can take into consideration, but uh I think, I almost took all of her comments and then I take back and do some correction, then I, then I give it to her again.

Mai indicated that some comments were on vocabulary and the grammar and some were on content. In terms of content, she indicated, for example, that Bain suggested she add a fifth recommendation to her conclusions, that the entrance examinations be pretested on native speakers, and Mai made that revision.

Teresa's Thesis Research

Teresa's research began during the quarter of Mead's seminar as she called several teachers she knew in Spain to ask for their participation and to begin planning logistics for the research. Teresa was calling on a social network to facilitate her research. When I asked how she knew the teachers, she replied:

> I'd been doing some, uh, how you call it's uh, like internship, in one of the institutions and then I knew, I knew … the chairman of the department of- in a high school, so I knew him, and I also knew the teachers there because they'd been former colleagues of mine at the university, so it wasn't very tough, and in the other, in the other institution, in the other high school, well I knew a lot of people, I still know them because I'd been a student there for like 9 years, and then since this is my hometown, you know, I know almost everybody, so it wasn't really … .

Teresa also noted that she had done most of her literature search before she went to Spain, starting in February, before Mead's seminar. After doing a search at the library, she identified books and articles she needed. She asked her parents to buy and send her some books from Spain and ordered some articles (particularly from journals published in Spain) through interlibrary loan. When Teresa arrived in Spain, she called the teachers to finalize arrangements for giving the questionnaire. They had already identified groups to fit her design. Teresa said it was difficult to arrange because of the time of year (a period devoted to testing) and because requesting parental consent was culturally quite odd. Nevertheless, she returned to the United States with the students' questionnaires completed as planned.

She first coded and tabulated their responses. After a couple of weeks off, she then "began really writing like, you know, introduction and the different parts." By August, she had begun to put "the different parts of my-my paper to my advisor's mailbox, you know to have feedback." At that point, Teresa ran into a problem: Her advisor (also Bain) did not provide any feedback on her drafts until November.

> I had some meetings with my advisor, yeah, but it wasn't really very helpful, I have to say that my my husband helped me more [she laughs, I laugh] than my advisor at that time, but anyway I had some- some meetings, but I was pretty frustrated because I didn't know if, what I- the content of what I was writing was ok or all that, so, you know, it's like going, I was putting stuff yes, since the beginning of August, almost every week or two weeks and I never received, till at the end I was writing a letter to this person saying, "ok, if you don't give any feedback, I have to go and look for someone else," and then finally um this person reacted or whatever, so this person correct everything up.

As she had during the seminar, Teresa continued to seek interactions, feedback, and aid from a range of people. When I asked if she had gotten any feedback from the committee before her oral, she said that there had not been enough time, but then went on to note that she had gotten a lot of help from one committee member, Margaret Shaw, because she had signed up with her for an independent study Fall quarter to work on the statistical analysis of her data. Teresa said she had easy access to Shaw, a Spanish professor who specialized in sociolinguistics, because she was a TA in Spanish ("so I could see her pretty often, and then you know it's like 'ok, do you have 5 minutes to ask you that?' while with the other people I had to set an appointment"). An acknowledgment in her thesis mentioned another person who had helped her; she explained:

> Hank was the the- this is a guy who works at the Spanish Department, so I- we work together and so she- he know what I was going through, because I didn't have any feedback and I was really mad at that, so he's an American guy and then he's been help me, helping me out in straightening thing (out) with my English.

She also noted that her husband, a researcher who "does a lot of stats," helped her both in choosing appropriate statistics ("I wasn't sure if I had to do a t-test here, or a t-test there, and he was helping me out,") and with how to use the statistical software. When I asked her what models she had used to develop a section on the history of Catalan, she replied that she had several friends who were historians at a university in Spain and that, while she was there conducting her research, she had asked them for some sources and copied the texts to read when she returned to the United States.

Teresa distributed her thesis to her committee before Thanksgiving and had her oral examination in early December. Although she passed in December, Teresa continued to work on the thesis (particularly revising language and formatting) and did not deposit it until March. When I asked why she had spent so much time revising her thesis after it passed, she replied:

> Well, because I wanted to make [laughs] sure that, I don't know, that uh, just if in the future someone would read it, I just wanted to make sure that everything was pretty much ok, so I could have done it, like I could have you know bound it like that, but I didn't want to do it, so you know I just went carefully through all the steps and all that.

Discussing her other acknowledgments, she noted that Tim, a fellow graduate student, had read through and responded to her whole thesis in that period, particularly helping to clarify the text in the Tables and that Doris, a new professor in the department, also helped her out, especially with the first section.

When I asked Teresa how she had decided on the arrangement of the chapters and what should be in each one, she pointed to a mix of textual and human resources. First, she noted that she had read three theses, including the one she critiqued in Mead's seminar and one another student had given her. Looking at their tables of contents, she developed an idea for how to structure her chapters. She also talked to her advisor and received further help. Describing how she decided on what topics to discuss in the chapters, her first account represents topics as givens or as what people would naturally be interested in, suggesting how thoroughly she had appropriated the special topics of sociolinguistics:

> I thought it would be good to have a chapter ( ) a part of that, about the historical perspective that, I think that's crucial to understand why- [she laughs], I mean why this person want to deal with Catalan and- and why these things happened there in Spain, if it's in a whole country where, with an official language, how come that Catalan, you know, is important, or was important historically, so I did that, and um about immigration and demographics … and I thought it was interesting to talk about immigration, immigration within the same country, why there was all these bunch of people coming from one, from some parts of Spain to the North, I mean why did this happen and all that, and about demographics as well, so that's why I did that, and- and uh schooling, hahh, since I was going to deal with schools in an area of Spain, and the system, well not really the system, but the programs have changed a lot during the last ten years since, 15 years in fact, since Catalan has been allowed, so I think it was interesting to talk about the different kinds of schools that that you can find.

I then asked her if the topics were typical of books and articles on sociolinguistics:

> Yeah, as I said, yeah, all- in all the articles that deal with sociolinguistics, there's always a part at the beginning that deals about historical issues, like for instance I've been reading um a lot about the um Hispanics groups in the United States, so in order, you know, to get the reader into the- into the topic, they would use uh, yeah, a lot of historic stuff, about historic, or demographics, or whatever, in which conditions did they live, what kind of cultural background do you have, what kind of social background, all that, and then after that, then yo-, they will go through the research, so I think that that's, I think that's crucial, because otherwise you don't know with which group are you dealing with.

Teresa also noted that her questionnaire items and contextual schemes were based on earlier research by Viladot and Fishman, but that she had revised them based on her personal knowledge of the area, as a speaker of Castilian and a teacher.

Mai's and Teresa's Thesis Research

Mai's and Teresa's research processes shared several features: the need to review the literature, a phone call home to request documents, problems

getting feedback from their advisor, meetings with the advisor and ultimately a committee. However, the similarities seem superficial in comparison to the differences. Mai's phone call completed her data collection,
whereas Teresa flew to Spain and spent an intense week administering the
questionnaire at several sites in Spain (a week that had required considerable planning and coordination with teachers and administrators ahead of
time). Mai's literature search involved browsing a few feet of shelving on
the seventh floor of a library, while Teresa conducted a more complex and
extensive search and also sought out sources from other people. Mai did not
engage her other committee members in the process of her research; Teresa
arranged an independent study with one of her committee members. After
finishing the oral exam, Mai makes a single change suggested by her
advisor, adding a paragraph to her thesis. After Teresa finishes the oral, she
works with another professor (Doris) and another graduate student (Tim)
to tighten up the introduction and, especially, to make the text of the tables
clearer. She continues to fine tune the thesis for three months. These
differences in processes were reflected in the texts themselves.

MODES OF APPROPRIATION IN TWO TEXTS

My initial sense of the differences between Mai's thesis and Teresa's was
evoked by their physical appearance and by a surface skimming of their
organization. When Mai gave me her thesis to copy, it consisted of two
stapled documents: the main body of the thesis (55 pages) and an appendix
of raw data (the test items she had analyzed, 52 pages). The thesis had a
cover page and then began immediately with a heading marked "Introduction." Teresa's thesis, in contrast, was hard bound in black (141 pages, 27
of which were appendices). Her cover page was followed by acknowledgments, a detailed Table of Contents, a list of Tables, and then a heading
for "Chapter 1." My first impression of Mai's thesis was that it resembled
a long term paper, whereas Teresa's resembled a dissertation. To further
explore the nature of these texts, I will focus on the ways Mai and Teresa
appropriated disciplinary texts and practices.

Mai's Text

Given Mai's simple literature search, I was easily able to obtain most of her
sources (simply by going to the same library stacks). As I analyzed her text,

I was struck by certain passages, such as the long list of purposes in the second sentence of this extract:

> In language testing, one must always ask two questions: (1) What is the purpose of testing? (2) What is the appropriate instrument to achieve this purpose? According to Ingram (1985), the purposes of language testing are the following: to measure proficiency; to give a quick group measure of proficiency; to conduct large-scale proficiency measurement; to measure "special purpose" proficiency; to measure achievement in "graded objectives" courses; to measure how well the learners are mastering what is being taught (formative assessment); to stream learners into courses; to diagnose learner's strengths and weaknesses, to evaluate a second language program, and to validate tests.

Comparing Mai's text to the source she cited (Ingram, 1985), I soon saw that each phrase in her list was copied word for word from a series of subheadings in Ingram's chapter (p. 258–266). I then saw that the first sentence in Mai's paragraph was also a word-for-word copy of one of Ingram's sentences (p. 256). Having found this example, I decided to look more carefully at how Mai was using source language from texts.

Figure 4.2 presents a side-by-side comparison of three texts: Mai's thesis, a selection from MacLaughlin (1985), and a selection from Erickson (1981).[9] Here again, Mai's text represents word-by-word borrowing from MacLaughlin. Although she only cites Erickson in these sentences, the first sentence of her paragraph began "According to MacLaughlin (1985)." There are five changes in Mai's text in comparison to MacLaughlin's: use of Erickson's last name instead of full name, use of numbers instead of bullets, use of *may* instead of *does* in point 2, the syntactic transformation of the initial noun phrase in point 4, and the deletion of reference to Erickson in the final sentence.

The way Mai used source text in Figure 4.2 was repeated throughout her thesis (particularly in the introductory sections). She tended to borrow chunks of text (ranging from sentences to paragraphs), making limited changes. This borrowing was usually (but not always) signaled by a citation at either the beginning or end of the chunk. Citations within the original source might be kept or not; quotations in source texts were sometimes kept but no longer marked (i.e., quotations marks or indentation were dropped and there was no citation of the source originally quoted). In some cases, Mai's paragraphs contained chunks from two different source texts, but this was fairly unusual.

---

[9]In this case, comparing MacLaughlin's text to Erickson's is also interesting.

Mai's thesis	MacLaughlin (1985, p. 220–221)	Erickson (1981, p. 7 and p. 10)
Advocates of a communicative competence approach make assumptions about language that have been largely ignored in traditional approaches to language assessment. Erickson (1981) argued that an appropriate model of language assessment assumes:	Besides the assumption of distinguishable underlying abilities, advocates of a communicative competence approach make assumptions about language that have been largely ignored in traditional approaches to language assessment. Joan Good Erickson (1981) argued that an appropriate model of language assessment assumes:	The model of language assessment is based on some commonly held assumptions regarding language that have prevailed, or, at least, met minimal challenge. These assumptions, listed below, do not appear to be used by most developers of discrete point tests.
1. Language is a symbolic, generative process that does not lend itself easily to formal assessment.	• Language is a symbolic, generative process that does not lend itself easily to formal assessment.	1. Language is a symbolic, generative process that does not lend itself easily to formal assessment.
2. Language is synergistic, so that any measure of the part may not give a picture of the whole.	• Language is synergistic, so that any measure of the part does not give a picture of the whole.	2. Language is synergistic, so that any measure of the part does not give a picture of the whole.
3. Language is a part of the total experiences of a child and is difficult to assess as an isolated part of development.	• Language is a part of the total experience of a child and is difficult to assess as an isolated part of development.	3. Language is a part of the total experiences of a child and is difficult to assess as an isolated part of development.
4. Both the quality and quantity of language use vary according to the setting, interactors, and topic.	• Language use (quality and quantity) varies according to the setting, interactors, and topic.	4. Language use (quality and quantity) varies according to the setting, interactors, and topic.
Language assessment should reflect the nature of the communication process and evaluate the major use of language—a verbal/ social communicative interaction in a natural setting.	Erickson maintained that language assessment should reflect the nature of the communication process and evaluate the major use of language—that of a verbal/social communicative interaction in a natural setting. Because an evaluator may not obtain all of the information needed from a natural setting, it may be necessary to use quasi-experimental and, in some cases, more formal approaches, in addition to observation.	Thus, a language assessment approach should indeed reflect the nature of the communication process and evaluate the major use language, that of a verbal/social communicative interaction in a natural setting. Because an evaluator may not obtain all of the information needed from a natural setting, it may be necessary to use quasi-experimental, and in some cases, more formal approaches in addition to observation.

FIG. 4.2. Comparisons of Mai's thesis with two other texts. **Bold print** marks common language between Mai's and MacLaughlin's texts; underlining, between MacLaughlin's and Erickson's.

Mai's bibliography listed 25 sources (13 books, 11 book chapters, one article, and one ERIC document). However, some items appeared to be secondary (like the citation to Erickson, 1981, in Fig. 4.2) or mistaken (e.g., chunks of text borrowed from a book chapter by Larson and Jones were attributed to a book by a different Jones). It is also worth noting that no authors were cited for more than one work in the bibliography, suggesting limited depth in her literature review. Another indication of her source use is that in the first 14 pages of her text (the introductory sections), Mai averaged 2.1 citations per page. Overall, Mai appeared to use a few sources heavily, borrowing with few changes chunks of text.

The nature of Mai's analysis and argument is suggested by the example shown in Figure 4.3. Mai's analysis involved reading through test items and attempting to judge them based on whether they tested what they claimed to be testing and on how well designed they were in qualitative terms. After

Some items have ambiguous choices for the right answer. For example:

(a) Facts and Figures, even when _____, can often be misleading.

    (A) accurate (B) mistaken (C) detailed (D) careful

    [correct answer: (A)]   (1981 III 20.)

(b)   The waiter took a very long time _____ us.

    (A) treating (B) awaiting (C) serving (D) dealing

    [correct answer: (C)]   (1983 III 16.)

In example (a), besides the given correct answer (A), the answer (C) can also be regarded as appropriate for the context of the sentence. As for example (b), the answer (B) is also fit for the sentence besides the given correct answer (C).

    For the following test item:

Whether _____ travel today is much more convenient than, say, fifty years ago.

(A) by land, sea, or air (B) by land, sea, or air, (C) by land or sea, or air (D) by land or sea, air

[correct answer: (B)]   (1985 II 22.)

The testee is supposed to know the correct usage of the conjunctive "or" and of punctuation, which have nothing to do with the comprehension of the sentence.

FIG. 4.3. An excerpt from Mai's analysis of reading test items.

24 pages of this kind of analysis, Mai summarized the analysis in a single paragraph, arguing that "most items are clear and unambiguous," that "some items do not meet the criterion that only one response is clearly the best," that "there is evidence that native speakers cannot get quite a few items correct," that most items were not important in that "they do not assess those general and relatively frequent expressions in normal use," that many items were "stilted and inauthentic," that reading and writing items were valid because they "seem to test what they are supposed to test," and that "speaking items fail to be valid in that they only require the testees to choose the correct answer on pronunciation and accent." This summary of findings seems at best loosely connected to the analyses Mai performed. For example, she provided no quantitative measures of "clear and unambiguous" items, never asked any native speakers to take the test, and did not compare test items to any kind of frequency measures of English language use to assess how common or unusual expressions tested might be. This paragraph summary was then followed by 10 pages of suggestions for improving the test (five suggestions representing fairly standard advice on language testing, like using native speakers to validate the test, being sure to evaluate the test well, and using authentic tasks), a half page of suggestions for further research, and a half-page conclusion.

Teresa's Text

To assess use of sources for Teresa was much more difficult because she used considerably more sources and her sources were multilingual (English, Spanish, and Catalan). Her bibliography listed 57 sources including 19 books (12 in Spanish or Catalan), 12 book chapters (4 in Spanish or Catalan), 23 articles (5 in Spanish or Catalan), and three other documents (two in Spanish or Catalan). Unlike Mai, Teresa cited authors for multiple works: Six authors were cited for two works in the bibliography and two authors for three works. In the introductory sections of her thesis (54 pages of text), Teresa averaged 3.1 citations per page.

   Figures 4.4 and 4.5 illustrate the ways Teresa appropriated language from source texts. She borrowed some chunks of text from sources and often followed organization and information closely. However, she used text selectively, deleting phrases and sentences, and synthetically, combining ideas and language from different source texts in a single paragraph and often in a single sentence. She used direct quotation sometimes and made obvious attempts to paraphrase text lexically and syntactically.

Teresa's thesis

e) Lexicon

There are many similarities between both Catalan and Castilian. In many cases simple deletion of final Castilian consonants will produce a Catalan word.

Catalan	Castilian	English
pa	*pan*	*'bread'*
accio	*accion*	*'action'*

However, there are differences that have their origin in differing earlier and later Latin forms:

Latin/Catalan	Latin/Castilian	English
*surtire/**sortir***	*salire/**salir***	*leave*
*pavore/**por***	*metus/**miedo***	*fear*

Both languages use two verbs corresponding to the English "to be": **ser** and **estar**. However in Catalan there is a basic difference in the semantic space assigned to each verb: **estar** is not used to indicate location, as it is in Castilian.

Woolard (pp. 147-148, 1989)

Lexicon. There are many similarities between the lexicons of Catalan and Castilian. Both bilingual children and adult learners often deduce phonological rules to transform Castilian words to Catalan and vice versa. The best-known and most generally applied is the deletion of final vowels or consonants from Castilian to produce Catalan forms, e.g.,:

Cast.	Cat.	
accion	***accio***	*'action'*
pan	***pa***	*'bread'*
disco	***disc***	*'record'...*

The most important differences between the Castilian and Catalan lexicons derive from earlier and later Latin forms (Sanchis Guarner 1980: 15-16), e.g.:

Latin>Cast.	Latin>Cat.	
*metus>**miedo***	*pavore>**por***	*fear*
*fervere>**hervir***	*bullire>**bullir***	*boil*
*salire>**salir***	*surtire>**sortir***	*leave...*

Catalan, like Castilian, distinguishes between two verbs corresponding to the English "to be": **ser** (also esser) and **estar**. However, the semantic distinction is subtle, and usage does not correspond to that in Castilian.... But generally, **estar** is not used to indicate location as it is in Castilian, and is never used to give the location of inanimate objects.

FIG. 4.4. Intertextual comparison of Teresa's thesis with Woolard (1989). Underlining indicates common text.

The character of Teresa's analysis is suggested by Figure 4.6. In this excerpt from her results, she is presenting the data related to the second of her nine research questions (concerning variations in language used by children from homes where both parents were Catalan speakers versus homes where both parents were Castilian speakers). The domains of language use are ones that other researchers had studied, aligning Teresa's findings to theirs. Her data appear to me to be very clearly, if sparsely, presented. After presenting the results for each research question in this fashion, Teresa turned to her last chapter "Summary, Conclusions, Implications, and Recommendations." She spends five pages reiterating the findings for her nine research questions and then a paragraph noting limitations of the study (e.g., self-reported data on language use, limited

Teresa's thesis

This **process** of reinstatement began to manifest **itself in the sixties** (Reinu, 1989) and reached its height in 1978 with **the promulgation of the Catalan Statue of Autonomy**, and **in 1983** with the **Linguistic Normalization Law** that considered **Catalan as the official language of Catalonia** (Mari, 1989)

Reinu (1989, p. 21)

The revival of Catalan, a **process** which began to show **itself in the sixties** (Ediciones 62, the "nova canco", independent theatre, etc.) received a considerable boost with the restoration of the *Generalitat*. The new political framework which arose from the constitution and the **Statute of Autonomy**, and the unanimous approval of the "**Linguistic Normalization Law**" in **Catalonia**, have been an important step forward.

Mari (1989, pp. 22-23)

Although Catalan did not formally recover its position as an official language until **the promulgation of the Catalan Statute of Autonomy** (1979), many Catalan institutions used it before this in their political and administrative activities, as did the *Generalitat* itself following its provisional restoration (1978). When **the Linguistic Normalization Law** stated **in 1983** that **Catalan, as the official language of Catalonia**, was to be the normal language of the local and autonomous administrations, it not only reflected popular feeling, but also the general tendency in all the Catalan administrations.

FIG. 4.5. Comparison of Teresa's thesis with two other texts. **Bold print** marks common language between Teresa's text and Reinu's or Mari's; underlining marks common language between Reinu's text and Mari's.

2. ARE THERE DIFFERENCES IN LANGUAGE USE IN DIFFERENT DOMAINS WITH HOMOGENEOUS CATALAN AND CASTILIAN FAMILIES?

To find out if differences in language use existed between these two groups, means were compared by using a t-test. In all the domains the differences were significant. For this comparison males and females were pooled together. See Table 6

TABLE 6—LANGUAGE USE ACROSS DOMAINS BY INDIVIDUALS FROM CATALAN AND CASTILIAN

DOMAINS	CATALAN GROUP (n = 56)	CASTILIAN GROUP (n = 42)	
	Mean (s.d.)	Mean (s.d.)	p. value
Home	1.13 (0.25)	4.50 (0.53)	0.0001
Neighb.	1.21 (0.41)	3.30 (1.30)	0.0001
School	1.23 (0.50)	2.70 (1.30)	0.0001
Free time	1.23 (0.48)	3.30 (1.20)	0.0001
P. transport	1.35 (0.72)	3.00 (1.50)	0.0001

Note: 1.0 = all Catalan , 5.0 = all Castilian. $p \leq 0.05$

SUMMARY: There seem to be important differences between the language used by people from the Catalan and the Castilian group. Members from both groups tend to use the language they mostly use at home in most of the domains.

FIG. 4.6. An excerpt from Teresa's analysis of data in her thesis.

sampling of schools, limited sampling of students from vocational schools). She next offers a half page of implications, which mainly identified groups that might use this kind of descriptive data. Finally, she ends the thesis with a page and a half of recommendations for further research.

Modes of Appropriation

Mai's final thesis text appears quite different from Teresa's along varied dimensions. Mai uses fewer sources than Teresa; uses mainly sources from books, whereas Teresa uses a mix of articles and books; uses only English sources, whereas Teresa uses ones in English, Catalan and Castilian; and shows less evidence of intertextual depth (e.g., no multiple sources for authors in the bibliography). In their writing, Mai and Teresa both borrow text from sources; however, Mai incorporates larger chunks, paraphrasing less and doing less to synthesize and integrate sources. Mai organizes her qualitative analysis of test items according to the sections of the test to address global research questions, whereas Teresa organizes her statistical findings to address nine specific research questions. Mai's summary of her findings and recommendations are loosely connected to her analysis, whereas Teresa's largely reiterate her findings. Although still rough in a number of ways, the organization and content of Teresa's thesis seems to be reaching toward that of a dissertation, as its physical format first suggested to me. Mai's thesis, on the other hand, seems a much more limited exercise in terms of the inquiry conducted, alignments to disciplinary discourses, and display of the textual conventions of dissertations and other research reports. Overall, Mai seems to be ventriloquating others' voices with limited evidence of participating in disciplinary practices of writing and knowledge making. Teresa, on the other hand, displays strong evidence of appropriating, aligning with, and becoming responsible for disciplinary practices.[10]

MODES OF APPROPRIATION AND FORMS
OF PARTICIPATION

In this chapter, I have briefly illustrated the differing modes of participation displayed by two NNES MA students in a language-education program. Mai's case, I would argue, illustrates a limited mode of participation centered on passing and procedural display, whereas Teresa's illustrates a richer mode of participation, including indications of deep participation. These modes of participation were certainly related to Mai and Teresa as persons acting in these contexts. However, I do not attribute the differences solely to their competencies or personalities, reducing differences in participation to questions of individual cognition and performance. Their differences also reflect the socially distributed functional systems through which they worked and in which they produced their research and their texts. Teresa was more tightly aligned with local and broader streams of

---

[10]Teresa's answer (quoted in part earlier) to my question about the topics of her introductory sections seems a telling indication of the depth of her appropriation.

disciplinary and professional activity than Mai, whose connections to such streams of activity seemed tenuous and irregular. Teresa's alignments amplified her work, whereas Mai's seemed to attenuate hers.

These differences in alignment appear in part as differences in relationships. When Hutchins (1995) studied the computation of navigational headings by teams on navy ships, he concluded that computational dependencies were first encountered by participants as interpersonal dependencies, and that, therefore, the structure of the team was critical to both performance and learning. He also found that relations in the team were interpersonal and not simply the formal fulfillment of roles (even in the hierarchical context of a military ship). Recent research on disciplinary enculturation has also pointed to the centrality of relationships (e.g., Belcher, 1994; Casanave, 1995; Chiseri-Strater, 1991). For example, examining three quite different mentoring relationships between professors and NNES graduate students at a U.S. university, Belcher (1994) found that conflicts of identity and discipline undermined two graduate students' transition to participation in disciplinary roles and forums, whereas in a third case, a smoother transition was effected as graduate student and professor–mentor entered into a deeply collaborative, mutually supportive relationship.

Mai's relationships with others in relevant communities of practices, her participation in meaning-making practices, appeared to be limited whether in Mead's seminar, in her out-of-class relations with other students and professors, or in her virtual encounters with others in texts. In Lave and Wenger's (1991) terms, she appeared to be relatively sequestered from participation and to find texts authoritative wholes with limited transparency. On the other hand, whether it was in developing her proposal, struggling with writing in English, or working through unfamiliar statistical analyses and presentations, Teresa's world seemed richly populated with helpful others. She also appeared to be deeply engaged intertextually with others. This engagement was visible in the origins of her research, in the ways she adapted previous questionnaires, in the connections she made between hers and earlier research on use of Catalan and Castilian in Spain, and in her coverage of typical sociolinguistic topics in her introductory chapters. In other words, Teresa displayed strong and growing access to disciplinary discourses, practices, and relationships and seemed to find texts reasonably transparent and appropriable.

In a number of respects, the data for this comparative analysis are not complete. I lack drafts and responses to drafts for the thesis texts, interviews with professors to explore how those texts were read and responded to, and the kind of text-based interviewing that might give weight and specificity to my sense that Mai's appropriations of others' texts reflected more limited learning and participation than Teresa's. Acknowledging these multiple limitations, I must also say that the analysis I have presented in this chapter of Teresa and Mai seems persuasive to me and that its limitations and intimations foreshadow two issues that I focus on in subsequent chapters. First, although the data for this analysis are less complete than data presented in chapters 2 and 3, it does cover a broader period, in particular shifting from performance on assigned writing tasks in a seminar to longer term personal, interpersonal, and institutional histories. Over the course of my research, I have come to believe that in order to understand writing and disciplinarity from a developmental perspective, it is important to take up perspectives that are longer in term, more diverse in settings, and, not incidentally, less grounded in dominant institutional perspectives. I return to this issue particularly in chapter 9. Second, the question of how to interpret Mai's and Teresa's appropriations of other texts and voices is, I believe, a central and troubling one for sociohistoric theories of disciplinary enculturation. As Scollon (1995) has noted, deeply rooted ideological commitments to the notion of originary authorship have left authorship and non-authorship (e.g., plagiarism) as relatively unexamined academic and disciplinary practices. If all learning involves appropriation, then we need much finer grained ways to analyze the varied qualities of appropriated voices, genres, and practices and what they imply for learning and social formation. For these reasons, I focus intensely in the next section (chaps. 5–8) on relationships among writing, authorship, and disciplinary enculturation. Chapter 8 in particular illustrates the value of bringing more definitive evidence to bear on the central question that can only be raised in this analysis of Mai's and Teresa's thesis research: What do particular modes of appropriation signify for trajectories of participation in disciplinary communities of practice?

PART III

Literate Activity and Mediated Authorship

5

Literate Activity, Scenes of Writing, and Mediated Authorship

Discussing notions of audience in socially oriented analyses of writing, Phelps (1990) observes that writing researchers and theorists have continued to be caught up in "the textual and the psychologized rhetorics where abstractions like the fictive audience (textual representation) and the cognitive audience (mental representation) are more salient than the actual exchanges of talk and text by which people more or less publicly draft and negotiate textual meanings" (p. 158). As writing research moved out of the laboratory to explore such exchanges of talk and text in naturalistic settings, it ran up against its own assumptive frameworks at a key interface between theory and methodology: the formation and representation of the object of study itself. As Brandt (1990; see also chap. 1) argued, researchers have often fixated on material texts rather than human activity in defining the nature of literacy. Witte (1985) noted a similar fixation in writing process research. His notion of pre-textual revision, in effect, questioned the whole edifice of objects of study that process researchers (e.g., Flower & Hayes, 1981) had erected around focal acts of transcription and the focal artifacts of texts. Witte (1992) extended his critique to studies of situated writing, arguing that historical streams of semiosis could not be arbitrarily fenced in by an a priori privileging of linguistic–textual artifacts and transcriptional processes.

The analyses offered in the last three chapters point to the complexity, heterogeneity, and particularity of academic writing tasks. The streams of salient activity that converge in these accounts of textual production and reception blend talking and listening, reading and writing, thinking and feeling, observing and acting. It is also clear that the historical trajectories of the artifacts, practices, and persons that interact in these scenes of writing implicate activity that is not only multimodal, but also temporally and spatially dispersed and distributed across multiple persons, artifacts, and sites. The unit of analysis then should not be that synecdochically foregrounded pair, transcription and text. Bateson (1972) argued vividly against accepting such commonsense units of analysis, contrasting as an example the everyday view of the self with a more dynamic, functional perspective:

> But what about"me"? Suppose I am a blind man, and I use a stick. I go tap, tap, tap. Where do *I* start? Is my mental system bounded at the handle of the stick? Does it start halfway up the stick? Does it start at the tip of the stick? But these are nonsense questions. The stick is a pathway along which transforms of difference are being transmitted. The way to delineate the system is to draw the limiting line in such a way that you do not cut any of these pathways in ways that leave things inexplicable. If what you are trying to explain is a given piece of behavior, such as the locomotion of a blind man, then, for this purpose, you will need the street, the stick, the man; the street, the stick, and so on, round and round. But when the blind man sits down to eat his lunch, his stick and its messages will no longer be relevant—if it is his eating you want to understand. (p. 459)

In this view, talk in the classroom, for example, may not be simply a context of and for writing; it may be writing. More precisely, this view suggests that transcriptions are events and texts are artifacts inextricably fused in functional systems of literate activity.

I am suggesting that an adequate account of writing must begin with three fundamental axioms. First, writing is situated. In other words, we must treat writing (and reading) as fully historical, recognizing that, as Brandt (1990) argues, writers and readers are inescapably situated in particular places and in the moment-to-moment flow of lived time. Second, writing is mediated. It is not solo activity, but a confluence of phylogenetic, cultural-historical, mesogenetic, ontogenetic, and microgenetic trajectories that weave together people, practices, artifacts, and institutions. Finally, as an important corollary of mediation, writing is dispersed. Focal texts and transcriptional events are no more autonomous than the spray thrown up by white water in a river, and like that spray, literate acts today are far downstream from their sociohistoric origins. This notion of writing as situated, mediated, and dispersed is the basis for what I am calling *literate activity*. Literate activity, in this sense, is not located *in* acts of reading and writing, but *as* cultural forms of life saturated with textuality, that is strongly motivated and mediated by texts.

Given this perspective, it becomes particularly important to examine the concrete nature of cultural spheres of literate activity. As was discussed in chapter 1, writing researchers have generally conceptualized disciplinarity in basically structuralist terms, seeing discourse communities as abstract, autonomous, spatialized structures of objects and rules, and disciplinary enculturation as transmission of those structures to largely passive novices. The analyses of the temporal and perspectival multiplicity of writing tasks in Mead's seminar, of the diverse texts and activities of Kohl's seminars, and of the distinct trajectories of participation that Mai and Teresa displayed in attaining an MA, all point to heterogeneity and particularity more than uniformity and generality. These analyses also illustrated ways that students and professors generated the texts, tasks, and contexts of seminars by drawing on diverse resources to align their literate activity.

A basic theme across many critiques of structuralism is the need to move from objects to events, from abstract systems to situated doing. When we shift from asking what language is to what it does, its constitutive functions, its context- and perspective-forming functions, come to the fore. These functions stake out the intersubjective grounds for aligning meaning making and action. Bruner (1986; see also Bruner & Lucariello, 1989) has identified one set of these linguistic resources in discussing subjunctivizing, a notion quite consistent with the Bakhtinian emphasis on the evaluative dimension of utterances (Bakhtin, 1986; Bakhtin & Medvedev, 1978; Voloshinov, 1973). Moreover, these constitutive functions (e.g., prolepsis, presupposition, implicature, subjectification) also appear to play key roles in socialization (Bruner, 1986; Bruner & Lucariello, 1989; Rommetveit, 1992; Stone, 1993). In analyzing Kohl's seminars, I suggested that topics, as semiotic artifacts intertextually indexing discourses, represent a key set of constitutive resources for disciplinarity. They fore-cast the shape of an activity, invoking its goals, and subtly working to coordinate and sustain joint, if partial, attention. Orienting to the shape of an activity in these ways may be a critical step toward eventually inhabiting those practices. The continuities that graduate students displayed in their work also suggested the need to look at ways that longer term, more durative forms of alignment and perspective setting shape trajectories of participation in disciplinary practices.

We cannot look only for interrelationships among communication, learning, socialization, and social formation: Rather, we must grapple with the fact that communication is learning is socialization is social formation, that literate activity is not only a process whereby texts are produced, exchanged, and used, but also part of a continuous sociohistoric process in which persons, artifacts, practices, institutions, and communities are being formed and reformed. This recognition, however, brings us to the threshold of a new problem. When writing is seen as activity that is sociohistorically situated, mediated, and dispersed, we run into an assumption more engrained than writing as transcription and text, the assumption of agency, of the writer as author.

As Phelps (1990) notes, poststructuralist, and particularly sociohistoric, theories have challenged dominant accounts of authorship and audience:

> [The concept of authorship] has been put into question by the dissolution of text in intertext, self in intersubjectivity and by the disappearance of every boundary that formerly separated (however permeably) mind from mind, mind from text, mind from material world, text from other text, text from talk, present experience from memory, object from context, and so on. In this world, audience is no longer the problem, but the given; it is ubiquitous. It is authorship we can no longer take for granted, once we understand ourselves to be so comprehensively invaded and possessed by the other, in the form of internalized language, genre, ideology (or alternatively, so diffused into the ambient flux of words). (p. 162)

Studying writing tasks situated in graduate seminars, I quickly confronted gaps between the tacit assumptions about authorship I had brought to my research and the complex histories of textual production and reception I was tracing.[1] Questions of authorship entail fundamental issues of agency. I approached these issues hesitantly, yet found I had to address them to understand literate activity and disciplinarity in these settings. In this chapter and the three that follow, I take up issues of authorship with a mix of theoretical and empirical sketches, working toward a sociohistoric framework that links writing, authorship, and disciplinary enculturation in literate activity.

SCENES OF WRITING

Writing Studies has actually constructed its objects of study, not simply from abstract transcription and text, but from a set of prototypical scenes that represent writing and authorship. Linda Brodkey (1987) has described and analyzed one key image, the solitary writer in the garret, a scene she called "the reigning trope for writing" in modern culture (p. 55). Brodkey describes a scene that invokes a repertoire not only of settings (the garret, study, library carrel, prison cell) and characters (in this case, the solitary literary writer), but also of typical plots and subjectivities. Brodkey's analysis of this synecdochic scene points to its grounding in modern-romantic notions of the writer as alienated artist, of writing as inspired transcription, and of texts as autonomous physical–semiotic objects released from

---

[1]Other researchers (e.g., Hull & Rose, 1989; Lunsford & Ede, 1990) have reported similar confrontations in their own research.

the scene of writing to make their own way in the world. Ironically, this scene has also been inscribed in writing process research, which methodologically asks people to write alone in bounded times and spaces and theoretically represents writing as individual cognition interacting with a material text.

The scene Brodkey has described remains a powerful, fundamental trope for writing both in specialized disciplinary and general cultural discourses; however, it must be set beside other scenes that organize our understanding of writing and authorship. As Phelps (1990) points out, Brodkey's solitary scribbler blends into another powerful scene, the abstract representation of writing as conversation. This image is dominated by the basic social unit of the dyad and motivated by the activity of exchanging messages. The writer makes a text for a reader in order to share her experiences or knowledge, to entertain the reader, or to persuade the reader. The reader receives the text, works diligently to decode its messages, and may sometimes even respond to the writer. This literate conversation is structured around the focal site of the text, either a mobile text that links a solitary writer to a solitary reader or a fixed text, spread flat on table or desk, the point where the reader's and writer's gazes intersect and they are intersubjectively fused. With texts represented as a kind of filtering medium for the conduit of messages, the natural plots of this scene revolve around clarity, implicitly governed by the initiating conditions of the writer as she inscribes ideas, more or less clearly, in the text. In this scene, the writer and reader enact a paradigmatic Gricean (1989) plot of cooperation, constructing a reciprocally shared conceptual world through the negotiated exchange of messages.

While Brodkey (1987) and Phelps (1990) have identified general sociocultural representations of writing, other scenes are grounded in particular social institutions. Especially relevant to this research are images tied to school, the workplace, and disciplines. Although the image of writing in school contains fragments of both the solitary writer (writing alone) and the writer–reader dyad (writing to the teacher), its dominant setting is the crowded classroom rather than the cell and its basic plot ruptures the symmetry and interchangeability of the writer–reader dyad. Acting as the prime mover in this institutional universe, the teacher motivates the writer, structures the writing (process and product) through assignment and monitoring, and then delivers a final judgment, evaluating student-writers and their textual products. Again, texts are powerfully foregrounded objects in this scene. However, the texts are no longer represented simply as the communicative conduits of the conversational scene: Student texts are seen as crystallizations of students' intelligence, knowledge, skills, attitudes, and effort, magic mirrors teachers gaze into to discover who is the most literate on the roster. The dominance of the teacher is reflected in the narrative time of school writing, a discontinuous representation organized from the teacher's perspective around a textualized version of the Initiation-Reply-Evaluation (IRE) structure of classroom discourse (Mehan, 1979): The teacher initiates writing (the assignment), the student replies (turning in a text), and the teacher evaluates (returning the student's text, usually with comments and grades).

The information workplace is another institutional site around which images of authorship have been forming, and graduate school, with its teaching and research assistantships, is also an information work site. The workplace writer is physically located in offices or laboratories and socially in bureaucratic structures. The workplace is a scene where documents cycle through a hierarchy of interlocking rings (internal and external) and claims of individual authorship are attenuated or suppressed.[2] The image of the workplace has also been generated out of cultural commonplaces of economics and business. With a Reaganite faith in the rationality of the market, workplace writing has been constructed within a discourse of authenticity; it is real writing, driven by bottom lines, and subjected to the "real world" evaluations of consumers, clients, or colleagues rather than the arbitrary criteria of school grades and test scores. In this institutional scene, texts carry sociorhetorical force. They function as potent tools of persuasion or as textual performatives, prized for what they do, their origins largely irrelevant except when origin itself enhances or threatens effect.

The final scene I discuss here, writing in the disciplines, is particularly relevant to writing in graduate school, a site permeated with the disciplinary writing of professors and students. As with workplace writing, images of disciplinary writing have been formed from a discourse of the real. Here, texts carry sociorhetorical forces designed to effect changes in the world, specifically in disciplinary knowledge and the application of that knowledge. However, disciplinary authors resemble the lone artists of Brodkey's garret rather than the in-corporated subjects of the workplace, an irony given that many of these authors produce texts in workplace laboratories and routinely publish with lists of co-authors in the tens or even hundreds (see

---

[2]For discussions of workplace writing, see Cross (1994), Duin and Hansen (1996), Freedman, Adam, and Smart (1994), Lunsford and Ede (1990), Odell and Goswami (1985), Spilka (1993).

Lunsford & Ede, 1990). Where the lone writer in the cell has been written as inspired artist and social visionary, the image of disciplinary authors has formed around scientific spheres of activity, with authors as a blend of inspired discoverers and publicists who plan persuasive campaigns by deploying finely honed arguments. The time of this narrative is irregular, with periods (often long) of backstage planning and preparation punctuated by powerful public texts that ignite realignments in disciplinary and public practice. In writing studies, the scene of disciplinary writing has been set in the broader field of a discourse community (where shared knowledge and rules unite "members").[3]

These five scenes of writing overlap and interact, generating a variety of hybrid representations, because they share considerable common ground. Each of these scenes isolates the object, "writing," by foregrounding transcription and text and filtering out most of the sociohistoric contexts, resources, and processes involved in textual production and reception. Each plays out a particular variation on the conduit model of communication. Each reflects the general representational bias that de Certeau (1984) described, the privileging of unified systems of production (the writing of texts, their goals) over the dispersed and heterogeneous tactics of consumption (the ways those texts are read or not read, used or not used, recontextualized in reception). Each scene constructs authors as autonomous originators—even if subject to constraints of clarity, impact, or correctness, situated in more social scenes of production, or accorded attenuated credit for authorship. Given these similarities, I think that Brodkey's (1987) reflections on the trope of the solitary writer apply to this collection of scenes as a whole:

> It is difficult to see or remember writing as other than it is portrayed in the scene of writing, since it is that picture which frames our experience and governs our memories. To see writing anew, to look at it from yet other vantage points, we must teach ourselves away from an image that we have come to think of as the reality of writing. It is not enough to say that it is only a picture, for such pictures provide us with a vocabulary for thinking about and explaining writing to ourselves and one another. (p. 57)

---

[3]This view of disciplinarity is particularly interesting because the image of consensual communities organized around impersonal knowledge and expertise is the outsider view of a discipline, its public face, which, Geisler (1994) argues, was historically constructed to develop and sustain the public authority of institutionalized expertise. Insider views of disciplinarity, on the other hand, typically involve personality, accident, group influences, everyday reasoning, history, and considerable conflict and uncertainty (e.g., Brodkey, 1987; Collins, 1985; Gilbert & Mulkay, 1984; Knorr-Cetina, 1981; Latour, 1987).

To develop a new vocabulary for literate activity in general and authorship in particular, we need to teach ourselves away from the dominant images of these scenes, first by questioning the assumptions within which they have been framed, and second, by developing carefully situated accounts of writing and authorship. In this chapter, I explore three theoretical frameworks that may aid in the work of reimagining authors and their activities. In the three chapters that follow, I explore case studies of authorship in a graduate sociology seminar, a site that blended school, workplace, and discipline.

COMPLICATING THE DYAD: ERVING GOFFMAN ON PARTICIPATION FRAMEWORKS.

It may seem odd to begin a reflection on authorship with the work of Erving Goffman, a microsociologist interested in face-to-face communication. However, in addition to a talent for uncovering sociocultural assumptions by posing concrete counter examples, Goffman had a powerful interest in how language indexed and constituted social alignments and positions. That blend of talent and interest was clearly expressed in Goffman's (1981) discussion of footings, "the alignment we take up to ourselves and others present as expressed in the way we manage the production or reception of an utterance" (p. 128). As Goffman worked to understand how footings were enacted and negotiated, he confronted the limitations of linguistic models of talk grounded in a folk model of conversation as a speaker–hearer dyad. His critique of this folk-linguistic model has clear implications for prototypical images of literacy as conversation.

Goffman (1981) identified two key problems with the speaker–hearer model of talk. First, its terms foreground only one channel of communication, the auditory. Exclusion of the visual channel creates a linear punctuated representation of time and action—talk as an archipelago of discrete turns, each dominated by one person. When the visual channel is acknowledged (with the addition of nonverbal communication and the material environment), communication in the dyad suddenly becomes constant and simultaneous. In addition, whereas the auditory fixes attention on language alone, with the visual, talk is opened to nonlinguistic contexts and activities. Second, the speaker–hearer model of talk deals with decontextualized, undifferentiated talk rather than a talk, a particular interaction situated within a concrete social encounter. It provides for only two generic, interchangeable roles (speaker and hearer) and isolates a single function, the exchange of messages to generate an intersubjective world. When talk is socially situated as activity, a wider field of roles opens up, including many that involve multiple participants and many that are asymmetrical and, hence, not interchangeable. A wider and more specific range of functions also becomes visible, many of which involve "coordinat[ing] action in what is already the shared world of a joint task" (Goffman, 1981, p. 141) rather than the creation of intersubjectivity from scratch.

To challenge the folk-linguistic model, Goffman invoked public scenes of talk with multiple participants (talk on a bus, in a hallway, on a street corner). Working from these public scenes, he first differentiated a set of generic roles for listeners, which he referred to as participation statuses, and collectively as participation structures. With multiple participants, there may be addressed and unaddressed recipients, and ratified participants need to be distinguished from the unratified (e.g., overhearers, eavesdroppers, even bystanders who simply see the talk). In such contexts, talk no longer flows across a single plane connecting the speaker to the hearer; multiple threads of talk are interwoven (including complex footings that arise from collusion, by-play among ratified participants, cross-play between ratified participants and bystanders, and side-play between bystanders). Going beyond this initial sketch of generic participation statuses and frameworks, Goffman emphasized that listeners assume culturally specific listening roles linked to culturally specific situations such as dinner parties, comedy routines, academic lectures, Protestant revival meetings, and broadcast media.

Goffman also analyzed the folk-linguistic notion of the speaker, suggesting that three roles are typically collapsed within that term: the *animator*, who actually utters the word; the *author*, who selects the sentiments and words; and the *principal*, whose positions are being represented in the words. In many instances of situated discourse, however, these roles are divided. For example, a presidential press secretary (the animator) might make an announcement of an environmental initiative that the President (the principal) intends to enact, reading words written by an EPA speech writer (author). Goffman refers to these configurations as production formats.

Goffman represents footings as very dynamic phenomena, shaped through two forms of lamination: vertical lamination, which arises through embedding (e.g., represented speech), and horizontal lamination, which occurs as participants take up multiple roles and activities, often simultaneously, with some active and others on hold. With embedding, Goffman extends the usual notion of represented speech, arguing that what is embedded is not only language, but social arrangements themselves (i.e., the particular participation frameworks and production formats of specific social activities).[4] In this sense, Goffman's view of embedding echoes Bakhtin's argument (1986) that utterances are cast in speech genres that embody typified social voices, relationships, and spheres of activity. For Goffman, the laminations of discourse allow for the complex, flexible transformations of footing and framing that are typical of everyday communication.

By situating talk in particular social activities and roles, Goffman moves beyond the folk-linguistic model of the speaker–hearer dyad and evokes a complexly textured image of multiple forms of participation in talk. Imagining the ways talk is subordinated to activity in many situations (e.g., medical examinations, service encounters in stores, mechanics' diagnosing and repairing an engine), Goffman concludes that the unit of analysis needed for understanding talk is situated social activity rather than a narrower notion like speech act or speech event.

Generating an image of literate acts isolated from social activities, roles, and histories, the writer–reader model in the scene of literacy as conversation suffers from many of the same problems that Goffman identified for the speaker–hearer model of talk. By situating writers and readers in streams of social activity, we can undertake a project analogous to Goffman's, the development of a more nuanced repertoire of terms, images, and narratives to describe diverse forms of participation in textual production and reception. Goffman's discussion has two important limitations in terms of such a project. First, Goffman treats the participation framework of listeners as separate from the production format of speakers. Second, an obvious limitation to Goffman's scheme is that one of the roles he has generated out of the speaker is still a relatively unproblematized and singular author, complicated only by embedding.

Dialogic models of discourse (e.g., Bakhtin, 1981, 1986; Duranti, 1986; Phelps, 1990) have argued that reception and production are reciprocal and mutually constitutive. If we return to the hypothetical example of the press secretary's announcement of an environmental initiative, we can consider how unlikely it is that a lone speech writer in the EPA would produce such a text. Even with the more likely scenario of multiple authors, we would

---

[4]It is important to recognize that represented speech is a common feature of everyday talk, not limited to more complex cultural spheres like the press secretary example. Tannen (1989) offers a useful discussion of the varied types of represented speech (which she refers to as constructed dialogue) found in everyday talk.

also need to consider how those authors recalled, anticipated, or actually sounded out particular ratified participants (including the principal in this case, the president) and bystanders (e.g., the press, the public, special interests); how the text was shaped to fit the genre of a particular administration's White House press briefings; and how the text echoed, responded to, or took into account prior texts. Considering this limitation and the potentially productive intersections between Goffman's notion of footings and Lave and Wenger's (1991) of learning as forms of participation in communities of practice, I use the term *participation* to refer to both production and reception. To address the givenness of authorship, I will shortly turn to LeFevre's (1987) rhetorical theory, which unpacks the author role itself by exploring the multiple forms of participation in invention. However, first, I consider some implications of Goffman's theory for accounts of writing grounded in the folk model of dyadic talk.

WRITING AS CONVERSATION: TEXTS, TURNS, AND SITUATED ACTIVITY

The folk-linguistic model of conversation that Goffman (1981) analyzes has carried over into models of writing in complex ways that are important to trace in some detail. Elements of the model have sometimes been incorporated directly into accounts of writing. They have also served as defining contrasts, as the opposite poles in dichotomous representations of orality and literacy. In this section, I explore contrasting and complementary representations of talk and text in Geisler's research on disciplinary writing and Bakhtin's accounts of spoken and written utterance.

Geisler's recent research (1991, 1994) illustrates the promise and problems likely to be encountered in the move toward a sociohistoric perspective on writing. Geisler (1994) calls for a shift from the spatialized cognitive process models of Flower and Hayes[5] toward a temporal activity-theoretic model in which academic writers' rhetorical practices—"projected in time through the structure of their activities" and mediated by an evolving series of textual artifacts—"interact with their developing understanding of domain content—as projected in space through the structure of their mental representations" (p. 124). Geisler also offers a powerful sociocultural contextualization of academic writing (rhetorical practice) and disciplinary

---

[5]Flower and Hayes (1981, 1984) illustrate the spatialized nature of models of writing typically derived from protocol analysis.

expertise (domain knowledge) in the emergent institutionalization of professions in the 19th and 20th centuries. To model writing as an active lived process rather than as abstract correspondences between structures of knowledge and texts, Geisler turns to a powerful analogy, the basic communicative activity of human culture, conversation. To account for disciplinary expertise, Geisler suggests that writing introduces a crucial change from the sequencing of conversation; thus, she proposes a quasi-conversational model for academic writing and disciplinary expertise. However, drawing on a view of expertise grounded in notions of discourse communities and on the folk-linguistic model of conversation, Geisler's account of writing and disciplinarity displays significant problems.

Geisler developed her model of writing as quasi-conversational activity through research that compared the writing of experts and novices in one discipline, philosophy. For experts, she recruited two PhD students (one a recent graduate) in philosophy to act as consultants. For novices, she recruited two undergraduates, not majoring in philosophy, to act as student employees. Geisler provided them with a common topic (medical paternalism), a common packet of readings (an introduction to the issues plus essays representing different perspectives), and similar tasks. All four participants were assigned the task of discussing the current state of thinking on medical paternalism, summarizing and evaluating definitions of the concept, and attempting to state conditions that would justify paternalism. For the experts, the task was to write "an article" for a popular magazine; for the novices, it was (somewhat paradoxically) to write a "long paper, term-paper length" for a popular magazine (Geisler, 1994, p. 133). The conditions of writing also varied. In this quasi-clinical design, all participants were asked to produce their texts in think-aloud sessions over the course of a semester, with interviews after each writing session; however, the experts worked at times and places of their choosing, whereas the novices worked in a university office at regularly scheduled hours.[6]

---

[6]From the perspective of activity theory, a central problem with this kind of quasi-clinical design rests in the multiple ways that the motives, goals, and operations of situated academic writing are disrupted, disallowed, and replaced with motives, goals, and operations imposed as part of the research activity itself. For example, in Geisler's design, whatever would lead PhD students in philosophy to write a popular article on medical paternalism is absent, replaced by cooperation in research activity. Likewise, for the novice writers, the usual motives and goals for producing a paper (grades, personal interests, graduation, specific histories of a course) are noticeably absent. In terms of operations, it is clear that neither the undergraduate students writing in a private office at regularly scheduled hours nor the PhD students writing a "popular article" on an assigned topic from a thin packet of pre-selected texts are using typical resources or are engaged in typical practices of writing and knowledge production (leaving aside the additional complication of the think-aloud procedure itself). In terms of the discussion

In her analysis, Geisler compared the sequences of writing-process categories derived from the writers' think-aloud protocols to conversation analytic analyses of turn-taking as adjacency pairs, like question–answer or request–agreement.[7] Equating texts with turns, Geisler posits a literate practice in which *writing* is treated as a first pair part and *revision* is the second pair part, but sandwiched between these text-turns are *reading*, *reflecting*, and *organizing*. For Geisler, it is this activity in the interstices of transcriptional turns (texts) that creates a space for reflection and, thus, explains the special potential of writing to produce expert thought. Geisler reconstructs, although somewhat provisionally, the great divide between orality and literacy in this gap between *writing* and *revision* (provisional because it depends on whether and how the gap is utilized).

However, Geisler's reliance on the folk model of conversation and the transcription-text-garret model of writing undercuts her attempt to treat writing as activity, producing instead a distilled, linear model of writing as solo action. In constructing the opposing pole of orality, Geisler begins with a deficit model of talk as immediate, unreflective, and turn-driven, as thought on the fly that cannot achieve depth and abstraction and that is locked down in one-dimensional linearity. The consequences of these models are quite visible in her analysis of the data. For example, Geisler (1991) mentions that her expert philosophers reported talking to their colleagues about their ideas. However, instead of incorporating this talk (or for that matter, the interviews that followed writing sessions for all four participiants) into her model of writing as activity, seeing it as historically relevant to the development of both their ideas and texts, she treats those conversations as a wholly separate process in which the products of expert, reflective literate practice are folded into the unreflective, "indigenous" space of conversation, thus enriching that space. In a similar fashion, Geisler

---

in chapter 3, these research tasks structure quite different semiotic genres from those present in either academic writing tasks tied to classrooms or to public professional writing. Of course, thrust into this novel activity, the participants must draw in some fashion on resources from their prior socialization (see van Mannen & Schein's, 1979, discussion of chains of socialization). Thus the problem is not that the design is decontextualized and will reveal nothing relevant about academic writing and expertise, but rather that it is so fully contextualized in another sphere of activity (social-psychological research) that what it reveals and what it does not reveal become very tangled analytic questions indeed. I am not suggesting that sociohistoric inquiry is limited to naturalistic research designs. In fact, much of the research has been conducted in laboratory settings. However, that research has typically involved investigation of microgenesis or the disruption of functional systems. Geisler's expert–novice design derives from another tradition, cognitive representationalism.

[7]See e.g., Sacks, Schegeloff, & Jefferson (1974) and Heritage (1984) on adjacency pairs.

(1994, 1991) identifies a central difference between experts and novices in ways they interact with the texts and their authors, particularly in how often they mention authors in their protocols and in how abstractly they represent authors' positions. In particular, Geisler (1994) suggests the undergraduate students were "operating in a world without interlocutors " because their texts and protocols displayed limited engagement with the authors they were assigned to respond to (p. 183). However, the protocols of one of the students (Leslie) were full of her arguments about, reflections on, and expressions of anger with doctors at a hospital who had refused to accept her grandfather's living will when he arrived there unconscious. Geisler discounts Leslie's highly dialogic encounters with those doctors because they involved her life experiences rather than the case studies given in the reading packet. My point here is not to equate Geisler's experts and her novices, not to discount differences in their literate practices, but to argue that representations of writing and expertise as activity need to be grounded in full accounts of literate activity. If we are committed to studying situated and mediated activity, what Hutchins (1995) refers to as *cognition in the wild*, then we need to take that activity as we find it functioning and not trim its contours to our domesticated folk categories.

Geisler's oral–literate dichotomy, however, is not the only model of conversation available. Bakhtin's approach to talk as utterance, for example, suggests a radically different view of the relevant temporal sequences. Consider, for example, the following invented (but hopefully plausible) interaction:

> Teacher: What is the capital of the United States?
> Student: Washington.
> Teacher: Right. Washington, D.C.

Conventional conversation analysis would propose a triadic structure for this segment of discourse, the IRE structure of a lesson (Mehan, 1979). This triadic structure is a culturally specialized elaboration of the dominant structure of adjacency pairs (e.g., question–answer with an optional third part for repair). Closer analysis might reveal how paralinguistic and gestural cues contribute to the regulation of turns, determine how certain rights (such as nominating who will talk next) are socially differentiated, and identify patterns of overtalk and latching. However, grounded in the problematic principle that the interactional record must display everything needed to achieve the communication (see Cicourel, 1981, and Hanks, 1996b, for critiques of this principle), conversation analysis stops (or at least claims to stop) with this expressed sequential interaction: an initiating event followed by a rejoinder followed by another rejoinder.

Bakhtin's (1986) sociohistorical account of conversation is interested in, but not limited to, the single plane of immediate linear sequence. For Bakhtin, the chain of utterances extends through space and especially time. From this perspective, the initiating move in the above example is itself already and necessarily a complex rejoinder to prior utterances. As Bakhtin (1986) notes, when we speak, we are not breaking an eternal silence. Thus, the teacher's question stands not as the first pair part of conversation analysis, but rather as an eddy far downstream in the historical currents of utterance, shaped intertextually by prior communicative events that define a range of probable significations for words, syntax, and prosodic elements and that contribute to the contextualization of the present situation as part of the sociocultural activity of schooling, of the role configuration as teacher to student, and of the information as askable within this culturally defined occasion. Likewise, the student's answering word, "Washington,"emerges out of a history that extends well beyond the teacher's single question. The student has to draw on some prior utterances to produce an acceptable answer and to avoid unacceptable rejoinders (e.g., "Why do you ask?" or "Good question. Look it up in the encyclopedia." or "I'm busy; bug off."). Moreover, the recipient design of each contribution in this little exchange is oriented to futures as well as pasts, each anticipating answers in word and action. And of course, the student has elected to cooperate in this exchange; she could, having known "the answer," chosen silence, irony, or insult as a reply. In this sense, *what is said* is produced, understood, and used against a background of *what has been said* and *what could have been said*.

Speech acts (in all senses, as locutions, illocutions, and perlocutions in context) do not stand alone. They are woven into the thickly layered fabric of our own situated and unfolding biographies; sedimented with traces of, to paraphrase Becker (1988), cultural forms and tools pushed into present use; and fixed in the evolving histories of everything from participants' fleeting definitions of situations to the long-term evolution of our species as organisms on this planet. Meaning is no more to be found in isolated linear sequences of conversational or literate acts than it is in isolated sentences.

On the other hand, although Bakhtin (1986) offered a richly layered account of talk as utterances situated in past-present-future chains of utterance, he also privileged the folk-linguistic model when he argued that utterances are defined by the real boundaries of turns, changes in speaker. Seeking a dialogic notion of writing, Bakhtin projected this model of talk as alternating speaker and listener to a model of written utterance (text) as a kind of extended turn-taking in absentia (a solution in this respect similar to Geisler's). Arguing that texts (works) are utterances in every sense like talk, Bakhtin (1986) says:

> The work is a link in the chain of speech communion. Like the rejoinder in a dialogue, it is related to other work-utterances: both those to which it responds and those that respond to it. At the same time, like the rejoinder in a dialogue, it is separated from them by the absolute boundaries created by a change of speaking subjects. (p. 76)

Like Geisler, Bakhtin here takes texts as equivalent to turns; however, in his case, the texts are public and probably authored by others. In a constructivist reinterpretation of the boundaries of written utterance, Nystrand (1990) relocates the boundary at the switch from the writer's construction of the text to the reader's construction of it. In other words, texts are dialogic because they involve the successive turns at meaning making of writers and readers.

Bakhtin might have generated a more Bakhtinian account of texts, and especially of the secondary genres of complex cultural communication, had he worked more from his own unit—utterance—than from the folk category of turn. The notion of utterance as situated, moment-to-moment talk saturated with response to past, present, and future events could have led to an equivalent understanding of writing as situated, moment-to-moment activity saturated with multiple forms of responsivity (cf. Brandt, 1990; Phelps, 1990). Although writing protocol research is problematic because of the methodological constraints its designs place on what writers do and the analytic limitations of its categorizations, such research should by now have disabused us from any image of textual production as a unified, homogenous unit—a turn. When writers are observed and asked (in interviews or protocols) to produce fine-grained descriptions of their writing processes, what appears is complex heterogeneous sequences of activity with multiple forms of responsivity (internal dialogue of the writer, reading and echoing of other texts, rereading of one's own text, physical actions and observations, others' readings of and responses to texts, anticipations of such readings, etc.). It is in this dense jungle of mediated, moment-to-moment activity and signification that we need to seek literacy in the wild.

In earlier Bakhtinian texts (Bakhtin & Medvedev, 1978; Voloshinov, 1973), the sociogenesis of consciousness was described in terms much like those Vygotsky (1978; 1987) was crafting at the same time (i.e., in the 1920s and 1930s). For example, Voloshinov (1973) argues that the word is interindividual, that inner speech in a transformation of external speech, and that consciousness is formed through interiorization of the culture's historically developed semiotic means. Utterance is, thus, described not only as external speech or text, but also as inner speech and text (with notions of inner speech, inner utterance, inner genre). In a striking statement of this notion, Voloshinov is discussing the finalization of spoken utterances, the question of how to identify their wholeness, but goes on to say:

> The process of speech, broadly understood as the process of inner and outer verbal life, goes on continuously. It knows neither beginning nor end. The outwardly actualized utterance is an island rising from the boundless sea of inner speech; the dimensions and forms of this island are determined by the particular *situation* of the utterance and its *audience*. (p. 96)

In this account, the chain of utterances is inner as well as external; thought and language are brought together in an integrated account. If we take utterance as always anchored in situated activity, then written utterance needs to stay much closer to the kind of moment-to-moment accounts that raw process protocols have displayed.

Bakhtin's (1986) account of works (texts) as utterance was likely motivated by more than analogies of talk and text. Central to his account of utterance and speech genre was the notion of composition, of construction of the whole and completion (see discussion in chap. 3). What is needed then is a way to bridge the gap between situated writing as utterance and the distinct wholeness that is realized, particularly for secondary genres, only over extended periods of time. To make this bridge requires, I would argue, an explicit recognition of the artifactuality of texts and of the textual mediation of literate activity. In this sense, Bakhtin's and Geisler's accounts could complement each other. Geisler's account could be enriched by incorporating a fully dialogic perspective. It is this kind of perspective, in terms of historical semiosis, that Witte (1992) contrasted with the narrower focus of situated writing. Bakhtin's accounts of written utterance could be enriched by engaging the situatedness of writing and the potential implications of textual mediation.

Seeing writing as situated, mediated, and dispersed in literate activity, we have an alternative way to account for what Geisler identifies as literate expertise and Bakhtin as the complexity of secondary genres. Secondary genres (in talk as well as text) are not secondary simply and circularly because they are embedded in highly organized spheres of activity. Genre and sphere alike become highly developed because of the concrete and sedimented nature of the mediated activity by, from, and within which they are constituted. The production, reception, and distribution of textual and other artifacts are central to such activity. Genres and spheres of activity are, thus, not products of the long, slow turns of individuals, but of long histories of socially distributed and mediated activity, within which utterances and other tools are worked and reworked, visited and revisited by multiple participants over time.

BEYOND TRANSCRIPTION AND TEXT:
LEFEVRE ON INVENTION

Much as the speaker–hearer model obscures the socially and materially situated activity that dominates face-to-face communication, the synecdochical extraction of the figure of writing from the messy ground of the lifeworld has suppressed ways that other texts, talk, perceptions, activities, and institutions might come into play in situated textual production and reception. This extraction of writing also generates the image of the autonomous author as one who make texts by transcribing words or being directly and substantively involved in that transcription. In *Invention as a Social Act* (1987), LeFevre works to reconstruct the object of modern rhetorical studies of writing by shifting attention from texts and acts of transcription to the social bases of invention.

Citing Foucault, LeFevre argues for a view of "discourse not as an isolated event, but rather a constant potentiality that is occasionally evidenced in speech or writing. The beginnings and ends of rhetorical acts are thus not clearly obvious or absolute" (p. 41). This perspective bears obvious relations to the earlier discussion of writing as dispersed in literate activity, emerging from streams of historical semiosis (e.g., inner and outer utterances). Viewing invention as a diffuse social process of meaning making rather than as bounded focal activity linked directly to transcription of a particular text, LeFevre (1987) set out to explore "the types of relationships that may exist between people who invent together or influence others' inventions" (p. 67).

To guide these explorations, she embraces the notion of "resonance" as a key concept:

> [Resonance] may occur when someone acts as a facilitator to assist or extend what is regarded as primarily another's invention, or when people are mutual collaborators at work on a task. Resonance also occurs when people provide a supportive social and intellectual environment that nurtures thought and enables ideas to be received, thus completing the inventive act. People who act as resonators help an inventor to locate himself or herself in a tradition and a community and to live in a way that is conducive to further invention. (p. 65)

LeFevre reviews several criteria (division of labor, control over decisions, distribution of credit) that might be used to classify the participation frameworks of collaborative invention. However, she also notes that authorship is not only diffused in concrete forms of social interaction as people invent together, it is also constituted by audiences that shape a text through reception and by the sociocultural legacies that constrain and enable it. In fact, LeFevre posits a continuum of social influences on invention, roughly divided into three domains: the internal dialogic, the collaborative, and the collective.

In the middle range of collaborative relationships, LeFevre identifies three categories of participation: inventing by interaction, joint invention, and contextual facilitation. In the first category, the inventor–rhetor is helped by others through interaction. Her examples invoke varied forms of help: a teacher responding to a student's text, a customer making a suggestion to a company on its product, a friend encouraging a novelist to write regularly, and a group brainstorming to generate ideas or solve a problem. Joint invention ratchets the level of mutual involvement a step higher. LeFevre points not only to traditional examples of acknowledged and unacknowledged co-authorship, but also to other participation frameworks: The multiple authorship that emerges from team science (with authorship lists sometimes in the hundreds), extended interactions among a group with a common project (e.g., the way Jefferson, Adams, Franklin, Washington, and others worked together to produce the U.S. constitution and other foundational documents of the U.S. political life), and the negotiated production of institutional documents (e.g., contracts between unions and corporations, political party platforms, international treaties). LeFevre's final category of collaborative invention, contextual facilitation, suggests broader rather than deeper forms of involvement. Here she points to specialized forums for publication (e.g., journals, book series, monographs, reviews), associations that develop around key sites (institutes, commercial enterprises, conferences, salons), and the individual sponsors, publishers, patrons, and others who take leading roles in establishing and sustaining such contexts for invention.

Beginning with a focus on meaning and resonance rather than transcription and text, LeFevre develops a complex map of forms of participation in collaborative invention. Some of these forms fit traditional models of authorship (e.g., co-authorship). Some, such as the interactions that occur as a teacher prompts and responds to a student's writing, occupy a recognized border zone, focusing, as they clearly do, on the key signifiers of authorship—texts and transcription. Others, however, such as supportive friends, general creativity groups, literary sponsors, and publishers, clearly fall well outside of traditional definitions of authorship.

These diverse forms of collaborative invention are flanked by the more private and more public poles of LeFevre's continuum. Describing the internal dialogic, she refers to the internalization of others or other perspectives, a process through which the self and other are co-constituted, establishing the internal ground for intersubjectivity. For the collective, she cites various forms of macrosocial control (e.g., normative expectations, the prohibition or promotion of particular notions), semiotic systems (particularly language), institutional and sociocultural formations (e.g., universities, disciplines, professions, social categorizations), economic and material conditions, funds of knowledge, and thought collectives.

LeFevre's examples, particularly in the middle range of collaboration, offer a richly diverse set of scenes for interrogating the participation frameworks of invention, and hence, authorship. However, her classification of the social grounds of invention remains anchored in a strong individualism. This individualism is most visible in the affective and evaluative orientation of the examples she offers to illustrate the categories. Her examples reflect a tacit moral universe where invention is best when closest to free individual choice. Flowing from her notion of resonance, LeFevre's representations of invention through interaction and joint invention are consistently consensual and positive.[8] Her discussion of contextual facilitation introduces a mild negative note, mentioning that an absence of resonance here could inhibit invention. However, when she turns to the collective, LeFevre offers dark, ambivalent characterizations of social forces, emphasizing ways that collectivities constrain invention through coercive prohibition, exemplified by the various ways women have been blocked from participation in cultural and scientific work.[9]

Conceptually, the centrality of the individual in LeFevre's continuum is seen in the distance between internalized representations of others and a collective resource like language. Although in a separate chapter LeFevre argues for a dialectical view of language as social and individual, her continuum of invention offers no space for such a dialectic because it is

---

[8]Spender's (1989) accounts of sexism in literary co-authorship, of the ways that authors such as F. Scott Fitzgerald appropriated women's words, work, and experiences, provide counter examples of joint invention as oppressive, coercive, and destructive.

[9]See Giddens (1984) for a discussion of representations of society in terms only of constraint. He argues that social forces and structures should be seen as simultaneously enabling and constraining.

anchored around the figure of the individual inventor–rhetor that tacitly drives the separation of internal dialogic, collaborative, and collective. At issue here is the appropriate unit of analysis. In the next section of this chapter, I turn to a sociohistoric perspective that explicitly challenges the traditional dichotomized notions of the individual and the social by considering them as interpenetrated. Taking up this kind of perspective would suggest that LeFevre's linear continuum be bent back on itself and twisted into a braid so that the boundaries between individual mind, situated social interaction, and sociocultural practices and structures intermingle and blur.

THE PERSON IN ACTIVITY: WERTSCH
ON MEDIATED AGENCY

A central thesis of Wertsch's *Voices of the Mind* (1991) is that the human sciences have suffered from a basic paradox: The dichotomy they have defined themselves around, the individual and society, offers problematic units of analysis, representing as autonomous and oppositional what is fundamentally an interpenetrated whole. Drawing on Taylor's analyses (1985, 1989) of the Western development of notions of agency and the self, Wertsch traces this paradox to a blend of everyday folk models of the person-as-actor with intellectual traditions that posit an atomistic, disengaged self. The construction of a sovereign, solitary self generates a complementary image of society as distant and depersonalized, strictly separated from concrete historical persons and their practices. Informed by Vygotskyan and Bakhtinian traditions, Wertsch argues that this paradox must be resolved by adopting two, more holistic, integrated units of analysis: mediated action and the individual-using-mediational-means (what Wertsch, Tulviste, & Hagstrom, 1993, call mediated agency).

Current Vygotskyan theory has settled on activity—that is, goal-oriented, tool-mediated actions in social and material worlds—as the basic unit of analysis (see chap. 1). Situated activity then is not simply a site where learning occurs, it is the object of learning (what will be creatively appropriated) and its subject (the source of consciousness, of the person). Here is where Bakhtin's insistence on the priority of concrete histories over abstract systems of knowledge is critical to a sociohistoric understanding of the person. From a Bakhtinian perspective, what is appropriated cannot be the abstract, impersonal, unified systems of language and culture precisely because no one ever encounters such systems. Thus, this view is not reducible to a common formulation of Mead's (1934) social psychology, the notion that we "internalize others" whom we then interact with in inner dialogue.[10] The person encounters language and culture only in partial, embodied forms, as particular historical persons, practices, artifacts, institutions, and events. From this sociohistoric perspective, social interactions (e.g., artifacts and practices as well as persons) are not gobbled up whole and recopied on the brain, but instead are transformatively appropriated as we orient ourselves in particular ways to the interactions (which are also orienting to us) and then, strongly influenced by motivational and affective issues, internalize fragments of our representations of this activity. Those fragments (already partial, interested, transformed) are not then stored as autonomous packages, but instead are woven into a fabric of presuppositions, stances, and orientations to action. This heterogeneous, situated, and dispersed image of socialization suggests an equally heterogeneous, situated, and dispersed notion of the self, of agency. For Wertsch, agency is, thus, hybrid and distributed, simultaneously historical and emergent, arising out of the complex intersections of a person's trajectory through a pluralistic sociohistoric landscape, the historical trajectories of the tools (mediational means) the person has transformatively appropriated, and the situated use of those tools in emergent interactions.

LITERATE ACTIVITY AND DISCIPLINARITY

When writing is located in literate activity, in multi-stranded histories that include speaking and listening, acting and observing, thinking and feeling, reading and writing, then, as LeFevre argues, it becomes difficult to identify whether a moment might figure in some "writing" process. With the understanding that literate activity is mediated and dispersed, time itself becomes problematic as activity weaves together multiple temporalities. That semiotic activity is mediated by textual technologies, is now immersed in literate forms of life, and is realized in part through writing is certainly

---

[10]Discussing how children are socialized into linguistic lamination, into *speaking for* not only other people, but also animals, dolls, and so on, Goffman (1981) argues:

> George Herbert Mead not withstanding, the child does not merely learn to refer to itself through a name for itself that others had first chosen; it learns just as early to embed the statements and mannerisms of a zoo-full of beings in its own verbal behavior....One might say that Mead had the wrong term: the child does not acquire a "generalized other" so much as a capacity to embed "particularized others"—which others, taken together, form a heterogeneous, accidental collection, a teething ring for utterances and not a ball team (p. 151).

important, significant, and worthy of our attention. Textual technologies do matter and they matter deeply. However, extracting writing (as transcription of texts) from full functional systems of literate activity breaks too many of the critical pathways.

Our language and narratives constantly invite us to treat historical persons (or some personified social entity like culture) as discrete actors or agents. The discursive resources available to see persons and societies as co-constituted in streams of situated activity, to describe agency as mediated and dispersed, are fragile and fragmented in comparison. Nevertheless, the notion of mediated agency is attractive, providing a way to retain a notion of the person as a particular source of agency without producing a bipolar world of detached autonomous selves and depersonalized societies. For the present discussion, it suggests a key unit of analysis for studies of literate activity is a notion of *mediated authorship* (a special case of Wertsch's mediated agency). The next three chapters offer situated accounts that explore how authorship was mediated in the literate activity of one disciplinary setting.

6

Images of Authorship in a Sociology Research Team

Although my studies in *Language Research* (see chaps. 2 and 4) had already begun to make classroom walls seem a bit porous (both spatially and temporally) and had suggested the need to attend more closely to students' goals and interpretations, the design of my next study (in *Geography*, *American Studies*, and *Sociology*) was still strongly grounded in the proto-typical image of classroom writing and authorship described in the last chapter.[1] Asking how academic writing tasks in a seminar were cued, interpreted, negotiated, produced, and finally evaluated by both the instructor and the students, the research was, in effect, meant to capture and contextualize in a fine-grained manner the literate sequences of initiations, replies, and evaluations that in total constituted the writing tasks for the seminars. However, one site, the seminar in sociology, proved particularly difficult to fit into that conventional classroom box.

From the prototypical perspective of classroom scenes, *Sociology* was anomalous in a number of ways. It was a topical seminar with no topic. The professor, Elaine West, was the principal investigator (PI) of a research project, the Adolescence Project (which I will refer to simply as the Project). All seven PhD students in the seminar were research assistants (RAs) in the Project, and West's two co-investigators (Professors Lynch and Harris) often sat in. The first session opened with West asking the students to review the work they planned to present. The students all indicated they would present texts based on the Project's data set. In every case, those texts were also directed to actual external contexts, including disciplinary forums (journal articles, conference papers, technical reports for grantors) as well as other institutional forums (preliminary examinations and disser-tation prospectuses). From the second session on, seminar meetings were

---

[1]See Appendix A for methodological details of the research presented in chapters 6 to 8.

primarily devoted to discussion of draft texts of the students' "own" work. (A student's draft was distributed to all seminar participants a day or two before they met.) When I asked students to provide me with drafts related to the work they would present in the seminar, several offered multiple drafts (as many as 11) of multiple documents (three was the maximum) they had produced (and often West had responded to) over periods of up to a year and a half. In short, *Sociology* was a seminar saturated with the participants' activities as a sociology research team.

Their status as a research team was also reflected in a complex web of other significant relationships. Five of the seven students were West's advisees. At least four had decided to use the Project's data for their dissertations. Three had already been listed as co-authors on conference papers or journal articles generated from the Project. The dominance of these extracurricular contexts was perhaps best reflected in the fact that West, Lynch, Harris, and five of the students had met biweekly as an unofficial seminar the two quarters before the official seminar.

As I began to analyze texts, transcripts of seminar sessions and inter-views, and fieldnotes, questions of authorship repeatedly emerged as central issues. With the complex streams of collaborative activity in the seminar and the Project, it was difficult to untangle whose ideas and whose work a particular text represented, to decide who was talking in a text. The data seemed designed to illustrate LeFevre's (1987) notion of invention as a constant potentiality. As my attempts to trace origins (who produced a text and whose communicative intentions and ideational content were inscribed in it) resulted in remarkably complex and uncertain histories of production, I began to refocus my attention to the issue of how the participants themselves produced representations of authorship (i.e., who was repre-sented as having produced a text, who was represented as being responsible for it, and what social practices had been employed in negotiating these representations).[2] Examining issues of representation led me to recognize

---

[2]Following up on Lunsford and Ede's (1990) citation of the work of Carpenter (1981), whose interest in forms of authorship arose from practical questions of library cataloging, I found not only an interesting discussion that unpacked multiple senses of writing (writing up, down, over, on, and in), but also a clear discussion of different grounds for authorship: origination versus representation, responsibility versus individual intention and work. Carpenter's discussion dovetails in interesting ways with recent arguments by Latour, Phelps, and Duranti. The distinction between origination and representation parallels Latour's (1993) analysis of modern science and society as constituted in part by the separation of hybrid practices of production that mix nature and society freely in heterogeneous networks from representational purifications that neatly separate nature and society. Considering the challenges of post-modern theory to originary authorship, Phelps (1990) proposes four basic notions for reconstruct-ing a theory of authorship: will, responsivity, work, and responsibility. In a different domain, Duranti

that I needed to account for the absence of authorship—non-authorship—as a positive accomplishment. Non-authorship took two forms in this community of practice: exclusion from authorship credit and allegations of plagiarism. This chapter then offers an initial sketch of some of the complex configurations and significations of authorship and non-authorship in this sociology seminar/research group, exploring the ways texts were produced, authorship was represented, and translations were made between production and representation.

REPRESENTATIONS: NEGOTIATING AUTHORSHIP
AND NON-AUTHORSHIP IN THE PROJECT

Figure 6.1 presents an official statement of authorship policies produced by West when the Project began. The policy statement is framed in a bureaucratic-legal discourse, offering a detailed explication of mechanisms for assigning authorship that strives to anticipate all eventualities. The statement constructs a hierarchical institutional universe headed by the entitled (marked by capital letters), the Principal Investigator/Project Manager and the Co-Investigator (parenthetically identified as West and Lynch, respectively). It identifies another, untitled, category of person, the graduate student, a designation that is neither capitalized nor specific to the Project (as "research assistant" would be). The modalities of the sentences tend to empower the titled heads of the project and to obligate the graduate students, laying out what the PI "will" and "may" (for possibility) do and what students "must" or "may" (for permission) do. Item 3 represents authorship in terms of positional rights; however, Item 4 seeks to rationalize authorship in terms of activity (contributions). The parenthetic elaboration in Item 4 of direct contributions as "conceptualization, data analysis, and writing" does not limit authorship to transcription (although in practice acts of writing and data analysis seemed more clearly defined and visible than conceptualization). However, what it omits is worth emphasizing because positions in the Project were clearly differentiated by research activities. Data collection and coding, two prominent activities for RAs in the Project,

---

1993) points to the Western cultural bias toward intentionality ("What do you mean?"). In his study of Samoan ethnopragmatics, he argues that Samoans "typically see talk and interpretation as activities for the assignment of responsibility rather than as exercises in reading 'other minds'" (p. 24). Noting how Western folk models of the individual, meaning, and communication have played out in linguistic theories, like speech act theory, he points to the parallels between the Samoan ideology and current sociohistoric theories.

are excluded (by omission from the elaboration) as contributions and hence as claims on authorship. The introductory paragraph ends by accounting for the policy on two quite different grounds: First, to ensure that contributions are acknowledged through authorship, and second, to communicate the rules governing use of the data.

August 25, 1988

Authorship Policies

It is expected that the data obtained from the Adolescence Project will be utilized by graduate students and other study personnel for papers presented at professional meetings, doctoral dissertations, journal articles, and other publications. The Principal Investigator or Co-Investigator may invite others to collaborate on papers on particular topics with them. Project personnel may also request (singly or with others) to use the data for specific purposes. The following policies were developed to assure that persons will be duly acknowledged, by authorship, for their contributions, and that all persons who wish to use the data are fully aware of the rules governing its use.

1.   The Principal Investigator (E. West) will act as "gatekeeper", giving permission to use the data for particular purposes, and making sure that domains of analysis are clear.

2.   All papers prepared by graduate students must be approved by the P.I. before they are submitted for presentation or publication.

3.   The Principal Investigator and Co-Investigator (E. West and D. Lynch) have the right to have their names appear on any papers derived from the data set. (However, they may choose to waive this right.)

Exception: Graduate students who use the data may be sole author of at least one publication derived from their Ph.D. dissertations. It is expected that in most cases more than one such publication will be sole-authored. Appropriate acknowledgement to all study personnel who assisted them should be made.

4.   The Project Manager and graduate students may author papers that they directly contribute to (conceptualization, data analysis, writing). Order of authors shall be determined by relative contribution, or if contributions are deemed equal, alphabetically or by mutual agreement.

5.   In the event of disputes regarding authorship or order of authors, the PI will resolve them.

FIG. 6.1. Authorship statement from the Adolescent Project.

This statement is about more than authorship; it is an object that constitutes part of the overall management of the Project and its research findings. In Bakhtin's terms, this policy and its projected practices represent centripetal forces–not only for representing authorship, but also for establishing social relations in the Project and controlling both what texts would be produced and what those texts would say. In an interview, West related her desire for control over analysis and publication to her concern that the Project not speak with conflicting and confused voices. The policy (particularly Items 1 and 2) places West at two critical gates, controlling access to the data and planned analyses at one end and funneling public texts through her at the other end.[3]

As the policy would suggest, multiple authorship was the norm for disciplinary publications in this group. The only single-authored publication was a conference paper for a special graduate student session. Authorship on institutional documents (i.e., preliminary examinations, dissertation prospectuses, dissertations) was always, by institutional definition, singular. During my research, four of the students in the seminar were working on preliminary examinations and dissertation prospectuses using the Project's data.

In practice, the authorship policy produced a two-tiered distribution of authorship credit. On one tier were West, Lynch, and two RAs (Sean and Lee), all of whom were regularly accorded authorship, particularly for journal articles. Among the seven journal articles that had been generated from the Project when my research ended, West had some level of authorship on six, while Lynch, Sean, and Lee were included as authors on five. In the second tier, authorship credit was rare. Among the other five graduate students in the seminar, only one (Linda) had been included as an author of a journal article. The prominence of West and Lynch in this hierarchy is not surprising: the policy statement accorded them the right to appear as authors on any publication (except for the noted exception related to dissertation work). However, the prominence of Sean and Lee (both PhD RAs with the Project for over two years) is more interesting.

Sean worked as the manager of data analysis, and Lee, a NNES student from Korea, as the database supervisor. Whenever reports were prepared,

---

[3]West's desire for control and her right to authorship may be typical features of research teams (see, e.g., Knorr-Cetina, 1981; Rymer, 1988). As PI, West was likely to be held both corporately and individually responsible for any work that came out of the Project. West's involvement in textual production fit all three of LeFevre's (1987) categories of collaboration, inventing by interaction, joint invention, and contextual facilitation.

Sean and Lee were called on to run statistical analyses. Their routine inclusion in authorship, thus, arose primarily because of their positions in the Project. While Sean's involvement in authorship often extended beyond running statistical analyses to writing and conceptualization, Lee indicated that he had never written a word on any of the six publications he "co-authored." When I asked what role he had played in writing these papers, he indicated that he had just done the data analysis:

> I read the drafts, but I didn't the paper, I just do the analysis and read the draft.... Sometimes she [West] gives me, usually she gives memo, and you do the analysis, I mean I do the analysis, and sometimes Elaine and I, or Elaine and I and David Lynch or, sometimes Sean too, get together and talk about strategy in terms of reviewing things for data analysis, and then proceed there, something like that.

Lee also noted that he was not particularly interested in these publications, that he was trying to distance himself from them in part because "it might be like downright lie."

At the bottom of the hierarchy were Linda, Thomas, Moira, and two students who had just joined the Project that semester. For Linda, Thomas, and Moira, non-authorship marked specific exclusions. It may not be surprising that Linda and Thomas, as seasonal data coders, were not routinely included in authorship. Moira, on the other hand, had worked as the manager of data collection for over two years. She was responsible for the annual distribution and collection of over 2,500 questionnaires to a group of adolescents and their parents or guardians, a task that often involved tracking people down because retention of the sample was crucial. Although she had held this key position in the Project almost as long as Sean and Lee had, her sustained managerial work was never reflected in or rewarded through authorship.

Of course, according to Item 4 on the authorship policy (Fig. 6.1), the work of Sean and Lee counted as direct contributions, whereas the work of Moira, Linda, and Thomas did not. The different kinds of work the RAs did also differed in visibility. However routine data analysis might be, each paper involved analyses that had to be requested, set up, run, examined, and passed on, making Sean and Lee's contributions part of an explicit and visible distribution of tasks. Data collection and coding, although essential, could become invisible because they never had to be specifically requested in the process of producing a particular text. The hierarchy of authorship also seemed to reflect disciplinary and sociocultural (e.g., gendered) con-structions of work. Whatever its explanations, Moira's exclusion from authorship, her non-authorship, should be seen as every bit as much an act, and thus subject to investigation, as Lee's authorship. In other words, both authorship and non-authorship need to be accounted for in terms of a situated politics of representation, a politics that stands in definite but complex relation to histories of production.

CO-PRODUCTION WITHOUT REPRESENTATION:
MOIRA'S CONFERENCE PAPER AND PRELIM

Moira, the manager of data analysis, was also the student who ended up producing the first single-authored publication from the Project, a paper for a special graduate student session at a national sociology conference. During the period of my research, Moira was actually working on two related documents—the conference paper, which I call *Arenas* (for its focus on a hypothesis related to "arenas of comfort") and a preliminary examination, which I call *Prelim*. Between November and July, Moira produced four drafts of *Prelim*, three of which West responded to, and seven drafts of *Arenas*, six of which West responded to. Work on the two documents was interleaved and passages of text migrated from one to the other. Here, I offer an initial glimpse into the history of production of these two single-authored texts, a history that is analyzed in greater depth and detail in chapter 8.

West's written responses to Moira's drafts were intense and repeated, consisting of both commentary (e.g., suggestions for revision, sources in the literature, questions) and actual textual revision. The revising West did was often quite extensive. Figure 6.2 presents one page of West's response to *Arenas 5*, the 22-page fifth draft of Moira's conference paper. I counted 17 responses on this page (out of 109 made to the whole draft). I would code all of these responses as text-revising.[4] If incorporated into the next draft, West's responses would add 106 words to this page (out of 332 she would add to the whole draft), delete 83 words (out of 567 she would delete from the whole), and rearrange one passage of the text (one of seven rearrangements proposed for the whole). Moira's typical reaction to this kind of response was to simply incorporate it into the next draft. Figure 6.3 presents the corresponding section of Moira's next draft of *Arenas* with West's words now represented in bold print. To be precise, Moira acted on all 17 of West's responses, adding 105 of the 106 words (the only exception being an error

---

[4]Broadly, I coded responses as text revising or commentary. Text revising effected actual changes to the text (corrections, substitutions, additions, deletions, explicitly signaled rearrangements). Commentary addressed the text without changing it (questions, expositions, directives, contextual issues).

The number of comfort domains available is ~~examined, with attention to~~ *shown in Table 2 by gender* ~~differences~~. The percent ~~described as~~ lacking any arena of comfort is very small all three years, at two percent or less. The modal ~~category~~ *number of comfort arenas is three;* ~~indicates that~~ most boys and girls find comfort in three domains. However, the distribution shows slightly different patterns for boys and girls, with more boys than girls ~~concentrated toward~~ *a t* the lower end of the distribution*s*. ~~As shown in Table 2,~~ Over the three year period, ~~approximately 31~~ *29 to 33* percent of *37 to 42* girls are described as having two or ~~less~~ *fewer* arenas of comfort, compared to ~~40~~ percent of boys*.* ~~reporting two or less comfort spheres. However, over time, the percentage of boys with four arenas of comfort increases, beginning with 11.5 percent in wave one, climbing to 16.4 percent in wave three.~~

[**foot-note this?] ~~One-way analysis of variance were~~ performed *Mean levels of* ~~comparing the number of comfort arenas to~~ six outcome variables (GPA, well-being, self-derogation, self-esteem, depressive affect, and self-efficacy). *were examined in relation to the number of comfort domains using analysis of variance. All our* In general, the cutoff point for significant differences (using Scheffe multiple comparison test) was between two and three, such that adolescents with three or four comfort domains had higher GPA's, greater perceived feelings of self worth and mastery, and were higher on the index of well-being.

~~The last question addressed by this~~ *over* ~~analyses are the advantages of having~~ A *B* *independent* ~~more arenas of comfort.~~ To assess the effects of the number of comfort arenas, this variable and four background control variables (socio-economic status, race, nativity, and family composition) were regressed on GPA and the five mental health constructs; well-being, self-derogation, self-esteem, depressive affect, and self-efficacy....

On the back of this page the comments below were written.

A) relationships were statistically significant and inspection of the means showed generally monotonic changes with the number of arenas of comfort

B) Though Simmons stresses the problems related to the absence of any comfort arena in coping with change, as we have seen, hardly any adolescents report no domain of comfort. We therefore assess whether advantages accrue to adolescents who have more arenas of comfort, in comparison to those with fewer arenas.

FIG. 6.2. Professor West's response to selected text from Moira's *Arenas 5*

West had made in describing a linear relationship as "monotonic"—which means flat), deleting all 83 words that had been crossed out, and making the rearrangement as indicated.

The number of comfort domains available is **shown, by** gender, **in Table 2.** The percent **(X)** lacking any arena of comfort is very small all three years, at two percent or less. The modal **number of comfort arenas is three;** most boys and girls find comfort in three domains. However, the distribution shows slightly different patterns for boys and girls, with more boys than girls **at** the lower end of the distributions. **(X)** Over the three year period, **29 to 33** percent of girls are described as having two or **fewer** arenas of comfort, compared to **37 to 42** percent of boys **(X). (X)**

Though Simmons stresses the problems related to the absence of any comfort arena in coping with change, as we have seen, hardly any adolescents report no domains of comfort. Therefore, we assess whether advantages accrue to adolescents who have more arenas of comfort, in comparison to those with fewer arenas. Mean **levels of** six outcome variables (GPA, well-being, self-derogation, self-esteem, depressive affect and self efficacy) **were examined in relation to the number of comfort domains, using analysis of variance. All relationships were statistically significant and inspection of the means showed generally** linear **changes with the number of arenas of comfort.** In general, the cutoff point for significant differences (using Scheffe multiple comparison test) was between two and three, such that adolescents with three or four comfort domains had higher GPA's, greater perceived feelings of self worth and mastery, and were higher on the index of well-being.

(X) To assess the **independent** effects of the number of comfort arenas, this variable and four background control variables (socio-economic status, race, nativity, and family composition) were regressed on the six dependent variables.

FIG. 6.3. Moira's *Arenas 6* revision of *Arenas 5* text from Figure 6.2. **Bold** print = West's revisions from *Arenas 5* incorporated into *Arenas 6.* (X) = Deletions suggested by West in *Arenas 5* and enacted in *Arenas 6.* Underline = Other changes between *Arenas 5 and 6,* presumably initiated by Moira.

West's words also traveled from *Arenas* to *Prelim.* Figure 6.4 illustrates how West's response to Moira's first draft of the conference paper, *Arenas 1,* worked and reworked collaboratively through subsequent rounds of response and revision, appeared six texts later in Moira's final preliminary examination (*Prelim 4*). Although West introduced considerably fewer changes in this paragraph than in the one seen in Figure 6.2, the changes still represent substantive revisions. For example, the pronoun *it* beginning the second, third, and fourth sentences in *Arenas 1* appears to refer in each case to the initial noun phrase of the first sentence, "a test of the arena of comfort hypothesis." However, with the incorporation of West's suggested revisions, those sentences in *Prelim 4* all refer to the arena of comfort hypothesis itself, not to a test of it. West's proposed deletion of "measures of" in the phrase "objective and subjective measures of change" might also be quite significant (see chap. 8 for further discussion of that revision). In addition to changes in meaning within the paragraph, West's marginal response on *Arenas 1* proposed repositioning the paragraph to a rhetorically prominent position, moving it from the middle to the end of the introductory section in the conference paper. Moira followed that suggestion and the

Arenas 1

A test of the arena of comfort hypothesis would make an important contribution to

several themes currently of interest in sociology, social psychology, and

developmental psychology. *This hypothesis* It addresses the need to examine contexts within which

individual development occurs (Gecas and Seff, 1990), and the impact of

interrelationships between life contexts on human development (Bronfenbrenner

198). It takes into account the influence of larger social structures on interpersonal

contexts, which in turn affect individual well-being. (Simmons, 1988; see also

House, 1981). Finally, it provides an opportunity to distinguish between objective

and subjective measures of *to* change and sort out the relative importance of each for

individual adjustment. The last point, concerning the difference between objective

and subjective measures of transition, marks a modification of the original

hypothesis laid out by Simmons and Blyth.

[margin note: place at end — Good summary]

Prelim 4

In summary, a test of the arena of comfort hypothesis would make an important contribution to several () **issues** currently of interest in sociology, social psychology, and developmental psychology. **This hypothesis** addresses the need to examine contexts within which individual development occurs (Gecas and Seff, 1990), and the impact of interrelationships between life contexts on human development (Bronfenbrenner 1980). *Especially relevant is Bronfenbrenner's concept of "mesosystems" which focuses on the interrelations between two or more context that the individual participates in.* The arena of comfort hypothesis takes into account the influence of **macro** social structures**, related to social class and ethnicity,** on interpersonal contexts, which in turn affect individual well-being (Elder et al., 1986; House and Mortimer, 1990; Simmons, in press ()). Finally, it provides an opportunity to distinguish between objective and subjective () change and **to** sort out the relative importance of each for individual adjustment.

FIG. 6.4. The evolution of a paragraph in Moira's texts. **Bold** print = West's revisions. () = Deletions suggested by West. Underline = Other changes in the text, presumably initiated by Moira. *Italic* = Revisions prompted by West's comment.

paragraph remained in that prominent position throughout subsequent drafts. Pasted from *Arenas 4* to *Prelim 2*, the same paragraph then served as the conclusion of the prelim in all subsequent drafts (incidentally displaying the perceived genre relation between the introduction of research reports and the preliminary examination as a whole).[5]

Figures 6.2, 6.3, and 6.4 illustrate the ways West's words and perspectives came to be embedded in Moira's texts through repeated cycles of response and revision. Although West's participation in the production of these texts is direct and involves the most basic authorial act (transcription of composed language on the text), Moira was represented as the sole author of both *Arenas* and *Prelim*. For these texts, West was represented as a non-author apparently because of institutional constraints: She could not co-author a paper designated for a graduate student session at a conference and certainly could not be represented as an author on Moira's preliminary examination. These examples also suggest how fluid contextual boundaries may be reflected in fluid textual boundaries. Text that West had revised/authored for the conference paper, with the document cycling processes typical for this disciplinary workplace, was then pasted into Moira's prelim exam. As a member of Moira's preliminary examination committee, West then judged Moira's prelim more in accordance with the context of school, as an object signifying Moira's disciplinary knowledge and communicative ability. In Moira's case, West crossed these boundaries between different institutionally situated activities with no signs of dissonance. Relations between production and representation, however, were not always so smooth. As we see later in this chapter, West did not always find the kind of tacit co-authorship displayed in Moira's texts acceptable in preliminary examinations.

TRANSLATIONS FROM PRODUCTION
TO REPRESENTATION: ATTRIBUTING AUTHORSHIP
TO PARK

I have already glossed the way authorship was attributed to Lee for his positional participation in data analysis. Another presentation in the seminar,

---

[5]To be more precise, this "paragraph" concluded the introduction–literature review in *Arenas 2*, but acting on another comment West made in response to that draft, Moira split off the final sentence ("The last point…") to introduce a new paragraph in *Arenas 3*. This two-paragraph structure at the end of the introductory section, although the content continued to be revised, was retained throughout all subsequent drafts of *Arenas*. Only the first of these two paragraphs was transferred from *Arenas 4* to *Prelim 2*.

that of Park, also a NNSE from Korea, illustrates how thin the grounds for such attributions might be. Park had obtained a BA (in Korea) and a master's degree in sociology (in the United States) and then transferred to Midwest University to obtain a PhD degree. He was in his second year of graduate study and had passed the preliminary stage of doctoral candidacy (a qualifying exam that only about one third of his cohort had taken and passed at the end of their first year). Park's main area of interest within sociology had been criminology; however, he also wanted very much to work as an RA rather than a TA. He had applied to and been hired onto the Project the quarter before the official seminar. Although the Project involved a new area, the sociological psychology of human development, with a particular emphasis on adolescence, Park intended to use the Project's data for his dissertation. After completing his PhD, he planned to seek a faculty position in Korea.

At the first meeting of the seminar, when West asked students to review what work they would do, the five students who had sat in on the informal seminars the previous two quarters responded by reviewing the research they were engaged in and the texts (prelims, prospectuses, or articles) they planned to distribute for group discussion. For Park and another new RA who entered the seminar without ongoing projects of their own, West explained that they would be drafting the literature review and data analysis of a technical report for one of the Project's funding sources. She also said she intended the report to eventually be worked up into an article. Park had been assigned the data analysis. At that point, Park asked if it would be possible to change topics. West indicated that they could talk about it later. Whether they did talk about it, I never found out. However, Park did present the tables he was assigned.

The session in which Park and the other student presented their work to the seminar began with discussion of the literature review. After several basic conceptual problems with that review had been hashed out, the discussion turned to Park's tables. The document Park distributed to the seminar was an 11-page handout consisting of a cover sheet listing variables and their abbreviations, followed by 10 pages of raw tables, each consisting of 30 rows and two to four columns of data. Park's writing on the handout was limited to the cover sheet description of variables (e.g., "1. 'B' in each variable represents students' attitudes about their part-time job *during the school year*") and to the table headings (e.g., "Relationship to Work Status"). That writing was likely derived from existing descriptions of the variables and the planned analyses.

Park began the discussion by asking a question. His references to "waves" refer to the years of the data, for example "wave 1" is the questionnaire data from the first year of the Project (see Appendix B for transcription conventions):

Park: I have a question here about the data analysis [6 s.; pages turning] uh, I didn't (distribute all) [1 s.] these output because I'm not sure the ( ) right or wrong, [4 s.], in here what I am trying to do is to compare between waves, controlling for [1 s.]
( ):   oh
Park: Edu- educational aspiration [2 s.], so in case of high aspiration, for example, comparing wave 1 and wave 2, [1 s.] I (chose) the student uh [1 s.] who has high aspiration in wave 1 and wave 2, in that case, what if the student [1 s.] uuhh have- igh high aspiration in wave 1 and in, [1 s.] and the low aspiration in wave 2 [7 s.] aaaahh [9 s.]
( ):   ( ) [1.5 s.] you mean what if their aspirations change.

A 48-second pause (quite a long silence in a seminar discussion) followed this last question as Park stood up, walked to the chalkboard, and began to write out (according to my fieldnotes) the following, evidently computer commands that describe selection of cases for the data he ran on aspirations: High Asp (T1, T2) Sel if W1C072E02 and W2C065E02 T-test pairs=BINT1 BINT2. Park continued:

Park: Well, I like to compare the wave 1 and wave 2 in the highest (region) [1 s.] in this case I chose [1 s.] only a student who have uh [5.5 s.; chalk sounds], who has a high aspiration in wave 1 and who has a high aspiration in wave 2, /but/
West: /Maybe/ you should tell us how you defined aspirations.
Park: (Here) (f) uh 2 means high aspiration
West: Yeah, but- but what does that mean, in terms of responses to survey questions? [7 s.]
Park: Uh, maybe high aspirations ( ) the uh- [2.5 s.]
West: They were planning to go to college? Is that what it means?
??:   / ( )/
Park: /Yeah/ right
West: Ok
Park: Low aspiration means if um less than or equal to high school degree
West: /Ok/
??:   /I see/

West: You're taking people (who) ( ) are hoping to go to college
Park: Yeah
West: Ok
Park: So my question is uh what if the student has a high aspiration in wave
            1 [1.s.] and low aspiration in wave 2, is that still (in)cluded here? Or
            [1.5 s.] included here? [1.5 s.]
West: Well, it would depend on what you were trying to show and what
            (you know), what you were, you know, the rationale behind this, [8.5
            s.] (why) er- were you thinking aspiration might be driving the
            values? or do you think the values might be driving the aspirations?
            or? [1 s.] or what [1.5 s.]
Park: Well, I don't know um, [2 s.] anyway the uh [1 s.] the figures included
            in (the) output is only the student who has a high aspiration in wave
            1 and who has a high aspiration in wave 2.

At this point, other participants, especially Sean, Lee, West, and Park's
co-presenter more or less took over the discussion, deriving from the tables
how many participants actually changed their aspirations (after Park did
not respond to West's first question on this topic). From this point on in
the conversation, Park was rarely consulted in the discussion of his tables
and, when consulted, was rarely able to respond with the information
requested.

The painfully long pauses that pepper the nine turns of Park's question
and his lack of response to substantive questioning on the rationales behind
his analytic decisions created a palpable sense of communicative breakdown.
The long 48-second pause as Park switched from speaking to writing may
have helped clarify his question, but did not do so immediately. Park just
wanted to know if it was appropriate to exclude from analysis students whose
aspirations were inconsistent, high in one year, low in the other. (It turned
out that Park's solution excluded more than 300 of 1,000 student respondents,
making it a questionable procedure for this group.) The sense of breakdown
was displayed in the seminar talk a few minutes after the exchanges just
quoted when West offered an account "to kind of clue up other people in- as
to how this project emerged the way it did." She began by noting that they
had had little time to work on the presentation and had considered postponing
it. Mentioning the literature review the other RA had done and her own
summaries of the data analysis, West then turned to Park's contribution:

And then Park would find the tables which showed the particular trends that I was
describing, and then just put in those few correlations or or t-tests, [someone laughs]
whatever, to illustrate what I'm trying to show in the report, [she laughs] but I um, I

indicated to Park that it might facilitate this uh, if he could have laid it all out, and then just in pencil, uh, indicated, you know, which correlations were significant and which weren't, so that he could uh, you know, see what the pattern was, and then uh organized just a few tables to show the trends, but- but actually you [Park] are presenting much more of the raw data and not gearing it as much to to the report, but we'll, you know, we'll work on that, we have time to develop it, here uh, you know, you can see more what's going on.

The amount and rawness of the data Park presented was not the only issue. West also pointed out that she had intended to focus on gender differences in her summary of the data; however, only three of Park's 10 tables provided data by gender. Much of the rest of the discussion focused on those tables. As attention was turned to them, basic questions were raised about those data as well and again Park was not able to answer those questions effectively. For example, when Lynch wondered about the signs in a column of numbers (saying he expected them all to be positive rather than negative), Park just restated the trend the table displayed rather than taking up the implicit question of its accuracy. After several indirect comments were not taken up by Park, Lynch finally switched to a directive, telling Park to run a particular data analysis to check the signs.

In short, Park was not able to participate very fully in a procedural display (see chap. 4) of "discussing the research." Not only did he have serious problems communicating his ideas to others and understanding what they were saying to him, he had also apparently misconstrued the assigned task. The problems were quite visible, prompting West to account for them in the seminar. Discussion of the research could continue only because others carried it out. Viewed over a longer period of time, Park's participation did not seem much deeper. When I interviewed him three months after his presentation (late in the summer), his comments reinforced the sense of minimal engagement. Asked how he had chosen the presentation, he replied that he had not chosen it, West had, and noted that "the other students [were] different, [they] continue the true work." Asked if he had worked on the data since the seminar presentation, he first said he had not, but then recalled: "there were some mistakes in my presentation of the tables, so professor gave me some kind of directions about how to correct, I corrected it and uh I just gave it to her."

In a text-based interview on the co-presentation, West offered a quite generic representation of Park, focusing more on his position in the Project than on his personal goals or abilities. She noted that Park and the other RA were new to the Project and that she did not feel that they should "be subject to the same requirement of producing a finished paper because they were at a great disadvantage given that the other students had had two quarters to develop their ideas." After reviewing the work they were assigned, West said that they would be continuing to work with her in the summer to co-author a paper and that she felt that Park and the other student had "kind of learned what it meant to integrate some empirical work with some theoretical considerations." She also emphasized that this seminar was a special kind of academic setting, noting that she had such different expectations from different students and that their products differed so markedly. She said that she accepted this diversity in the spirit of professional training, of getting at the students where they were, and that that was why she had chosen to designate the course pass–fail. Turning to Park specifically, she said only that she thought he would be working on the Project for his dissertation and concluded, "I don't really have a sense of his, you know, writing capacity as of this point."

Park's participation in the seminar seemed to be dominated by passing (see chap. 4). He received credit for the seminar, which although it was pass–fail also fulfilled an advanced (hands-on) research requirement, in exchange for attending most seminar sessions silently and for setting up, running, and distributing fairly raw data he had been assigned to run, data that he seemed to understand quite partially and that he had great trouble discussing. His performance was a far cry from the goals West had initially invoked, a final or near-final draft of a major project (prelim, prospectus, article, conference paper) with some data analyzed. It also contrasted sharply with the work of five more senior RAs. Park himself distinguished between the assigned task he did and "the true work" of other students in the seminar. West's interview comments on Park were oriented to justifying the institutional translation of this performance in terms of his position in the Project and his projected work in the future.[6]

---

[6]Passing the course did provide Park with continuing institutional access (failing it would have been a serious problem). This low-demand participation could potentially be of value, particularly for NNSE. Lave and Wenger (1991) found that apprentices often begin with a period of very peripheral participation in a social practice. They suggest that this period can give newcomers a holistic sense of the community of practice and begin the development of social relationships with community members. Some theories of second language acquisition (e.g., Krashen, 1981) have also recommended low-demand participation (even silence) in the initial phases of langiage acquisition. Because of Park's limited linguistic and discursive resources for engaging in complex disciplinary talk, his access to participation was severely circumscribed. In fact, I found it difficult to communicate with Park in a one-to-one interview. Thus, he might have benefited from this mode of participation if it gave him the time and resources he needed to participate more fully in the opportunity spaces the Project afforded. West's stance toward Park's performance seemed at least partially motivated by this kind of reasoning. Whether Park's passing is best viewed as nurture or neglect, however, depends on its ultimate outcome. In Park's case, that outcome stretched beyond the limits of this research. During my research, Park's passing clearly involved very limited participation in sociological practices.

Park's case displays how institutional position in the Project and quite limited participation in producing the tables for a seminar discussion were translated into an attribution of authorship. This translation was more than a temporary convenience for the seminar. Months after the seminar was over, West continued to count Park as one of the co-authors who were working on turning the finished technical report into a journal article. Although my data collection ended at this point and I cannot attest in any way to Park's subsequent contributions, I have noted that the planned journal article was eventually published and that Park appeared as the third author.

TRANSLATIONS FROM PRODUCTION
TO REPRESENTATION: PRIOR TEXT AND PLAGIARISM

The fairly settled representations of authorship in public texts obscure the potential complications for participants in translating the flux of productive activity, such as the co-production of Moira's texts through response–revision rounds, into represented authorship. In this section, I present a paired comparison of two instances of students' using prior text, one of which was treated as an appropriate use of boilerplate, the second of which was identified as problematic, at the least, borderline plagiarism. In other words, this comparison explores the shifting surfaces of authorship and non-authorship at the interface of production and representation.

The text that follows is the entire section entitled DATA SOURCE from Moira's *Arenas 2*.

> DATA SOURCE
> Is it okay to lift this from another AP paper?
> The data were collected in the first, second and third waves of a a four-year longitudinal investigation of the developmental...

In response to Moira's question of whether this section could be lifted from another AP (Adolescence Project) paper, West simply wrote "OK" in the margin. In the next draft, *Arenas 3*, Moira had expanded this section to 83 lines of text (eight paragraphs, about 3 1/2 pages). However, in her written response to *Arenas 3*, West then crossed out without comment 71 of the 83 lines, deleting five of eight paragraphs completely and most of two other paragraphs.

In a text-based interview, West was presented with a copy of Moira's *Arenas 3*. As she flipped through the text, she came across these crossed out passages and without my prompting offered an explanation for her extensive deletion:

> So this was the first one [referring to the text, perhaps thinking it was *Arenas 1*], and here I really felt that she had way too much on the sample, and she had taken this from some other papers that we had done, and I think that's all right so, it's sort of like boilerplate in uh-, you know, lift descriptions of the sample, I don't expect students to have original writing, so that's why I crossed all that ( ), in this particular format I guess—this was a preliminary draft for the [conference] paper—that the people there would not be interested in all that detail, so I just crossed it out …

West went on to explain that she had carefully crafted a standard description of the subjects and the data's statistical characteristics and saw no value in having students rewrite that description from scratch. Here again she may also have been interested in controlling representations of the Project's data (varying only levels of detail). In any case, this was an instance where "lifting" language was acceptable, even desirable. West accounts for her deletion of most of the lifted text as simply a practical judgment of the level of detail appropriate for the audience at a particular conference.

However, in another case, lifted language was represented very differently. In a memo attached to a draft of Linda's preliminary examination, West wrote in part:

> Secondly, some of the passages are clearly lifted from Houston et al. Since you did some of that preview, and I then rewrote the material and added more information, it would be more appropriate for you to paraphrase that paper or place material in quotes. Since that was a joint endeavor, and your prelim (and dissertation) are supposed to be your own work, it is best to avoid duplication that is word for word.

"Houston et al." referred to a journal article, on which Linda was listed as second author and West as fourth. In light of the extensive text revising/authoring that West did for Moira's conference paper and the relationship between that paper and Moira's prelim, I found it interesting to see West asserting in this memo that the prelim and dissertation "are supposed to be your own work."

Asked in a discourse-based interview to comment on West's memo, Linda replied:

> I talked with her after that, after I saw that comment, what I did is I went back to all my original writings for that paper, and uh, I- you know, I just went back to the very beginning, to like my first draft, second draft of those, and took it [i.e., the text in her draft prelim] from that, it just so happened that we [i.e., Houston et al.] took just about everything that I wrote or you know the majority of it, well she [West] made some correction for the paper that was published, but really when I went back to my drafts,

it was what I had written, and that's what I took um, but to avoid any problems at all for the prelim ... I went and made another draft ... I just went through and put quotes, by everything, I figured that would just save any- any trouble, and I was under a time crunch, and I didn't want to go argue about it with them ... anytime I put anything from them, even though I had written it from draft 1, I put quotes, since it was already published, that's all i did, I put quotes, I mean, paragraphs, you know.... but I figured "so what? I wrote it in the beginning," you know, and we had talked about that, and she said "well, that's fine, if it goes back to your first draft, that's fine," but I thought "well, I'm not going to you know go over it again and get in trouble"

Linda concluded that the quotes satisfied West's (and possibly others') concerns about this use of text; however, she was clearly frustrated, insisting that she had written the words originally and liked them, that it was only because the text had been published that she had run into trouble, and that, although the comments suggested she had acted inappropriately, she did not think she had lifted language or done anything wrong.

My fieldnotes report on a conversation with West (about three weeks before my interview with Linda) in which I asked her about these two cases. She noted that Moira had used a standard description of the data set, whereas Linda was copying sections from the literature review of an article. Indicating that she was "shocked" to see the borrowed text in Linda's prelim, West recalled, as she had in the memo, that Linda had given her some rough notes on sources, which she, West, had added to, written up, and shaped into a review of the literature.

These two cases of lifted language suggest the complexities of making situated judgments of authorship and non-authorship. On the one hand, West authorizes Moira's use of prior text (as boilerplate that Moira had played no part in producing) for a public text, the conference paper, presented in a disciplinary forum. On the other hand, West is shocked by Linda's use, for an institutional document (her prelim), of prior text that she both participated in producing and had been officially credited with in represented co-authorship.

The conflict between West's challenges to Linda's authorship and Linda's implicit and explicit claims to authorship were played out in two representational domains: attributions of textual production and appeals to the norms of authorship. West represents Linda's participation in production as limited, indicating that Linda "did some of the preview," producing only rough notes that West had then added to and written up. Linda represents production quite differently, asserting that her own initial draft was used almost word for word in the published article and that what she had pasted into her prelim was from her original draft. West also invokes an institutional norm for student authorship, "the prelim (and dissertation) are supposed to be your own work." Linda tacitly invokes a different norm: The words you write belong to you.

The norm of individual work that West invoked in the memo certainly had considerable institutional force, but also had an obviously problematic relationship to literate practice in this setting (consider Moira's prelim). The "rule" in this case could not be governing practice, but it might be operating as an interpretive scheme within a repertoire (cf. Gilbert & Mulkay, 1984), as a flexible resource for assigning representations of authorship. Why different schemes applied to Moira and Linda is uncertain. The difference might reflect disciplinary traditions in which methodological ideas and text are seen as more public, more routine, less authored than conceptual ideas and text. It might also reflect the difference in West's general assessment of Moira and Linda. Over the previous months, Moira had made rapid progress on her preliminary examination and her dissertation prospectus, while also working on her first conference presentation. West clearly felt good about Moira, describing her work as "outstanding." On the other hand, in our first interview, West stated that she was very worried about Linda's progress, unhappy with her writing for the seminar, and beginning to question her ability to complete the PhD. As Hull, Rose, Fraser, and Castellano (1991) reported in their study, a teacher's perception of problems and errors in a text may be, in part, a function of her confidence in the student. The differences might also relate to the specific ways that West came to represent textual production in her memory (although we would still need to account for those memory differences).

In any case, the analyses sketched in this episode offer a glimpse into the ways authorship and non-authorship (and, not incidentally, disciplinary participation) were negotiated as complex links were forged between situated histories of textual production and situated histories of the representation of that production. These accounts focus on LeFevre's middle range of collaborative inventional processes. While this kind of social distribution of invention among people and over time is a key element in the notion of mediated authorship, it is nevertheless only a partial account of mediation. Chapter 7 turns to the question of how sociohistorically developed resources sedimented in artifacts, practices, and institutions also participate in authorship.

7

Voices in the Networks: Distributed Agency in Streams of Activity

The accounts of chapter 6 begin to situate authorship in the socially distributed activities of collaborative invention and authorship attribution. Although these accounts complicate simple, idealized images of the solitary writer or the writer–reader in literate conversation, they still fall well within our broader sociocultural repertoire of accounts—structures of cooperative team work (or, for that matter, forced labor). As narratives, they conform to the conventional folk model of action that locates agency in individuals: People act individually, even if in concert; things are acted on; and the environment is a stage, a fixed passive context, on which action take places. To articulate a fuller account of mediated authorship, I must take up the harder task of describing ways that sociohistoric tools-in-use actively participate in authorship, ways that they operate to enable, channel, and constrain both the substance and participation frameworks of literate invention. I can list diverse tools implicated in the Project sociologists' work: disciplinary and everyday language, genres, and concepts; mathematical systems; computer hardware and software; psychometric and sociometric scales; the nested institutional structures of seminar, research team, department, university, profession, and state; social identities; institutional forums for disciplinary communication (conferences, journals, books); and so on. Proximal or distal, such tools-in-use must form the fabric of literate practices and textual artifacts. However, to move beyond chanting such lists of mediational means as a kind of sociohistoric mantra, we need to weave tools into specific accounts of writing, to give these silent tools a voice in the constitution of activity.

Because mediation is at the heart of mediated authorship, our ways of understanding mediation are a central issue here. Following Vygotsky's notion of psychological and material tool mediation, Bruner (1990) and

Wertsch (1991) have argued that each person's activity is mediated by what they refer to as a cultural toolkit, a collection of cultural artifacts and practices. These toolkits are, to a large extent, culturally prefabricated, already there for human actors. However, cultures do not dispense standard toolkits to all their members. "Cultures" are mosaics of highly differentiated historical streams of activity, and even within a particular stream of activity, participants' experiences are still perspectival, at best partially shared. For example, in the most closely knit, egalitarian nuclear family, each member will have differential access to and participation in "common" experiences and practices. Most social contexts impose additional differentiation as social categorizations (e.g., of gender, ethnicity, class, generation, group affiliation) further shape access to and participation in social practices. Finally, psychological tools (artifacts and practices) cannot simply be passed from person to person; they must be appropriated. In a sense, the nature of cultural toolkits, and hence of mediated authorship, hinges especially on our accounts of appropriation.

Extending Bakhtin's argument that what is appropriated in language learning is situated historical utterance rather than Saussure's abstract *langue*, I would suggest that all psychological tools are encountered in particular and concrete forms and appropriated dialogically. Central to appropriation is a person's affective and evaluative orientations to a tool: Tools may be encountered, partially appropriated, and then rejected. In other words, people develop varied dispositions toward and senses of ownership over the psychological tools they encounter and (to some degree) appropriate. Nor is appropriation a one-time event. Once initially appropriated, a tool begins a life that can take a variety of courses. Without further use, the tool may be lost. With further use, it is transformed as familiarity increases depth of access or facility of use, as new contexts of use arise, and as emergent properties or improvised functions are reappropriated. In this lifetime, the tool, its relations to an evolving toolkit, and the sociomaterial contexts of its use are all changing. In other words, appropriation is always a selective, partial, transformative, and ongoing process, not a one-shot transmission.[1]

As was noted in chapter 1, an account of appropriation cannot be limited to internalization, but must include externalization and coordination as well.

---

[1]Discussing transmission in science and technology, Latour (1987) contrasts humans metaphorically to material conductors and semi-conductors, characterizing us as unpredictable *multi-conductors,* who ignore, drop, deflect, modify, add to, corrupt, and recontextualize the claims and objects we encounter (and, of course, often do several of these things simultaneously).

For many activities, what is appropriated is not a way of acting independently, but of acting-with. Externalizations of speech, writing, drawing, and modeling produce external artifacts that then enter into and structure subsequent courses of action.[2] Much activity involves continuous interaction with external objects. I do not, for example, internalize the piano when I learn to play it, the car when I learn to drive it, the computer and its graphic software when I learn to draw with them, or the mountain cliff when I learn to climb it. In each case, I learn to act-with these objects, not to act independently. I may be able to pantomime the activity, say of driving, but the pantomime will differ from actual driving (and not just because I do not travel anywhere). In some cases, acting-with can be so extensively internalized that the activity can go forward without the external objects (e.g., playing chess mentally, memorizing a text so that it can be recited instead of read). Inner speech is an exceptional example of such internalization. It is important to note that as internalization points to the sociogenesis of the person, externalization points to the sociogenesis of the tools themselves as the sedimented artifacts of human activity.

What emerges from such situated processes of appropriation and use is not a kit of uniform psychological tools, but of tools forged in a variable geometry of centripetal and centrifugal forces. In this chapter, I explore the ways that such tools mediate authorship, particularly analyzing ways that functional systems of literate activity in *Sociology* mediated the authorship (agency) of a graduate student as he developed his dissertation research. However, that analysis first requires careful reflection on the central trope of tool use and on strategies for analyzing the role of tools in activity. Central to the argument of this chapter is the fundamental recognition that the process of sedimentation in tools (artifacts, practices, and institutions), like that of appropriation in persons, transforms concrete situated activity into tacit, abbreviated, and presuppositional forms.

"IF I HAD A HAMMER ... ": REFLECTIONS ON ARTIFACTS, ACTIVITIES, AND AGENCY

The humanist psychologist Abraham Maslow is reported to have said, "If the only tool you have is a hammer, you tend to treat everything as a nail."

---

[2]In spite of our images of language as internalized dictionaries and grammar books (see chap. 1), talk is an acting-with practice. Clark's (1992) research on referencing as co-action is an example of the different view of talk that emerges when its processes are examined.

Although Maslow was interested in helping people to overcome the role of habitual thought and behavior patterns on the road to greater self actualization, this aphorism captures a central insight of sociohistoric theories, the way that human culture is transmitted and transformed through the historical development and situated use of mediational means (tools or artifacts) in systems of activity. For sociohistoric theories, such means include not only physical objects like hammers, computers, books, and buildings, but also more dispersed, less tangible phenomena, like languages, bodies of knowledge, institutions, and situated practices. Holland and Cole (1995) use the hammer to illustrate ways that a tool comes to embody both a theory of a task and of the persons who will engage in it:

> The generic function of hammers is to connect two or more objects by driving a nail (or its equivalent) through them. Although hammers can be used for a (restricted variety) of other tasks (those where hitting something is functional, as in war; as a door jam or a paperweight), their shapes are predominantly shaped by their nail-driving function. In Gibson's (1979) terms, hammers "afford" hitting nails. (p. 482)

From a different perspective, this last sentence echoes Maslow's aphorism.

A key concept for Gibson's (1979) ecological psychology, *affordance* is the notion that things objectively, but relationally, invite particular perceptions and actions. For example, a flat horizontal surface may afford sitting, lying, standing on, or running over for a person. If the surface is water, those affordances disappear for the person, but at least the last two remain for a water bug. Because an affordance combines features of the environment with capacities and activities of the organism, affordances are fundamentally relational and, thus, complex, fluid, and multiple.

> The fact that a stone is a missile does not imply that it cannot be other things as well. It can be a paperweight, a bookend, a hammer, or a pendulum bob. It can be piled on another rock to make a cairn or a stone wall.... The theory of affordances rescues us from the philosophical muddle of assuming fixed classes of objects, each defined by its common features and then given a name. As Ludwig Wittgenstein knew, you *cannot* specify the necessary and sufficient features of a class of things to which a name is given. They have only a "family resemblance." But this does not mean you cannot learn how to use things and perceive their uses. (Gibson, 1979, p. 134)

In addition to surfaces, objects, and tools, Gibson extended the notion of affordance to organisms (e.g., a person's embodied behaviors afford particular perceptions and actions to another person). His notion of ecological affordances embraced cultural phenomena as well. For example, he suggested that a post box "affords letter-mailing to a letter-writing human in a community with a postal system" (p. 139).

Holland and Cole (1995) also stress the cultural elaboration of tools, pointing to ways hammers have been tailored to specific tasks:

> Despite a common objective—to drive nails and fasten two objects together—the differences between hammers bespeak a difference in the appropriate way to mediate activity; it would be as ludicrous to use a sledgehammer to fasten a picture hanger as to use a tack hammer to drive spikes into railroad ties. And so it is with all forms of mediated activity: the principle of mediation implies that each new combination of goals, conditions, and mediational means constitutes a distinctive functional system of behavior (Luria, 1928; Vygotsky, 1929). And in so doing, the functional system "affords" certain tasks and presumes certain types of people. (pp. 482–483)

Holland and Cole's point is that a hammer presupposes not only nails, but particular sociohistoric ensembles (cultural types of structures, construction materials, processes, people).[3] Like other artifacts then, a hammer is an externalized objectification of sociohistoric activity in the world, embodying the co-evolution of tools and worlds.

Without losing these insights, however, I want to pause at this point to explore some problematic baggage that may travel with the trope of tools. Holland and Cole (1995) actually suggest not only that hammers embody and afford, but that they *impose*, a theory of task and person. However, to treat nail hammering (and its ensemble) as *the* function of hammers, we must fix a perspective that privileges nail hammering (even if that perspective is, as I would agree it is, invited by the hammer and its makers). Especially when we fix such perspectives tacitly, we risk an overdetermined and incomplete account of tools and their contexts. This risk can be illustrated in two ways.

First, as Holland and Cole note, but seem to dismiss as unimportant, hammers, like other tools, can be flexibly transformed through being recruited into other activities. As a weighty object, the hammer could be used as a paperweight, a piece of exercise equipment, or a handy weapon. It might be fused into a modern sculpture or displayed as a cultural icon in a museum or as part of an educational project (e.g., on blacksmithing). Although these other uses of hammers may not be intended in their design and may be restricted, both statistically and functionally (i.e., I can't imagine using hammers to wash dishes), such uses are neither finite nor

---

[3]As Jarmon and Bogen (1996) have demonstrated, what hammers afford in the way of nail driving is not transparent. In a videotaped study of how novice hammerers at a Habitat for Humanity site learned and were taught the affordances of the hammer, Jarmon and Bogen foreground the complex ensemble involved (the way to hold the body and move the arm, rhythms of striking, the kinds of materials used in construction, the ways nails enter wood, etc.).

terribly exotic.[4] As Gibson (1979) suggested for stones, the hammer affords all these uses, whether intended or not.

Second, the problem with tacit perspective fixing becomes even clearer when we consider the functions for which hammers have been designed. Holland and Cole (1995) state that the generic function of hammers is to drive nails or some equivalent in order to connect two objects, and their examples of specialized hammers all fit this generic function. However, hammers are not and have not been so limited. Beginning with neolithic stonework and extending to ancient and modern metalworking, first hammerstones and then metal hammers have been used to shape and form other tools.[5] The blacksmith's hammer is one example. Hammers have also been used to break up rocks in settings as varied as ancient copper mines, prisoner chain gangs, and modern geologists' fieldwork. One line of hammer-like devices, mallets, have been used for millennia in joinery (connecting objects, especially furniture, without nails or pegs) and in woodworking and stonecarving as part of the operations of chiseling. The specialization of hammers is often expressed in the total design of the tool. The familiar hammer with a curved nail-pulling claw is only one such tool. Ripping hammers, used in demolition, have straight claws. Bricklayer's hammers, used for cutting, scoring, and breaking bricks, include a sharp bit end (not a claw) as well as a face. In addition, there are a variety of hammer-like devices built into machines: power-driven hammers for mining and metalworking, pile drivers, the hammers of a piano. The examples of mallets and piano hammers also raise the issue of how to relate our conventions for naming to the tools themselves. In a sense, what we now call hammers fit into a family of percussive devices with blurred Wittgensteinian lines. In any case, the diversity of prefabricated forms and functions for *hammers* alone suggests that in fixing a perspective, we are privileging a cultural prototype (the most familiar use for hammers in current U.S. society, and particularly in noncraft-oriented academic circles, probably does involve nail hitting). Moreover, our everyday model for use of any tool involves an

---

[4]Of course, the hammer has also come to have a variety of graphic or verbal significations. Associated with manual labor, the hammer was incorporated into Marxist symbology, prominently on the hammer and sickle flag of the former Soviet Union. As a metadiscursive trope, we can *hammer* points home or *hammer* someone's argument into pieces. Probably combining its leftist labor association with its metadiscursive uses, the hammer is repeatedly mentioned in the well-known folk song alluded to in the heading of this section.

[5]See, for example, Blackburn (1974); Singer, Holmyard, and Hall (1954); and Singer, Holmyard, Hall, and Williams (1957) for more on hammers and their history.

external tool and a tool user, reinforcing rather than softening the boundaries between subjects and mediators in activity. Thus, prototypical perspectives are an issue to take seriously in thinking about cultural tools and toolkits if we want to avoid problematic reifications not only of tools, but of associated tasks, persons, and contexts.

The trope of tool use emphasizes the instrumental, functional character of semiotic and material culture. It can point usefully to ways that artifacts come to embody histories of activity and to afford congruent activities (including congruent goals, subjective stances, and so on). To avoid the problematic baggage of this trope, we can return to the larger point Holland and Cole (1995) were making, that "each new combination of goals, conditions, and mediational means constitutes a distinctive functional system of behavior" (pp. 482–483). Whereas Luria (1979) talked about functional systems in terms of invariant goals and outcomes being variably achieved, Newman, Griffin, and Cole (1989) point to the likelihood of variations in goals and outcomes as well, suggesting a more perspectival, negotiated view of functional systems. Beyond that, I see a need to distinguish between two senses of functional system, a distinction analogous to the one Bakhtin (1986) draws between concrete utterances and their typifications (speech genres). On the one hand, a functional system can refer to a particular situated functional system. To paraphrase another aphorism, we can never step in the same stream of activity twice; every instance of situated activity involves some variation in goals, conditions, and mediational means, and, even in the course of a brief action, goals, conditions, and means are dynamic and perspectival. On the other hand, a functional system can be typified (i.e., relatively stabilized or prefabricated). Situated functional systems align with other instances to form typified functional systems not only by the principle of family resemblance, but also by cultural-historical co-genesis. One way functional systems can become stabilized is through sedimentation and prefabrication, the tailoring of tools.

A STRATEGY FOR ANALYZING TOOLS: REANIMATING VOICES IN HISTORY

In action research that examined the use of a computer mathematics game in classrooms in the United States and Russia, Griffin, Belyaeva, Soldatova and the Velikhov-Hamburg Collective (1993) found that the structure of the computer program was shaping not only the options available within the game and its practice sessions, but also the ways students interacted with the program, other students, and instructors. In other words, the program was strongly affording particular constructions of contexts, academic tasks, and participant roles. Most tellingly, it discouraged practices (repetition and reanalysis of solutions; collaborative learning) that instructors and researchers desired. To account for the active role the program played in constituting the contexts of instruction, Griffin et al. (1993) turned to the history of the program and realized that embedded in the game were the programmers' ideological perspectives on learning: "Part of our contexts had been 'prefabricated' by the programmers of the software; their contributions about what could and should be done in the educational context were revealed in screen displays. The programmers had to be treated as 'hidden' members of the communicative interactions, with distant but powerful 'voices'" (p. 126). Embodied in the computer game, the frozen "voices" of the programmers presupposed and thus shaped the communicative contexts of its live users (students and teachers).

In an ethnographic analysis of biochemical research at the Salk Institute, Latour and Woolgar (1986) also explored prefabrication. Arguing that scientific knowledge was achieved in the construction of chains of inscriptions, they described how each inscriptional artifact simplified and codified results that could then be incorporated as *black boxes* (unexamined givens) in the construction of cascading networks (e.g., observations recorded as columns of data turned into tables and graphs incorporated in scientific articles cited in subsequent articles and grant applications leading to funding of further observations). In addition to these textual artifacts, they also noted the durable inscription of theories and facts in the scientific instruments (like the spectrometer) and objects (like radioactive isotopes) that co-produced many of the "original" inscriptions.[6]

To reopen textual and material black boxes, Latour (1987) proposes a strategy of following the actors, particularly of tracing artifacts to earlier stages of their development before they became black boxed. With this strategy, which points outward to widening networks, to other times, places, and activities, Latour was able to illustrate substantial differences between science and technology in the making and science and technology as made. For this network analysis, he also argues that humans and non-humans must be treated symmetrically. In recent actant-network theory (e.g., Callon, 1996; Latour, 1993) the symmetrical treatment of non-humans as full

---

[6]For example, they describe the mass spectrometer as "the reified part of a whole field of physics … an actual piece of furniture which incorporates the majority of an earlier body of scientific activity" (p. 242).

subjects has led to a reconceptualization of epistemological issues as questions of ontological politics, in which processes of consultation must legitimate representation, "speaking for" others, whether human or non-human. In this ontological politics, non-humans can be said to be *re*animated because they regain the status they held before modernity (Latour, 1993).

Griffin et al's (1993) analysis of the computer program and Latour and Woolgar's (1986; also Latour, 1987) of biochemical research represent separate traditions, but display a significant convergence in their strategy for analyzing sedimented artifacts.[7] That strategy could be seen as an expansion of Vygotsky's genetic methodology from the sociogenesis of persons to the sociogenesis of functional systems and their diverse elements. The basic strategy involves: (a) identifying the elements of a functional system of activity; (b) tracing the histories of some key elements, especially to recover the particular motives, goals, values, and practices interiorized in material and semiotic artifacts and practices as affordances; and (c) reanimating artifacts, treating them as participants with a voice in constituting contexts of activity. In Latour's theory, this reanimation is linked to the principle of symmetry, which proposes that people and things be treated equally as semiotic actants. In sociohistoric traditions, reanimation involves the recovery of the cultural-historic, institutional, and individual origins of artifacts, with no implication of Latourian symmetry.

REANIMATING TOOLS IN THE LITERATE ACTIVITY OF *SOCIOLOGY*

To examine ways that artifacts, practices, persons, and institutions mediated authorship in *Sociology*, I first explore the sociogenesis of several key mediational means. By returning to critical moments in which such means as the seminar, sociology as a discipline, psychosocial scales, funded research projects, and sociological genres were visibly in the making, I hope to reconstruct their sedimented affordances. I then analyze how one student's dissertation research was formed and re-formed in interaction with such means. Together, these analyses are designed to reanimate voices

---

[7]This strategy is also clearly articulated in Engestrom (1993) and Hutchins (1995). Hutchins, for example, argues: "We may attempt to put temporal bounds on the computation that we observe now, today, in any way we like, but we will not understand that computation until we follow its history back and see how structure has been accumulated over centuries in the organization of the material and ideational means in which the computation is actually implemented" (p. 168).

hardened in the networks of disciplinarity, to suggest how such voices are appropriated in situated activity, and to explore the construction of situated and typified functional systems.

The Seminar as a Progressive Institution

One of the background contexts much in need of reanimation is the institution of the seminar itself. Its history indexes critical sociohistorical changes in the function of the academy and disciplines, changes that have helped define modern societies. The last three decades of the 1800s saw a rapid growth of universities and disciplines in the United States and the spread of new forms of educational and disciplinary activity, particularly emanating from universities and institutes in Germany. In this new activity, universities were seen as sites for the production of new and socially useful knowledge through original research; traditional roles were reconfigured as faculty became knowledge producers and students, their active apprentices; and instructional practices shifted to serious dialogue (rather than oral exercises) and written (as opposed to oral) examination (see e.g., Clark, 1989; Gellert, 1993; Hoskin, 1993; Leventhal, 1986; McClelland, 1980). One of the early figures in this German development, Wilhelm von Humboldt, wrote, "The relationship between teacher and student ... is changing. The former does not exist for the sake of the latter. They are both at the university for the sake of science and scholarship" (quoted in Gellert, 1993, p. 8). Where von Humboldt's comments point to the internal reorganization of knowledge practices (science and scholarship), the role of knowledge in society was itself in flux, emerging as the driving force for two metanarratives of progress, the modernization of the secular nation–state and the personal growth of the autonomous individual.

The seminar in the humanities and emerging social sciences and the laboratory in the physical sciences were basic manifestations of this new progressive educational practice. In the late 1800s, U.S. universities began to develop graduate education and faculty scholarship in line with this new configuration of higher education. The sociology seminar and the departmental program it was part of were descendants of those early German seminars. They renewed the fundamental practices of having students present written work for critical review (oral and written) by peers and professors and of requiring students to advance through a sequence of institutional written examinations that would culminate in the writing of a piece of original research.

Sociology

In the wake of these new modes of knowledge production and their institutionalization in higher education, disciplines underwent an intense period of re-formation, marked by increasing specialization, professionalization, and differentiation. As one of these institutionalized disciplines, sociology was about a century old when I began research in the Project/seminar. One of the founders of sociology in the U.S. was Albion Small, the first chair of the first sociology department in the world and the first editor of the first sociology journal in the United States. Small also helped to found in 1905, and later served as an early president of, the American Sociology Society (later Association). Under his institutional leadership, the University of Chicago became the dominant school of sociology in the United States in the early decades of this century.[8]

As Small promoted sociology in the 1890s, he had to work hard to constitute disciplinarity, to establish his vision of sociology as a science of society against other competing sociologies (Marxism, social welfare movements, Christian sociology). The boundary work (Gieryn, 1983) that Small engaged in is striking to a reader a century later. In the preface to one of the first sociology textbooks, Small and Vincent (1894) contrasted what people had so far thought about social forces and facts (which was "interesting") with the "positive knowledge" of society to be derived from "the method of observation and induction" (p. 15). Later in the preface, they warned of two dangers to scientific sociology. The first was the "destructive dogmas" of social revolutionaries (à la the French Revolution). They argued that "the teacher must impress the pupil with the belief that his primary task is not to reform society, but to understand society" (p. 19). The second danger they pointed to was "the possibility that certain mystical preachers will be mistaken for sociologists" (p. 19). In 1894, when Small wrote to William Harper, the President of the University of Chicago, to request funding for a journal of sociology, he struck a similar note in his arguments, for example:

> 3. Sociology is the most recent, the most difficult, the most complex and the most misunderstood of all the sciences pertaining to society. Every silly and mischievous doctrine which agitators advertise, claims Sociology as its sponsor. A scientific journal of Sociology could be of practical service in every issue, in discrediting pseudo-sociology and in forcing social doctrinaires back to accredited facts and principles. (Dibble, 1975, p. 164)

---

[8]See Turner and Turner (1990) on the early institutional history of sociology in the United States.

In France, Durkheim was also concerned that readers might confuse scientific sociology with other varieties of social thought. In the preface of his 1895 monograph *The Rules of Sociological Method* (Durkheim, 1982), he worked to distinguish sociology from common sense reasoning, moral judgment, and philosophical speculation. This policing of sociology's borders did not quickly subside with its institutionalization. Discussing the teaching of another Chicago sociologist, Robert Park (who played an intellectual role comparable to Small's institutional role), Faris (1967) notes that "more than once he drove students to anger or tears by growling such reproofs as, 'You're another one of those damn do-gooders'" (p. 35).

Central to the early foundational texts of sociology was the notion that a science of society must be developed to offer surer, more objective knowledge than everyday opinion, philosophical speculation, or partisan politics. A key element in both Small's and Durkheim's view of this science was the use of statistical methodologies for ascertaining social facts. Almost a century later, the sociologists of the Project worked in a field, however complex and contested, that was established and widely institutionalized in college departments, textbooks, professional associations, conferences, journals, and disciplinary literature. As disciplinary topics, scientific objectivity, statistical methodology, and potential social benefits remained highly visible; however, much of the boundary work had become sedimented and presupposed. Thus, the Project sociologists never had to warn readers not to confuse their work with, say, liberation theology.[9]

Empirical Sociology, Graduate Education, and Research Institutes.

As Turner and Turner (1990) note, from its beginnings sociological research generally involved some kind of survey methodology for the collection, tabulation, analysis, and reporting of data on communities, groups, and institutions. This kind of research activity is labor intensive and provided an impetus for institutional formations that would distribute the work. As Bulmer (1984) notes, Robert Park and Ernest Burgess, the leading scholar–mentors in Chicago sociology in the 1920s, were particularly active in developing institutional forums (i.e., the Society for Social Research and the Local Community Research Committee) to complement seminars. Like seminars, those forums integrated the tasks of producing social research,

---

[9]On the other hand, in seminar talk there was explicit discussion of how to construct and maintain boundaries between psychology and sociology.

sociologists, and sociology as a discipline.

The need for such forums was the focus of the 1962 presidential address to the American Sociological Association (ASA). Paul Lazarsfeld (1993), a mathematician turned sociologist who led in the development of quantitative empirical research (i.e., a combination of surveying and statistical analysis), argued for the value of research institutes tied to universities:

> They provide technical training to graduate students who are empirically inclined; the projects give students opportunities for closer contact with senior sociologists; the data collected for practical purposes furnish material for dissertations through more detailed study, or what is sometimes called secondary analysis; the members of a Department with an effective institute can give substance to their lectures with an enviable array of actual data; skills of intellectual cooperation and division of labor are developed; chances for early publications by younger sociologists are enhanced. (pp. 267–268)

The Project was not precisely an institute in Lazarsfeld's sense; however, with its multi-year grant, the Project did create an institute-like structure. Its research was funded as a result of the social–disciplinary negotiation of a refereed grant proposal (see Myers, 1990, for provocative case studies of such negotiations in biology). It attracted a number of graduate students and several faculty members to the issues the Project was addressing and the data it was producing. With this mix of senior and junior members, *Sociology* functioned as a site of disciplinary enculturation as well as of knowledge production. Seminar sessions could be seen as what Ochs, Smith, and Taylor (1989) call an opportunity space, "a temporal, spatial, and social moment which provides for the possibility of joint activity" (pp. 238–239).[10] Because it was aligned with multiple institutional activities (other courses, departmental advising and examination, the Project, disciplinary forums), the seminar provided occasions in which students' draft texts were responded to by a group that was known and knowledgeable, interested and responsible.[11] The seminar sessions of the Project, both informal and formal, certainly did provide most of the benefits that Lazarsfeld listed. As a typified functional system, this team structure had complex properties, dividing research labor but also working to coordinate joint

---

[10]Analyses of bedtime story practices (e.g., Heath, 1982), sharing time in elementary classrooms (e.g., Cazden, Michaels, & Tabor, 1985; Wertsch & Minick, 1990), and family narratives at the dinner table (e.g., Ochs, Taylor, Rudolph, & Smith, 1992) have suggested the importance of everyday opportunity spaces in the acquisition of sociocultural values and practices associated with schooling and literacy.

[11]Ochs et al. (1992) argue that, in such familiar settings (marked by trust and shared subject

attention and activity, bringing multiple perspectives and talents to bear on a particular problem space but also channeling that multiplicity through the personal lenses of the principal investigator.

Elaine West, PI

Sociological and sociohistoric theory (e.g., Bakhtin, 1986; Cole, 1983; Crane, 1972) alike emphasize the role of dominant individuals, whether they are referred to as elites or authoritative voices, in the establishment, maintenance, and transformation of social formations. In this sense, the historical production of certain kinds of people is central to the development and stabilization of literate and disciplinary activity. In his 1962 ASA address, Lazarsfeld (1993) stressed the critical role played by the administrator of a research institute, emphasizing the position's challenging intersection of institutional and intellectual functions. As the principal investigator of the Project, West's voice was certainly a dominant one both institutionally and intellectually across time and contexts. She was centrally involved in designing the research; securing its funding; hiring its employees; overseeing data collection and analysis; controlling access to the data; supervising, teaching, and mentoring its RA–students; and responding to and co-authoring its institutional and disciplinary publications.

In designing the Project, West (with input from Lynch and others) had selected from a range of potential problems to address and methods to utilize. These choices became sedimented in the Project and routinely appeared in the special topics (see chap. 3) that participants stressed. Topically, some of the key disciplinary values the Project offered were that it would address a set of established questions through a longitudinal panel design rather than a cross-sectional or trend design,[12] would work with a large sample of adolescents, would collect data related to multiple contexts (including questionnaires for parents and guardians), and would use sophis-

---

knowledge), people are more likely to take risks and to engage in the kinds of complex linguistic, cognitive, and social interactions central to theory building and critical thinking. Certainly, the negotiation of Sean's prospectus in the seminar displayed this kind of risky, complex discursive play (see Prior, 1994).

[12]In panel designs, surveys or questionnaires are administered two or more times to a single set of subjects in order to analyze change. In the 1940s, Lazarsfeld (see 1993) had argued for the value of panel research over cross-sectional designs (where a single survey samples groups at different points in some process, such as freshmen and seniors in a college) or longitudinal trend studies (where repeated surveys are done, but with different respondents).

ticated statistical analyses of the data.[13] Vesting these various forms of power in a single person (see Fig. 6.1 for a partial codification of West's roles) represents a centripetal strategy, not in the sense that West was functioning as the sole originator of the ideas and issues the Project addressed, but in the sense that her social formation as a person, her particular dialogic appropriation of activities, was being expressed in her actions. For her own dissertation research, West had done secondary analysis on another large longitudinal data set (also a panel). Thus, in leading the Project, she was assuming full responsibility, the role of principal investigator initiating her own data set, within the kind of institutional structure in which her own sociological practices had been formed.[14]

Measures, Designs, and Data

During World War II (WWII), social research received massive infusions of government money as it studied issues of morale at home and abroad (Turner & Turner, 1990). In the aftermath of the war, sociology in the U.S. experienced considerable growth and benefited from increased funding (foundation and federal). In this period, a new style of social research also emerged, one that rejected macrosocial theorizing and sought instead to tackle intermediate problems. For example, in the 1940s, Lazarsfeld's research practices used descriptive statistical analyses of survey and questionnaire data to relate measures of individual psychology to measures of social contexts. When this kind of approach to research was recast by others around hypothesis testing and the use of statistical tests of significance, the result was a robust research literature:

> The spread of this new research format was dramatic. An enormous number of quantitative studies of this kind were produced. ... By 1965, no less than 2500 "measures" had been invented and reported in the sociological literature, and an enormous body of methodological folklore had grown up about the pitfalls of various methods, samples, and statistical techniques. (Turner & Turner, 1990, p. 116)

As Turner and Turner note, a key element in such research is the selection

---

[13]These topical emphases could be seen when West deleted most of the boilerplate on data sources from Moira's conference paper (see chap. 6). The text West left, because she felt it would be important for the audience at the conference, emphasized the panel design, the size of the adolescent sample, the retention rate of subjects, and the completeness of the parent–guardian sample.

[14]Perhaps as Lazarsfeld suggested in his 1962 address (Lazarsfeld, 1993), learning to do sociology in a research team does help develop future scholar–administrators.

of measures (questionnaire items), many of which take the form of standard psychometric and sociometric scales.[15] Although it employed the next generation of statistical methods and the depth of the research literature on its measures had increased markedly over the decades, the Project was clearly an outgrowth of this post-WWII research tradition.

Like Griffin et al.'s (1993) computer programs or Latour and Woolgar's (1986) scientific instruments, these measures, developed collectively over time, carry sedimented voices. They have particular wordings, address particular interests, are associated with an intertextual history of use and outcomes, and are grounded in particular theoretical systems, terms, and concerns. Drawing on Fleck's (1979) notion of active and passive constraints, Bazerman (1988) has argued that, when scientists seek to construct and negotiate reliably reconstitutable objects, they must contend with both the "active" constraints of social and rhetorical work and resources and the "passive" constraints of the world. In different terms, Latour's (1987) actant-network theory offers a similar perspective, arguing that scientists must mobilize human and non-human allies as they seek to fabricate mobile, stabilized objects and theories. In Pickering's (1995) terms, these kinds of captures of agency are always mediated and involve the development of interactive stabilizations (e.g., finding items that people respond to with some consistency). Thus, the data, that amalgam of measures, participants' responses, coding, and descriptive displays, speak in multiple tongues.[16] As we see in the next section, its affordances have a major voice in the Project sociologists' representations of their work and the world.

Genre

All of the texts produced by the participants in the seminar displayed organizational, topical, and stylistic features of a basic textual form of science and social science, the experimental report (see, e.g., Bazerman, 1988; Myers, 1990; Swales, 1990).[17] Experimental report genres are constructed from particular social voices as well as formal arrangements

---

[15]The importance of measures in this kind of research is displayed in Miller's (1991) *Handbook of Research Design and Social Measurement*, where 249 pages are devoted to scales.

[16]Latour's (1993) references to quasi-objects and quasi-subjects seem to address a similar point (although I am not sure how this mixing is reflected in a semiotic actant). Ilyenkov's arguments on the ideality of the material-artifactual world are perhaps more relevant here (see Bakhurst, 1991).

[17]The research reports produced in the Project represent genres with a long history. Bazerman (1988)

and rhetorical moves. As Wertsch (1990) notes, science has been articulated in a distinctive voice, what he calls the Western voice of rationality. The texts from the seminar took up this voice. Thus, personal experience, narrative, informal registers, situational contexts, and signals of emotion were normally absent from such texts, although they were often highly visible in interview accounts of goals and decisions and in the seminar negotiation of research plans and texts (see Prior, 1994). As in other scientific settings (e.g., Knorr-Cetina, 1981; Latour & Woolgar, 1986), research decisions with strong local influences were represented as canonical and traditional, as reasonably driven by the prior literature, public interest, and the nature of the data to be analyzed.

Turner and Turner (1990) sketch the typical organizational schemes and content that have characterized empirical sociological reports since the 1950s:

> The typical study done under this model was a dissertation or journal article that had the following form: a review of the "theory" behind the problem (usually no more than a few remarks on the interest of a past master in some more or less closely related problem, and at times no more than a reference to the previous research on the subject); a formulation of a "hypothesis" and discussion of the sample, the "design" of the research, and the methods of measurement or operationalizing the "concepts"; the presentation of the findings, usually presented in tables and accompanied by a discussion of the statistical methods that produced a judgment of significance; and a conclusion that suggested some researchable implications of the finding. (p. 115)

Their description aligns well with the kinds of texts the Project sociologists produced. However, the sociologists of the Project/seminar were working more in a system of genres (Bazerman, 1994b) that included tabular presentations of data, research memos, draft and final versions of grant proposals, conference papers, technical reports, journal articles, preliminary examinations, dissertation prospectuses, and dissertations.

---

documents some early events in their formation. His accounts trace the substantial influence of situated historical actors such as Oldenburg, the correspondent turned editor who worked to establish *The Philosophical Transactions* as a forum for scientific exchange; Newton, whose desire to publicize his findings on optics led to an early exemplar of the scientific report as a problem-solving narrative; and Newton's critics (Hooke, Moray, Paides, and Huygens), whose questioning of Newton's claims and experiments triggered responses from Newton (embodied in his *Optiks*) that seem to have reset the parameters of scientific practice and argument. As he weaves the biographies of scientists and editors into a story of the co-genesis of scientific genres and practices, Bazerman foregrounds ways that practices crystallized in emerging genres were refracted through the particular biographical lenses of key actors in their development. Engestrom and Escalante's (1995) account of the sociogenesis and failed stabilization of Postal Buddy also points to the role of particular personalities, like the company's CEO and particular officials of the postal service, in the trajectory of its development. Interpenetration, in other words, is a two-way street.

In the design of graduate examination and advancement, the generic structure of the research article was distributed across a progressive sequence of three institutional texts. Preliminary examinations were treated as elaborated versions of the conceptual introduction (including identification of problems, a review of the literature, and identification of specific researchable questions). In the dissertation prospectus, the research space (Swales, 1990) identified in the prelim was then succinctly summarized and operationalized in a research plan. Finally, review, methodology, results, and discussion would all be put together in the dissertation itself. Each of these institutional genres resembled some disciplinary genres as well. The prelim review of the literature could be related to review articles in journals and books. The prospectus was similar to grant proposals and, at least some, conference proposals.[18] It was also expected, as the authorship policy indicated (see Fig. 6.1) , that the dissertation might be a source for one or more research articles. For the late 20th-century sociologists of the Project, the voices, textual forms, and social uses of these institutional and disciplinary genres were largely off-the-shelf tools, some assembly required.

Like the authorship policy for the Project (see chap. 6), genres also extended beyond textual representations to shape literate activity. For example, the textual division of conceptual–disciplinary argumentation, measures, and analyses was partially mirrored in students' research activities, as they wrote literature reviews and proposals before they ran and analyzed data. In this sense then, generic topics worked to stabilize not only texts, but literate activity as well.

Sociology Across a Century

The differences between the sociological practices, texts, and contexts of a Durkheim or Small writing in the 1890s and those of West, Lynch, Sean, Moira, and others in the Project in the 1990s are clearly not simply individual. Disciplinary concepts, texts, genres, persons, institutions, and communities were significantly prefabricated by the 1990s. Those prefabrications afforded quite different problem spaces (see Hutchins, 1995) for the Project's sociologists from those of Small and Durkheim. However, prefabrication is also presupposition: The means the Project sociologists

---

[18]Moira's conference proposal (*Arenas 4*) included the literature review, research questions, and methodology. After the proposal was accepted, she ran the data and then prepared the results and discussion. However, Moira's data did not cooperate and she had to revise the research questions and analyses as well as write up results and discussion (see footnote 27, also chap. 8).

employed had sedimented within them the voices of Small, Durkheim, Lazarsfeld, and many others who as producers, patrons, or consumers of sociology participated in their development. The relative durability of these sociohistorical projects is illustrated in an article where West and a co-author from another institution reflected on the field of sociological psychology. Two of their final three paragraphs stressed the need for longitudinal and panel studies in order to understand the complex interactions between macrosocial forces and individual development. The value of such research was linked to the production of disciplinary knowledge, the continued vitality of the discipline, and possible applications to understanding and shaping social change in the United States and internationally (especially the rapidly changing Eastern Europe of the late 1980s). The Project was, thus, tracing particular trajectories within the larger (blurred) fields of sociology, and the sociologists associated with the Project were all, to varying ways, aligning to those trajectories. In the next section, these histories are woven together as I trace one stream of activity within the Project in more detail. One way to gauge the extent to which these artifacts, practices, and institutions mediate authorship is to imagine the writing without them. In the case that follows, it is difficult to imagine the student writing at all without these historical legacies.

SEAN'S DISSERTATION ACTIVITY: AFFORDING AND MANGLING A RESEARCH PLAN

Wertsch's (1991) person-acting-with-mediated-means engaged in mediated action is an apt description of literate activity in *Sociology*, as long as it is not seen through static images of homogeneous activity structures and possessed toolkits that elide the complexities arising as multiple streams of historical activity collide in the agency-saturated field of the present moment and are propelled into the future. In an earlier article (Prior, 1994), I traced in some detail the way the dissertation prospectus of one of the students in the seminar, Sean, was jointly revised in the talk of a two-hour seminar session and retrospectively revised in practice. I also noted the way that the text of Sean's prospectus attenuated everyday discourses and the local and biographical contextualizations, enhancing and claiming disciplinary ones instead. That analysis displayed ways that Sean's authorship, specifically his revision, was socially distributed in the Project's interactions. Here, I am revisiting Sean's dissertation prospectus to explore ways that Sean's authorship of the prospectus and ultimately his dissertation were mediated by artifacts, practices, and institutions as well as persons. In the previous section of this chapter, I traced (very partially) histories of several key tools that participated in the development of Sean's research and associated texts. Here, I focus on how these heterogeneous elements were aligned in his research and how agency was distributed in those alignments. To pursue these issues, I first sketch some of the particular affordances in the ecology of Sean's research and then look at how his initial dissertation plan was mangled as it encountered dissident readings from other seminar participants and as the data were consulted and had their say.

Affording Sean's Dissertation

 Sean's own account of how he developed his dissertation research fits well with actant-network accounts of forging heterogeneous links to establish a stable and winning network. It also suggests the value of considering institutional and intertextual affordances. In an interview, Sean offered the following account for his engagement with the eventual topic of his dissertation prospectus:

> I've been working on this project for about 2 1/2 years as the data analyst, and I had to come up with a dissertation area, and the Project was designed to um investigate the effects of adolescent work experience on psychological functioning, and I knew that there were five main indicators of psychological functioning and I just decided to pick one of them and that would be my dissertation topic, ok? ... so anyway I just said, you know, "I'm interested in depression," well, as part of the Project we had a prototypic analysis, it's a standard way we have of looking at each of the five outcomes, so Elaine just said, "Well, good, why don't you start the prototypic analysis on depression."

When I asked if he had been interested in depression before he came to the Project, Sean said that he had not and then provided a more elaborated account of how he "just decided to pick one" of the five variables:

> It was more of looking at the five variables and deciding what I was going to do, basically the three biggies as far as I could see were self-esteem, self-efficacy, and depression, self-esteem, I know first hand, was just a very complicated literature, it's gigantic, and there are some very serious complications with the whole idea of self-esteem, so I didn't want to get into that ... and also there's a lot of good work that's been done on self-esteem, so it would be difficult for me to make a contribution in that area ... self-efficacy was actually a very good variable, but someone already took it, ... Professor Lynch, he already had self-esteem, er self-efficacy, and so I felt as though depression would be my best shot.

Sean also noted in both research interviews and seminar discussions that gender was a "hot topic," so it was not surprising that his proposal focused on gender and depression.

After he selected depressive affect as his variable, Sean began work on a set of texts. Sean, as first author (with West, Lynch, and Lee as co-authors), worked on a conference paper that examined depressive affect and adolescent work. Under West's guidance (including the kind of editing and rewriting seen with Moira in Figs. 6.2 and 6.3), he next took the lead in revising that paper to submit it to a journal and, after the journal's first review, in revising and resubmitting it. During this period, Sean was also writing an extensive review of the literature on depression and depressive affect in the multiple drafts of his prelim examination. An early draft of the prelim had been distributed and discussed in the first quarter of the informal seminar. When the seminar met to discuss his draft prospectus, Sean had just completed a final revision of the journal article and had just passed his prelims. Sean was, thus, working intensely within the tightly coupled system of research genres. However, the idealized institutional progression of linked texts and research activities for students was reversed here with Sean writing conference papers and research articles before he had completed his prelim, prospectus, and dissertation.

As Sean's accounts make clear, his dissertation activity was deeply embedded in the Project's activity. Sean's roles as research assistant, seminar student, degree candidate, and professional sociologist were tightly aligned within the overlapping structures of the Project, seminar, and program. His research was enabled and enriched by the collaborative activity of the Project/seminar team over a number of years in designing the Project, funding its implementation, collecting and coding data, and analyzing those data. This kind of continuity and coordination of activity (or the lack thereof) may be a key factor in graduate study and the transitions to disciplinary and professional work (see chaps. 2, 4, and 9). As was noted in chapter 6, Sean's institutional position as a data analyst particularly afforded possibilities for deep participation in disciplinary practices (or at least for getting disciplinary credit in terms of authorship). Sean's prior learning, capacities, and orientations allowed him to take advantage of this positional affordance. (In contrast, Lee and Park, also positioned as data analysts, seemed less able to access potentials beyond the purely positional.) The structure of coordinated interests that arose in this nested context also engendered a kind of positional mutuality that attracted the attention and support of others, particularly West, toward Sean.

The convergent coordination of Sean's activity in the Project can be situated in larger scale institutional alignments. The streams of activity within the Project were predicated on the cyclic concentration and conversion of symbolic and material capital (see Latour & Woolgar, 1986). Without the financial support of a major grant, the Project could not have existed. The combination of a coveted research assistantship (as opposed to a teaching position) and potential access to the Project's data for a dissertation recruited students to West as well as to the Project. Several students indicated, for example, that they became West's advisees because they had been employed in the Project. Moreover, without the Project, few, if any, of these students would have been exposed to West's disciplinary (as opposed to classroom) practices.[19] Without considerable disciplinary capital (publications, a faculty position at a major research university, awards and honors, previous successful experience with this kind of research, etc.), West would not have been a likely candidate for such a grant. Finally, as was sketched in the previous section, in the larger contexts of historical relations between social inquiry as a science and its application to public policy, it is not incidental that the Project proposed employing state-of-the-art statistical analysis to quantitative data on a large panel of adolescents and their parents in order to relate psychological and social variables and to address issues of public interest (e.g., how adolescent work might affect self-esteem or high school grades). In short, the Project was constituted in a heterogeneous web of relations formed around personal, interpersonal, institutional, and sociocultural histories.

Sean's selection of and inquiry into depressive affect was multiply afforded by local resources (the Project, his position, the variables measured in the Project's research, the responses of participants, his need for a dissertation, negotiations with West and other researchers, seminar response to his draft) as well as by broader, largely intertextual and institutional, resources (e.g., the fields of psychology and sociology, existing forums for publication, the development of research groups and their funding, graduate study in sociology, the literatures on self-esteem and depression, "issues" in the field).[20] As the previous section suggests, most

---

[19]West reported that she had never taught a seminar like this one (i.e., no readings, no set lecture, mainly response to student texts). She attributed its structure to the Project, noting that she typically worked intensely with only one or two students at a time (as they were dissertating or working under small grants), whereas now she was working intensely with a whole group.

[20]Based on textual analysis, Swales (1990) suggested that the first rhetorical move of a research

of these prefabricated resources of sociology were largely developed in the century before Sean's writing. These affordances structured what paths Sean did not take as well as those he did.

Mangling Sean's Hypotheses

In his analyses of scientific and technological developments, Pickering (1995) emphasizes the contingency and unpredictability of extending culture in real time, of the way plans and projects are buffeted, shaped, and reshaped by heterogeneous fields of material and human agencies in a dialectical dance of accommodations and resistances. He pays particular attention to the way conceptual models evolve and change in response to historical processes of accommodation and resistance. Likening these processes to what happened when clothes were squeezed through the mangle (the rollers that wrung them out on early washers), Pickering refers to this dance of agencies as the *mangle of practice*. The patterns of mangling that Pickering presents in case studies of Morpugo's search for the quark, Glaser's development of the bubble chamber, and the introduction of numerically controlled tooling in General Electric's aircraft division reminded me of what I observed as Sean moved from his draft prospectus to his final research. Here, I want to present a brief description of the mangling of Sean's dissertation plans, particularly as embodied in his hypotheses and his proposed analysis. Through this mangling, multiple agencies—sociohistorically distributed across persons, practices, artifacts, and institutions—came to participate in Sean's writing and his research.

In his prelim, Sean had identified a researchable question: Why do adolescent girls (and women) suffer from greater depressed mood than adolescent boys (and men)? Sean hypothesized that the observed differences in depressed mood might come from differences in "the sense-making aspects of the gender role identity" and how that sense making played out in supportive communication. Sean developed seven hypotheses for his prospectus, but his fourth hypothesis was really the core of his plan:

---

article is to create a research space: establishing a territory, establishing a niche, and occupying the niche. As Larson (1984) notes, classifications of discourse based on features of texts may differ greatly from those that also take into account topical and contextual features of the rhetorical situation. Sean's accounts of selecting depressive affect evoke a complex rhetorical situation in which Sean had to adapt (not establish) a niche embedded in the structure of the Project and then align that niche to both the multiple spaces afforded by disciplinary literatures and the ongoing work of other researchers in the Project. Swales's account then might be revised and extended to incorporate the collective and historical activity of the research group and the field. In other words, ecologies and niches are developed through distributed activity as well as the rhetorical action of individuals.

(4) Expressive social support will have negative implications for depressed mood, especially among girls; among females, these effects will be more pronounced among same-sex dyads.

In the seminar, Sean introduced this hypothesis by saying it involved "what happens when girls get together and engage in social support."[21] Sean's proposed answer to his prelim question was that girls (more than boys) would tend to be expressive, that what girls (more than boys) expressed was likely to be negative and introspective (rumination), and that when anyone expresses negativity, others are likely to deny it, making the person feel even worse.

Sean's hypothesis turned out to be highly controversial and triggered an extended debate on two topical terrains: the social ramifications of Sean's representations of girls and boys, and the disciplinary question of whether the Project's measures could be construed as measures of expressive and instrumental social support, and especially, whether they provided any data on what happened in communicative interactions. The following comments by West touch on both these issues and also illustrate the way in which arguments relevant to each were expressed in the seminar discussion:

West: =It seems like the critical issue is what's happening in these inter-
           changes, and if in fact it does generate kind of, you know, [1 s]
           mutual gloom and /negativity/
Sean: /umhm/
West: You know you tell me about your problems and that makes me more
           depressed, and I'll tell you about mine and you'll get more de-
           pressed, and then I'll say "I'm depressed" and you'll say [laughing]
           "There's no reason to be you know," [8 seconds of West and others
           laughing; multiple voices] and and you know but- but that may not
           happen, and then, you know, in a lot of cases, um, you know, people
           do want to sort of let off steam, and that is cathartic and uh, but we
           have no idea what's happening in these dyads.

Bracketed by references to the question of measures (enunciated in disci-plinary terms of *dyads* and *interchanges*), West parodies Sean's repre-sentation of girls' talk in a everyday voice (a hypothetical scenario with

---

[21]Note the double-voiced nature of Sean's representation, the mix of everyday discourse, "girls getting together," with disciplinary discourse, "engaging in social support."

constructed dialogue, followed by that colloquial truism about letting off steam). Under this kind of intense critique, at one point in the seminar, Sean decided to drop hypothesis four. However, another graduate student (Thomas) continued to question him on his "theory."

Thomas: I mean, there's just a general theoretical issue here, are you saying that that uh, the ways that girls support each other is dysfunctional, the ways boys support each other is more functional?

Something like this pointed question seemed to underlie much of the opposition to Sean's hypothesis and to be reflected discursively in the everyday grounds of its critique.

The second key issue, over appropriate ways of representing and using the Project's measures, was argued in markedly more disciplinary voices. For example, shortly after parodying Sean's basic story of girl talk, West was suggesting the following to Sean:

But the problem is that if you set forth the hypothesis and your measures aren't very good, if you don't confirm your hypothesis, you don't know if it's because your measures or the hypothesis is wrong.... I think what's (clear you're) going to find is that closeness, and you know these variables, will have positive effects on lots of outcomes, just like they always seem to do in the literature.

In these comments, we see West questioning Sean's hypotheses in terms of hypothesis testing, if–then reasoning, the naming of measures,[22] and intertextual allusions to the research literature (where a history of positive outcomes for measures of "closeness" contrasts with Sean's negative expectations).

Sean was also proposing to use a cutting-edge statistical technique, hierarchical linear modeling (HLM), in his analysis. However, aligning his proposed social support variables, the Project's measures, and that statistical model turned out to be quite complicated. To get a sense of how this part of the seminar discussion developed, I include a brief excerpt, in which Lynch, West, and Sean are discussing how to develop a model for Sean's data.[23] Throughout this discussion, Lynch repeatedly evoked a hypothetical

---

[22]West is contesting Sean's representation of the Project's measures as "social support" measures, referring to them instead as measures of "closeness." It is useful to note here that Sean's measures were selected by West and were derived from questionnaire items like (italics added), "How *close* do you feel to your best friend of the opposite sex?"

[23]Lynch was seen as the expert on these statistics and their applications in this group.

(perhaps familiar) model (not Sean's) involving analysis of *students* in *classes* in *schools* to clarify issues of level in the HLM analysis. In the following excerpt, Sean has just suggested using a diagnostic scale of gender in his equations in place of (or in addition to) actual biological sex, and Sean, Lynch, and West are beginning to work out how to conceptualize and implement such an analysis:

Sean: No, no, this is HLM, it's four dummies representing gender diagnosticity at the second level[24]

Lynch: Nope, that doesn't do anything for you, I mean that- I mean that gives us perfect collinearity in the *b*'s, we already know what the *b* is for each group

Sean: Ok one- ok once we estimate /just the-/

Lynch: /That would-/that would be like this, if- if schools were my second level, I would put in a dummy variable for each school, now that's redundant information

Sean: Ok

Lynch: Because I already know, I've already put these (under some schools), I know what school they're in, that's how they got in the group,

Sean: Ok, so

Lynch: So to predict the *b* based on that is just totally redundant information

Sean: Ok

West: So what- what do you propose now? I mean I guess /I'm ( ) /

Lynch: I'd just leave the alpha/ in there

Sean: The gamma you mean

Lynch: The gamma, excuse me, yes

Sean: And ok what is /the gamma/

Lynch: /Most- most/ of these are going to be just a gamma, by the way

Sean: I (didn't) mean- ok, so, the gamma will tell us the average difference between the groups

Lynch: Right

Sean: We've got four groups

Lynch: Yeah

Sean: The average difference between the four groups, and what will that mean?

---

[24]In this conversation, "dummies" refers to dummy variables in an equation; the *b*'s, gammas, and alphas also represent variables in the HLM equations.

After working out how to use HLM for Sean's proposed hypotheses in an extended discussion, Lynch concluded by stressing the riskiness of the approach and how time consuming it might be. Because Sean needed to finish his dissertation within half a year of this proposal in order to take a postdoctoral position he had been offered, he was very wary of such risk and decided not to use HLM. However, Sean and West, in separate interviews, recalled how exciting and valuable this session had been because of the way Lynch had clarified analytic strategies with HLM.

As these examples suggest, the seminar talk was highly heterogeneous. The plausibility and acceptability of Sean's concepts and methods were tested by translating them into hypothetical everyday narratives and asking if those narratives were consonant with participants' common sense; by relating them intertextually to findings in the literature; by comparing them to canonical models of scientific reasoning; by exploring local issues, such as whether Sean's measures and models meshed with the Project's; and by generating scenarios of both institutional and research events (e.g., the upcoming prospectus meeting, possible outcomes in running the data). From this nonlinear and heterogeneous discussion, Sean emerged with significant changes to his prospectus plan.

Pickering (1995) notes that path dependence is a central characteristic of the mangle of practice. That the outcome of the seminar response was path dependent, contingent on the concrete, sequential unfolding of that particular afternoon's talk is suggested by West's candidate revisions of Sean's fourth hypothesis. In the seminar, West offered five distinct revisions: (1) drop the hypothesis; (2) keep the hypothesis, but don't develop it as a major contribution; (3) state the hypothesis as one that emerges from the literature, but then indicate that it could not be tested with the Project's measures; (4) evaluate the hypothesis only for a subset of girls who score highest on depressed mood; and (5) revise the hypothesis to say that social support will be beneficial for boys and girls, but more beneficial for boys than girls. West's final suggestion came very shortly after Thomas questioned the representation of girls as dysfunctional (again, this was after Sean had stated that he would definitely drop the whole hypothesis):

Sean: We should assume that social support has positive effect- that
          would explain hypothesis 5, but in the case of girls it doesn't
          because it's- because it's expressive it's-and because they ruminate,
          it's just another occasion for them to ruminate and so it's dysfunc-
          tional
West: Well maybe /you could/

Thomas:	/That so-/ go ahead
West:	Now maybe you (could) state this in a somewhat weaker form, and to just say that you would expect that the uh positive implications of social support or uh (effect)would be weaker- would be less for girls than for boys because some girls may be engaging in these processes that you don't- you don't expect so much for boys
Sean:	How do you- "the positive aspects of expressive support will be greater"
West:	No /what you say is/=
Sean:	/"Will be less for"/
West:	=Is that- is that, you know, you're expecting (that) social support will have a negative effect on depressive affect, you could say that that negative effect would be stronger for boys than for girls[25]
Lynch:	That's not really what he's saying, is it?

Sean's final hypothesis echoed West's fifth proposed reformulation:

(4)The negative, causal relationship between instrumental support and depressed mood for boys will be stronger than the negative, causal relationship between expressive social support and depressed mood for girls.

In revising this hypothesis, Sean was reversing his argument. His hypothesis had suggested that expressive support was bad, increasing girls' depressive affect; the revised hypothesis suggests that it is good, decreasing their depressive affect, although this decrease is less than the decrease instrumental support provides for boys. In relation to this inversion, Sean also revised his presentation of the literature that supported the hypotheses. Citation of the theory that related depression to denial of negativity disappeared. Gone too was a detailed description of findings that girls' social support was positively associated with drug abuse. (The most prominent source in that description went from a paragraph summary of findings to a parenthetic citation in a list.) Three new sources were cited to highlight the beneficial effect of social support, a point that West had repeatedly stressed in the seminar response.

However, more serious mangling was in store. Asked in an interview what results he had found, Sean laughed and described the fate of his final hypotheses:

---

[25]In formulating precise language for this hypothesis, West also shifts from Sean's everyday use of *positive* and *negative* (as good and bad) to a technical, mathematical usage (where negative simply means lower numerically).

Sean: When you get down to the empirical business of it, Paul, the very
           first thing you have to do is establish that there is indeed an
           instrumental and expressive support, there isn't. [laughing] So the
           whole thing was blown out of the water within one week of analysis
Paul: [laughing] So that's what you're writing up now, or did you do
           something different?
Sean: [Sean discussed what he did find and then returned to the prospec-
           tus]But see when the committee met to talk about the prospectus,
           the actual committee, what they sai-, the- Ray Scott is a statistician
           type of guy and he said, "You know Sean this argument is too well
           specified because, you know," and like he saw what was going to
           happen right away, he said, "you know, at every step you're assum-
           ing that something will definitely be true and that's not, that's not a
           good way to construct an argu-, you should leave arguments open
           so one way or the other you'll be able to do something" so the
           committee, it was kinda weird, the committee said, you know, "The
           hell with this prospectus, you know, go do something on social
           support, stressors, and adolescence, [laughing] we'll see you in a
           couple months." so I went out and sure enough it failed, and I came
           in, told Elaine, she goes, "Ok, well, go back and do it, you know,
           keep going" so...

In narrating his prospectus meeting (which took place three days after the
seminar discussion of his prospectus), Sean first represents the voice of Ray
Scott and then the whole committee (West, Lynch, and Scott) to the effect
that they had anticipated that his analytic strategy would blow up, but had
said "the hell with the prospectus" and authorized him to just "go do
something on social support, stressors, and adolescence." Finally, Sean
narrates a discussion with West in which he announces that he cannot test
his hypotheses and she tells him to "go back and do it." Reflecting on her
study of situated action in a science lab, Knorr-Cetina (1981) concluded,
"If there is a principle which seems to govern laboratory action, it is
scientists' concern with making things 'work,' which points to a principle
of success rather than truth" (p. 4).[26]

Sean's account describes how his planned analysis failed as soon as he

---

[26]Sean's representation of Scott's advice ("leave arguments open so one way or another you'll be
able to do something") is an explicit formulation of this principle of success. That Sean's dissertation
did not even have to tell the story of his failed analysis before it moved on to his eventual research seems
a lesson in the same curriculum.

began to run the data, an electronic artifact, composed from respondents' answers to particular questionnaire items and the coding of those responses. Basically, the data told him, evidently with greater authority than West or Lynch could muster in the seminar response, that they were not measures of expressive and instrumental social support.[27]

In the short period between Sean's presentation of his draft in the seminar, his committee meeting to vet his proposal, and his initial run of the data, Sean's hypotheses are intensively mangled, first by his colleagues in the seminar and then by the data. The outcome is mixed. Sean and others have rehearsed and learned about sociological practices as they worked through his prospectus. Institutionally, Sean has advanced and will soon finish his dissertation and move on to a prestigious postdoctoral position. Conceptually, however, his hypothetical framework is largely overthrown as his plans run into multiple and heterogeneous resistances in practice.

FORGING HETEROGENEOUS NETWORKS IN SOCIOLOGY

In an anthology of behind-the-scenes narratives of sociological research, James Coleman (1967), a leading sociologist in the kind of survey research

---

[27]For her conference paper (and ultimately dissertation), Moira also proposed making secondary use of the data from these scales. However, in her case too, appropriating the voices frozen in these scales turned out not to be an easy affair. After her conference proposal (a conceptual introduction, research questions, a projected methodology, and a timetable for completion of the research) had been accepted, Moira ran into trouble when the analyses were run. Instead of simply adding the results and discussion to her final paper, Moira had to go back and substantially revise the goals and projected analyses of the research. When I asked her to discuss these revisions, she recalled that she had planned to analyze the relationship between objective change and subjective discomfort. However, her plan ran into data elicited by problematic indicators (questionnaire items) and her attempts to reconfigure those indicators into new constructs seemed to fail:

> But I don't know that I have sensitive enough indicators within each of the contexts to pick up that [subjective perception of] change, and I might not have good enough change indicators, and so, like for the school context and for the family context, I have to really do some piecing together, I've used the one indicator that I can use to try to get at that change, and I don't know if it was good enough, and I don't know if my comfort indicator is good enough, so, so far the analysis didn't pan out, although I found some interesting things, it wasn't what I expected so I toned that down completely [we laugh] in the second paper ... and also um the focus of the- an arena of comfort as a mediator, comfort as a mediator or buffer to changes in other contexts, I wasn't able to look at that yet.

Moira's comments and her revised texts further display the way the Project's data, that composite of measures and the responses 2,500 participants made to them, shaped what questions she was able to address, what arguments she could make, and what texts she could write.

the Project also represents, describes the development of his first major research project in the 1950s, a project that led to the publication of *The Adolescent Society*. His narrative displays the highly laminated and heterogeneous trajectory of his research process, including his initial belief that the critical political issue for the future involved not socialism (ownership of the means of production) but pluralism (distribution of those means); his involvement as a graduate student researcher in a large study of a labor union; his methodological training (especially from Paul Lazarsfeld) at the Bureau for Applied Social Research at Columbia; the early development of methods for contextual analysis (which he would employ and extend); a dinner conversation with his wife and another couple about their wildly divergent high school lives (which prompted him to select high schools as the site of his research); sources of funding and their interests (several foundations turned him down before he got a grant from the Office of Education); a range of material resources (e.g., number and quality of research assistants, his teaching schedule, the presence of a Univac computer); co-researchers' interests and work; presentations and papers early in his analysis of the data that were directed at audiences whose primary interests were educational processes rather than political pluralism; the data (what they allowed him to study, the unexpected results he got, limitations and trends); and his own need to synthesize and write up the research. As with Sean's hypotheses, both Coleman's initial impetus for the research (to study pluralism) and his specific hypotheses were intensely mangled in the process of doing the research: instead of governing the research, they served as initial moves in an unstable, open-ended process. Coleman (1967) notes that his narrative, especially the disjunction between the rationales and hypotheses that the research was designed to address and the rationales and hypotheses it finally did address, does not fit positivistic accounts of the research process. However, he suggests there may be empirical value in following the data rather than imposing preconceived notions on it. I cite Coleman's narrative at length here because it suggests that Sean was being socialized into durable social practices of a community of practice rather than being a party to some local, idiosyncratic aberration in those practices.

   The previous section offers a picture of the intertextual and institutional affordances that mediated Sean's work, of ways that his textual and research practices were socially distributed in the Project team (focally in processes of response to texts, but also in the historical accumulation of its resources), and of ways that the data (a sedimented artifact of participants' responses to questionnaire items) spoke, reshaping Sean's already mangled research plans. Acting in concert, this ensemble of mediational means (e.g., genres, measures, the intertextual literatures of the field, the organization of the research team) seemed to have had a somewhat paradoxical effect. On the one hand, the institutional demand for "original" work and the generic demand for an extended initial focus on conceptualization (in the prelim and the prospectus) prompted Sean (like other students) to innovate to some degree, creating a more centrifugal space. On the other hand, the disciplinary positioning embedded in the Project, the generic forms and voices of experimental reports, the standard measures (in interaction evidently with the respondents' reading and response practices), and written and oral responses to the prelim and prospectus, particularly from West and Lynch, seemed to constrain that innovation, to operate as conservative centripetal forces. In this case, Sean began exploring somewhat novel constructs in the early stages of his work on the prelim and dissertation proposal; however, the measures, the data, and the seminar response to his draft left Sean with little of his conceptualization or disciplinary positioning intact. Moreover, the Project's design anticipated a range of disciplinary forums and issues for the work that would emerge from it, and Sean, even when he sought to examine his most novel constructs through the data, still operated within that embedded disciplinary positioning.

In the seminar and his subsequent activity, Sean was rehearsing practices as well as using artifactual resources. A key set of practices revolved around sociological reasoning and representation. In the seminar, Sean's dissertation hypotheses were exposed to a four-way alignment. First, his story was subjected to a folk psychological, common sensical, critique. In this case, the critique was fairly harsh. As Edmondson (1984) has noted, personal sense making is often evoked in the margins of sociological rhetoric, buried in examples that are socially emblematic or in the practice of telling hypothetical "someone" stories. In the seminar talk, this layer of everyday personal sense making was made explicit and rehearsed. Second, Sean's story was articulated against the intertextual affordances of the literature. Sean's strongest argument in the seminar discussion was the well-established finding that starting in adolescence, girls and then women report significantly higher levels of depressive affect than boys and men. On the other hand, the literature on "closeness" suggested to West that Sean's expectations for the effects of his indicators were unlikely to be realized. Third, his conceptual models needed to be aligned to specific measures and statistical procedures and ultimately to the actual data of the Project. Finally, all of these alignments had to be articulated to the interpersonal and social relations of the research group. In each of these alignments, Sean's authorship and agency were distributed.

VOICES IN THE NETWORKS

In this chapter, I have pointed to a common strategy in sociohistoric theory and science studies, that of tracing and reanimating voices in networks of people, artifacts, practices, and institutions. However, I see critical differences between these approaches, differences that point to their potential to complement each other. In the sociohistoric work emerging from Vygotsky's circle, the emphasis has been on ontogenesis, on the development of the person. Attention to the development of mediational means has generally been secondary and fragmentary in contrast.[28] Actant-network theory's focus on science and technology—its attention to machines, theories, laboratory and workplace practices, and scientific objects—has led it to serious theoretical and methodological consideration of things, to a principled and systematic investigation of their sociogenesis. The actant-network principle of symmetry can help provoke the systematic application of the genetic approach of sociohistoric research to understanding the development of artifacts, practices, institutions, and communities as well as persons. In this chapter, I have pointed to correspondences between appropriation (the development of the person) and sedimentation (the development of things), to the way both processes are marked by transformations, especially toward abbreviated and presuppositional forms. Another notion, which has so far been applied only to ontogenesis, is that of *leading activity* (e.g., Leont'ev, 1981a). As play and school have been seen as leading activities in the ontogenesis of modern Western children, oral and written presentations for seminars, conferences, and academic publication could be seen as leading activities in the sociogenesis of disciplinary artifacts, practices, and institutions (see Bazerman, 1988; Ochs, Jacoby, & Gonzales, 1994).

On the other hand, it is precisely this focus on the sociogenesis of the person that sociohistoric theory can offer actant-network approaches. As Latour (1987, 1996) follows the actors, some (e.g., machines and theories) are routinely traced back into their developmental phases to uncover the

---

[28]Sustained treatments of the development of mediational means have recently appeared (e.g., Bazerman, 1988; Cole, 1995; Engestrom, 1993; Cole & Engestrom, 1993; Griffin, et al., 1993; Hutchins, 1995; Moll & Greenberg, 1990; Wertsch, 1995).

perspectives, interests, and contextual presuppositions inscribed in them. However, human actors are rarely (and then only marginally) taken up from this developmental perspective. For example, when Latour (1988) set out to decenter Pasteur and relocate his legacy in a network of allied actors, he relied primarily on fairly conventional models of human actors. Latour did distinguish two Pasteurs: "Pasteur," a floating social signifier, and the embodied Pasteur. "Pasteur" is a discursive space capable of soaking up the causal attributions of its allies and, hence, becoming a transcendental historical figure. However, the apparent price Latour paid for achieving a decentered "Pasteur" was allowing other human allies, like the hygenicist Richet, to operate without quotes as full subjects. Moreover, the embodied Pasteur repeatedly claims center stage, where he is written, within a conventional image of disciplinary authorship, as an exemplary blend of ideational inspiration and strategic genius, a kind of guerrilla scientist–rhetor. In short, actant-network theory appears to operate largely on conventional models of agency, although it extends these models unconventionally to non-humans. It achieves a collective agency by multiplying autonomous agents in competitive networks of alliance and conflict, whereas sociohistoric theory sees collective agency as an outcome of interpenetration arising through processes of internalization, externalization, and alignment. By treating mediational means as potentially constitutive of persons and not simply as external tools, sociohistoric theory diffuses agency across traditional boundaries. When Latour (1987) traced machines, theories, and scientific objects back in time, he noted the vast differences between science as made and science in the making. The notion of sociogenesis suggests that it is equally important to trace back humans, to see them in the making as well.

Finally, another difference in these two traditions is important to note. Actant-network theory took a marked semiotic turn in the late 1980s. Interested in tracing the heterogeneity of networks and treating humans and non-humans symmetrically, Latour, Callon, and others decided to treat all as semiotic actants. Callon (1996), extending the notion of inscription (Latour & Woolgar, 1986), talks about ways that networks become hardened through representation as delegation. In this view, representation–delegation becomes the category that must account for the production of tools, texts, people, and institutions. In contrast, sociohistoric theory has consistently rejected the abstraction of concrete historical activity to a textual-verbal plane of representation. Following the actors may be a common strategy, but in sociohistoric terms, what is traced is a heterogeneous network of productive activity, fully embodied in space-time, not a synchronous textual representation.[29]

Combining these approaches calls for research that traces the dialogic intermingling of voices in these networks of production, that integrates the sociogenesis of all of the elements in functional systems. To move from the question of how functional systems mediate the production and authorship of texts to how participation in literate activity mediates the ongoing sociogenesis of functional systems themselves, I turn in the next chapter to an analysis of rounds of response and revision between West and Moira, examining their co-authorship as the mediated production of identities and institutions as well as of texts and knowledge.

---

[29]Pickering's (1995) notion of material agency rejects the semiotic turn from within science studies. He allies his notions of material agency and the mangle more to Law's (1987) discussion of heterogeneous engineering where "without detours through semiotics, [Law] invokes natural forces as part of an actor-network account of the Portuguese maritime expansion" (p. 13).

8

A Microhistory of Mediated Authorship and Disciplinary Enculturation: Tracing Authoritative and Internally Persuasive Discourses

Grounded in models of writing and learning that emphasize texts and transmission (see chaps. 1 and 5), studies of connections between written response and textual revision (e.g., Beason, 1993; Michaels, 1987; Onore, 1989; Sperling & Freedman, 1987; Ziv, 1984) have generally focused on how student writers interpret responses and how they act on them as displayed by changes in subsequent texts. The notion of mediated authorship treats the basic terms of such interactions (the people, their words, and their texts) as dialogically open and interpenetrated. It asks what footings the speaker/writer takes to her words, whose voices are present in an utterance, and how those voices are being (re)appropriated. These questions work to foreground developmental issues, particularly the ways such textual exchanges mediate the historical (re)production of persons and communities of practice.

Reporting on writing and learning in an undergraduate anthropology course, Herrington (1992) takes up a sociohistoric perspective to examine how students and instructors composed social selves through writing, response, and revision. She describes how a struggling student, Kate, was responded to (and subsequently revised texts) in ways markedly different from those observed for a more successful student, Sally. Teaching assistants in the course rewrote passages of Kate's, but not Sally's, papers.[1] For

---

[1]Rewriting as a form of response (e.g., as illustrated in Fig. 6.2) has also been found in other research across varied settings: elementary (e.g., Michaels 1987), secondary, (e.g., Sperling & Freedman, 1987), undergraduate (e.g., Ziv, 1984), and graduate/disciplinary (e.g., Blakeslee, 1997; Knorr-Cetina, 1981).

her part, Kate took a fairly passive stance, usually just incorporating that response into subsequent drafts. In her analysis, Herrington came to question the value of rewriting-as-response for Kate, finding that Kate did not always understand the bases for the instructor-authored revisions that she made. For example, on one paper, when the instructor deleted Kate's challenges to the fairness of regulating Eskimo hunting, Kate complied with the specific deletion in her revision, but then reintroduced the same issue elsewhere in the text.[2] Herrington's analysis suggests that, although Kate's texts changed to reflect the authoritative discourse of the instructors, Kate evidently did not. Herrington's concern with how students "compose themselves" in the discipline could be read in a narrow sense (e.g., creating a textual persona appropriate to a discipline, developing self-confidence to express "one's own" ideas). While those senses are relevant, I would argue that an interest in composing selves asks writing researchers to consider the more funda-mental issue of how students, instructors, and communities of practices are themselves being (re)produced through this kind of mediated authorship.

As soon as I began to analyze West's responses to Moira's texts and her revisions (see Figs. 6.2 and 6.3), I started to wonder who was talking in these texts. With process analysis of the texts, I could trace how West's words were incorporated or not by Moira in subsequent drafts. Such analysis shed light on the surface of response and revision, on the circulation of words among texts, but said little on the deeper issue of what Moira made of those response-initiated revisions, how she understood and felt about them, and what she was appropriating from this literate activity. To explore these issues, I could not simply ask whether Moira's texts were increasingly conforming to a specialized disciplinary register (see Berkenkotter et al., 1988). Instead, I needed an approach to language, such as Bakhtin's (1981, 1986; also see discussions in chaps. 1 and 3), that sees words as coming not from abstract lexicons but from other people, as representing not discrete semiotic objects, but dynamic arenas within which diverse personal and social significations may converge, clash, and co-exist.

With his notion of authoritative and internally persuasive discourses, Bakhtin (1981) was seeking a framework that would fuse accounts of the person's dialogic appropriation of social languages and the society's (re)production of the person:

---

[2]Han's focused uptake of Mead's version of her research problem illustrated a similar process arising in oral response (see chap. 2).

Both the authority of discourse and its internal persuasiveness may be united in a single word—one that is *simultaneously* authoritative and internally persuasive—despite the profound differences between these two categories of alien discourse. But such unity is rarely a given—it happens more frequently that an individual's becoming, an ideological process, is characterized by a sharp gap between these two categories: in one, the authoritative word (religious, political, moral, the word of a father, of adults and of teachers, etc.) that does not know internal persuasiveness, in the other the internally persuasive word that is denied all privilege, backed up by no authority at all, and is frequently not even acknowledged in society (not by public opinion, nor by scholarly norms, nor by criticism), not even in the legal code. The struggle and dialogic interrelationship of these categories of ideological discourse are what usually determine the history of an individual ideological consciousness. (p. 342)

For Bakhtin, what is internally persuasive is not the static expression of an autonomous self, but a dynamic product of historically situated interactions. If, as in Voloshinov's (1973; see quote in chap. 5) metaphor, thought and language are a boundless sea (of inner speech) dotted with islands (external-ized utterances), the interplay of authoritative and internally persuasive discourses are powerful forces (gravitation, wind, rain, rivers), constantly churning up the surface of the sea and producing its deep currents. This interplay, Bakhtin suggests, is the basic semiotic mechanism of human development as others' words, practices, and worlds are slowly and selec-tively reaccentuated and interwoven into the evolving formation of a par-ticular personal consciousness.

Bakhtin's (1981) definition of the internally persuasive word as half someone else's is practically identical to his description of "the word in language" (see quote in chap. 1).

In the everyday rounds of our consciousness, the internally persuasive word is half-ours and half-someone else's ... it enters into an intense interaction, a struggle with other internally persuasive discourses. Our ideological development is just such an intense struggle within us for hegemony among various available verbal and ideological points of view, approaches, directions, and values. The semantic structure of an internally persuasive discourse is not finite, it is open; in each of the new contexts that dialogize it, this discourse is able to reveal ever newer ways to mean. (pp. 345–346)

If we reverse Bakhtin's depiction of the internally persuasive word as owned, open, interactive, and productive, authoritative discourse can be defined as language associated with some form of social authority, language that is relatively alien, closed, and unproductive, not well understood or integrated in the person's consciousness.[3] In this sense, authoritative discourse is akin

---

[3]As with many of Bakhtin's concepts, other formulations of these notions could be derived from

to notions of inert knowledge (cf. Freire, 1970; Spiro, Vispoel, Schmitz, Samarapungavan, & Boerger, 1987).

To trace the interplay of authoritative and internally persuasive discourses in this microhistory of literate interactions (the response rounds between West and Moira), I needed to go beyond intertextual analysis of the circulation of words in texts, to develop a careful rendering of West and Moira's situated activities and their reflexive understanding of their textually mediated activity. Thus, I first sketch some salient personal, interpersonal, and institutional histories that afforded, and are indexed in, the exchanges between West and Moira. I then present a close analysis of ways that Moira incorporated or resisted West's responses, tracing how their words came to intermingle in the texts, and exploring the extent to which West's responses were authoritative or became internally persuasive to Moira. Asking whether the revisions West authored became internally persuasive to Moira is a way of asking what Moira was learning from, and being enculturated into, through these textual exchanges. As Lave and Wenger (1991) argue, enculturation always implicates cultural formation as the participation of a person reciprocally shapes the community of practice. Thus, I conclude this analysis by considering how Moira and West's co-participation in these literate practices mediated the ongoing development of West, the Project, the department, and the discipline.

AFFORDING THE RESPONSE ROUNDS

In chapters 6 and 7, I described some of the ways West's and Moira's interactions could be situated in institutional and disciplinary streams of activity. Before turning to a detailed analysis of the response rounds and what they signified, however, I will outline some of the personal, interper-

---

other statements he made. His accounts of authoritative discourse were often skewed toward the most distant and oppressive forms of social authority in his time (i.e., Church, State) and toward formal issues (e.g., specialized scripts and languages, discrete representation of speech).

> Authoritative discourse permits no play with the context framing it, no play with its borders, no gradual and flexible transitions, no spontaneously creative stylizing variants on it. It enters our verbal consciousness as a compact and indivisible mass; one must either totally affirm it, or totally reject it. It is indissolubly fused with its authority—with political power, an institution, a person—and it stands or falls together with that authority. (Bakhtin, 1981, p. 343)

Although this absolutist description might suggest that authoritative and internally persuasive discourses are distinct binary categories in a formal taxonomy, Bakhtin's representations of internally persuasive discourse and language in general do not accord with such a dichotomy.

sonal, and institutional histories that afforded West's responses to Moira and Moira's uptake of those responses.

Moira

When the seminar began, Moira had interacted with West almost daily for two years through her position as manager of data collection in the Project. Her supervision of the annual collection of questionnaire data from a group of more than 1,000 students and their parents or guardians was critical to the Project's success: Its panel design (see chap. 7, footnote 12) depended on a high retention rate so that comparisons could be made across different waves (years) of the data. Data collection often involved multiple contacts by mail, phone, and even in person in some cases. Moira was evidently performing this task well as retention in the fourth year of the Project remained more than 90%. However, as was discussed in chapter 6, Moira's work did not receive credit in the form of routine co-authorship. In fact, she was not listed as co-author on any of the 15 publications (conference papers and journal articles) that had been generated from the Project before the seminar. Moira's conference paper (*Arenas*) would be not only her first publication, but also the first single-authored publication to come out of the Project (because it was being submitted to a special graduate student session).

For Moira, the Project had originally offered a valuable work setting where she could develop her research skills. When she began graduate study, Moira had a strong interest in adolescent risk (e.g., risk for problems like drug abuse, school failure, teenage pregnancy, criminal behavior, and psychological or social dysfunction). However, finding research opportunities had proved difficult. Her first advisor's specialization was criminology, but his research focused on adults, not adolescents. Moira explored working with a professor in education on a study of academic enculturation at the university level, but that research stalled. Finally, Moira switched advisors and topics, to work with West and to use the Project's data. Having just begun to develop her dissertation topic in the fall, Moira did not feel like an authority in the spring: "I still feel like a real dummy in the area; it didn't seem like I had enough opportunity just to read, so I don't feel like an expert and that can certainly diminish my confidence in my writing." Throughout Moira's account of her search for a dissertation topic, two key themes were repeated: pursuit of her own interests (in adolescent socialization and risk) and the need to find a professor–mentor already engaged in relevant research. Indicating that the education professor had not kept her informed or expressed much interest in her research, Moira concluded, "I need somebody that's direct to work with and committed to me."

Moira's representations of her writing skills and her graduate studies also provide useful contexts for her perception of and reactions to West's response. Moira indicated that she really appreciated West's intense editing because she had not gotten any feedback on her writing either in undergraduate or graduate school, adding that she found writing "a real struggle–it's probably the thing I like to do the least just because of that, not getting any information about how I write, what's wrong, what's right." She recalled how embarrassed she had been when she shared the first draft of her prelim in the unofficial fall seminar, saying it was not only the first time she had shared her writing with a group, but the first time she had really shared "anything that I was interested in."

In an interview, Moira described her graduate education with clear disappointment. She recalled how excited she had been to start graduate school, expecting that she would be "able to go to class and discuss some ideas" in an environment where professors and students interacted more as peers. Her high expectations were not realized in practice:

> I found that some of the graduate seminars weren't any different than my undergrad experiences were, it was straight lecture, and instead of having um, discussions, it was more like, giving your- giving an answer and hoping that it was correct so nobody would humiliate you, you know, I mean it just seemed like it was so tense that I wasn't learning anything, it was- I was more worried about my reputation as a graduate student than- than really being able to filter through some ideas and get anything out of the classes, and the amount of the material that you're expected to assimilate within a short period of time is ridiculous

Moira's comments painted a portrait of a depressed (and depressing) atmosphere for learning, dominated by material to assimilate (rather than discussion and reflection) and driven by the needs to maintain face and to manage time under a heavy load of reading and teaching. For Moira, her interactions with West and the Project/seminar were a radical break. She was finally learning what her fellow students were interested in, engaging in collegial intellectual conversation, working with an engaged mentor–professor, and getting the opportunity to develop her ability to communicate in writing and speaking. In fact, Moira felt as though she had made it: "I finally have somebody that's paying attention to my work and giving me feedback on it, so it's gotten better." She concluded: "It's a shame I couldn't have experienced that the four years prior."

Moira indicated that she typically accepted West's editing without question, unless she felt that West's rewording was "ambiguous" or didn't "seem to be my thoughts." In accounting for this compliance, Moira stressed two factors: West's expertise (e.g., "I figure she's had a lot more experience writing and reading this stuff, so I tend to go along with her suggestions") and timing (she often had only a day or two between receiving West's written response and the point at which a revised text was due). Moira did offer a more ambiguous account of West's response at one point in a discourse-based interview:

Moira: Sometimes I read my papers after- a few months after I write them, I'm like, "Did I write this? This doesn't sound like me." [Moira laughing, dramatized voice]
Paul: Everybody does that
Moira: Yeah?
Paul: Yeah, I think so
Moira: and Elaine is such a good editor, sometimes I take her changes unquestioningly
Paul: Umhm
Moira: and that's probably not good, I mean there's a few times I haven't, and then she still comes back and says [Moira slightly mimics West's voice] "Now, I don't think you understand the difference between" [Paul laughs, Moira laughs] "All right, Elaine" [said tensely, re-signedly]

Moira has an image of what she "sounds like" and finds that her texts often do not match that image. She connects this dissonance in part to West's "editing." In this passage, Moira evokes the asymmetry of her relationship with West in a constructed dialogue (Tannen, 1989), animating West's voice and her own. West's words ("Now, I don't think … ") are spoken in a measured, calm, well-enunciated, formal register—a stereotypical voice of rational academic authority. Moira's own voice is audibly under pressure, squeezed, tense, and subservient. The ironic resigned tone of this constructed dialogue and its realization in socially stereotyped voices of power and status were rare signs that Moira might feel uneasy with West's responses. The main thrust of Moira's interview comments and her behavior indicated acceptance and gratitude, particularly in comparison to her negative appraisal of much of the rest of her academic experience.

West

West was a highly productive sociologist, deeply engaged in an intense period of writing and responding to writing.[4] The 14 Project publications (eight conference presentations and six journal articles) West had co-authored in the two years before the seminar offer a useful image of her disciplinary writing practices. All 14 were multiply authored, with any-where from two to five authors on each paper. In this period, counting only her writing related to the Project, West had co-authored with two other professors and 13 graduate students. In the few cases I observed of this collaborative writing, West delegated drafting to others, contributing mainly in initial planning of the papers, and then reviewing and rewriting, often extensively and repeatedly, others' draft texts.[5] In other words, the practices of response and revision seen in Moira's texts (e.g., Figs. 6.2, 6.3, and 6.4) were typical of much of her writing in relation to the Project. However, it is important to recall that Moira was the sole author of the conference paper and that her other text, the preliminary examination, was not only singly authored, but also represented an institutional test of Moira's scholarly potential. In these exchanges then, West might have responded more as a teacher–mentor to a graduate student than as a principal investi-gator and co-author.

When I asked West what her goals were in responding to student writing, she painted a complex portrait. She noted that her goals varied depending on factors like the student's level and native language, but then offered a general goal that oriented her responses: "to move [students] forward and to help them create the best paper that they can." She represented her role metaphorically as that of a journal editor who would treat "students as if they're professionals in the field." When I asked her whether rewriting students' texts was one of her normal response practices in seminars or was more a function of the Project, she responded that she generally did rewrite, explaining:

---

[4]As was suggested in chapter 7, West's work was located in a somewhat interdisciplinary speciali-zation, sociological psychology. Her research methodology involved complex statistical analyses of questionnaire items, particularly in panel designs. Topically, she focused on connections between psychological development and social contexts. Her questions were also oriented toward issues of public concern and public policy.

[5]The practice of having RAs (or other junior participants) produce draft text that the principal investigator then works with appears to be common practice in research teams. For other examples, see Blakeslee (1997), Knorr-Cetina (1981), and Rymer (1988).

because I think that if you write down a way of making it clearer, then the student learns, you know, the phraseology to make it clear, and so usually it's of that nature, it's more like editing than- but because I'm principal investigator, if I notice that they've really made a mistake in the way they describe the data, sometimes that happens, they get confused about the findings or something, then I cross it out and write in the correct response, and I think that's better than just saying "this is wrong," and then, you know, the student doesn't know.[6]

Because this professional standard did not "always come out really well" for the students, West was concerned that they not become too discouraged, particularly when they had worked hard and gone through multiple drafts. To avoid discouragement, she said she tried to be supportive and to get them to realize that they were not alone, that "even faculty members send things to journals and have their work criticized and have their writing corrected." Working closely as co-authors with West, at least some of the students could learn that lesson first hand.

West also displayed considerable familiarity with Moira's work, placing it in biographical contexts that fit precisely with Moira's own accounts (recalling both her interest in "deviance" and in educational sociology). When West was explaining why she rewrote students' texts in general, she illustrated her points in part by pointing to Moira (and Sean) and the disciplinary contexts for her response:

And also because these students are, you know, they're kind of on the verge of entering their academic careers, and, you know, some closer than others, but in the case of Moira and Sean, they've been, you know, submitting papers to meetings and, you know, ( ) journals, and so I want to make it as good as it can be, you know, for their own sake, as well as because they're representing the Project.

West was working with a number of students, but seemed especially pleased with Moira's progress. In the text-based interview on Moira's papers, West began with an evaluation: "This was a very good set of papers, I was, you know, quite impressed with Moira." After looking over Moira's papers, she volunteered this characterization of Moira's reaction to her responses: "She's been really responsive, I mean it's great to have a student who, you know, will read everything and take it all into consideration, and

---

[6]In these interviews, both West and Moira describe response in terms of clarity and correctness. These representations accord well with Ball, Dice, and Bartholomae's (1990) argument that response to students in disciplinary courses typically presents the contingent, contestable nature of disciplinary discourses as issues of the generic clarity of the writing or unproblematic facticity.

then, you know, do it really much better the next time, and so I have been very gratified, you know, by Moira." Recalling the short time Moira had spent on her research topic, West described Moira's performance as outstanding, particularly noting "the clarity of her writing" and "her ability to pull together a lot of rather diverse literature." West assessed Moira's progress in disciplinary as well as departmental contexts, saying that she had "very high hopes for Moira in terms of her contribution to the profession and her ability to get a very good job" and that, although Moira was still wrestling with her dissertation prospectus, she was making "very good progress" on it.

The Zone of a Situated Relationship

As Minick et al. (1993) argue (see chap. 1), it is important to reconceptualize zones of development as simultaneously more personal, more interpersonal, and more institutional than has been conventional in sociohistoric research to date. The particular histories that converged as West responded to and Moira revised this series of texts provide some insights into the modes of participation within which these textual exchanges were embedded. West was certainly no anonymous authority to Moira, any more than Moira was just another novice. West knew quite a bit about Moira, her research topics, and the contexts her texts would be read in. Moira's routine acceptance of West's proposed revisions was not simply a matter of West's institutional capital. Moira trusted West, a trust grounded in her daily experiences as well as in formal institutional positions. As their textual exchanges unfolded, the words West and Moira wrote could be variously indexed in the seminar, departmental exams, the Project, the norm of collaborative writing in the Project, Moira's projected career as sociologist, the interpersonal relationship between Moira and West, Moira's earlier experiences of school and writing, and West's position in the department and discipline. Thus, West responded to Moira's texts from complexly laminated activity footings, seeking to teach Moira but required to test her as a student and able to direct her as an employee, seeking to help Moira represent herself well as a sociologist but also to represent the Project well in a public forum and ensure it did not speak in too many voices (see chap. 6). The zones of development within which Moira and West interacted were laced together and supported by an interpersonal web of practical relations characterized by mutual knowledge, mutual interests, trust, and even liking.

TRACING AUTHORITATIVE AND INTERNALLY
PERSUASIVE DISCOURSES IN RESPONSE ROUNDS

At the time of the seminar, Moira was working on two closely related documents. Figure 8.1 displays the specific corpus of texts and responses that this case examines. The exchanges began in November with the first draft of a preliminary examination (*Prelim 1*) that Moira presented to the unofficial seminar. They resumed in March with four drafts of Moira's conference paper, which I call *Arenas* because of its focus on the "arena of comfort hypothesis." *Arenas 4* was the conference proposal she submitted, a final draft of sorts. It did not include actual results, but outlined planned analyses. In April, Moira produced and West responded to two more drafts of her prelim, building closely on her work on *Arenas*. (For example, several key paragraphs were pasted from *Arenas 4* into *Prelim 2*.) At the end of April, Moira presented *Prelim 3* and part of *Arenas 4* to the seminar. In May,

Paper	Date	Length/Response
Prelim 1	November	24 pages (West's responses on 17)
Arenas 1	March 2	6 pages (West's responses on all)
West memo	March 7	(West's 2-page memo in response to *Arenas 1*)
Arenas 2	March 11	10 pages (West's responses on all)
Arenas 3	March 13	18 pages (West's responses on 13)
Arenas 4	March ?	18 pages (Lessing's responses on 12)*
(*Arenas 4* submitted as a proposal to a professional conference.)		
Prelim 2	April 27	19 pages (West's responses on and a cover memo)
Prelim 3	April 30	26 pages (West's responses on 23)
Arenas 4 (partial)	April 30	10 pages (West's responses on 6)
(The two texts above were stapled together and presented to the seminar on May 3.)		
Prelim 4	May 21	37 pages (Final text, passed by committee)
Arenas 5	July 9	22 pages (West's responses on 18)
Arenas 6	July	25 pages (West's responses on 14)
Arenas 7	July	25 pages

(*Arenas 7* was submitted to the session organizer and a discussant in late July.)

FIG. 8.1. A chronology of Moira's texts and West's responses. * Lessing was a sociologist from another institution who responded to Moira's paper.

Moira produced the fourth and final draft of the prelim, which was passed by her committee. In July, her proposal accepted by the conference and her data now run, Moira produced three more drafts of *Arenas*. Because Moira's analysis of the data did not turn out as planned, she could neither run the analyses nor address the questions she had described in her conference proposal (*Arenas 4*). Thus, she had to extensively revise the introduction and analysis sections, not just add the results and discussion sections. (The page displayed in Fig. 6.2 was from *Arenas 5,* the first of these July drafts.) *Arenas 7* was submitted to the session organizer and a discussant before the conference. In analyzing this series of textual exchanges, I pursued two basic strategies to trace the extent to which West's responses were authoritative or internally persuasive to Moira: intertextual analysis and parallel discourse-based interviews.

Intertextual Analysis

Intertextual analysis involved tracing how West's responses were acted on by Moira across these response rounds. Figures 6.2 and 6.3 presented a very straightforward example of how West's words and ideas entered into Moira's text. Because my initial analysis uncovered many similar examples of response–revision connections, I became particularly interested in any deviations Moira made from West's suggested revisions, any signs of resistance or unprompted revision.

In some cases, such intertextual tracing was less straightforward. For example, in responding to *Arenas 1*, West only crossed out the *s* in *adolescents* in the second sentence of Moira's abstract; however, in *Arenas 2*, that sentence was extensively revised.

> *Arenas 1* (Abstract, sentence 2)
> It is hypothesized that objectively measured transitions in multiple contexts will have an adverse impact on adolescents adjustment, and this response will depend on the actor's subjective perceptions and interpretation of the changes as negative.
> *Arenas 2* (Abstract, sentence 2; italics added to mark changes)
> It is hypothesized that *change in any given life arena* will have *less* adverse *psychological and behavioral consequences if the adolescent has an "arena of comfort" in another domain, characterized by lack of change and satisfaction.*

Had Moira initiated a major revision of this sentence? At first, I thought so. However, West's response to another sentence—from page 3 of *Arenas 1*—suggested a different story. That response is represented at the top of Figure 8.2. West's revision was incorporated without change in *Arenas 2,*

Arenas 1 (p. 3, sentence 5)

The revised hypothesis is that ~~simultaneous~~ change in ~~all~~ [any given] life arenas will have [less] ~~psych & behavioral~~ adverse consequences if the adolescent ~~perceives the changes to be undesirable and~~ [has an "arena of comfort" in another domain, characterized by lack of change and] ~~disruptive.~~ [satisfaction.]

Arenas 2 (p. 3, sentence 11)	*Arenas 2* (Abstract, sentence 2)
The revised hypothesis is that change in **any given** life arena will have **less** adverse **psychological and behavioral** consequences if the adolescent **has an** **"arena of comfort" in another** **domain, characterized by lack of** **change and satisfaction.**	It is hypothesized that <u>change in</u> **any** **given** <u>life arena</u> will have **less** adverse **psychological and behavioral** <u>consequences if the adolescent</u> **has an** **"arena of comfort" in another** **domain, characterized by lack of** **change and satisfaction.**

FIG. 8.2. From text to text—Tracing West's words in Moira's texts. The bold print represents words inserted from West's written response to Moira's sentence 5 on page 3 of *Arenas 1*; the double-underlined text represents words inserted from the original language of Moira's sentence 5 on page 3 of *Arenas 1*.

as shown in the bottom left of Figure 8.2—the bold print indicating West's words. The sentence on the bottom right of Figure 8.2 is the second sentence from the abstract again, the same as the one above, only now the bold print and underlining highlight the borrowing from the page 3 sentence, revealing a complex blend of Moira's and West's words.

Two important points emerge from this example. First, Moira did not simply incorporate West's language mechanically into her revisions. Changes at one textual site sometimes triggered changes at another site (also see footnote 8). Second, the apparently seamless and uniform abstract of *Arenas 2* evaporates under analysis, replaced by a textured, dialogic, historic construction.[7] The questions of who is speaking here and whose meanings are being conveyed have already become complex. For this analysis, I treat "Moira" and "West" as sources of these words. However, in what sense is Moira the author of "it is hypothesized that," or West, of a phrase like "psychological and behavioral," with its obvious allusion to

---

[7]The problem of who is talking here is similar to the one Wittgenstein (1958) noted with regard to recognizing the diverse functions of language: "Of course, what confuses us is the uniform appearance of words when we hear them spoken or meet them in script and print" (p. 6).

disciplinary taxonomies, not to mention the explicitly cited references to the "arena of comfort"? In other words, an intertextual analysis of the responses to and revisions of texts may partially reveal the concrete, historical co-production of Moira's text, but can only hint at the longer chains of utterance and activity that Moira and West are extending.

Figure 8.3 displays another complex use of West's words. In addition to responses written on the text of *Arenas 1*, West also responded with a separate two-page memo (see the chronology in Fig. 8.1). Moira incorporated parts of that memo fairly directly into her next draft, *Arenas 2*. In Figure 8.3, the boxes with arrows connecting them show how closely Moira's text echoes West's. For example, in Point A on the left, West says "whether objective change leads to subjective discomfort (dissatisfaction)" and in Point 1 in *Arenas 2* on the right, Moira says "whether objective change leads to subjective discomfort, represented by path A." If you compare B to 2, D to 3, E to 4, and G to 5, you will see additional examples of this borrowing. Although these comparisons do reveal some deviations from West's words, those deviations seem relatively minor and one case, the addition of "and psychological" after "behavioral" in Points 2 and 5 of *Arenas 2*, could be traced to West's responses in other parts of the text.[8]

This analysis also uncovers a more striking and rare example of deviation, what I would label resistance. West's memo proposed a model (the diagram at the top of Fig. 8.3) quite different from Moira's in *Arenas 1*.[9] Derived from a generic model used in the Project, Moira's initial model had listed contexts (family, peers, work, and school) on the left, psychological constructs (self-esteem and self-efficacy) in the middle, and "negative behavioral outcomes" on the right. That model suggested examining a chain of influences—from the contexts to the intervening psychological variables to the final behavioral outcomes. The model West proposed in the memo directly introduced the constructs (subjective and objective change, arenas of comfort) that Moira was interested in examining. However, Moira did not accept all of West's model. Arrow C in West's model connected objective change to behavioral maladjustment, a connection elaborated in

---

[8]These additions seem to represent another example of generalization. Following West's insertion of "psychological and behavioral" as modifiers for "consequences" in that page 3 sentence (Fig. 8.2), Moira made similar changes to several other sentences in *Arenas 2*, including those displayed in points 2 and 5 of Figure 8.3. Moira's omission of West's "behavioral" in her *Arenas 2* diagram (also in Fig. 8.3) may, as we will see, represent a more complex generalization of West's response.

[9]These diagram models are quite consequential in this kind of research as they encode hypotheses about relations between variables and determine specific statistical analyses.

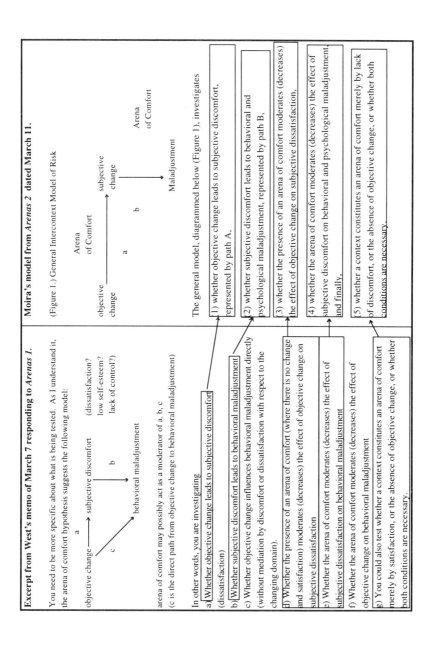

FIG. 8.3. From text to text—West's memo as source text for Moira's *Arenas 2*. I reformatted the text of *Arenas 2* to make comparisons clearer. Figure 1 followed the text presented here and the text appeared as a normal paragraph. Boxes and arrows are added for emphasis.

Points C and F. Moira did not reproduce Arrow C in her *Arenas 2* model, nor were Points C and F incorporated into her text. To understand why Moira resisted these particular points in West's memo, I first analyzed her texts and interview transcripts. Slowly, I began to see that Moira had a critical project in this work.

Figure 8.4 presents several extracts from the first draft of Moira's preliminary examination, a rough "personalized" document that Moira reported feeling embarrassed to share with the participants in the informal Fall seminar. These passages (particularly those I have underlined) express Moira's dissatisfaction with the passive and determined representation of adolescents she found in the literature on adolescent risk and with the emphasis on environmental and physiological rather than psychological factors. Additional evidence emerged from interviews with Moira. When I asked if she had been interested in adolescent risk before she started working in the Project, Moira replied as follows:

Moira: It was interesting to me, and, just from a lot of interesting personal history, it was close to my heart, but nothing I really thought I could pursue

Paul: Umhm, did you get interested then in the arena of comfort, as the focus?

Moira: Um, I don't know, I wish I had rational plans for a lot of this stuff, but it seems like it just happens, um I think because I was disappointed in the- in how much attention is paid to the family when- when you look at an er- maladjustment in adolescence, it seems like they're- it's- they're so quick to blame the family, so "Here's this screwed up family," it seemed like you're basically doomed and um, there's some mention of teachers, or adults in the community, grandparents, other- other people, other contexts that can help the child to adjust or to overcome some of the deficits of the family, but not much attention to that, and I think it needs to be paid more attention to- because obviously there's a lot of kids that are growing up in screwy families and they make it.

Moira's unelaborated personal experience (apparently a reference to problems in her own family) had contributed to a dissonant and critical reading of the adolescent risk literature. Her critical themes were also visible in the texts already discussed. For example, that second sentence from the abstract of *Arenas 1* suggested that adolescents' responses to change would "depend on the actor's subjective perceptions and interpretation of the changes as negative." Also note that in the sentence from page 3 of *Arenas 1* (see Fig. 8.2), Moira represented her work as the "revised hypothesis" that adverse consequences of change will result only "if the adolescent perceives the changes to be undesirable and disruptive."

Evidence of Moira's critique in these sentences was erased when she accepted West's revisions, but becomes visible again in the absence from

Prelim 1 (page 2)

Throughout the literature review I will outline what is lacking in the research as applied to my problem. Briefly, based on the reading I have done so far <u>there is little emphasis on the adolescent experience</u>. <u>Seldom is the adolescent treated like an active participant</u> capable of evaluating his/her own circumstances and actions. <u>The literature seems to concentrate more on environmental inputs than the psychological characteristics</u> crucial to rising above structural adversities, or succumbing to their negative effects.

Prelim 1 (page 4)

Throughout the literature, <u>development is treated like something that just happens, as though it is a neutral process that the individual is little concerned with or unaware of.</u> Development takes place in a normative context, and the adolescent is supposed to turn out a certain way. The adolescent is being trained to fit into society, and has some sense of awareness that he/she is being molded a particular way. By the time they reach adolescence they are forming evaluations of the socialization process, and it's future implications for them. <u>The notion of interaction between the adolescent and his/her environment is included, but there is no sense of individual judgment or choice.</u> When attention is paid to the individual, I get the sense that there is <u>more interest in the power of physiological characteristics than the psychological influences on adaptation</u>. <u>This passive view of the adolescent ignores the possibility of resistance, and that resistance may be adaptive.</u>

Prelim 1 (page 8)

<u>The risk model appears to be based on a conception of development as a process of adaptation, with the goal of fitting in and accepting existing norms</u>. <u>Can the definition of risk be flexible enough to accommodate individual orientations to social integration and the case of the resistant adolescent whose aspirations do not conform to a normative path</u>? As noted above, <u>the idea of risk is usually associated with behavioral outcomes, but</u> I also had to keep in mind that other factors may come into play in influencing adolescents aspirations. <u>Psychological variables may be more central</u>.

FIG. 8.4. Excerpts from Moira's critique of the literature in *Prelim 1*. Underlining added for analytic emphasis.

Arenas 2 of Arrow C and Points C and F from West's memo. The submersion of Moira's critical project that occurs through these response rounds is interestingly reminiscent not only of Herrington's (1992) description of Kate, but also of Myers's (1990) intertextual analyses of writing in biology. Myers noted that his biologists' projects, visions, and motivations (particularly Bloch's) were most visible in early writing with limited circulation. As more public texts emerged from processes of review and revision, those individual issues and goals tended to be replaced in the texts by issues and goals with higher consensus (or at least greater familiarity) among key members of the community.

Discourse-Based Interviews

Intertextual analysis revealed many examples of West's words being incorporated into Moira's papers (e.g., Figs. 6.2, 6.4, 8.2, and 8.3), and a very few examples of Moira resisting West's words (e.g., Fig. 8.3). However, intertextual evidence alone said little about Moira's ideological and evaluative orientation to West's words in her texts. To what extent were West's words internally persuasive to Moira? Tensions between students' perspectives and goals and professors' have figured prominently in accounts of disciplinary enculturation (e.g., Berkenkotter, et al. 1988; Casanave, 1995; Cazden, 1992; Chiseri-Strater, 1991; Prior, 1991). Thus, the question of internal persuasiveness seems critical to understanding these response rounds as learning and enculturating exchanges.

To address that question, I turned to a second methodological strategy: parallel discourse-based interviews. Discourse-based interviewing (Odell, et al., 1983) was developed to help uncover writers' tacit knowledge of and motivations for texts. This technique typically involves presenting one or more alternatives for some passage(s) of a text to the writer (or possibly someone else), asking if she would accept the alternative(s), and asking her to explain why or why not. In this case, I was able to conduct discourse-based interviews on Moira's texts with both Moira and West. In addition to offering alternatives I had generated, I included alternatives taken from earlier drafts that had been revised. Most of these prior draft alternatives were ones that Moira had authored, West had rewritten in her response, and Moira had accepted in her revision.

I prepared three texts for the discourse-based interviews. Using clean copies of the three final texts (*Arenas 4* and *7* and *Prelim 4*), I introduced 36 alternatives (in some cases two alternatives in a single sentence). Moira responded to the full set of alternatives in her interview. However, because I was interviewing West on other students' texts and her time was limited (see Appendix A), I only presented 21 of those alternatives to West. Among the alternatives, I offered Moira 16 opportunities to replace revisions West had written and she had copied with her original language. In seven of the 16 cases, Moira chose to return to her original language, not realizing that was what she was doing. In five cases, she chose to retain West's revisions. She expressed no preference in two cases and rejected both in two others. Evidently, when West's authority was removed from the revisions, some became much less compelling, while others appeared to have become more internally persuasive. *interesting !*

In her interview, West was offered nine of the same alternatives (changes that placed Moira's original texts against West's revisions). West chose to keep her own revisions seven times, to return to Moira's wording once, and to reject both once. Although these quantitative data are suggestive, to explore whether the changes were internally persuasive to Moira, I was primarily interested in comparing the reasons they offered and the extent to which those reasons matched. The complex patterns of convergence and divergence that emerged from that analysis suggest varied blends of the authoritative and the internally persuasive.

In some cases, West and Moira displayed strong convergence, agreeing closely on explanations. For example, in *Arenas 4*, one sentence read in part, "It takes into account the influence of larger social structures." That sentence was pasted into the text of *Prelim 2*. In responding to *Prelim 3*, West crossed out *larger* and replaced it with *macro*. Figure 8.5 presents a prompt from the discourse-based interview on *Arenas 4*, offering the same alternative, crossing out *larger* and suggesting *macro*.[10] Both West and Moira accepted this proposed change and used similar reasoning to explain their acceptance. Although West elaborated on the revision a bit more, Moira and West both accounted for their acceptance of *macro* primarily by saying it is a word used in the literature. Here we see a convergence of the authoritative and the internally persuasive around a word rich in intertextual allusions to sociological literature and debate.[11]

Convergence, however, was not a given. A sentence in *Prelim 4* listed

---

[10] In most cases, the alternatives were Moira's original text. In this prompt, the alternative is actually West's proposed revision to a later draft that Moira did accept.

[11] For example, see Knorr-Cetina and Cicourel's (1981) book *Advances in Social Theory and Methodology: Toward an Integration of Micro- and Macro-Sociologies*.

macro
It takes into account the influence of [larger] social structures....

Moira: *See "macro" a lot here,*	West: I think "macro" is fine and um
"macro" is fine,	Paul: because?
and *that's certainly used in the*	West: well, *it's just a term that utilized*
literature, so macro would be a good	and here we're contrasting "macro" with
change, I have no idea why I used larger	"micro," focus on the individual, so
	actually "macro" is probably a better
	choice

FIG. 8.5 Moira and West respond to a proposed change in *Arenas 4*.

eight categories of risk factors for adolescent problems, one of which was "hereditary influences." In *Prelim 2*, Moira had originally written "potential hereditary influences." In responding to *Prelim 2*, West, without comment, had crossed out the word *potential*. In a prompt from Moira's discourse-based interview on *Prelim 4*, I proposed adding *potential* back in before "hereditary influences." Moira accepted the alternative quickly, saying that she would keep it because she was "more on the socializing end of the continuum." She joked that her opinion should be obvious given her choice of field and then added that she was "still on the nurture end" although she was being challenged by some of her recent experiences as a mother. The word *potential* clearly signaled for Moira a position on the nature-nurture debate, a debate she saw as relevant to her discipline, sociology, and also to her everyday experience of the world as a new parent. In this example then, when offered her own word without the authority of West's pen, Moira quickly reclaimed and defended her original inclusion of *potential*, a fairly clear sign that authoritative discourse had operated without convergence.

Figure 8.6 presents a more complicated case. The proposed alternative, "operationalized, this becomes a bit tricky," is actually Moira's language from *Arenas 1*; the printed, crossed-out text is a substitution West had written in and Moira then included in all subsequent drafts of *Arenas*. Moira rejected both the alternative and West's revised language, whereas West rejected the alternative and kept her wording. However, Moira no longer felt comfortable describing the issue as one of *operationalization*, as she had in *Arenas 1*, seeing it instead as *theoretical*. In fact, in spite of their different decisions, both agreed that the real issue was theory, not opera-tionalization. Thus, on that issue, we see clear convergence. Both Moira and West also mentioned some benefits to *simplifying* the language, but Moira seemed more attached to her original tone, particularly preferring the word *tricky* to *problematic*. In other words, Moira had found the content of West's words internally persuasive, but was resisting West's voice and what it indexed socially.

This resistance to voice was displayed even more clearly in Moira's response to another prompt. In Figure 8.7, the crossed-out words are West's; the proposed alternative is a slight modification of Moira's original sentence, which had read, "We now turn from environmental change to

operationalized, this becomes tricky.
However, [the relationship between objective change and subjective discomfort, and their implications for psychological and behavioral adjustment, remain problematic].

Moira	**West**
ok, hm, I like the change, because this was so wordy, but I don't know if it gets at it ( ) because I don't know if it was necessarily in her operationalization I mean because it- *the article I was reading was more theoretical argument than an operationalization, so er uh, or empirical work, so since she's never tested it herself, I don't think that "operationalize" would be the right word* but I would definitely accept revamping this sentence and simplifying it *I like this because of the "tricky" but "operationalize" is probably not the right word*	here I would think that the new wording is simpler, so that's a benefit of it, but the referent to "this" is unclear because uh, and *I think that the revision changes the meaning of the sentence, because what you're initially talking about here are the relationships among variables, a theoretical connection whereas the new wording introduces the issue of measurement* and uh, and and it's a- it's ano- *it's another issue, so I think I would reject that alternative*

FIG. 8.6. Moira and West reply to a proposed change in *Arenas 4.*

We will now turn from environmental to developmental stressors. [To fully understand the etiology of risk, one must have knowledge of] the concept of

developmental stress, or "normative crises" as coined by Erikson (1968), which

recognizes that in normal development, some stages are more problematic than others.

Moira: All right, I have to think about this one, yeah I kinda like that change,

Paul: Because?

Moira: because it's smoother, and this is really academic sounding,

[Moira makes a face and laughs]

Paul: I should have a videotape [Moira laughs, Paul laughs] catch the yuk face

Moira: "To fully understand the etiology of risk, one must have knowledge of"

[Moira reads in a formal manner, carefully enunciating words with a slight East Coast

accent] it just sounds very wordy and remote or something

FIG. 8.7. Moira replies to a prompt in *Prelim 4*.

developmental transitions."[12] Moira and West both accepted the proposed change, but Moira's response displayed much stronger affect. She characterized the printed text as "academic," accenting that word as a clear negative and reinforcing it nonverbally with a repulsed expression, what I term in the transcript "a yuk face." She then reads the printed text in a stereotyped elite voice and finally describes it as "very wordy" and "remote."

At the end of the discourse-based portion of the interview, I explained where the alternatives had come from and told Moira that she had sometimes rejected revisions West had initiated and she had incorporated into her texts. As we discussed reasons for such rejections, Moira talked about the voice of sociology:

You've obviously compared my writing to other people in this Project, and I think mine is probably less of the real hard sociological jargon, and it's really hard for me to talk to like that- it's hard, it's- I can read and I understand it, but it- I can't talk that way, it's just really difficult, um, and I don't know if that's just me, because I wasn't raised speaking in that tone or, um, my family isn't all that sophisticated, and um,

---

[12]Because I altered Moira's original language in this prompt, it was not counted as one of the 16 that set Moira's original text against West's revisions.

we're also very nonverbal in a lot of our communication because we've had to be over the years for a lot of different reasons, so um even talking to Elaine, the first- when I was first working with- for her was extremely intimidating, and I don't think she's an intimidating person necessarily, but just that she's the- you know, the expert in the field, and I felt like, it'd be- like my ideas were unimportant or that I couldn't articulate myself in a way that she could understand me, it was really frustrating and it still is to a certain extent, but it's improved.

Moira's affective resistance to West's words points to an important issue. Words do not operate only on a one-dimensional continuum of propositional persuasiveness; they also index social identities and affiliations. Although Moira appears to find the conceptual content of West's words persuasive in these last two examples, her comments also reflect considerable resistance, expressed most clearly in affect—through paralinguistic and nonverbal channels—to the social implications of those words.

That Moira accepted West's proposed revisions in her texts and then took so many back when they were anonymously offered in the interviews points to their authoritativeness. That Moira and West often agreed in their decisions and reasoning, particularly on conceptual issues, points to the way these exchanges fostered centripetal learning and enculturation (the convergence of the authoritative and the internally persuasive). That Moira sometimes cringed at and even parodied the language suggests tensions in her enculturation, particularly around issues of social identity and affiliation.

TWO-WAY STREETS AND NARRATIVE STRATEGIES

Although I began my analysis to explore whether West's words were becoming internally persuasive to Moira, in analyzing the discourse-based interviews, I also found indications that Moira's texts and talk were influencing West. Although the changes were subtle, these data do offer an important glimpse of enculturation as a two-way street.

Figure 8.8 shows Moira's and West's reactions in a discourse-based interview to a proposed change in the model. This prompt is basically the reverse of the other proposed alternatives: Now I am asking them if they would accept a change Moira had rejected, West's memo formulation of the model with Arrow C, which Moira had omitted in revision (see Fig. 8.3). To my surprise, West and Moira both rejected this change. However, their reasons reveal an interesting difference. Moira reasserts the arguments she had first made in *Prelim 1*, stating her belief that "there has to be some reaction by the individual." West, on the other hand, still contends that Arrow C is well motivated ("in fact, there is a direct effect, but she didn't

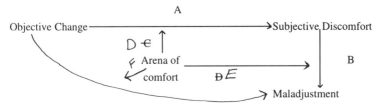

FIG. 8.8. Moira and West reply to proposed changes in *Arenas 4*.

Moira

I think, we had talked through that before, and like *like could something happen? could there be a change in the context and that would spur some type of maladjustment? But I guess I think it has to- there has to be some reaction by the individual so I didn't include that path,* um, there will likely be a lot of changes to this model once I really start getting into the data, things get more clarified, so I think that would be, I would probably not include that, <u>although,</u> based on my preliminary analysis, the subjective-objective didn't pan out in the family context the way I've looked at it so far, so what's happening seems to be more like that

West

ok, this is uh, this is what the theory would lead to think, the effect of this on this, objective change on maladjustment, is mediated by subjective discomfort, but it could be that subjective discomfort doesn't have any ( ) and then, *in- in fact there is a direct effect, but she didn't draw that in,* but that's the alternative,view, *I mean I think what- here she's doing is highlighting the causal connections that are posited by this theory and leaving out you know this alternative*

Paul: would you accept that as a change in the model?

well, uh, *I think that as stated what she's trying to do here is to depict what the theoretical linkages are, that are specified by this, you know, particular work, you know, by Simons and Blyth,* and so therefore I think that it it's good as it stands

draw it"), but goes on to suggest that Moira was attempting to depict the causal connections posited by this theory, that she is in fact just following Simmons and Blyth in this. However, if we go back to West's memo response to *Arenas 1* (Fig. 8.3), we see that she had introduced her diagram of the model, which included Arrow C, saying: "As I understand it, the arena of comfort hypothesis [of Simmons and Blyth] suggests the following model." Thus, it appears that West's representation of the arena of comfort hypothesis has shifted.[13]

To analyze what was happening in this last case, I turned to a notion Myers (1990) developed in his analysis of the translation of technical texts in biology into their popular counterparts. Myers suggested that the technical texts told a "narrative of science" whereas the popular texts told a "narrative of nature." For example, one of the technical texts that he analyzed (by Williams and Gilbert in *Science*) told the story of an experiment with butterflies and vines to test the concept of co-evolution. The popular version of this text (by Gilbert in *Scientific American*) told the story from the personified perspectives of female butterflies searching for safe places to lay eggs and of vines seeking to defend themselves from eggs and caterpillars.

Looking at Moira's and West's accounts of why they reject Arrow C, I saw an analogous distinction at work. Moira explained why she rejected the change in terms of a "narrative of society" ("there has to be some reaction by the individual"), whereas West rejected the change in terms of a "narrative of sociology" ("what she is trying to do here is to depict the theoretical linkages"). These narrative strategies could reflect preferences tied to expertise (i.e., West, as expert, might naturally prefer narratives of sociology); however, other data from the intertextual analysis led me to question that interpretation.

Figure 8.9 traces the evolution of two sentences from *Arenas 1* to *Arenas 3*. In *Arenas 1*, Moira introduced the sentence we looked at in Figure 8.2 from page 3 with "the revised hypothesis" and in the next sentence went on to suggest that this revised hypothesis would allow an examination of "objective and subjective measures of change." I have already discussed, in relation to Figure 8.2, the changes that West introduced into this first sentence. In responding to the second sentence of *Arenas 1*, West crossed out "measures of." Moira accepted West's proposed revisions. Thus, in *Arenas 2*, the second sentence indicates that the revised hypothesis would examine "objective and subjective changes." In responding to *Arenas 2*, West substituted "Following Simmons' formulation, we hypothesize" for "the revised hypothesis is." Although the subject of the next sentence, "this hypothesis," does not change in *Arenas 3*, its meaning has altered, as the

---

[13]I do not infer from this evidence that West has undergone a fundamental conversion in her representations of adolescent agency. Her interview comment ("in fact, there is a direct effect") makes it clear that is not the case. However, it does appear that her representation of the hypothesis has altered, even if only in that she can assign a wider range of interpretations to it.

Arenas 1

The revised hypothesis is that simultaneous change in all life arenas will have adverse consequences if the adolescent perceives the changes to be undesirable and disruptive. This hypothesis alludes to the interplay between objective and subjective measures of change.

Arenas 2

The revised hypothesis is that (**X**) change in **any given** life arena(**x**) will have **less** adverse **psychological and behavioral** consequences if the adolescent **has an "arena of comfort" in another domain, characterized by lack of change and satisfaction**. This hypothesis alludes to the interplay between objective and subjective (**X**) change**s** which we will attempt to capture in this analysis.

Arenas 3

Following Simmons' formulation, we hypothesize that (**X**) change in **any given** life arena(**x**) will have **less** adverse **psychological and behavioral** consequences **if the adolescent has an "arena of comfort" in another domain characterized by** *stability* **(lack of change***) **and satisfaction**. This hypothesis alludes to the interplay between objective and subjective (**X**) change**s** (**X**).

FIG. 8.9. Cumulative changes in Arenas. **Bold** print = West's revisions. ***Bold print italic*** = West's revisions of her previous revisions. (X) = Deletion of a word or phrase by West. (x) = Deletion of a letter by West.

hypothesis now refers to Simmons's original hypothesis rather than Moira's revision of Simmons.

In the whole text of *Arenas 1*, Moira identified her contribution to the arena of comfort hypothesis at three points as an exploration of the relation between objective and subjective *measures* of change.[14] In the first round of response, West deleted "measures of" in two of three cases. (The third case remained through *Arenas 4*, but disappeared when the whole paragraph was deleted in *Arenas 5*.) I read these changes as the reverse of the example

---

[14]The other two examples can be seen in Figure 6.4.

from the discourse-based interview. Here, Moira is telling a narrative of sociology, challenging sociological practice in fact, whereas West is simultaneously rewriting the text as a narrative of society and repositioning Moira's contribution as following rather than revising Simmons's arena of comfort hypothesis. At the end of these exchanges, it appears that Moira believes she is modifying Simmons and Blyth's arena of comfort hypothesis by exploring *subjective measures* of change, whereas West believes Moira is just following that hypothesis out, making explicit what it always implied, by exploring *subjective change*. In the end, Moira's and West's views co-exist almost imperceptibly both in Moira's texts and in their agreement on issues such as not including Arrow C in the model. Moira's text is, thus, seen as a dialogic blend not only of Moira's and West's words, but also of their worlds.

MEDIATED AUTHORSHIP AND DISCIPLINARY ENCULTURATION

In the earlier analysis of the ways Mai and Teresa appropriated language from texts (chap. 4), I raised the question of how to describe the varied qualities of appropriation and their implications for learning, for participation in communities of practice. The kind of analysis pursued in this chapter of the degree to which appropriation was internally persuasive or authoritative offers one way to explore that question.

This analysis has displayed how through multiple response rounds, West's words came to populate Moira's texts, altering not only their style, but also their content, their motives, what they indexed socially, and what disciplinary discourses they referred to intertextually. Over the course of seven drafts, *Arenas* was incrementally refashioned toward West's voices, what she found internally persuasive. Moreover, West mediated Moira's authorship not only through her written responses, but through her sedimented work in weaving together the functional systems of the Project itself (everything from securing institutional funding and hiring RAs to constructing the Project's design, selecting measures, and ordering specific analyses). The way those prefabricated resources of typified functional systems mediated Moira's literate activity may have influenced Moira and her texts as much as (perhaps more than) West's written responses did. As was noted previously (see chap. 7, footnote 27), Moira's desire to emphasize adolescent agency through the arena of comfort hypothesis was complicated by the lack of appropriate indicators (questionnaire items) in the Project's data.

As in Sean's case (chap. 7), the mediation of Moira's authorship involved dialogic interactions not only with other people's voices, but with the voices sedimented in networks of artifacts, practices, and institutions.

On the other hand, analysis of these exchanges did display Moira's overt resistance to West's proposed revisions on the issue of objective change, her covert resistance to West's tone, and some signs of her reciprocal influence on West's own discourse. To summarize, I might say that in spite of almost total compliance with West's proposed revisions, Moira continued to be an active agent in this discourse, working to maintain ownership of her texts and research. However, that formulation implies a simple agonistic dualism, Moira's words struggling with West's. What I see is more complex and intriguing. At several points, West actually helped Moira to shape an argument closer to the personal views she expressed in *Prelim 1*. For example, West's memo model emphasized Moira's central concerns much more sharply than Moira's initial model in *Arenas 1*. Likewise, although Moira had argued repeatedly in her first text (*Prelim 1*, see Fig. 8.4) against approaches to adolescent coping that stressed the environment and behavior at the expense of psychological perspectives, it was West's insertion of "psychological and behavioral" before "consequences" in one place (Fig. 8.2) that seemed to prompt Moira to include "psychological" and avoid "behavioral" in other parts of her text (e.g., Fig. 8.3). In addition, as the discourse-based interviews suggested, Moira came to find at least the propositional content of a number of West's revisions internally persuasive.

West's and Moira's participation in the streams of activity that surrounded the production of Moira's texts seems to have influenced West, the Project, and other institutions as well as Moira. Moira's dissonant reading of the adolescent risk literature, signaled first in *Prelim 1*, triggered not only this series of texts, but also an extended (sometimes public) instructional interaction, a tacit co-authorship, a theoretical dialogue, and a new thread of research and potential publication in the Project—one not planned for by West. Data were statistically analyzed in ways they otherwise would not have been. West was almost certainly led to think about the arena of comfort hypothesis more than she otherwise would have. Moira's persistent critique of objective *measures* of change and passive views of adolescents encouraged West to reconsider how objective change is related to subjective discomfort in this hypothesis. In a shift from her memo, West ends up reading, or at least being able to read, the arena of comfort hypothesis as one that had already implicitly emphasized the subjective response of adolescents and challenged unmediated objective influence.

As Moira and West participate in these streams of activity, the quality of Moira's participation in the Project shifts perceptibly, as is indexed in the intensity and momentum of textual production and reception displayed by the chronology of texts (Fig. 8.1). Over the course of the year, Moira moves from being an employee engaged in logistical support of the research (with no authorship credit) to one of two students West thinks of as "on the verge of entering their academic careers," as actively engaged in the communicative forums of the discipline (major conferences and refereed journals). That the other student was Sean (see chap. 7) suggests how much ground Moira had gained. Departmentally, this activity moved Moira through her preliminary examination and toward her dissertation prospectus. Finally, Moira's questions about adolescent risk and arenas of comfort were beginning to move into disciplinary forums (see Fig. 8.1), with texts of *Arenas* read by Lessing (a sociologist at another institution) and by the organizer and discussant of the conference session, and finally heard by those who attended the session where Moira presented her paper.

Considering the implications of these data for disciplinary enculturation, I would make a symmetrical argument. Moira's influence on West, the Project, and communities of sociological practice is unlikely to represent a significant event in the history of sociology or even necessarily of West and the Project. Likewise, I would not argue that these interactions radically restructured what was internally persuasive to Moira or her modes of participation in sociology, although I believe they clearly represent what I refer to as deep participation. My argument is that this analysis makes visible processes that are usually significant to persons and disciplines only when extrapolated over time and across multiple settings. This microhistory of mediated authorship suggests how relative newcomers to disciplines change as they appropriate discourses and practices and enter into new relations within functional systems of activity, but it also suggests how such newcomers, particularly at key sites like major research institutions, might exert their own centripetal force as their ideologies are dialogically received and accommodated to as well as altered. In other words, what is internally persuasive to a student, particularly to cohorts of students, may accrue authority (see also Casanave, 1995).

The question of who is talking leads not only to authorship and agency, but also to the historical production of functional systems and the role of writing in that production. As this microhistory displays, the activity of the Project/seminar was heavily mediated by and oriented to textual artifacts. Moira's texts and authorship, for example, were extensively mediated not only by West's response texts, but by an intertextually linked arrays of questionnaires, raw data, coded data, statistically transformed data, memos, drafts of publications, and published papers. In turn, Moira's texts (both draft and final) became part of this chain of works. However, the chain was not limited to texts, but located in laminated literate activity, including diverse histories of talk, reading, observation, action, thinking, and feeling as well as writing. The brief analyses in chapter 6, Sean's case in chapter 7, and Moira's in this chapter display ways that literate activity created opportunity spaces within which sociological discourses and practices could be foregrounded and rehearsed. As they produced these texts, the Project sociologists had to, for example, align their everyday activity and understanding with disciplinary discourses through specific representational practices and to make things work when planned analyses or routine procedures failed. Through this literate activity in the seminar, all of the participants had opportunities to (re)appropriate various conceptual tools, embodied ways of acting, affective and motivational orientations, goal structures, communicative practices, and so on. In their production of cultural events like *a seminar discussion of a prospectus* or *the co-authoring of a conference presentation*, participants were both indexing and (re)constituting the laminated institutional spheres of activity of a university, a department, a specific seminar, the Project, and sociology conferences and journals. At the same time, they were indexing and reconstituting their positions and relations in these spheres. If disciplinary enculturation typically refers to the transmission of specialized knowledge and discourse to novices, these accounts support a view of enculturation as a continuous, heterogeneous process of becoming, the historical co-genesis of persons, artifacts, practices, institutions, and communities through everyday mediations of activity and agency.

PART IV

Redrawing the Maps of Writing and Disciplinarity

9

Laminations of Activity: Chronotopes and Lilah

Bakhtin's theoretical work consistently expressed his desire to develop a dialogic, sociohistorically situated understanding of language. Like his more familiar notions of utterance and speech genre, his discussion of the chronotope (literally time-place) reflected that project. Bakhtin (1981) suggests that chronotopes are foundational elements in a theory of language as history rather than system. Rooted in concrete events involving particular times, places, people, and actions, he argues, "language, as a treasure house of images, is fundamentally chronotopic (p. 251). In this sense, any situated activity is chronotopic. However, Bakhtin was especially interested in typified chronotopes. For example, he argued that literary (and other) genres are powerfully prefigured by the stock of typified chronotopes available to represent real time-space in texts. For Bakhtin, these chronotopes do not simply associate particular times and places with cultural events (e.g., breakfast in the morning in the kitchen), but construct subjectified, perspectival, motivated situations, associating plots, motifs, persons (with exterior behavior and interior consciousness), classes of objects, affective atmospheres, and evaluative orientations. In other words, these typified chronotopes invoke full narrative worlds, saturated with sociohistoric forms of life.

Perhaps because much of Bakhtin's discussion focused on chronotopic representation in literary genres, his notion of chronotopes has primarily been taken up for analysis of narrative representation in novels, short stories, and films. However, Bakhtin made it clear that he understood typified representations to be grounded in real-life embodied chronotopes (i.e., in actual concrete histories). For example, he pointed to relations between powerful social institutions like the Greek public square or the Roman family and the representational modes of literary and rhetorical genres. He also highlighted, in a postscript to his original essay, the embodied chronotopes of the reader and the author, the situated activities of producing and renewing a text. Thus, when Bakhtin talked of a chronotope, such as that of the road, he was ultimately invoking not only representations of roads in varied genres, but also actual histories of roads and travel, and the dialogic interactions between such embodied experiences and their representations. In short, Bakhtin was deeply interested in the interpenetration and co-evolution of embodied and representational chronotopes.[1]

In chapter 5, I described five prototypical scenes that have dominated writing research and theory. Here, I am suggesting that those scenes can be productively reconceptualized as typified representational chronotopes. Examining those scenes as chronotopes rather than prototypes offers two critical advantages. First, the notion of chronotopes is holistic, historical, and oriented to full narratives, whereas the notion of prototypes has been developed largely in terms of category formation (Rosch & Lloyd, 1978). Narrative, as Bruner and Lucariello (1989; see also Bruner, 1986, 1990) suggests, is not simply an externalized discursive form, but a mode of inner understanding that is basic to our ontological grounding in the world, to making sense of the flow of experience. Second, while both prototypes and chronotopes relate situated experience to internalized representation, prototype theory is grounded in cognitive representationalism (see Dreyfus, 1992; Hutchins, 1995) and is, thus, more oriented to objectifying perspectives and notions of internalization as one-way transmission. Formed within Bakhtin's framework, the notion of chronotopes is more sensitive to dialogic multiplicities, affective and evaluative orientations, and the intermingling of representation and world. In his analysis of literary genres, Bakhtin (1981) argued that chronotopes are "the organizing centers for the fundamental narrative events of the novel... the place where the knots of narrative are tied and untied" (p. 250). Considering the interanimation of embodied chronotopes (of writing researchers, their participants, and the readers of their texts) and representational chronotopes (of writing research in talk and text), I would argue that chronotopes are the organizing centers of writing research, driving the way objects and sites are bounded, defined, and animated in "natural" sequences of action that obscure the fuller ecology of literate activity.

---

[1]Discussing the dialogic interactions of real and represented worlds around literature, Bakhtin (1981) argued:

> The work and the world represented in it enter the real world and enrich it, and the real world enters the work and its world as part of the process of its creation, as well as part of its subsequent life, in a continual renewing of the work through the creative perception of listeners and readers. Of course this process of exchange is itself chronotopic: it occurs first and foremost in the historically developing social world. (p. 254)

THE CHRONOTOPE OF THE CLASSROOM
AND ITS CONTRADICTIONS

As was suggested in chapter 5, the representational chronotope of writing in the classroom centers on a textual version of Initiation–Reply–Evaluation (IRE) discourse in which the teacher initiates the writing task (assignment), the student replies (text), and the teacher then responds to or evaluates the text (evaluation). In this institutional discourse, students' texts function less as messages than as tests, read to assess students' intelligence, knowledge, effort, and attitude. Like the scenes described in Chapter 5, chronotopes are laminated, not pure. As Bakhtin (1981) noted, "Chronotopes are mutually inclusive, they co-exist, they may be interwoven with, replace or oppose one another, contradict one another or find themselves in more complex interrelationships…. The general characteristic of these interactions is that they are *dialogical* (in the broadest use of the word)" (p. 252). The chronotope of the classroom envelopes the chronotopes of the solitary writer in the garret and of the writer–reader dyad (see chap. 5). In this dialogic interaction, the enveloped chronotopes are reinflected. The solitary artist–writer is now the lone student acting under orders, doing homework for school rather than being engaged in personal expression and social critique. With the student writing to the teacher, the writer–reader dyad becomes highly asymmetrical and involves routine violations of Grice's (1989) cooperative principle, as in the frequent demand that student writers not take common ground as common or that they write texts to a certain length regardless of relevance or quality. What I have come to realize in reflecting on my research is that almost hard-wired into the chronotope of the classroom are the authoritative perspectives of the institution and the teacher. In this representational chronotope, people exist in their institutional capacities (as teachers or students), and the IRE scheme of assignment, text, and evaluation offers an image of student writing solely from the teacher's desk.

The power of this representational chronotope and its privileging must be understood in relation to the embodied chronotopes of researchers, participants, and readers. In my own case, as I undertook research into academic writing, I was approaching a social institution as familiar and dominant as Bakhtin's family to the Roman or public square to the Greek. From pre-school at age 4 through completion of a master's degree in applied linguistics at age 24, I had spent large parts of many days of each year as a student in classrooms or, outside the class itself, doing the assigned work of school. I returned to the role of student at age 33 for four more years as I pursued my PhD. For most of the past 18 years, I have also experienced classrooms from the other official role, that of teacher. As I note in Appendix A, many of the questions and concerns that initially shaped this research were provoked by my experiences as a teacher. Finally, the privileging of institutional perspectives in this chronotope is furthered naturalized because the participants of this research (professors and graduate students) and almost anyone who reads it will also have come through similar institutional histories.

That it seems natural to study writing in the academy from the institution's perspective is clearly visible in existing research. When I began my first pilot study of writing in seminars (see Appendix A), the salience of teacher and text in this chronotope was so powerful that I expected to be able to define the "real" writing tasks of the seminar simply by relating students' texts to the professor's responses, goals, and values (note the absence of students here). That the professor seemed to be responding to the students and events in the seminar as well as to the texts surprised me; however, I was unable to document it because I had not collected relevant data. As I analyzed the relevant data in my next study (of *Language Research*, see chap. 2), I was struck by the active ways students pursued diverse goals and their own projects as they undertook writing tasks. In other words, I had tacitly assumed students would simply try to match the professor's assigned task. Although these findings should have been obvious from my own experiences as a student, I had to struggle to articulate them. The problem, I suspect, was that they did not accord with the institutional perspective inscribed in the representational chronotope of the classroom.

I see evidence of the same kind of assumptive framing and privileging in others' research as well. Whether surveying instructors' assignments (e.g., Bridgeman and Carlson, 1983; Horowitz, 1986b, Rose, 1983) or engaging in naturalistic inquiry (e.g., Herrington, 1985, 1988; Walvoord & McCarthy, 1990), the assignment–text–evaluation structure of the classroom chronotope has provided the basic map of the territory. For example, while Flower et al. (1990) carefully documented the complex menu of options that students might pursue when assigned a summary writing task, they assumed that task representations were simply determined by student understanding of the task, derived from prior experience with classrooms and summary writing. That students might represent the teacher's task one way but carry it out another way was not considered. Not distinguishing task representation from task implementation (see chap. 2 for an analysis of the multiple faces of the task), this view effectively equated student agency with error or academic incompetence. Nor did they examine the instructor's representations of the tasks and contexts or how the summary assignment and its contexts had been cued in the history of the course. Treating instruction as transparent and unproblematic illustrates the way instructors' perspectives are naturalized. The discussion of Walvoord and McCarthy's (1990) methods and interpretations in chapter 1 pointed to similar assumptions in their research.

One way to conceptualize the consequences of these assumptions is to consider how they obscure dialogic lamination in two complementary planes. *Horizontally*, they sever relations of the classroom to other times and places, and *vertically* they present persons only in their institutional capacities, obscuring other activity footings or social identities within the classroom itself.[2] In my first two studies (see chap. 2 and Appendix A), I was progressively recognizing that teachers' and students' literate activities were profoundly contextualized in their lives, that students' writing and instructors' responses were shaped by personal and interpersonal as well as institutional and disciplinary contexts. My last research project pushed those recognitions further. For example, the sociology seminar (chaps. 6–8) complicated the object of my research because the chronotope of the classroom was so overshadowed by the chronotopes of the research project, disciplinary conferences and publications, and institutional examinations. When I entered the seminar, I knew nothing about the Project except that students were going to be writing from "a common data set." When I asked Sean (see chap. 7) to provide texts related to his prospectus, I received not notes, drafts, and the odd earlier paper I had expected, but thick packets of multiple drafts of multiple texts (some dating back almost a year) with multiple responses from West and others. Likewise, as I watched Park's presentation for the seminar (see chap. 6), it was difficult to account for what he did (or how he was ultimately graded) from the perspective of the assigned task in the seminar. As I followed the data in *Sociology*, the object of my inquiry shifted radically, from the one-dimensional chronotope of the classroom where professor and students were negotiating writing tasks to

---

[2]Focusing on actant-network theory, Starr (1991) argues persuasively for *not* accepting privileged institutional perspectives, noting the many ways such perspectives obscure the full relations of a dominant institutionalized network, particularly its relations with "others." Starr argues that research should attend carefully to heterogeneity and perspective, to shifting identities and social orders, to which actors benefit from stabilized networks as well as to which actors make up the networks. Her argument that people always hold multiple memberships and are multiply positioned (and multiply marginalized) fits well with the notion of vertical lamination.

a complexly laminated and dynamic activity setting. To understand the texts I was collecting, I had to expand the purview of the research horizontally (looking beyond the classroom) and to deepen the analysis vertically (seeing the multiplicity of activity footings, identities, and relationships that motivated the work). In the end, the seminar came to seem the most ephemeral of the relevant chronotopic framings for the literate activity of this group.

Although *Sociology* and other sites produced palpable tensions between the chronotopic framing of my research and the narratives of literate activity I was developing, the case of Lilah, a student in *American Studies* (see chap. 3), triggered a fuller awareness of the theoretical and methodological implications of those tensions. A first-year graduate student in American Studies, Lilah produced a text for Kohl's seminar on field research that resembled a number of other students' texts. Like Sarah's (described in chap. 3), it was strongly aligned to the special topics of the course (a neighborhood, ethnicity, interviewing, questions). However, Lilah was the only student in my research who agreed to do a process log on her writing, and her log pointed to a much more complex tale of her work. During the quarter, Lilah provided 23 entries of varying length and format (from essay-like paragraphs on focused topics to telegraphic lists of ideas for papers), totaling 73 handwritten pages of text. In the instructions for the process logs, I had asked Lilah to keep all drafts and notes, to describe her writing for Kohl's seminar, and to discuss any reading or conversation related to that writing. I had also expressed an interest in related writing done in the past or concurrently.

Although I had anticipated that writing, reading, and talk in other academic and non-academic settings would be involved in her writing for *American Studies* and was interested in such connections, I was still asking essentially how these other things related to the focal writing task of Kohl's seminar. Where I had tacitly accepted the privileged perspective of institutional production (see de Certeau, 1984) and granted the seminar a fairly autonomous and dominant space on that official map, the literate activity Lilah described did not respect the borders of the institutional territories she sometimes inhabited. Like the texts of *Sociology*, Lilah's logs led me to widen the scope of my inquiry, influencing the texts I analyzed (texts she wrote for three courses over two semesters) and the topics of our research interviews (which included those courses and professors and also varied biographical topics). More fundamentally, Lilah's logs relocated the perspective of the inquiry in ways that challenged my initial framing. The horizontal and vertical laminations her log entries pointed to produced a

clash of chronotopes, with not only methodological implications for research designs, but substantive implications for understanding writing and
disciplinarity.

REMAPPING THE TERRITORY/INHABITING A LIFEWORLD

With her first two log entries, Lilah began to construct a map of her
academic writing quite different from the one I, as researcher, had imagined.
In her first entry, Lilah wrote about her quarter's work. Her text moved
seamlessly from the research project for Kohl's seminar to a paper on
Chicano ethnicity she had written for an immigration history seminar with
Professor Marini the previous quarter, and a related paper she would write
for Marini in the continuation of that history seminar. It also pointed to ways
that Lilah's home and community spheres of activity as well as special
topics of the seminars (see chap. 3) were intermingling in Lilah's representations of these tasks:[3]

> *As for more stressful thoughts—what about all these papers coming up and how can
> I break them down to make them more manageable?*

> *I'm thinking that for Kohl's project, I'll study North Midwest City since I will also be
> continuing work on a paper about Chicano ethnicity in another class. With the other
> paper, I studied how definitions of ethnicity changed through the 70's & 80's and how
> in much of the non-Chicano lit ethnicity was judged functional if the ethnic group
> prospered in the U.S., dysfunctional if they fared poorly. Obviously, that's the more
> conservative spectrum of scholarship, but I think money is a pretty embedded standard
> for lots of things in the U.S. So with the North Midwest City research, I think I'd like
> to get a feel for how businesses interact with the community and what impact they
> have on notions of ethnicity, if they have any impact at all. They must in some way
> since business leaders are often community leaders*

> *One of these days, I really want to get at how the businessman sometimes turns himself
> into a mythic, natural figure as in the case of the Raynor Street Titan, who is this
> year's North Wind, I think. Greg brought a button home with a drawing of this guy
> looking like Father Wind—cheeks puffed and some sage-like hat on his head. I think
> he sells insurance when he's not being the North Wind. Anyway, I think this self or
> cultural transformation is fascinating, and I wonder if this happens in other commu-
> nities.*

In this log, Lilah reports that she plans to align Kohl's assignment with her

---

[3]Log entries in this chapter are presented in italics. All names of local persons, institutions, and
places have been changed to pseudonyms in Lilah's log entries and texts reproduced here.

work for Marini by selecting a Chicano neighborhood for her field research. This initial alignment is soon fused as she decides to make research on North Midwest City's Cinco de Mayo celebration the focus of both Kohl's and Marini's papers. Her reflections also index the work of her husband, Greg, who was involved in community economic development. Links to Greg, and through him to home and local community, appear explicitly in her discussion of the North Wind button he brought home, which she connects to disciplinary topics like myth, self transformation, and community. They appear implicitly in the previous paragraph, where she talks about her interest in exploring how business leaders shape community and ethnicity, a topic that she ultimately would highlight in her papers for both Kohl and Marini.

Lilah's second log entry (presented in full below) charted a wider course as she moved associationally back and forth among Kohl's task, a seminar on Native American studies with Ron Nash (part of another two-quarter sequence), Marini's history paper the previous quarter, her own ethnic identity, and her life experiences:

Still haven't done any more reading, and haven't concretized my project, but that's the beauty of Kohl's philosophy on the quarter system—not long enough for finished products. I love that! It's so freeing. I feel like I'm really going to be able to simply observe and record and think—not become an overnight expert. Of course, there's nothing simple about observing and recording. I've been learning this in my class with Ron Nash. The article for this week on the problems non-native writers have when they try to write native-centered histories emphasized this. How easy it is to jump to the other side before you've really examined your own.

I think I sort of did this in my choice of topics last quarter in immigration history. I wanted to be the outsider/insider and get Chicano history into the picture of immigration history. And in some ways it's not a bad move. I mean, in the same way that Native Americans are often portrayed as dead, historical figures, so too is immigration history all focused on something that is over. Ethnicity lives on—that's stressed. But the reality of immigration, its imminence in current Am. history, is downplayed, made invisible. I probably did the same thing, though, in that I focused on more established Chicano historians (only read English texts) and really didn't look at the complexities of an immigration that continues daily. More accurately, a migration.

Anyway, the article this week talked about dealing with one's own culture first before claiming authority in another. Maybe, though, I don't know what my culture is, so I keep bouncing off of others to get a sense of possibilities. Or maybe I don't want to acknowledge what I am. German seems so boring and Americanized. My mother talks about some distant French Huguenot relations and some Italian ties too. There's also the mysterious Bohemian link. Even identifying it doesn't interest me. Perhaps one's culture is what one gravitates towards, what holds resonance. Travelling through Germany I never felt much. Watching <u>Aguirre</u> and <u>Stroszek</u> (I can't remember director) was a different matter, though. Then I was glad to be German—there was *something stubbornly eccentric I loved about those characters. Moreover, there was an abundance of mental illness in those films, an appreciation for its depths and unnavigable reaches that made them resonate with me and my family history.*

So this whole notion of culture as nationality or ethnicity eludes me. I don't know where to begin to start deconstructing myself as an oppressor, as part of the oppressive group. Experiences as a white teacher in an all-black high have given me more insights into my own oppressive stereotypes and notions about education. But I'm getting tired and hungry.

Lilah's log entry traces a kaleidoscopic trajectory of chronotopes, of pasts, presents, and projected futures, personal and global, situated and abstract. This trajectory achieves coherence through the continuity of her own biography and through central topics, especially ethnicity and course work.

Ethnicity is an interesting topical thread in these two log entries, a discursive shifter that indexes and weaves together a heterogeneous chronotopic network associated with Lilah's work. Ethnicity is a disciplinary topic associated with texts in immigration history and Native American studies. Institutionally, ethnicity is associated with the academic tasks of her courses, talk about ethnicity in class, study of it in her field research, and writing about it for seminar papers. However, ethnicity is not limited to academic and disciplinary spheres of activity. It also appears briefly as a concrete social issue, nationally of ethnic relations and histories in the United States and locally of the North Midwest City Chicano neighborhood where Lilah plans to study. Ethnicity also emerges as part of Lilah's own (ambiguous) identity, something she connects to the family she grew up in, her travels in Germany, German films she identified with, and her experiences working as a White teacher in an all-Black high school. What ethnicity indexes across these contexts is not simply propositional or referential; Lilah signals affective and evaluative orientations with each link. In these log entries, Lilah sketches a dense chronotopic network, and each jump in time and place (pointing to the horizontal lamination of her activity) foregrounds particular scenes, activities, relationships and aspects of her identity, indexing the vertical lamination of her multiple activity footings.

Even in these early log entries, Kohl's task is being deprivileged by Lilah's perspective. On Lilah's map, writing for all her classes ("all these papers") are found in one territory. And why not? From her perspective, they all happen on her time, in the lifeworld she inhabits. On Lilah's map, Kohl's seminar and its tasks appear as just another stop on her daily circuits of activity, circuits that go beyond school to other sites and beyond the present to remembered pasts and projected futures. In the next sections, I explore how these chronotopic laminations played out in Lilah's literate activity over the next several months.

AN OVERVIEW OF LILAH'S LITERATE ACTIVITY
FOR THREE SEMINARS

Lilah's literate activity for her three seminars that quarter was tightly linked. For the history seminar the previous quarter, Marini had asked students to write on a topic they would then research in greater depth the following quarter. In her first two logs, Lilah notes that she had written a paper focusing on Chicano ethnicity and economics. She also describes her decision to align that second paper for Marini with her work for Kohl's seminar by studying a Chicano neighborhood. In the next entries, Lilah reports her decision to make the annual Cinco de Mayo parade in the North Midwest City the common topic of her papers for Kohl and Marini. With her work on Cinco de Mayo, Lilah maintained a coherent focus over the quarter. She conducted five interviews with community activists, attended the neighborhood celebration, went to a reception–party held to commemorate a new relationship between community organizers and the state historical society, and read varied sources on Chicano ethnicity. For Ron Nash's seminar, her log documents a protracted struggle to identify a good topic.

For Kohl, Lilah turned in the brief draft "outline" he requested in the eighth week, got his feedback, and then turned the final paper in on time. In the final paper (with headings for each section to evoke the outline), Lilah recounted how she had decided to do research on ethnicity using Cinco de Mayo as a focal point for examining issues of community and control, described the parade itself, and then (in a section titled "History") discussed the histories of local Cinco de Mayo celebrations as related by three Chicano community leaders she interviewed. Lilah went on to describe the geography of the North Side (in a section called "Time and Place"). Her next section ("Comparisons") compared the Cinco de Mayo celebration with a local Norwegian-American celebration as described in a journal article Marini had introduced in his class. She concluded with a section on methodology, a bibliographic essay discussing her sources, and a list of questions she had used as a guide in conducting her interviews.

The paper for Marini on Cinco de Mayo was delayed. The final draft I received was titled "Penultimate, as yet untitled draft on Cinco de Mayo." Lilah had presented her research in the seminar, turned her draft in to

Marini (two weeks after quarter ended), and received his written and oral responses to it. However, she still had not written the final draft when we conducted our last interview several months later. In the draft for Marini (a paper without headings), she emphasized the interviews she had conducted (as she had in Kohl's paper), but cited more textual sources (newspapers, articles, and books). Some sections of this paper (e.g., the comparison with the Norwegian-American celebration) were taken directly or with minimal modification from the paper she had turned in to Kohl several weeks earlier.

Nash assigned students a single paper (with no drafts) to be turned in at the end of his two-quarter seminar. Lilah spent much of the second quarter in search of a topic for his paper. She first considered analyzing depictions of Native-American women in the fiction of Native-American women authors. Halfway through the quarter, she became interested in the exotic biography of a turn-of-the-century Native-American girl who was adopted by a spiritualist Euro-American family and became a psychic medium in their seances. Her initial enthusiasm dimmed when she read a critical review of the biography. A week later, Lilah was watching Bill Moyers interview Sam Keen on television. She began to connect Keen's adoption of Native-American spirituality, the use of the Native-American girl as a psychic medium, New-Age interest in Native-American culture, and comments a student in Nash's class had made on colonialist processes of cultural appropriation. Through this associative and analogic process, Lilah arrived at her topic, an examination of "White shamanism" focusing on the writings of Sam Keen and Frank Waters. She settled on this topic just three weeks before the end of the quarter. Her final paper for Nash, began with three epigraphs, a four-line quote from Frank Waters's *The Book of the Hopi*, a 14-line quote from Sam Keen's *Your Mythic Journey*, and a three-line quote from Yeats's "The Second Coming." She structured her paper on White shamanism by analyzing quotes from first Waters and then Keen, pointing to biases and unintentional ironies in their work. Interspersed with this analysis was a general critique of White shamanism and Euro-American uses of Native-American culture.

FOLLOW THE TACO: DINNER, RESEARCH, HISTORY, AND CULTURAL COMMODIFICATION

Drawing on the "follow the actors" strategy that Latour (1987, 1996) employs to trace heterogeneous networks (see also chap. 7), I will explore the laminated trajectories of Lilah's literate activity this quarter by partially tracing a single thread in her work, a thread constructed around Mexican food and, particularly, the taco. In an early log entry, after she has decided to study Cinco de Mayo, Lilah recounts a conversation from Nash's seminar:

> *One woman is writing her paper on Tex-Mex cuisine. As it happens, the year Tex-Mex became big was also the year when illegal aliens and cracking down on border control was the hot political issue. She thinks it has something to do with imperialist nostalgia—desire for cultural artifacts of destroyed or subjugated peoples. It's also a commodification of culture—a way of getting "goods" from another culture without the people.*
>
> *Someone mentioned that she should go to the International Festival and look at how that is commodified. Suddenly, ethnicity = food, i.e., something consumable. This is what I'm wondering about with Cinco de Mayo. What's used to present ethnicity? And is the festival really about ethnicity or more about commodification of an ethnic community that makes it more palatable to the larger <u>American</u> community? I've always felt a little disappointed with these events that claim to be international and end up just featuring different dances, clothes, foods. But until today I didn't know why. Really, they lose their cultural differentness by putting it into a shape Americans can buy.*

In this entry, Lilah aligns another student's discussion of the cultural politics of Tex-Mex cuisine, her own interests in ethnicity and Cinco de Mayo, and her disappointment with international events she had attended. With this topical network forged, ethnic food as cultural commodification emerges as a possible theme for her work on Cinco de Mayo. Following the taco as Lilah works through this theme offers us a partial window into the dialogic interanimation of embodied and represented chronotopes in her literate activity.

Lilah's next log entry reports that she and her husband went to a Mexican restaurant on the North side to check out the neighborhood. She writes that the food was fantastic and describes the restaurant, its customers, and what the neighborhood looked like at night. Was Lilah out for a family dinner or doing research for her papers? I would argue both and probably more as well. This dinner, like any event, was laminated, part or potentially part of multiple streams of activity, not a single stream, even when seen just from Lilah's perspective.

In an interview she conducts for her research the next week, Matthew Huerida offers a different view of Cinco de Mayo, one that challenges the equation of ethnic food, festivals, and cultural imperialism she developed in Nash's seminar. Her log notes:

I can't remember what I was saying some time ago about postmodern interpretations of ethnicity and ethnic festivals—something cynical, I believe, about it all being reduced to food and dance or something, but I got a very different feeling about it from talking to Huerida. He admitted a lot has been lost by making the festival bigger and more public (formerly they had to be small and quiet so as not to rouse racism in mainly Anglo communities), but at the same time it's a chance for better understanding between different groups of people. It's not much, but it's something. And I got the feeling that it's important young Latinos experience it.

In another interview, Santos, the business leader who organized the more public Cinco de Mayo celebration, also complicates Lilah's expectations. In the log, she writes:

Much more interesting than I had expected. He doesn't sound simply like an opportunist. It seems like he heard a lot of people in the community call for more than activist leadership. When asked for his solution to the problem of economic and general neighborhood deterioration, he gave it—Cinco de Mayo. The rest is history.

In Lilah's interviews, the community activists offer her somewhat conflicting histories of Cinco de Mayo, but uniformly challenge the views of ethnicity she has encountered in her classes. She finds that she likes the people she is interviewing and feels sympathetic to their world views, making it harder to see them through cynical lenses.

Lilah's papers for Marini and Kohl eventually take up the theme of food and ethnicity, particularly the figure of the taco. The flavor of these entries also reflects her assessment of Kohl and Marini as audiences for her work. In Kohl's paper (see Fig. 9.1), Lilah writes about the varied accounts of the history of Cinco de Mayo celebrations in Midwest City in a fairly informal and somewhat playful style (notice particularly her taco tropes). In Marini's paper (see Fig. 9.2), the taco also appears, but in less frequent and less playful guise. After relating Santos's account for how the community came to accept his plan to use Cinco de Mayo as a way to revitalize the North Side Latino community, Lilah presents a more historical account (Excerpt 1) that links Santos, Cinco de Mayo, and the taco, offering a succinct and specific account of the taco's benefits. Near the end of Marini's paper, Lilah makes one last, parenthetic allusion to the taco (Excerpt 2). When I asked Lilah in an interview at the end of the quarter how she chose to represent the battle between the taco and the historical event in Kohl's paper, she replied:

Um, Santos mentioned, he said, he said that, I don't know, he told the business community, "What can we sell? We can sell the taco." you know, [she laughs, I laugh],

If the example of Cinco de Mayo is at all representative, it seems, then, that history is a matter of who owns cultural symbols. Not only will Santos's version of Cinco de Mayo's genesis and role in the community most likely stand as the authoritative text on the event, but his ability to successfully wield cultural symbols will, to an extent, determine what facets of Chicano/Latino culture the State Historical Society chooses to present. Successful use of cultural symbols becomes in this case and in this culture, a numbers game, to a large extent. So, when Santos says he and others have "learned how to read and write—how to present ourselves to the community," Santos is talking about how to get the sort of recognition he wants for the North Side. As it happens, Santos's cultural symbol has been the taco, a much more marketable commodity than that elusive slice of history, the 1862 battle at Puebla, Mexico that Santos's critics would like to wield. In short, the debate on Cinco de Mayo is not one of culture versus commericalization, but about which cultural symbols to use and how to use them.

It gets murky, here, though. The taco versus the battle at Puebla seems a pretty pathetic contest on the face of it. And yet, in the waning years of the twentieth century, in Midwest City, the taco has seemingly won out. The victorious taco is now opening the doors of the SHS [the State Historical Society] and, if Santos has his way, there will be more than migrant stories representing Chicano/Latino history in the state. By the year 2000, Santos wants to read about the "true contributions of Hispanics—success stories." Utilizing vehicles like the SHS, Santos believes that he can ensure a certain kind of change regarding the community's self-perception and outsiders' perceptions. Tacos become success stories and installations at the SHS in this scenario. And revitalization of the past means more certainty for the future, for Santos's point of view.

FIG. 9.1.   Following the taco in Lilah's final paper for Kohl.

like I, that really hit a note because all these older people were saying, "you know what kind of (foods) were there? Oh, there were *tacos*," [said disparagingly] you know, this *anglicized* stuff, whereas like Santos was reveling in it or something, I don't know, I think that's why it was so ironic, here's this taco, it *is* what has sold the festival, I think, and it is what has interested the State Historical Society [I laugh, she laughs], I don't get it all, but it's the taco that becomes history ... which might be my thesis with Marini, can the taco become history?

Excerpt 1:

Of course, the rest is "history." When Santos finally got festival plans off the ground in 1981 and local businesses asked him which ethnic aspect to market, he suggested the taco, and, as it turns out, the taco has seemingly brought in grants and revenues to the community (over two million in 1990),[14] bought Santos a voice in governmental affairs and history-making, and returned control of the community back to local businesses.

Excerpt 2:

Seen in this light, Cinco de Mayo in its present form—made intelligible for the larger community through the use of the taco—is exactly about learning how to read and write in this cultural milieu, as Santos says. It also carries within it resistance to "the powers that be" (establishment? government?) in that it defies the history of invisibility reflected in the destruction of the flats.

FIG. 9.2.   Following the taco in Lilah's penultimate draft for Marini.

Following the taco across these varied scenes, activities, and texts points to the lamination and diffusion of Lilah's literate activity. Where is writing and research happening in this chronotopic network, and who is doing it? Chicano ethnicity and Cinco de Mayo could be points of origin for this network, but the streams of activity that led her to these topics were diverse and diffuse (as the next section suggests). Mexican food and ethnicity happen to come up in Nash's course in relation to commodification, colonialism, and cultural decline. However, her appropriation of these topics is complicated by the interviews she conducts with Huerida, Santos, and other Chicano leaders. Her papers for Marini and Kohl and her interview comments to me present related, but variously inflected accounts of the taco. Finally, there is that ambiguous dinner at a Mexican restaurant. The twisting trails of the taco in Lilah's literate activity trace trajectories of chronotopic lamination that are profoundly perspectival, mediated, and dialogic.

MULTIPLE ALIGNMENTS, MULTIPLE IDENTITIES: THE HETEROGENEITY OF SITUATED ACTIVITY

In one of the first ethnographies of higher education, Becker et al. (1961) found that a central issue for new medical students was deciding the amount and direction of effort they would expend in their studies. Their analysis suggested that early medical school experiences produced an intense role conflict, which was resolved as the students dropped their initial orientation to learning as preparation for professional practice in favor of an orientation to learning as passing tests and classes. Chin (1994) described a similar tension emerging in the writing of first-year journalism students. However, in her analysis, the students resolved the tension differently, disengaging from school writing they had come to see as unreal and engaging more intensively in building a portfolio of actual published work. Analyzing the ways Lilah negotiated the demands of the three seminars, I found a more complex set of tensions and resolutions, in which personal and interpersonal as well as institutional and disciplinary activity footings formed multivalent, multidimensional grounds for alignment.

Lilah's process logs suggested that she was more concerned with Ron Nash's paper than Marini's and more with Marini's than Kohl's. In an interview on the final day of the quarter, we discussed how she had selected topics and decided on level of effort in the three seminars. She began by saying that she had put a lot more time into writing Nash's paper (10–12 full days) than Kohl's (two days or so). (Note that Lilah only counts the time she put into writing up the paper, not doing the research.) When I asked why her effort was so different, she pointed to the professors' different personalities.

For Kohl, Lilah stressed his lack of interest and energy:

> I think there's just the sense that Ko- in Arthur's class that, it's like he's taught it years and years and years, and um I don't know, I didn't get the sense that he was really all that interested in what I might have to say or want to do, I got- I felt that he was very open and encouraging, and you know um kinda- kinda good as like a first-year coach, or something like that … and I- and I guess what I think is good is that he didn't tell us, "This is the way you do it," so that therefore we have to think about it on our own … but I think he was just so loose and so sort of undemanding that I didn't charge up, I didn't have that adrenaline, um, I didn't worry too much about a grade either, you know, I'm not- well and I don't really care whether I get a B or not, cause I didn't, I didn't put in the work so I didn't- I think it'll be fair if I got a B, but I've also heard that he's very very nonchalant about his grading too.

For Marini, Lilah repeatedly alluded to the strictness of his deadlines and the inflexibility of his expectations. She indicated that Marini's definite stances toward work and knowledge motivated her to keep up with the work, but also to be resistant. In the introduction to Kohl's paper, Lilah wrote that she had chosen, in Marini's course, to study Chicano ethnicity to be contrary. In an interview, I asked why she wanted to be contrary:

Because I love, I love being that, I ( ) you know, that's another case of personality things, I mean, there's something about his [Marini's] personality that I just want to challenge … it was something about just his whole course that I wanted to challenge, I think it's that- that straight historical approach that I resist, and I think it's also his kind of, oh, what's the right word, it's not arrogance, but it's that sense of knowing things, you know where, or like, so "so-and-so's article isn't any good because he didn't do research the right way and it-" I don't know, I don't know how to characterize that exactly, but um, see that's- that's a weird thing because it's almost like I did the op-, it's almost like that Nash and Marini's personalities worked on me in opposite ways because in Marini's class I did the contrary thing, everybody else, most everybody else did like European immigration research topics, and in Nash's class I did the safe thing, which was to stick with the Native- Native American topics, and I think that actually I care more about Nash's opinion of me, you know, maybe he's in my department, I've thought just fleetingly about him as an advisor because I'm more interested in creative kind of plays in the middle of creative and academic writing, and maybe he would be the person open to that, but um so so I really- I just function differently in different environments.

As in these comments, Lilah consistently expressed the most positive motivations for Nash. She noted that Nash was a writer, someone who enjoyed the language and would appreciate prose that was "fun." She was also attracted to Nash's strong personal commitment to his scholarship. Nash was a Native American studying how Native Americans have been researched and represented by others.[4]

Another indication of her representations of the professors could be seen in how she imagined Kohl and Nash as readers. In an interview after the semester, when she mentioned that she had felt "freer" writing for Kohl, I asked if she was confident that Kohl would be happy with her paper, if she could imagine his response as something like "What's this? This is strange. It's a C." She responded:

I can't imagine that, yeah, that would, that would blow me away, and his- then I'd totally misread his personality, no, I imagine comments like uh "Well, I think your questions are good" you know, and "I think you got a good start on this," well, I'm not even sure he'll do anything on this, I- I actually think he's the sort, he reads it and puts a grade on it, for the final copy or whatever, when he doesn't have to hand it back to you, so yeah, whereas with Nash, I imagine getting comments like, "this doesn't make sense," "Yipes" for a sentence or something, you know.

Lilah's comments point to a number of practical factors that motivate her

---

[4]Chapter 3 noted the way students in *American Studies* displayed the practice of using personal identity as a disciplinary topic. Nash was a local example of this practice among the faculty.

uptake of the seminar writing tasks, including her own interests and pre-
ferred stances, grades, and institutional relationships (who is in her department, who might be her advisor). One of the central factors, however, seems
to be a kind of interpersonal attunement with the professors that was
strongly affective and evaluative. Although she likes Kohl's open approach
to research, she finds him distant, disconnected, not motivating. She sees
him as going through the motions and imagines him as an uninterested and
unappreciative audience. She says Marini's strict deadlines motivate her,
but his certainties also provoke her desire to be contrary. She ends up not
only being contrary in her selection of a non-European topic, but also in
meeting his deadlines (her final paper unfinished three months after the
quarter has ended). Lilah represents Nash as a kindred spirit, a creative
writer with a sense of humour, an interested, engaged, critical reader. Where
the chronotope of the classroom foregrounds the institutional roles of
teacher and student, Lilah's diverse appraisals of Kohl, Marini, and Nash
point to finer grained interpersonal attunements, rooted in embodied and
projected interactions and in participants' multiple identities (displaying
one kind of consequence of vertical lamination).

In my analysis, however, I found the story of engagement that Lilah told
was only partly consistent with her texts and activities. Lilah consistently
stated that Kohl's task and Kohl himself were not motivating. At one point
during the quarter, she wondered if she would be making any progress at
all on her field research if she were not also doing it for Marini. As her
interviews suggested, she did not seem particularly intent on putting up a
good front for Kohl (e.g., compare the tone of her papers for Marini and
Kohl in Figs. 9.1 and 9.2). Nevertheless, my analysis indicated that Lilah's
work for Marini's paper was shaped by Kohl's task much more than her
work for Kohl was shaped by Marini's.

Lilah's paper for Kohl was strongly aligned to the special topics that Kohl
had cued in *American Studies*. She focused on the research process, emphasized interviews as sources, and used headings (suggesting the idea of an
outline). The content of the sections also displayed her alignment. "Time
and Place" was a heading that practically quoted Kohl's repeated argument
that history and geography, time and place, must be viewed holistically. In
that section, Lilah drew on a geography student's MA thesis to describe the
geography and history of North Midwest City. Lilah also displayed alignment in her uptake of Kohl's written response to her draft. In the seminar,
Kohl emphasized the importance of a comparative perspective in field
research, suggesting that students might want to compare their sites in

Midwest City with those in other cities. In her draft outline, Lilah had included a section titled "Comparative Perspective," a kind of placeholder where she wrote that she might use an article on Cinco de Mayo in San Francisco for comparisons. Responding to her draft, Kohl suggested another approach: "You may be interested in comparing Cinco de Mayo with other ethnic celebrations as well as with other Chicano/Latino expositions. In M.C. Swedish, Norwegian and Irish national celebrations have a long history." In her final paper, Lilah followed Kohl's suggestion for that section, comparing Cinco de Mayo with the history of a Norse-American celebration in Midwest City.

Lilah said she selected the northside neighborhood and then Cinco de Mayo because she had proposed studying Chicano ethnicity in Marini's seminar. However, she also noted that she chose Chicano ethnicity to resist Marini's emphasis on European immigration, and nothing in the earlier paper she had written for Marini suggested that Lilah was contemplating, or Marini seeking, research on a local neighborhood using ethnographic field methods. Moreover, with only slight revision, the section on comparison that Kohl had proposed and shaped through his written response to her draft appears in Lilah's penultimate draft for Marini. Finally, the views of the Chicano community leaders in interviews cued by Kohl's task deeply informed Lilah's whole analysis of Cinco de Mayo and ethnicity. Given the direction of these influences, Lilah's description of her final presentation on Cinco de Mayo in Marini's seminar, and Marini's response to it, is not terribly surprising:

> *I presented my research at the last class (and thank goodness it really was the last class!). And he seemed a bit frustrated that I hadn't done more, that I'd listened more to the activists (who lament the loss of culture in Cinco de Mayo). He had the same perspective as Kohl—there's no loss, only change. I feel like that's easy to say for an outsider. It still seems to me that traditional notion of history. Historians define what is or is not going on; participants only inarticulately sense or react to things.*

She goes on to note that Marini stressed the need to find documents to back up all the interviews, glossing his attitude as "It's not valid if it's not written." Seeking basic procedural display with Kohl's task and intending to make it contribute to her work for Marini, Lilah ends up aligning more with Kohl than Marini, displaying forms of disciplinarity that make her work problematic and frustrating from Marini's perspective. Why? In part, Lilah's engagement was shaped by her long-term interest in business leaders' roles in community formation (see her first log entry). However, more fundamentally, Kohl's task proleptically structured practices and afforded experiences, such as the open-ended interviews with those business leaders, that indexed Kohl's own orientations to research. In other words, as Kohl's task representations mediated Lilah's literate activity, the sedimented, abbreviated voices of social and disciplinary networks that Kohl had appropriated were being reappropriated, largely tacitly, by Lilah.

The complexities of these situated alignments also became visible in the reception of Lilah's work. When I called to set up a final interview several months after the end of the quarter, Lilah had not picked up Kohl's paper. She picked it up the day before the interview. I asked Lilah to comment on Kohl's written response, a final summary comment at the end of the paper (see Fig. 9.3). Asked how she understood the response, how valuable it was, and what she would do with it, she replied:

> Ok, well this first paragraph was um really the only thing that I took as a commentary on my writing, the rest of it seems to go off into what he thinks the whole, the whole topic is, and so out of this paragraph I get just the fact that he liked my questions, he liked the fact that I questioned a lot, um, I- I mean I'm- I'm reading into this a little bit, but I get the sense that he probably liked a certain openness towards the whole project that he saw there, um, which is what I pretty much predicted, um, and I guess it was nice to find out that he wasn't a whole lot different than what I had anticipated him to be, and um that was really nice because I felt that the Ron Nash thing that um actually he, in his comments, he was quite a bit different than who I knew him to be in the classroom as a teacher and all that, and I was, I was kinda upset by the, you know the um, the uh, whatever, the jump there, something, but um, so it was it was nice to feel like um with Kohl I was on pretty solid ground there, um, at the same time, I don't find much of anything challenging in- in that paragraph, um I don't feel motivated to go on and do more stuff as a result of these comments.

Lilah sees little of value in Kohl's comment, beyond the comforting sense that she had read him correctly. However, in her earlier interview (quoted previously), Lilah had imagined Kohl as an uninterested reader, suggesting he would probably just write a grade on the paper. She may discount his substantive responses in the second and third paragraphs, but nothing she said earlier implied she was expecting Kohl to engage substantively.

In her comments on Kohl, Lilah also introduced the topic of Ron Nash's upsetting response to her paper, and I asked her to explain what had happened:

> Well, I got a B minus, and um it was just like a paragraph of comments, said something like, "you rai- you raise interesting ideas and you argue points well, but um the main problem with the paper is that you keep going back to explication of these two people's works and um or the narrative or something keeps turning back to explication, and that it's a little hard to talk about white shamanism without giving some kind of a nod to Lynn Andrews and Carlos Castenada" and that it would be a stronger paper if I had

You have written a very perceptive account, both of the subject and the process of research. I both enjoyed and have great interest in your account of "finding out."

I believe the major theme is that of "identity." The North Side Community has great time depth relatively—goes back to World War I and the twenties. The University's interest—both faculty and students goes back to the late sixties when the minority departments were set up and student recruitment and community research were started in the neighborhood.

The University Chicano community and the North Side community did not overlap. The students were overwhelmingly recent migrants and activist. The North Side community was old, stable, family oriented, work oriented and was not particularly linked to the University either as students, faculty or educationally interested in the University curriculum as opposed to technical-vocational job orientation. It was this separation that led to various attempts to create consciousness and identity. Your players and participants all have different motives and goals—and therefore, different, yet true views of Cinco de Mayo in this state.

FIG. 9.3. Kohl's written response to Lilah's final paper.

used more sources, so um... but then at the end it was like, well that "you should have explicated more" sort of you know, or "you should have brought in more books, done the same thing with more more," and um, and it also just kinda felt like um, an easy criticism to level, like you know, "Sure this is fine, but you should have done more"... but I guess the surprise factor was that, was that, you know in class he just sounded, he- he was a lot more ... seemingly more accepting of ideas for ideas sake, you know, and um never gave us like any standard format that he wanted this paper in, never said you know, "Hey, don't want you to explicate stuff" or "I do want you to" or- he just said "Write a good paper" you know.

She also noted that Nash's written response (a final paragraph and two brief marginal comments on her 20-page text) were much less engaged that she had expected. She had expected him to respond more extensively and intensely than he did, to focus more on substance than technical structure, to appreciate that she was "going pretty far out" with her ideas, and to grade more positively than he did. Asked if this response had changed her thinking on Nash as a possible advisor, she replied that it definitely had, that he was not going to be her advisor. Lilah concluded the interview by wondering how she would complete her degree, whether she was even in the right department.

As Lilah's alignments to her professors and their tasks were laminated, interviews with Kohl suggested his reading and response were shaped by comparable chronotopic lamination, indexing multiple activities and identities. Looking at Lilah's paper in a text-based interview, his first comment was: "Yeah I was particularly interested in this." He then related at some length his own interactions with the North-Side Hispanic community as well as the historical contexts of Hispanic migration to the state and Anglo-Hispanic racial tensions. He recalled his role in the 1960s with university programs designed to attract minority students and faculty. He then returned to Lilah's paper:

> So here again, I was deeply involved in this paper [he laughs, I laugh] I couldn't keep my own ideas out of it, so I found it fascinating in what she had found out about the fifth of May, in the sense that it was a commercial build up and not an ethnic thing.

Asked if the conflicting stories of the University and the North-Side Chicano leaders that Lilah described had evoked some of his own experiences in the 1960s, Kohl responded with a long discussion of his personal experiences and then returned to Lilah's paper:

> So I can't read this without reading myself onto every page and getting involved, it isn't organized the way I told them to organize it, she has not done an outline, she hasn't done anything in depth particularly, she just wrote about what she was doing, and it came across quite well, [pause] that's what I liked about this American Studies class, it involved me.

Kohl continued talking about programs he had been involved in during the 1960s to recruit Hispanic students and faculty, saying in part:

> I always used to say to the Puerto Ricans when I reported on these projects back in the 60s, that there was (no learning time) and when we first recruited students for the minority departments, it was a farce in a sense, we were just giving them jobs, and they rotated these jobs, I mean a person couldn't last longer than six months, "Now it's somebody else's turn to have this thing," and if I had told the regents that all we were doing was bringing color onto campus and rotating these people—they weren't (graduating), I don't know what they would have said, I think they realize it now, but there was no learning period, you just went out into the street and had to do what you had to do, nobody- they couldn't tell you what to do, they didn't know what to do, and you didn't know what to do, so this has brought back a lot of memories.

Ironically, it appears that the professor who appreciated Lilah's comments the most was Kohl, who read himself onto every page and wanted to reward the interesting work students like Lilah had presented him.

Lilah's multiple alignments in her academic work provided one index of the lamination of the classroom, its chronotopic heterogeneity. Another index becomes visible in the chronotopic traces of Kohl's own fieldwork, his administrative experience at the university, and his lifelong involvement in the communities of Midwest City in his reading of and response to the texts Lilah and other students wrote. This analysis suggests that the typified representational chronotope of the classroom would figure the identities and alignments of both Lilah and Kohl much too narrowly.

CONSTRUCTING DISCIPLINARITY:
FILTERING CHRONOTOPES

With all of this heterogeneity and lamination of literate activity, it is worth returning to the issue of how disciplinarity is produced and sustained. In the sociology seminar (see chaps. 7 and 8), complexly dialogic processes of production were routinely transformed as they were textualized. In that transformation, local, personal, and everyday elements were omitted, attenuated, or recontextualized in disciplinary discourses. Thus, Moira's conference paper on arenas of comfort contained little of her critique of sociology or her attempt to revise that hypothesis and made no mention of her family history. Likewise, no trace of the argument over girls' depression that surrounded Sean's prospectus ever appeared in his texts. Disciplinarity was constructed by representationally foregrounding disciplinary contexts, relations, and identities.[5] This process, one in which embodied and representational chronotopes are selectively filtered and transformed, could be seen even in Lilah's relatively informal reports of her research and in Kohl's written response on Lilah's paper.

In the course of one of her Cinco de Mayo interviews, Lilah was invited to attend a reception–lecture at a mansion turned community center (the Ian K. Watt House). Lilah went expecting an anonymous, informal lecture; her log presents the scene this way:

---

[5] See Collins (1985), Knorr-Cetina (1981), Latour & Woolgar (1986), Myers (1990), and Prior (1994) for additional examples of these representational practices.

I went to the Ian K. Watt House last night for Sanchez's talk. It wasn't a lecture per se. I came in tennis shoes and shruggy clothes, expecting to get a corner spot and dutifully take notes. Instead, there were name tags, mariachi music, and waiters circulating with hors d'ouvres. People were in dresses and suits; there was this buzz of excitement because many people there had been a part of pulling it off.... The talk didn't start for about 45 minutes, and feeling sorely out of place, I wandered around the mansion, making myself at home in the master bathroom.

Santos spoke first about the new partnership between his community organization and the Historical Society to develop resources on Chicano and Latino history in the state. Then another community leader (Sanchez) gave a talk on Cinco de Mayo. After Sanchez talked, there was some entertainment. In the process log, Lilah wrote:

Then a little girl (6 years old) in Spanish costume belted out "La Bamba," even doing a little shimmy during the guitar riff. I was reminded of how my oldest brother used to pay me a nickel to dance to rock and roll when I was little. How odd the way adults foist their world and their sexual preoccupations on kids who have no idea what things actually mean.

In her penultimate draft for Marini, after reporting and analyzing the main events of that evening, Lilah mentions the entertainment as well:

On a lighter note, the event concluded with a performance by Miriam Martinez, a six-year-old with the voice of Linda Ronstadt, who is on her way to a national talent contest. After a few hearty *canciones*, she launched into "La Bamba," shimmying her way through the guitar riff. From the hors d'ouevres on silver platters to the sequins on Miriam's costume, it all seemed amazing to me. How had Cinco de Mayo arrived at Ian K. Watt's mansion? What could Zaragosa and Horatio Alger have in common?

Lilah's associations of the young girl's performance with a disturbing family memory are buried and hidden in her text for Marini, the word "shimmying" being at most a weak, uncertain trace of her evaluative response to the event. In her paper, that memory and evaluation lead quickly back to *history*, in this case juxtaposing Chicano ethnicity and privileged Americana.

A similar transformation appears in Kohl's response to Lilah's work (see Fig. 9.3), where he presents his personal memories, particularly of the history of the Chicano community on campus, in an I-evacuated, objectified, historical fashion quite different from the personal storytelling he displayed in our interviews. Although he explicitly expresses interest in Lilah's paper, without any account for why he found it so, his comment could be, and was, read as empty. The transformation of the embodied chronotopes of disciplinary activity into representational chronotopes of disciplinary texts clearly involves some very selective filtering. However, it would be as problematic to equate disciplinarity only with its representation as it would be to discount representation. Disciplinarity, I argue, can only exist in the total relationship between the embodied chronotopes of historical activity, the representational chronotopes of inner as well as outer speech, and the transformative practices that mediate them.[6]

A VIEW FROM SOMEWHERE ELSE: THINKING CHRONOTOPICALLY ABOUT WRITING RESEARCH

Lilah's process log and the other scenes, activities, and perspectives it indexed led me to an account of her literate activity that disrupted the conventional chronotopic representation of writing in the classroom. Her literate activity wove together not only events in *American Studies* that particular quarter, but in other coursework from that and previous quarters, anticipations of future academic work and relationships, her home life, and her biography. These alignments marked not simply her institutional role as student, but her multiple identities and relations with others and the world. Kohl's responses to Lilah's text (and to other students') also indexed other places, times, identities, and relations. For Kohl, Lilah's text evoked memories of lived experiences as well as intertextual connections, memories that were affectively and intellectually charged. Although the disciplinary topics of American Studies and the local focus of Kohl's task certainly made personal salience of topical content more likely, even the most abstract meanings can only enter life, as Bakhtin suggested, through people's situated experience. In different ways, both Lilah's work and Kohl's responses to it point to the importance of affect, identity, interpersonal attunement, and particular biographical experiences in academic work. To echo Bateson's (1972) blind person and stick analogy (quoted in chap. 5), I would argue that bounding Lilah's activity or Kohl's around some official version of the seminar's writing task severs critical pathways in their streams of activity.

---

[6]Focusing on literary work, Bakhtin (1981) sketches this kind of total relationship between the world narrated in the work and the event of narration:

These events take place in different times (which are marked by different durations as well) and in different places, but at the same time these two events are indissolubly united in a single but complex event that we might call the work in the totality of all its events, including the external material givenness of the work, and its text, and the world represented in the text, and the author-creator and the listener or reader; thus we perceive the fullness of the work in all its wholeness and indivisibility, but at the same time we understand the diversity of the elements that constitute it. (p. 255)

What Lilah's logs taught me was the need to rethink the framing of my research, to rethink the chronotopic presuppositions embedded in my designs and analysis. Over the course of several studies, I had come to see the need to examine writing and disciplinarity first as situated, then as perspectival, and finally as mediated, but had not recognized that I had largely fenced all these recognitions into an a priori context, the conventional chronotope of the classroom. A reflexive attention to such chronotopes, to ways they foreground not only roles, sites, and cycles of activity but also subjectified perspectives and evaluative orientations, could serve as a valuable resource in planning, undertaking, and writing up research on literate activity in the academy (and elsewhere). Where my research design developed somewhat fortuitously as the expectations of my chronotopic framing were problematized by first one research experience and then another (see Appendix A), intentional attempts to breach conventional representational chronotopes of writing, to work against rather than with the socioculturally given definitions of sites and activities, could offer significant opportunities to counter the privileging of institutional perspectives in studies of writing and disciplinarity.

One way to reimagine chronotopes is to shift perspectives. For example, instead of beginning an analysis with the role of teacher and student, the site of the classroom, and the instructor's assigned tasks as givens and asking how the student engages in that task, research might begin with the student, the cyclic activities of a day in the life, and ask where (if anywhere) the task might appear or be salient in that day. The notion of functional systems (see chaps. 1 and 7) also suggests the value of taking up the perspectives, and tracing the historical trajectories, of specific artifacts, practices, and institutions as well as of persons. As Latour (1987) and Callon (1996) have argued, elements of such heterogeneous networks should be followed through time and space without respect for the borders of our privileged cultural maps. The notion of chronotopes suggests the need to understand writing and disciplinarity not only as activity situated somewhere, but as activity linked—through mediation and sedimentation—to networks of other times and places and, thus, laminated with multiple activity footings. In designing research, the notion of chronotopes points to perspectival framing as well as particular perspectives found in foregrounded activity. This understanding of the interpenetration and co-evolution of embodied and representational chronotopes argues for reflexively interrogating perspectival frames, for intentionally varying somewheres to produce richer accounts of the complex laminations of literate activity and disciplinarity.

10

Writing/Disciplinarity: A Sociohistoric Approach

In chapter 1, I contrasted structuralist representations of communication, knowledge, learning, persons, and communities as abstract and objectified with sociohistoric perspectives that treat these terms as concrete and heterogeneous. In that chapter, I also introduced the activity perspective I pursue throughout the book. That theoretical perspective has been elaborated through exploration of specific notions in subsequent chapters: task multiplicity (chap. 2), semiotic genres (chap. 3), trajectories of participation (chap. 4), literate activity and mediated authorship (chap. 5), authorship and non-authorship (chap. 6), the sociogenesis of functional systems (chap. 7), authoritative and internally persuasive discourse (chap. 8), and, finally, laminations and chronotopes (chap. 9). These variations on the theme of writing and disciplinarity as activity could be read as the structural framework of the book.

However, I could also turn that structure inside out and argue that this book has been constructed around the case studies of writing situated in graduate seminars. Working out the stories those case studies tell certainly was the touchstone for the theoretical perspectives. Whether tracing the complexities of academic writing tasks in *Language Research*, the distribution of authorship in *Sociology*, or the laminations of Lilah's writing for three seminars, analysis of these case studies required multiple alignments of data and interpretive frameworks, ultimately across as well as within the cases. The data to be aligned included observational and audiotaped transcripts from the seminar sessions, students' texts, professors' written responses, and transcripts of interviews with students and professors. The interpretive frameworks to be aligned included my own everyday understandings of academic work, a variety of disciplinary discourses, and the particularities of situated addressivity (as analyses and texts were produced over time in response to real and imagined readers). Working through the case studies, I repeatedly ran into the engrained affordances of folk-structuralist discourses, tripping over words like task, writing, genre, context, discipline, and community, each of which seemed to transform dynamic processes into objects and to dissolve heterogeneities. Late in the analysis, I came to realize how deeply the privileged institutional perspectives of school were sedimented in my research design.

Writing with and against such diverse discursive currents shaped both my analysis and my theoretical engagements. After weaving and reweaving the multiple alignments of data and interpretive framework in my own laminated literate activity, I have arrived at a point of relative stabilization. Individually and collectively, as thick descriptions of activity and as theoretical analyses, as specific textualizations and as representations of the fuller set of data collected, case studies that initially seemed hard to understand and harder still to communicate have come together to tell stories. In the process, a theoretical perspective that initially consisted of little more than my strong resonance with a few texts (especially Bakhtin, 1981) has broadened, deepened, and taken root.

At this point, I am planning new research on literate activity and disciplinarity. I know I will continue emphasizing the situatedness of activity. In fact, having gone from no observation to observational note-taking to audiotaping (see Appendix A), I now see the need to better capture activity in its embodied forms by videotaping. However, what I expect to be most significant in the design and conduct of my future research flows from the theoretical perspectives I have arrived at through this research, particularly the notions of functional systems, lamination, and chronotopic reflexivity. With these perspectives, I will need to move beyond situated activity to trace histories of some of the heterogeneous elements of the functional systems found in that activity. Tracing what I have called voices in the networks will allow me to explore the sedimented affordances of those elements. I will also need to move beyond sites and activities defined by privileged institutional discourses to sites and activities that index other perspectives. Pursuing the chronotopic laminations of writing and disciplinarity seems to lead inexorably into full cultural-historical lifeworlds of people and their communities of practice. In other words, I still see that studying literate activity and disciplinarity requires attention to the kinds of detailed microhistories of persons and practices displayed in the case studies of this book. However, I also see that it calls for much more extensive historical tracing of artifacts, practices, and institutions (as was very partially explored in chap. 7) and of the chronotopic laminations of that activity (as suggested by Lilah's case in chap. 9).

As I anticipate the complex alignments this future research promises, I expect what is now stabilized will be further mangled, though I trust not unrecognizably so. I could say, "Stay tuned." However, since disciplinarity is an architecture for mind and society that is oriented to producing change and complexity, it is probably better to echo Pickering's (1995) notion of practice as interactive stabilization and say, "Keep tuning." In this final chapter, I briefly summarize what these case studies from an activity perspective have suggested about writing and disciplinarity and then conclude with a reflexive exploration of some of the chronotopic laminations of my own work.

WRITING/DISCIPLINARITY AS ACTIVITY

Whether describing the complex processes through which professors and students aligned around the semiotic genres of seminar writing tasks, the diversity of performances that counted as appropriate and successful instances of a task, the situated practices that linked texts to representations of authorship, or the laminations that shaped writing, response, and disciplinary knowledge, the case studies in this book document that writing in the academy is *activity*. In other words, writing and disciplinarity are locally situated, extensively mediated, deeply laminated, and highly heterogeneous.

For example, when *Sociology* met to discuss Sean's prospectus, the focal event was talk about text. As illustrated in chapter 7, that talk contributed to the revision of Sean's text in terms of what was deleted from it, what was added, and what was changed. Even specific lexical choices (e.g., West's use of "negative" and "stronger" when she reformulated Sean's hypothesis) came to be incorporated into the text. That writing is dispersed in this fashion stretches the boundaries of text-and-transcription models. Likewise, when West parodied Sean's "story" with a counter-story, the everyday discursive grounds of her argument stretched the typical representation of disciplinarity as autonomous, as separate from the lifeworld. That the seminar response to Sean's prospectus simultaneously involved an opportunity space for disciplinary enculturation, a seminar writing task, departmental gate keeping, and lines of research in the Project and possibly in disciplinary journals complicates any approach that treats writing, knowledge, and social formation as separate issues. That Sean's dissertation prospectus ends up looking like procedural display rather than a charter document for his research suggests an additional layer of questions about what was going on in the seminar. Nevertheless, the seminar was text-focused talk, intended by its participants to be aligned to these multiple streams of activity, to have these kinds of consequences.

However, what are we to make of Sean's and West's claim that what was most significant in that afternoon's talk was really Lynch's discussion of statistical strategies related to hierarchical linear modeling (HLM), a discussion prompted by unusual analytic issues in Sean's proposed research? Both Sean and West said in interviews that they had imagined new and exciting kinds of analyses after they had left the seminar. It could well be that this incidental discussion of HLM, a statistical approach deleted from Sean's final prospectus, was more consequential as a link in other chains of literate invention than any part of the focal response to Sean's prospectus. The potential importance of the HLM discussion in that afternoon's talk shifts attention from focal to dispersed activity. It reinforces LeFevre's (1987) argument that invention is a constant potentiality woven into the whole fabric of social life. This kind of dispersion is also suggested by Voloshinov's (1973) image of the boundless semiotic ocean of inner and externalized utterance and by Witte's (1992) call for a theory of writing grounded in a constructive semiotic. Of course, the discussion of HLM did happen in a seminar, so the dispersion appears in a social space where disciplinarity at least is foregrounded.

However, the literate work of disciplinarity (focal or dispersed) was not limited to such institutionalized sites. Mai, Teresa, and Han, for example, all related their research plans to their own experiences as students and teachers. More radically, how do we incorporate in a tale of academic writing the kind of events that Lilah describes: her Mexican dinner, the button her husband brought home with the business leader depicted as the North Wind, the shimmying 6-year-old singer she viewed at the Watt mansion, the discussion in Nash's course of Tex-Mex cuisine, or that Bill Moyers interview with Sam Keen? How should we figure in the family experiences that Moira alludes to and that seem to provide such a powerful ground of and motive for her work? Those experiences not only drew her interest to adolescent risk and drove her critical reading of the literature, but grounded her views so strongly that she resisted West's depiction of objective change, even though she routinely trusted and accepted West's other revisions, represented West as an expert, and described herself as a "dummy" in the area. Where do we place Kohl's experiences growing up in Midwest City and interacting with Chicano students, faculty, and community leaders in the 1960s, experiences that so shaped his reading of Lilah's paper? It is this kind of evidence that led me to argue that writing and disciplinarity are laminated, not autonomous, that every moment implicates multiple activities, weaves together multiple histories, and exists within the chronotopic networks of lifeworlds where boundaries of time and space are highly permeable (see also Bazerman's, 1994a, discussion of kairos).

The case studies, particularly of Mai and Teresa in chapter 4, of Sean in chapter 7, of Moira in chapter 8, and of Lilah in chapter 9 point to another permeable boundary, that of the person. As I traced quite different trajectories of participation and modes of discursive appropriation in seminars, what united all of these trajectories was that students' work was so clearly aligned to and mediated by the work of others (whether in joint activity or through the appropriation of others' artifacts). The distinctions between Moira, Mai, and Teresa in the quality of their appropriations and participation were striking, but hard to describe. All were appropriating others' words in their texts. Indeed, how else could anyone align with and produce a recognizable discourse? However, the specific nature of those appropriations, their contextualizations, and their consequences differed along multiple dimensions. The dialogic nature of appropriation points to the need to develop a nuanced vocabulary for the forms of appropriation and participation that constitute situated learning in laminated communities of practice. The analysis of internally persuasive and authoritative discourses in Moira's and West's response rounds represents an initial attempt to address that issue. In any case, as mediated activity implies mediated agency (Wertsch, 1991), literate activity implies mediated authorship.

Finally, if laminations and heterogeneities make disciplines open and relational, the question arises of how centripetal enculturation is achieved. A central notion here is that of co-genesis, the long-term alignments of typified functional systems. Structuration (Giddens, 1984) from this sociohistoric perspective implies not just the widespread circulation of isolated mediational means, but the widespread circulation of typified functional systems. Co-genesis points to the co-evolution of people, tools, and worlds. It creates not shared culture, but affordances for alignment in what Rommetveit (1985) identified as "pluralistic, only fragmentarily known, and only partially shared" worlds (p. 183). Long-term, widespread co-genetic processes can be identified in historical frameworks. For example, Hoskin (1993) and Hoskin and Macve (1993) not only link the development in Germany of new forms of education in the late 1700s with the intensification of disciplinarity at the turn of the next century, but extend the linkages further, noting the way the same educational practices were applied in corporations and government of that period to manage larger and larger scale enterprises. Significantly, their analysis traces specific people, artifacts, and practices across particular institutions. Pickering (1993) points to the intense discontinuities of physics that flowed from World War II, arguing that those discontinuities arose because the military enfolded physics, forming a new system that altered both disciplinary and military practice. Van Nostrand (1997) explores another face of this system in his studies of generic activity and knowledge construction at the interface of military research-and-development programs with scientific research. Each of these analyses points to the durable alignments that emerge co-genetically in typified functional systems.

On the local level, such co-genetic processes are visible in many ways. The examination in chapter 7 of the durable, local, and situated alignments and affordances of Sociology points to this kind of co-genesis. The routine way Kohl and the students in his seminars oriented to the institutional activity of schooling and coordinated their activity around his assignments marks their co-participation in co-genetic functional systems. Lilah's paper on White Shamanism suggests the thickness of such alignments. Taking a course on representations of Native Americans taught by a Native American, she comes across the biography of the adopted girl, watches Moyers interview Keen on TV, and encounters the topic of ethnicity in every class, at home, at work, and in the community. If disciplinarity is a heterogeneous network, the forging of its links is afforded not simply by powers of recruitment or principles of family resemblance, but by the prefabricated affordances of co-genetic alignment that arise from the fact that functional systems are the unit of development, not individual and isolated persons or tools.

The case studies and theoretical reflections in this book argue that analyses of academic writing as texts and transcriptions and of disciplines as discourse communities have taken up problematic units of analysis. I have proposed literate activity and disciplinarity as alternative units of analysis. Both units reflect the fundamental notion of activity, where activity is understood as sociohistorically organized functional systems that weave together heterogeneous trajectories of persons, practices, artifacts, institutions, and communities.

INTERSUBJECTIVITY: MIXING UP THE CHRONOTOPES

In chapter 1, I suggested that models of intersubjectivity are at the core of different approaches to human activity. I described the conduit metaphor of communication as the foundation of structuralist views of knowledge, learning, community, and the person. I described a dialogic perspective on intersubjectivity as the alternative foundation of sociohistoric approaches. I have also developed the argument throughout this book, most clearly articulated in chapter 9, that disciplinarity involves the embodied chrono-topes of laminated activity as well as the representational chronotopes of its entextualized semiotic genres. Thus, I want to conclude by reflexively exploring two important streams in my own literate and disciplinary activity, streams that have provoked my thinking about intersubjectivity and nurtured central themes of this book: notions of alignment, footings, lamination, functional systems, affect, and embodiment. The first stream involves my teaching and the second involves my participation as a participant in another research project.

Teaching English Grammar Sociohistorically?

As a new Writing Studies professor at the University of Illinois, one of my first course assignments was a descriptive English grammar course for undergraduates, a course the state mandates for English Education majors. This course presented several dilemmas to me. First, the state mandate presupposes that language arts instruction in schools should include healthy doses of explicit study of traditional grammar, a notion that has been questioned quite seriously by existing research and theory. Second, as chapter 1 displayed, I am quite skeptical of the structuralist language theories that have generated the grammars that teachers in schools are supposed to transmit to their students. Finally, I knew of no tradition for the sociohistoric study of language that I could easily adopt or adapt to a course on descriptive English grammar. My solution to this dilemma was to develop a course designed to help students understand the history of the language and to become sensitive to its situated, dialogic, and specialized forms. If, as Wittgenstein (1958) argues, we normally do not notice the multiple language games that inhabit our diverse forms of life because they are clothed in the common garb of language, my goal in the course has been to illuminate that cloth in ways that would make visible its complex textures and diverse materials.

To illuminate these textures of language, I have worked to structure experiences that disrupt the routines of language. One of the examples that I present in class for discussion has to do with tropes in everyday language. Here is the scenario. In class, I write on the board the following sentence: *Bosnia could be another Vietnam.* I then ask the students if they understand this sentence, and they all do. I ask what they understand of it, and they hesitate because asking them to account for such a transparent meaning is puzzling (is there a trick here?) and may well be a merely rhetorical question after all. In that hesitation, I begin to offer alternatives. "So it means that Bosnia could be a major rice exporter?" Laughter. It never means that after all, and I know it won't. "That Bosnia could be a southeast Asian country?" No. More laughter. Even without initial discussion, everyone has understood that "Bosnia could be another Vietnam" should be unpacked to mean something like: "If the United States gets militarily involved in the war of Bosnia in the 1990s, then it could face the kind of serious military and political problems that occurred when the U.S. became militarily involved in the war in Vietnam in the 1960s and 1970s." In other words, "Bosnia" and "Vietnam" in that simple sentence are acting as metonymic expressions for particular historical events as seen from the perspective of the United States.

I then write a second sentence on the board: *Zimbabwe could be another Zambia.* I ask if everyone understands this sentence, and so far, no one has gotten it. I explain my sense of it briefly, that after gaining independence from its colonial status, the technological, economic, and political infrastructure in Zambia quickly eroded, creating a variety of civil problems, and that Zimbabwe, which became independent years after Zambia, could follow a similar path.[1]

These contrasting examples illustrate not only everyday metonymy, but also point to the intertextuality (not the dictionary definitions of terms) that allows students to register an understanding of the first trope and not the second. These examples and their reception also become an illustration of intersubjective practices because I constructed them expecting just the kinds of responses I got. How could I achieve such sure intersubjectivity? Is it because I know my audience so well? I developed the examples in my first year of teaching at the University of Illinois and have repeated them without change ever since. Audience knowledge in this case could not mean personal knowledge of the other people or even extensive interaction with a group. Is it because Vietnam and Bosnia are shared knowledge? If so, then what is the knowledge we share? Audience and shared knowledge are relevant, but have to be qualified in critical ways.

---

[1] I borrowed this metonymy from the novelist Doris Lessing's (1992) autobiographical account of her return to Zimbabwe, where she had grown up. I have to confess I read the book more because of my interest in Lessing than in Zimbabwe.

First, the students and I do not in fact share the same knowledge of, the same intertextual allusions to, Vietnam. For example, some students have seen *Full Metal Jacket*; some have not. Some have heard stories about the war from family members; some have not. Some have studied the war in courses or read novels of it or watched TV programs like *China Beach*; some have not. I remember watching the war on TV as a child and participating in a few small protests against it as a high school student, whereas very few of my students have any actual memory of the years of the Vietnam war. Where I might trace U.S. involvement to the rearming of the Japanese and support of French recolonization in 1945, others recall that the war began sometime in the 1960s (or was it the 1970s?), nor do we all agree on how to gist the story of the war, on what evaluative orientation to take on it. For some, Vietnam was a righteous war against evil communists, lost because of timid leadership and internal betrayal at home. For others, Vietnam was an unjust and imperialistic invasion that was defeated by courageous freedom fighters in Vietnam and righteous protesters at home. And, of course, these differences speak volumes about students' identities and affiliations. If these kinds of diverse, even conflicting, representations and evaluative orientations can count as shared knowledge, then shared knowledge works.

Second, there is still the question of how I knew that this knowledge would be shared or not. My initial answer was that I had lived in the United States long enough to know that Vietnam is widely discussed as a troubled war, so I expect that the students will have seen some film or TV program, read some books or stories, heard some conversations, studied the war in high school history, and so on. On the other hand, I know that African news rarely appears on TV or in movies (with the exception perhaps of South African apartheid) and that Africa is not a common topic in schools. After I had worked through this activity with half a dozen classes, I came across Clark's *Arenas of Language Use* (1992) and was excited to see that his research on the mutual knowledge question was struggling with similar issues and that his answers fit my sense of what kind of knowledge I was employing. Clark argues that mutual knowledge cannot be accounted for in terms of the shared knowledge paradigm (*I know x, you know x, I know you know x, you know I know x, I know you know I know x*, etc.). In place of that solution, Clark proposes co-presence heuristics, including physical, linguistic, and community membership forms of co-presence. It is this last category, community membership, that echoed my account of how I could anticipate which metonymy the students would understand as if it were transparent and which they would find incomprehensible. I revisit Clark's account of mutual knowledge in the final section of this chapter, but first I turn to the second, and more powerful, stream of activity that has shaped my understanding of intersubjectivity, situated activity, and sociogenesis.

Cindy Magic and the Invisible Cheetahs

In the past two years, my understanding of communication and development has been deeply affected by my wife's research on footings (Hengst 1995, 1996). As a speech pathologist with a strong orientation to semiotics, Julie had become very interested in the complex communicative settings she often participated in, settings where, for example, people with ALS (amyotrophic lateral sclerosis, also called Lou Gehrig's disease) were communicating with her and family members using augmentative technologies or where a client with aphasia, a family member, a student clinician, and she, as a clinical supervisor, were interacting in a therapy setting. When she began work on her PhD, she quickly became interested in Goffman's (1981) notion of footings because he did not privilege language and he emphasized the lamination and multiplicity of activity. Looking for a convenient site where she could explore method and theory for a situated analysis of footings, she decided to study a role-playing game that I play with our two daughters. The game, *Cindy Magic*, had been invented about four years earlier during a long car ride with our oldest daughter Nora (aged 8 at the time of Julie's research). The game originally began as an adaptation of the Disney movie *101 Dalmatians*, but other than having an evil character named Cruella de Vil who kidnaps animals and people, its scenarios bear little relation to the movie. The main characters in fact are the Magic sisters who constantly oppose Cruella de Vil. The game was mostly played in the car when doing errands or around the house when doing chores. As Nora grew older and the game developed a history, it had become much more complex. About a year before Julie's research, our youngest daughter, Anna, had begun to play the game (she was aged 4 at the time of the study). However, when Anna began to engage in it, the complex plots proved too difficult for her. In fact, it became hard to sustain the game with them both.

Julie videotaped several games and transcribed verbal and nonverbal interactions. Figure 10.1 is an adapted transcript from one episode of one of those games. The game is being played in the living room of our home. At the same time we are playing, we are also folding clothes and putting them in a basket. In Segments 29 to 37, Cruella de Vil and her henchmen (the hunters) have come to kidnap the Magic sisters (the heroes of the game) and the Magics are calling on the Cheetahs (who routinely help save the Magics from Cruella de Vil and the hunters). P, N, and A stand for Paul,

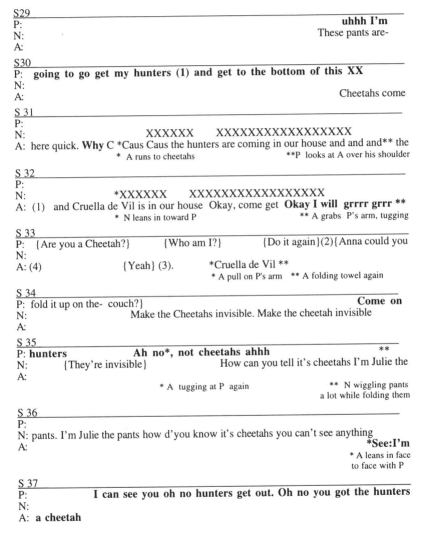

S29
P: **uhhh I'm**
N: .   These pants are-
A:

S30
P: **going to go get my hunters (1) and get to the bottom of this XX**
N:
A: Cheetahs come

S 31
P:
N: XXXXXX   XXXXXXXXXXXXXXXXX
A: here quick. **Why** C *Caus Caus the hunters are coming in our house and and and** the
                    * A runs to cheetahs   **P looks at A over his shoulder

S 32
P:
N: *XXXXXX   XXXXXXXXXXXXXXXX
A: (1)   and Cruella de Vil is in our house Okay, come get **Okay I will grrrr grrr **
                    * N leans in toward P   ** A grabs P's arm, tugging

S 33
P: {Are you a Cheetah?}   {Who am I?}   {Do it again}(2){Anna could you
N:
A: (4)   {Yeah} (3).   *Cruella de Vil **
                                    * A pull on P's arm ** A folding towel again

S 34
P: fold it up on the- couch?}   **Come on**
N: Make the Cheetahs invisible. Make the cheetah invisible
A:

S 35
P: **hunters**   **Ah no*, not cheetahs ahhh**   **
N: {They're invisible}   How can you tell it's cheetahs I'm Julie the
A:
            * A tugging at P again   ** N wiggling pants
                                                        a lot while folding them

S 36
P:
N: pants. I'm Julie the pants how d'you know it's cheetahs you can't see anything
A: *See:I'm**
                                                        * A leans in face
                                                        to face with P

S 37
P: **I can see you oh no hunters get out. Oh no you got the hunters**
N:
A: **a cheetah**

FIG. 10.1.   Cindy Magic and the Invisible Cheetahs. Adapted from Hengst (1996). Standard print, bold print, and brackets all indicate particular registers. Respectively, they represent speaking in main character (e.g., Anna as Jane), in secondary character (e.g., Anna as a cheetah), and as everyday self (e.g., Anna as Anna). X = unintelligible. This transcript has been simplified in several ways (e.g., proxemic boxes have been dropped).

Nora, and Anna. Each of us plays multiple characters, but our typical roles in the game have Nora as the oldest sister (Mary), me as the middle sister (Elizabeth), and Anna as the youngest sister (Jane). In this episode, I also act as Cruella de Vil and the hunters and Anna and Nora act as Cheetahs. Of course, we also break out of the game and speak as ourselves sometimes.

Julie's interest was in identifying the communicative resources we employed to manage these multiple footings, particularly given our very asymmetrical communicative capacities and roles. A key resource Julie identified was a kind of immediate accommodation that she called *reflection*, the matching of another person's words, voice quality, rate of speech, postural orientation, gestures, actions, and so on. Reflection could involve a single or multiple resources and could be divided (e.g., postural orientation could reflect one participant while words reflected another). In Figure 10.1, a problem emerges when Nora suggests making the cheetahs invisible. [Note that "P(CdV)" refers to Paul playing Cruella de Vil, A(Jane) means Anna playing Jane, and so on.] Julie analyzes this episode in the following terms:

> Paul then, in S29–30, reflects Nora's shift back to a familiar topic and begins to speak again as Cruella de Vil. P(CdV) introduces another topic familiar to the game in general and reports that Cruella is going to get her hunters to help her. A(Jane) ratifies this topic (i.e., the hunters) by proposing a routine solution familiar to all the participants. In previous episodes, when the characters are fighting Cruella de Vil, they recruit more help as Cruella recruits more villains. So, a typical response to Cruella de Vil calling on her evil hunters is for the Magic sisters to call on their talking cheetahs or their robots. A(Jane) does this by using linguistic and paralinguistic resources (i.e., speaking as "Jane" and as the "cheetahs") and by physically acting out the scene, running behind Paul to talk to the cheetahs and then acting out the role of a cheetah attacking P(CdV) in S32. During this time (from S30–33), Nora folds clothes, watches the action, and whispers conspiratorially to Paul (probably making suggestions—as Nora—about how to play out the game). Paul appears to lose the thread of the game, and in S33 he breaks out of character to clarify what is happening. In his interview, he agreed that Anna moving so quickly and speaking in different voices confused him, even though it was a familiar scenario. It is interesting that while Paul was out of character in S33 he also spoke briefly to Anna, monitoring/directing the folding clothes activity ("Anna could you fold it up on the couch?") This was the only time he directly managed the household chore during this game episode.

> In S34, N(Mary) directs the others to "Make the Cheetahs invisible." Paul ignored her remark and in S35 made it clear that he knew it was cheetahs that were attacking him ("Ah no, not cheetahs ahh"). Anna, too, seemed to ignore the suggestion by not responding verbally or nonverbally and by continuing to act out the cheetahs the way she had been. N(Mary) did not let it drop, though. In S35–36 she incorporates the notion of invisible cheetahs into her talk when she (speaking as Mary) says to Cruella "...how d'you know it's cheetahs, you can't see anything." This time A(cheetah) does respond. She was watching N(Mary) when she spoke and, immediately after she

finished, A(cheetah) moved around directly in front of P(CdV), held his face to hers in both her hands, practically nose to nose, and said "See:I'm a cheetah." Paul immediately reflected A(cheetah)'s words saying "I can see you." The word "see" can be traced from N(Mary)'s utterance to A(cheetah)'s and then P(CdV)'s. Paul reported in his interview that part of his reluctance to take up Nora's idea was his concern that Anna did not understand what it meant for the cheetahs to be invisible. It was not clear to him whether she was actively blocking Nora's idea or if she just did not understand the notion. Nora, on the other hand, saw this as one more time that Anna clearly refused to play the game her way. She interpreted Anna's immediate display of her visibility ("See:I'm a cheetah") as a refusal to be invisible. Nora, however, dropped the idea of invisible cheetahs and returned to playing out the idea of only the Magic sisters being invisible.

In my interview with Anna, she was not able to talk about whether she understood what Nora meant when she wanted the cheetahs to be invisible. However, the discourse itself supports both interpretations. Clearly, Nora's interpretation is easy to see. She had to present her idea three times before anyone responded to it, and then, when Anna did respond to it, she did so by doing the exact opposite, one way to use the resources to block an idea. However, if she did not understand the notion of invisibility as Nora did, Anna could have been trying to take up Nora's idea. Anna only responded after N(Mary) stopped using the word "invisible" and shifted to the words "you can't see anything." Anna's immediate response, then, could be seen as fixing the problem (i.e., that Cruella de Vil couldn't see the cheetahs), thus ratifying Nora's idea, and making sure that P(CdV) could see her.

When I asked Anna to act out what an invisible cheetah would be like, she closed her eyes and said that the cheetah couldn't see anyone. This suggests that Paul's interpretation, based on both his understanding of Anna's abilities and on her ambiguous behavior, was probably more accurate than Nora's. But either way, the invisible cheetahs did not get played out and the episode continued without it. (Hengst, 1996, pp. 20–21)

As a participant in this research, I watched the videotapes and read the transcripts with the eyes of a parent, responded to them in interviews as a participant, thought about them as a researcher with similar interests, and talked to Julie about the research at length in all of these roles. I was struck by the kind of alignments that appeared to be happening in this episode around words like "see" and the way multiple interpretations of what a word signified or what was happening in the game could be sustained and coordinated. I was also struck by the way Anna used her available resources to participate, grabbing my face to be sure that Cruella de Vil would see the cheetah attacking her. Julie's research led me to think more than I otherwise would have about Goffman's (1981) footings and Vygotsky's (1978) analyses of play. I connected Cindy Magic to Cole's (1995, 1996) work on tertiary artifacts (play-like worlds such as the Fifth Dimension). I also began to see relationships between the communicative processes Julie identified in her analysis of these episodes of Cindy Magic and the kinds of alignments that I was analyzing between Liz and Kohl on *genre de vie*, around the notion of "an outline" in *American Studies*, or in Mead and Han's co-construction of the problem for her proposal in *Language Research*.

FINAL (RE)ALIGNMENTS

Long descriptions of one of my classroom lessons and of my wife's research on a family game may seem like a detour from the business of concluding a book on literate activity and disciplinarity in the academy, but they are in fact a direct path to the conclusion. I have argued that literate activity and disciplinarity are situated, mediated, and dispersed, that they do not respect official cultural boundaries and conventional representational chronotopes, but emerge out of deeply laminated lifeworlds. As streams of activity in which I have participated, interactions in my grammar class and my wife's research on Cindy Magic have shaped the way I describe and understand the diverse participation frameworks of situated literate activity in the academy and their consequences. This seeming detour, in other words, indexes some of the heterogeneity, lamination, and mediation of my own research (see also Appendix A). It would be dishonest as well as difficult to claim a purified representation of my own disciplinarity in light of the conclusions I have reached on the lamination of others' disciplinarity. Grounded in notions of dialogic activity, sociohistoric analysis should not proceed without reflexively examining and (to some extent) displaying its own practices of knowledge and text making.

I have also come to see the relation between Clark's (1992) view of intersubjectivity and Hengst's (1995, 1996) accounts of the situated nego-tiation of footings as emblematic of an important theoretical distinction. When I first read Clark's (1992) discussion of co-presence heuristics, I was struck by how well his account matched my classroom discussion of Bosnia, Vietnam, Zimbabwe, and Zambia. I seemed to be drawing on precisely the kinds of heuristic searches into community membership co-presence that he proposed. However, his account resonates less well with the intersubjec-tive practices of *Cindy Magic and the Invisible Cheetahs*. The difference, I believe, marks a distinction between an account of intersubjectivity as a heuristic cognitive process (which matched my set-piece intellectual point in the institutionalized space of the classroom) and an account of activity in which coordinations operate with varying degrees of intersubjectivity and in which embodied actions, affective orientations, motivations, interpersonal relationships, and artifactual mediations figure as strongly as propositional practices. The problem is that this later kind of activity is the only kind available, even in classrooms: However we represent it, we are always, and can only be, in embodied, situated, motivated streams of historical activity. Moreover, the episode of *Cindy Magic and the Invisible Cheetahs* foregrounds the developmental issues that have been a key impetus for this research.

In short, Clark's (1992) co-presence heuristics still emphasize *what people know*, whereas sociohistoric orientations to activity emphasize *how people, tools, and worlds come to be and act in the world.* Instead of looking to multiple forms of cognitive co-presence, this research suggests the need to explore distributed practices of alignment at all levels, from the kind of durable institutionalized alignments that were visible in the analysis of *Sociology* to the kind of fleeting alignments that Lilah made as she watched Bill Moyers one night on TV. If we wish to understand literate activity and disciplinarity, then we must follow the currents of such historical activity wherever they lead. At this point, I would say they lead to dynamic processes of appropriation, externalization, and alignment in and through which persons, artifacts, practices, institutions, and communities are being produced, reproduced, and transformed in complexly laminated social and material worlds.

Appendix A

Situating the Research: Multiple Exposures of a Methodology

Discussions of methodology are typically placed early in research reports, as methodology is supposed to form, along with identification of a problem or question and review of any relevant literature, the origins of the research. Studies of laboratory science (e.g., Amman & Knorr-Cetina, 1990; Collins, 1985; Knorr-Cetina, 1981; Latour & Woolgar, 1986; Pickering, 1995) have challenged this idealized linear representation of scientific methodology. They have described laboratory practices as complexly situated, often emergent and improvisational, and they have documented how inadequate and often inaccurate textual accounts of those practices are. For example, they have shown that textual accounts often present endpoints (methods, question, and findings) as the origins of the research. This discussion of research methodology is positioned as an appendix because it is hybrid, involving origins and plans, emergent processes of implementation, and endpoints of the research.

The basic goal of this Appendix is to provide a sociohistorically oriented account of the literate activity of this research. Much as I describe the multiple origins of Mai and Teresa's research in chapter 4 or Lilah's in chapter 9, I first offer three accounts of the origins of this research. Together, these accounts point to the laminated and heterogeneous nature of this research. I then trace the implementation of the research, providing further details on sites and methods and on how the research was, in Pickering's (1995) terms (see chap. 7), mangled in practice. Finally, I discuss the analysis and writing of this research from a practice perspective. Even reflexive accounts of methodology tend to focus on providing post-hoc biographical and intellectual contextualizations for the research or descriptions of the situations of research. Such accounts do represent a significant advance over decontextualized canonical accounts of method-ologies; however, they continue to elide fundamental issues of interpretive practice. I suspect the problem is that interpretive practices are too situated

288

Elide- to omit or suppress

and too mundane. The genesis of an interpretation often appears to be locked up in a black-box activity glossed as, "I read/saw x and thought y." In the final section of this Appendix, I evoke some of the mundane interpretive practices I have engaged in during this research. This Appendix then offers multiple exposures of a heterogeneous research process. I hope that, combined with the images of the data and research offered throughout the book, this Appendix provides a sense of this research as practical activity, helps readers to engage dialogically (whether critically or with appreciation) with the case studies presented here, and offers material of some use to other researchers studying literate activity and disciplinarity.

ORIGINS

In this book, I am analyzing data I gathered primarily in the course of two research studies I conducted as a PhD student. The first study was conducted in an education seminar, *Language Research* (see chaps. 2 and 4; chap. 2, footnote 3 provides details of the methods). The second study was conducted in four seminars, three of which (*Geography*, *American Studies*, and *Sociology*) are discussed here (see chaps. 3, 6, 7, 8, and 9). These two research studies were preceded by a pilot project. In this section of the Appendix, I present three accounts of the origins of this research. The first account is a dissertation proposal for the second study. As I began that study, I wrote up several research proposals for different audiences, each somewhat different. Where the proposal presents a relatively synoptic disciplinary account of the research, locating it in a linear trajectory of knowledge accumulation, the second account is autobiographical, situating the research in my experience as an ESL instructor at the University of Wisconsin (UW)–Madison. The final account of the origins of this research is a narrative of progressive discovery, a disciplinary detective story in which the object is to locate the academic writing task and the plot revolves around successively better locations.

Account 1: A Qualitative Research Proposal in Experimental Dress

The text that follows is a large excerpt from one research proposal for the second study, excluding only a title page, qualifications for conducting the research, and the references (all of which are listed in the references for this book). This proposal provides one image of the questions this research addressed, its disciplinary and institutional contextualizations, and its methodology. I have not revised the text, so it presents the kind of evidence that is often rewritten in reports to accord with what actually happened and what was eventually found (cf. Knorr-Cetina, 1981; Latour & Woolgar, 1986).

Statement of the problem

Recognition of the importance of context in understanding first and second language writing has grown over the last decade, yet situated studies of writing in the university (outside of composition programs) remain few. Fewer still have involved international students or looked at the writing of graduate students. In addition, existing studies have explored a limited range of settings and emphasized a limited set of sources for data on context. Thus, more research that uses multiple sources of data is needed to understand how academic writing is socially constructed in advanced graduate courses that include students with varying language and cultural backgrounds.

Background and rationale

Research on the academic needs of non-native speakers of English (NNSE) in university setting has so far relied on several approaches: intuitive cultural analyses (e.g., Kaplan, 1966), surveys or interviews (e.g., Bridgeman & Carlson, 1983; Johns, 1981; Ostler, 1983),[1] textual analysis of classroom writing prompts (e.g., Braine, 1989; Horowitz, 1986a, 1986b), textual analysis of professional genres (e.g., Swales, 1990; Swales & Najjar, 1987), professor judgments of manipulated student essays (e.g., Santos, 1988), and comparison of student writing with professional genres (e.g., Howe, 1990). Several studies have employed multiple methodologies. For example, Tarone, Dwyer, Gillette, & Icke (1981) combined textual analyses of professional genres with subject specialist interviews and Sorenson (1985) combined interviews with professors, analysis of students' writing with professor commentary on it, and analysis of course syllabi. English for academic purposes (EAP) composition specialists have also looked to a comparable body of literature in first language studies (e.g., Bazerman, 1988; Myers, 1989, 1990). While these methods have generated valuable data on beliefs and textual products, they provide only indirect evidence on the classroom contexts and processes within which students actually write and are evaluated.

After a decade in which composition research and theory emphasized cognitive studies of composing processes generally conducted in clinical settings (North, 1986),[2] in the 1980s composition theorists increasingly turned their attention to the importance of the social and personal contexts of writing in natural settings (Bizzell, 1982; Beach & Bridwell, 1984; Bartholomae, 1985; Faigley, 1985; Anson, 1988). While this shift in focus and research strategy has been reflected in a number of naturalistic, contextualized studies of early literacy (e.g., Heath, 1983; Dyson, 1988), situated study of writing in the disciplines (as opposed to in composition programs) at the university level has been limited. A few studies have directly investigated writing in disciplinary courses: most notably studies of a two-course, senior engineering sequence (Herrington, 1985), an undergraduate literature class (Herrington,

---

[1]This citation refers to Ostler, 1980.

[2]This citation refers to North, 1987.

1988), and an experimental graduate course on introspective studies of writing (Sternglass & Pugh, 1986; Sternglass, 1989). Several case studies have also been reported, including ones of a graduate student in his first year of a rhetoric program (Berkenkotter, Huckin, & Ackerman, 1988); of two students writing simultaneously for an English composition course and disciplinary courses (Faigley & Hansen, 1985); of an undergraduate student taking English and biology courses in his first two years (McCarthy, 1987); of a returning, adult student in an upper-level literature class (Doheny-Farina, 1989; Clark & Doheny-Farina, 1990); and of 13 freshman students in seven different courses (Nelson, 1990). Taken as a whole, these studies suggest that classrooms are complex environments, that task expectations are communicated through explicit and implicit processes, and that different disciplines (and even different classes within a discipline) have different expectations, reflected in varying criteria for evaluating student work.

However, these situated studies of writing in university classrooms have several limitations. First, most have emphasized one or two sources of data, not integrating data from classroom interactions, students' and teachers' perceptions and expectations, students' composing processes, students' texts, and professor's response. Second, most have focused on initial adjustment to a context, not looking at more advanced levels of expertise and enculturation. Studies of natural writing processes (e.g., Nelson and Hayes, 1988) and of the effects of disciplinary enculturation (Jolliffe and Brier, 1988) suggest that important differences exist between novice and advanced writers in academic settings. Third, none of the above studies has examined the role of international students or NNSE, groups whose different language and cultural backgrounds raise important theoretical and practical questions.

In a previous study (Prior, in press [3]), I found evidence of very complex relationships between classroom contexts, students' writing, and the professor's response. First, the study suggested that there are many perspectives to take on academic writing tasks, that the origins, contexts, undertakings, and responses to such tasks are complex and socially situated. Second, it suggested that advanced disciplinary enculturation may be marked by several important trends and issues, focusing on the emergence of students as subjects in the discourse, the increased historicity of writing, and tensions inherent in disciplinary microsocieties between reproduction and change, authority and personal judgment. Third, international students (all NNSE) appeared to function much as the U.S. students (all native speakers of English); however, they were clearly responded to in this seminar as a special group and their generally lower pattern of grades suggested that NNSE face greater difficulties, especially when language problems and limited patterns of class participation coincided. Finally, evidence from that study raised theoretical questions about the notion of "discourse communities."

In this study, I plan to extend my previous study by investigating a different discipline and examining three issues either not covered or given less attention in the pilot study:[4] the history of students' composing, the disciplinary/departmental context, and the students' interpretation of the professor's response.

Statement of specific research goals

The goal of this research is to extend theory and research by: 1) seeking to develop a more complete account of the writing context in a university course, 2) investigating

---

[3] This citation refers to Prior, 1991.

[4] Here I am referring to the study in *Language Research* as the pilot.

writing at advanced levels of disciplinary enculturation, and 3) investigating the special situation of international students in this context. The general goals will be addressed through a focus on the following seven questions, which emerged from the pilot study:

1) What are the disciplinary and institutional contexts for this class?
2) What are the professor's goals and rationales for the writing tasks in this class?
3) How does the professor communicate expectations for form and content?
4) How do students interpret writing tasks?
5) How do students undertake writing tasks throughout the quarter?
6) How does the professor evaluate and respond to the students' final written texts?
7) How do the students interpret the professor's written response?

Method

Subjects. The primary subjects of this study will be the students and professor of an advanced graduate seminar in a disciplinary course. The seminar selected will have to be an advanced course in the discipline, involve significant writing by the students, and include both U.S. and international students (some of whom speak English as a second language). A subset of the students in the class will be focal students, whose work will be followed more intensively. In addition to the primary subjects in the seminar, other graduate students and faculty in the department will be secondary subjects: all will be asked to complete a questionnaire and some will be asked for follow-up interviews.

Design. The research design employed is ethnographic. Different sources of data and different methods are used to realize a triangulated and contextualized perspective on students' writing and the professor's response to it. The design is particularly aimed at gathering data that have received less attention in previous studies: classroom interactions, the social and personal contexts of participants, and the professor's responses to student writing.

Instrumentation. Data for this study will be gathered from seven main sources:

1) Class observations. Extensive field notes will be taken in the classes and (if permission is granted to do so) audiotape recordings will be made of all class sessions. All class documents will be collected. Selected class episodes will be transcribed for further analysis.

2) Questionnaires. Questionnaires will be given to students to determine their national origin, native language, academic background and goals, disciplinary affiliations, and goals for the seminar. A similar questionnaire will be given to the professor. The purpose of these questionnaires will be to identify important individual variables and to examine the structure of the seminar participants' discourse communities. Other students and faculty in the department will also be given a related questionnaire, with less emphasis on personal data.

3) Interviews. Students in the seminar will be asked to discuss the writing assignments, their perceptions of the professors' expectations, their own goals in writing, their reasons for selecting topics, problems or questions they have with either the content or the forms for the assignments, and their perceptions of how the professor will grade/respond to their writing. The professor will be asked about the goals of the writing assignments, how he consciously communicates his expectations for the

assignments, his general perceptions of students' understanding (or lack of understanding) of the expectations, and his goals in responding to student writing. Semi-structured interviews with students and faculty in the department will explore issues raised from the questionnaire and from the seminar. In addition, I will ask these interviewees to bring documents (e.g., papers, syllabi, writing assignments) and use those as cues to discuss experiences in particular classes.

4) Writing process logs and interviews. A focal set of students in the seminar will be asked to maintain a complete set of their drafts and to keep a writing process log recording their interpretation of writing tasks and discussing what reading and writing they do for each paper. The process logs will be turned in weekly and followed up with interviews every three weeks to explore issues that emerge in them. (See Nelson, 1990, and Sternglass, 1989, for discussion of process logs).

5) Students' written assignments. Students' final texts with comments and grades on them from the professor will be analyzed for evidence of how they understood and undertook the tasks and how contexts influenced their texts. In addition, the professor's written responses will be analyzed. Issues that emerge from this analysis will be followed up, particularly in the text-based interviews.

6) Text-based interviews with the professor. I will interview the professor about a sample of the papers, selected for their relevance to research questions which emerge from initial analysis of the texts. The interviews will follow a modified version of the discourse-based interview procedure (Odell, Goswami, & Herrington, 1983), focusing on selected professor responses as well as the students' texts (Prior, in press). I may also ask the professor to record retrospective protocols on selected students' papers immediately after reading and responding to them.

7) Text-based interviews with the students. Finally, I will use similar text-based interviews with some students to explore their understanding of the professor's written comments on, and evaluations of, their papers. I will also explore what (if any) actions the students take as a result of the professor's comments.

Data analysis. The various sources of data will be analyzed qualitatively using different interpretive and rhetorical schemes to attempt to arrive at a rich, contextualized description of writing in this class. Among the areas I anticipate looking at are: how classroom interactions affect final written papers; how students' goals for writing and their task-investment strategies (Nelson & Hayes, 1988; Nelson, 1990) affect their writing; how assigned readings, class documents and classroom interactions communicate special topics (eide in classical rhetoric) of the discipline (Miller & Selzer, 1985) and how those special topics are reflected in the students' texts and the professor's responses; how the professor's responses relate to his/her goals and expectations; how the professor's knowledge of students affects response to them; how students' writing relates to professional genres; and whether the class and department are best characterized as "discourse communities." This design and the analysis employ three of the four types of triangulation Denzin (1989) suggests: data, method, and theory.

Rereading this proposal, I am struck by how hybrid a text it is. The topical section headings and subheadings are designed for experimental or quantitative research, but in this case qualitative content is grafted into this schema. For example, in the section on instruments, probably intended for tests and specific devices, my physical and psychological attendance at seminars is represented as an "instrument." The final section on data analysis, probably intended for issues of reliability, coding, and inferential or descriptive statistics, opens by stating that the analysis will be qualitative and integrative, lists topical issues that will be examined, and closes by asserting that the research involves three of Denzin's four categories of triangulation. The topics for this proposal were structured by the institutional context, a college of education where the only recommended format for dissertation proposals was derived from social scientific research practices. As Knorr-Cetina (1981) noted, textual descriptions of research replace local and more laminated histories (personal, interpersonal, and institutional) with purified disciplinary motives, rationales, and contexts. As a textual projection of disciplinarity, this proposal displays the same kind of textual transformations that I would later identify in Sean's and other students' writing (see chaps. 7, 8, 9; Prior 1994). The next account resituates this research in earlier histories of my teaching experience.

Account 2: Autobiographical Origins

In the decade before I began my doctoral program, I taught ESL first at Indiana University–Bloomington, then in Saudi Arabia, and finally at the UW–Madison. Those teaching experiences led me to form many of the basic questions and orientations that would ultimately motivate and inform my research.

As I taught, I became increasingly concerned with a basic issue: How did my classes relate to the academic needs of my students? This question came into particularly clear focus at UW, where I coordinated and taught ESL composition courses for undergraduate and graduate students (most of whom were already taking academic courses) from diverse disciplines and with diverse educational and cultural backgrounds. Many of the students seemed quite successful in their academic work, but displayed a complex array of problems with writing, everything from formal problems of grammar and mechanics to problems with the use and understanding of various lexical items to discursive problems such as establishing a culturally appropriate voice or using sources without plagiarism. One path that led to my research began with my observations, interactions, and reflections on writing and academic discourse as a teacher in this setting, particularly centered around three areas: use of sources in writing, library research, and descriptions of academic culture.

Many of the students in my ESL classes had striking problems writing from sources, particularly with distinguishing who was talking in the text (i.e., between an author expressing her ideas and presenting those of others) and with copying chunks—sometimes large—of source texts into their summaries, often without any signal that they were reporting someone else's ideas. Actually, I became aware of and concerned about this problem almost by accident. In my second semester at UW, I was teaching an advanced ESL composition course (undergrad and grad) with an inherited syllabus that asked students to write paragraphs in rhetorical modes (e.g., comparison, definition, cause–effect) based on their personal knowledge or experience. One day I decided to have the students summarize a *Newsweek* editorial. The summaries I received were disturbing. On the surface, they were written as though they were personal experience essays, with no language signaling authorship or even referring to *Newsweek*. Most of the summaries missed the point of the editorial as I read it, which was particularly striking given that most had also directly copied entire sentences from the editorial into the "summary." Extending these practices to writing for disciplinary courses, I was troubled. I concluded that my students would plagiarize horribly in their academic writing. In the next class, I told them that they had plagiarized, explained what the institutional penalties for plagiarism were, stated in strong terms that I did not expect to see them plagiarize again, and assigned another summary.

When that second batch of summaries I assigned came in with the same kind of extensive plagiarism, I began to reassess the problem. I made up a handout that included some sample student summaries with the language they had copied directly from the article presented in bold print.[5] As we looked closely through these examples, students repeatedly expressed incredulity that what I was showing them was, in fact, plagiarism. Several said that they had been explicitly taught to do what I was identifying as plagiarism. One student explained the two-step the procedure he had been taught for summarizing: (1) locate the topic sentence of each paragraph; and (2) copy those topic sentences onto the paper. Beyond issues of copying, I found that students knew little about the basic lexical, semantic, syntactic, and mechanical resources in English for representing quotation, paraphrase,

---

[5]These ways of reading and typographically representing intertextuality eventually became critical practices in my research (see chaps. 4, 6, and 8).

summary, and citation. I concluded that what I was dealing with involved both a complex cross-cultural difference in use of sources and a specialized functional domain of language (represented speech) that students had limited understanding of and control over. On both scores, the problem was something I could address through teaching.

My understanding of the use of sources was challenged more radically a few years later when I sat around a table with two colleagues (William Perry and Susan Ranney) assessing a set of essays from a reading–writing placement examination we were piloting for international students at UW–Madison. A basic goal of the new exam was to help us diagnose whether students knew how to "use sources appropriately" in a U.S. university context. As we scored the essays, we soon realized that we were not agreeing on the critical dimension, "use of sources." Talking over the texts we had scored differently, we quickly recognized the reason for our divergence: Each of us had a different definition of plagiarism. At one extreme was the view that students were plagiarizing if their summary closely followed the organizational structure or sequence of topics of the source text; at the other extreme was a fairly liberal tolerance for the transfer of unquoted chunks of text into the summary. What became clear that Saturday afternoon as we sat around a table in an empty classroom was that plagiarism was a cross-culturally variable construct not only for our students, but also for us, as we had naively taken for granted in many conversations that it referenced our shared perceptions and values.

A second critical experience with issues of academic discourse arose as I attempted to orient international students to "U.S. academic culture." Revising an ESL course on spoken language for graduates and undergraduates, Bill Perry and I decided to focus more on cultural orientation and communicative uses of language than pronunciation and listening comprehension drills. For the designated language laboratory section, we used a set of tapes developed by Mason (1983). The tapes presented lectures and interviews that contrasted higher education in different regions of the world (e.g., Europe, the Middle East, East and West Africa, East Asia, and Latin America) with that in the United States. Four interviews were with professors who had grown up as citizens of a country in the region, immigrated late in their education to the United States, and were working as faculty at a U.S. university. These successful intercultural travelers seemed ideally placed to help new arrivals with issues of academic and cultural adjustment.

As we discussed these taped lectures with one another and our students, it soon became apparent that marked differences existed between the interpretations of insider and outsider audiences. As an outsider audience to other educational systems, Bill and I initially accepted descriptions of these systems; however, students from those regions pointed out that their own educational experiences had differed, often radically, from those described by the lecturers. On the other hand, as an insider audience for the United States, we often disagreed with assertions about U.S. higher education (e.g., that U.S. professors expect and are pleased when students disagree with them in class, an assertion that illustrated the egalitarian and participatory nature of U.S. academic culture). Our students, on the other hand, generally accepted these assertions, often enthusiastically amplifying them with their own experiences. Many reported, for example, that U.S. students did not display any signs of deference, status, or respect for professors. With critical insider audiences for both sides of these cross-cultural comparisons, what started as an attempt to orient students into U.S. academic culture became a forum for critical reflection on "cultural and intercultural accounts," an opportunity to examine the gaps between their relative simplicity and definiteness and the complex particularities of personal experience.

A third critical incident involved use of libraries, typically considered an important skill for academic writing. Many of the students in my classes came from countries where finances and policies limited access to libraries, so that a university graduate might never have searched for information in a research library. Finding that the usual combination of some classroom talk about library research with a tour was not enough for our students, we arranged with reference librarians for a hands-on session where students could practice using periodical indexes and other resources. In those sessions, most students had great difficulties with the varied typographical cuing systems that signaled divisions between and within entries. Some had striking difficulties orienting their activity to the library's physical or social organization. An experience that became emblematic for me of the tacit and situated nature of cultural knowledge came when I followed an undergraduate student from Indonesia as he walked out into the stacks to locate a bound periodical. Staring intently at the paper that held a call number he had found in an index, he finally stopped, looked up from his paper, and asked me what he was supposed to *do* with this number. I pointed up to the white cards attached to the sides of the metal stacks and his eyes lit up as he realized that the call numbers related to these cards. I then pointed out how the spines of the bound periodicals also had call numbers on them. With that knowledge, he quickly found the journal he was looking for. Two points struck me about this event. First, I realized the multiple obstacles to access that the student had experienced that day, from the typeface cues of the periodical index to the mysteries of an on-line computer catalog to the locational cues on stacks and spines. Second, I realized I would never have included the advice, "Look up," into any conceivable lesson on library research. It was too tacit, too physical, too basic. To me, libraries were transparent spaces.

As I left the UW and headed to the University of Minnesota to work on a PhD, I took a set of questions and perspectives that had arisen in these contexts of my work as a teacher. I was interested in academic and disciplinary enculturation into ways of reading and writing, speaking and listening, sensing and acting, but was also skeptical of abstract, unified portrayals of academic culture, trained through my own intercultural orientations to counterpose the particular to the universal, the idiosyncratic counterexample to the generic type, the complexity of individualized interpretations to the taken-for-granted codes of cultural rhetorics. I was interested in practical issues of how to teach and assess specialized literate abilities, but also suspected that the social, the cultural, and the conversational played major roles in literate access and success. I believed that knowledge was inextricably tied to language, but saw knowledge as often tacit and experiential rather than explicit and propositional. Clear continuities are visible between those experiences, my later research, and my ultimate theoretical orientation. It should not be surprising, given these biographic snapshots, that I would soon be attracted to sociohistoric critiques of structuralism or theories of practice and especially to Bakhtin's work. However, as much as those questions and perspectives established an orientation for my research, they did not mark out a clear trail for my inquiry, as the next account makes clear.

Account 3: Where's the Task? The Co-Evolution
of Theory, Research, and Methodology

Doyle (1983) defined academic tasks in terms of three elements: the products students produce, the operations students undertake, and the resources available to students for accomplishing their work. He went on, however, to say that academic tasks are fundamentally altered when they are placed within the social organization and history of the classroom. To explore how academic writing tasks are accomplished within such specific sociohistoric contexts, I conducted three qualitative studies of writing and response in graduate seminars. Over the course of these three studies, my understanding of both academic writing tasks and my own task as a researcher altered fundamentally.

As I planned a pilot study of writing tasks in a curriculum seminar in education, I hoped that a close examination of professor response might provide some key insights missed by earlier studies that looked at what professors assigned (e.g., Bridgeman & Carlson, 1983; Horowitz, 1986b), what students wrote (e.g., Herrington, 1985, 1988), or what professors wrote (e.g., Swales, 1990), but not at how professors read and evaluated student writing. I was motivated by a felt sense that, as Doyle (1983) suggested, "The answers a teacher actually accepts and rewards define the real tasks in classrooms" (p. 182). In this pilot study, I sought "the task" (assuming that there was *one*) mainly by examining the professor's goals, written responses, grades, and values. I collected students' final drafts with the professor's comments and grades on them, conducted semi-structured interviews with the professor about his goals and expectations for the seminar and the papers, and distributed questionnaires asking students about their backgrounds and their perceptions of tasks in the seminar. In the analysis, I developed a coding scheme for the professor's responses. I then categorized each response and counted the words in it. With this data, I could look at the kinds and amount of response the professor made on each paper. Hoping to identify what features of texts triggered particular responses, my approach at this time was consistent with many early studies of response (e.g., Diederich, 1974; Freedman, 1979, 1984; Harris, 1977; Rafoth & Rubin, 1984), which tacitly assumed that features of texts controlled instructor responses.

As I attempted to integrate the quantitative and categorical analysis of the professor's response with his accounts of his goals and practices, I became puzzled by what appeared to be anomalies. For example, although he had indicated that substantive response was critical and content-oriented comments generally peppered the margins of his students' papers, one A paper had no written response to content until the final summary comment. Seeing no explanation in the student's text for this departure from his usual response practices, I turned to the limited contextual data I had, the student question-naires. There I found that, when asked to describe the writing assignments for the seminar, the student with the A paper and no marginal content comments had written beyond the space provided, adding a two-page essay in which she argued that the professor's emphasis on the personal and his ambiguous descriptions of writing tasks amounted to an unethical form of psychological experimentation. I speculated that the professor's reserved response to her writing might reflect an uncomfortable interpersonal relationship established through classroom interactions. That thought forced me to question my as-sumption that the instructor was responding to the text alone, to suspect that his responses, Doyle's bottom lines of acceptance and reward, were also shaped by his appraisal of the students, grounded in classroom interactions. I also noted that Herrington (1988) and Doheny-Farina (1989) had both suggested that the substance and style of professors' classroom interactions were tacitly reflected in the form, topics, and argumentation found in students' writing. Thus, my central methodological conclusion from the pilot study was that I needed a more ethnographic, more contextualized research design to explore how the intellectual and social history of classroom interactions played out in both the students' writing and the professor's response.

With these goals in mind, I revised the methodology for my next study, adding classroom observation, semi-structured interviews with students about their writing for the seminar, and text-based interviews with the professor. Observation would allow me to examine ways that the students' writing and the professor's responses were being shaped by classroom contexts. The text-based interviews with the professor would allow me to explore reasons behind written responses, particularly to examine whether the professor was reading and responding to the students as well as texts. Finally, the addition of student interviews would provide more information on the contexts and intentions behind their texts, data that I thought would be helpful in understanding the professor's response.

Following the same professor into a graduate seminar on second languages education (*Language Research*), I began this second study (see chaps. 2 and 4; Prior, 1991) with the intention once again of discovering and describing *the* academic writing tasks of the seminar through careful examination of the professor's response and evaluation. However, any notion of "the writing task" evaporated as I confronted the multiple images of the seminar's writing tasks offered by participants. I first attempted to categorize this task multiplicity. However, I saw that even an expanded series of task categories (*stated, restated, inferred, understood, negotiated, undertaken, read,* and *responded to*) failed to capture the multiplicity, as each category varied with time, person, and setting. Given this analysis, I concluded that academic writing tasks in a seminar were multiple, indeterminate, and historically constituted.

Results from *Language Research*, particularly task multiplicity, the prominence of students' ongoing projects, and the close connections between classroom talk and students' texts, led to further revisions of my research design. First, to understand how students interpreted and acted on professor response, I decided to conduct text-based interviews with students after they received responses from the professor and particularly to examine any revisions or other consequences of that response. Second, to more fully understand students' literate processes, goals, and representations of context, I planned to collect drafts and process logs if possible and to expand the depth of student interviews. Finally, I decided to capture the details of critical classroom interactions by audiotaping seminar sessions whenever possible. As that research design was implemented, my plan to investigate "another seminar" serendipitously turned into a study of four seminars in quite different disciplinary–departmental settings.

MANGLING A RESEARCH DESIGN

Individually or in combination, the accounts I have provided can only offer perspectives on the history of this research, suggesting the complexity of biographical, institutional, and sociocultural trajectories woven in it. In this section, I turn from research designs to implementation of the final research, beginning with access stories.

Negotiating Access

The canonical first step in an ethnographic study is negotiating access to a research site. Pratt (1986) provides an interesting perspective on access stories in ethnography. However, stories of Evans-Pritchard meeting the Nuer or Firth meeting the Tikopia (see Pratt, 1986) are not a good model for ethnographic research undertaken at a U.S. university. My first contacts did not involve native canoes raucously entering the water to greet my arriving ship or complex negotiations with native porters to arrange transport of gear into the back country. Instead, it started with the prosaic activities of reading a university timetable, calling a university registrar to determine numbers of U.S. and international graduate students in particular departments, negotiating with the indigenous inhabitants of a Committee for the Review of the Use of Human Subjects, and sitting in front of a Macintosh computer producing the myriad documents that accompany ethnography in a bureaucratic setting.[6]

My letters and follow-up phone calls to department chairs provided me names of approximately 20 professors to contact. Letters to those professors and follow-up phone calls to some of them resulted in serious discussions

———————

[6]Among the documents I produced in the two months preceding the research and in the first month of data collection were the following: a dissertation proposal for my thesis panel, a thesis statement for the graduate school, a letter to the Committee for the Review of the Use of Human Subjects requesting approval for modifications to my previously approved methodology, a mail merge list of selected

with six professors. For several professors, time was a serious concern. My original plan had envisaged about five hours of interview time with professors. When I first discussed the research with Elaine West, a sociology professor, she indicated that a five-hour commitment was simply too much. I thanked her for having considered participation. After getting off the phone, I discussed the conversation with my wife. Told that the professor had already asked the students if she should invite me to present my research to them, Julie suggested that I was crazy to pass up a site where the professor was taking the research so seriously. I was working at that time as an RA in the Center for Interdisciplinary Studies of Writing for Lillian Bridwell-Bowles, who was also a reader for my dissertation. I stepped into her office the next day and asked how she would feel about such changes in the design. She said that ethnographic research designs need to be flexible. I reconsidered my decision, called Professor West back that day, explained that I had had second thoughts, and asked if she would still be willing to consider the research if I limited interviewing to two hours. She agreed, fortunately, as the sociology seminar proved to be a particularly productive and provocative site (see chaps. 6–8).

In some instances, conversations with professors about potential sites did not lead to access. In a team-taught course, one professor decided not to participate because of concerns about how the research would influence a pedagogically experimental course and because she had just begun a term as editor of a major journal. In another case, I chose not to pursue a potential site in the School of Business because the professor described a course dominated by group work in class and out. I had not planned for, and was uncertain I had the resources for, data collection in a setting so different from those I had studied. In the end, I had four potential sites: *Agricultural Economics* taught by Bill Rice and Thomas Mann; *Sociology*, taught by Elaine West; and two seminars taught by Arthur Kohl, *Geography* and *American Studies*. (Here, I will only discuss the latter three seminars I report on in this book.) Not knowing what kind of enrollment each class would have or what level of participation (if any) students would agree to, I decided to approach all four seminars and then select the most promising site.

department chairs and a mail merge letter to those chairs requesting their assistance in identifying appropriate courses, a mail merge list of professors and a mail merge letter to them introducing the research, a one-page description of the research and a one-page bio-statement to accompany those letters, an informed consent form for students, an informed consent form for professors, a one-page description of paid participation for students doing process logs, an initial questionnaire for students, an initial questionnaire for professors, an application for graduate school funds to pay for research expenses, and an application for a dissertation fellowship.

Entering Sociology.   I took an elevator up to the 12th floor of a tower and entered a well-furnished, modern conference room that adjoined West's office and provided a panoramic view of the campus and the city. Seven PhD students and West sat around the table. At the beginning of the first session, West introduced me, and I explained my research, handed out the informed consent forms and a sheet explaining paid participation for process logs, and answered several students' questions. Then West suggested that they should discuss whether they wanted to participate among themselves and asked me to leave the room. After about five minutes, she invited me back in and indicated that the class had agreed to the research. I sat down, collected all of the informed consent forms (except those from the two professors who were absent and an undergraduate student who occasionally attended), and began taking notes. The remainder of that session, the students reviewed what research they intended to present in the seminar. At the next session, the second professor signed the consent form. The third professor, an anthropologist who attended less than half of the sessions, refused to read the consent form and simply gave me verbal permission to record his comments in class.

Entering Geography.   I arrived at Arthur Kohl's geography seminar on a spring evening. Five students sat around a table in a room filled with maps and globes. As introductions were done, I briefly introduced myself. Then Kohl began discussing the course and contextualizing its content in both the historical development of geography and the departmental program. The remainder of the class was primarily lecture. Near the end, I passed out my materials. Several students needed to run to catch buses; a couple signed the forms. I left not knowing if I would have access to this seminar. The next week, two of the five students were gone, and another had arrived. Enrollment then remained at four students, but from the third week on two other students regularly sat in.

Entering American Studies.   The afternoon following the first meeting of *Geography*, I also entered Kohl's *American Studies*. It met that day in a small basement room in an old building. Eighteen students were crowded around a long table and in chairs lined against the wall; most seemed to know one another. I recognized one student who had also been in *Geography* the night before. Before class, another student walked over to where I was sitting, shook my hand, and introduced himself as "the C.E.O. here." Professor Kohl then entered and began lecturing. Unlike the previous night, students (one in particular) interrupted his lecture with questions and comments (sometimes ironic). Then I was introduced. I began to explain my research. The student who had been in *Geography* the night before immediately asked if it would not be biased for me to study two classes with the same professor. I responded that all studies were biased and that it would be interesting to see the same professor in two different contexts. He followed up by saying that Kohl would be the same in each class; I answered that the students would be different. That much was already quite obvious. Then the student who had been questioning Kohl so intensely began questioning me. He asked what I was doing there, how I had gotten there, if I should have gotten students' permission to attend at all, and so on. I responded to each question, but my responses did not seem to satisfy his concerns. After several exchanges, Kohl regained the floor, saying he had invited me, but that they did not have to participate if they didn't want to, and that I would pass around information at the end of class. Next, he asked students to introduce themselves and to discuss their research interests. It was the third quarter the seminar had met; most of the students had taken it the previous two quarters with another professor. The remainder of the class period was taken up with students talking about their research interests, some student-to-student interaction, and some short lectures by Kohl in response to the topics being raised, mostly talking about local neighborhoods and their histories.

At the end of the class, I passed out my informed consent forms. A few people looked them over and signed them; most did not. Class ended; people began talking. I went up to the student who had questioned me so sharply. Another student was talking to him, one who had expressed interest in the research and offered to help out. She was talking to him about a photograph on the front cover of a book; the image showed an ethnographer in a tent writing notes with natives in the background who are looking not at the ethnographer, but at the camera. I asked him if he had any other questions, and he told me that the other student had convinced him to participate by arguing that they needed to experience what it was like to be studied as well as what it was like to study others. He went on to say he was concerned I would disrupt the strong group cohesion the class had developed over the previous two quarters, but that he would reluctantly consent.

Design as an Open-Ended Process

In chapter 7, I use Pickering's (1995) notion of the mangle of practice to discuss how Sean's dissertation prospectus was reshaped and redirected as he encountered seminar responses and the data itself. My design was also mangled in practice as it encountered the people and contexts of my study. Informed consent was anything but routine in three of the four settings. In several cases, I had to draft out individualized contracts with students to clarify what data I could collect, analyze, and report. In *American Studies*, I did not get signed consent from everyone until the final week of the quarter. My desire to use process logs ran into overwhelming passive resistance. Even with the carrot of paid participation, out of approximately 60 students in the four seminars, only four expressed any interest in doing process logs and by the fourth week of the research, three of those four had begged out of the task. The one student who did process logs (Lilah in chap. 9) participated fully, but did not want to be paid. My plan to select one site was complicated by uncertainties about students' consent and the quality of data as well as my growing interest in all four settings: I decided to conduct research, with varying degrees of intensity, in all four seminars. To make up for the increased demands of observation and data collection, I decided to allocate less time for the departmental component of the design.

Specific interviews provided another good example of the mangling of the methodology. The substance of the semi-structured and text-based interviews with students varied with the particular data available, with what kinds of analyses I had begun to pursue, and with the contexts of the interview. In the case of Moira in the sociology seminar (see chaps. 6 and 8), I had available seven drafts of her conference paper and four drafts of her preliminary examination. As I traced how West's responses came to be incorporated into Moira's drafts (see Figs. 6.2 and 6.3 for examples), I began to wonder if Moira really agreed with the changes. Thus, in preparing for Moira's discourse-based interview (Odell, et al., 1983), I developed a number of prompts that would give Moira the opportunity to replace West's words with her own earlier language. On the other hand, in an interview with Lee, a NNSE in the same sociology seminar, I had only a single text, a rough draft of part of his prelim exam, which he had presented in the seminar. In doing a text-based interview with him, I was particularly interested in examining how he understood West's marginal comments and editing and whether he had acted on them or thought them through, so I conducted a very different text-based interview. I asked Lee to read West's written responses, discuss what they meant, and then say how he had or would react to those comments. I also asked him to read selected passages as he had written them and then again as West had edited them, to discuss why he thought West had made those changes, and finally to say how he had acted or would act on them and why. In the case of Lilah (see chap. 9), the only student who carried through with the process log, three lengthy interviews ranged wide as I attempted to understand the connections among three courses in which she was doing related work. In a text-based portion of one interview with Lilah, we looked at the introductions to her final papers from all three seminars and discussed how stylistic and topical choices in those introductions reflected her perceptions of the three professors and her goals for the papers.

My approach to interviews with professors was similarly tailored. The nature of the data and of the relationships developed with each professor were quite different. West had been very concerned with time so I worked to be very efficient in these interviews, to juggle my interest in understanding her background, goals, and contexts with my interest in getting text-based and discourse-based interviews. Our interviews were rapid-fire, very businesslike but cordial. When my time had run out and I had turned off the tape recorder, West would continue discussing the research with me, offering additional insights into her contexts and sounding out my reactions to the seminar. I conducted several types of text-based interview with West. For Moira's papers, I used some of the same passages I had asked Moira about (excluding some to save time), whereas for Lee, I asked West to comment on her marginal responses and editing and to indicate how important she felt each comment was. Professor Kohl had put no general limits on his time. In interviews, he leaned back in his chair and gazed out the window or around the room, offering long, reflective answers, often including stories of experiences throughout his career. In the text-based portion of the interviews, I simply asked him to comment on students' work and his response because his attitude toward it as in-progress and his general avoidance of marginal and interlinear comments or editing did not lend themselves to a discourse-based interview. In other words, asking him highly specific questions about the language of the texts simply did not seem to me to reflect his approach to those texts.

RESEARCH AS INTERPRETIVE PRACTICE

In addition to showing how my initial research design was mangled as I encountered a variety of unexpected contingencies and as my own goals, resources, and conditions evolved, the last section suggests how inadequate references to conventional research tools (e.g., semi-structured interview, discourse-based interview, intertextual analysis, process tracing) may be.

As dialogic activity, research involves the construction of meaning out of prior experiences, current emergent events, and anticipations of future responses, a process occurring in concrete moments of observation, reading, writing, talk, and listening. I believe it is important to examine research practices as situated and mediated activity. Here, I turn to analysis and writing to consider them from an activity perspective.

Obviously, interpretation involves practices of thinking, a phenomenon I experience as a mixture of inner voices and images, some recalled, some constructed. Some of this inner speech had a clearly directive character. For example, at a number of points I reminded myself that the goal of my research was interpretation. This reminder directed my attention to issues of understanding in data collection and analysis. If other voices had prevailed, voices reminding me to seek reliable and objective data, the research would have unfolded in a very different fashion. Some voices were more particular. For example, as I discussed my research plans with Lillian Bridwell-Bowles one day, she stressed the value of empathy and identification as interpretive strategies. She illustrated these strategies with a story about another ethnographer who found out that a woman she had interviewed had invented liberally as she described her biography. The ethnographer was amazed and angry—until she recalled a time she had been "creative" with her own credentials; then her understanding increased. For some reason, this story stuck. At a number of points in the research, I encountered practices that I initially reacted to negatively. Searching my experience to see if I could find similar practices, perhaps in different settings, I often did. Taking these imaginative leaps into another's experience through reflections on my own contributed much to my interpretations, and this strategy was regularly triggered by memories of that conversation with Lilly.

I frequently play out internalized hypothetical dialogues with others. In some cases, these dialogues represent replays of past interactions or anticipations of future interactions. For example, in preparing for research interviews, I would imagine questions I might ask and possible answers. In some cases, they are more hypothetical. As I have written up the research for conference presentations, articles, and finally this book, I have imagined people's questions, objections, and reactions (grounded to varying degrees in my experience with them). Those responses and my attempted answers to them often sent me back to the data or to reading. Sometimes they merged with my writing, as I would try to capture fragments from an internalized dialogue. In any case, these inner dialogues are typical features of my thinking and invention.

Finally, images also seem to play an important role in my thinking. Some of the images represent memories of experiences, and the images often seemed to trigger affective as well as visual memories. As I think about the participants in this research, I often recall images of them in different settings and recall how I felt in those settings as well. For example, my interpretation of Moira's interviews emerged in part from images and affective memories of that interview. I have also found myself creating metaphorical images throughout the interpretive process. I have repeatedly struggled with tropic images to capture my sense of the complexity, multiplicity, and temporality of interacting histories that make up classroom interactions. Those images are often of weaving, of interwoven strands, of textured fabrics; recently, images of streams and fluids have become more common. These images seem to shape both interpretation and textual production. It is difficult to trace the role they play in the analysis and the text (although a lexical count of related words, like my use of *weave* and *streams*, would offer some evidence).

In my proposal and subsequent reports, I have said that my approach to analysis is primarily interpretive, but what does that mean? Latour and Woolgar (1986) argue that the biologists they studied were involved in complexly layered processes of inscription. Thus, an experiment would end up with inscriptions derived from spectrometers, other devices, and laboratory logs, and these inscriptions might then be mixed with others to produce an article. In a similar sense, ethnographic research produces multiple inscriptions: student texts, interview transcripts, class transcripts, professor responses, notes, analytic codings, and so on. One approach to dealing with such data is reduction, the reinscription of these texts into a simpler set of categories. However, I felt that such reductions helped produce exactly the kind of reified structuralist analysis I was questioning.

The approach I decided to pursue was to integrate multiple data sources, to bring them together to facilitate an overall interpretation of the results. Basically, integrative analysis involved bringing multiple texts together at one place and time and reading across texts. For example, as I analyzed transcripts from discourse-based interviews with Moira and West on Moira's texts, I extracted the discourse-based sections and produced a single document that included each bracketed passage, the proposed changes, Moira's reactions to the proposed change and West's reactions to the proposed change. This textual alignment allowed me to see patterns in the data I would have missed otherwise. I also had gone through all of West's interviews and produced an index of names and general topics. As I was writing up the analysis of Moira's case, I used this index to make a separate document that included all of the comments that West had made about Moira (those elicited in text-based interviews and any that arose in the semi-structured parts of the interview). In addition, I had a full set of working copies of the numbered drafts of *Arenas* and *Prelim* (see chap 8), on which I had marked in red ink any changes from previous drafts; an analysis I had made on separate sheets in which I arranged sentence-by-sentence comparisons of language from the abstracts of the first four drafts of the Moira's conference paper; and the entire transcript of Moira's interview, again with a general topical index to aid access. Much of the analysis and write up of Moira's case involved reading and rereading across these multiple inscriptions. The tools of integrative analysis that I developed were designed to facilitate the display and comparison of these inscriptions and to ease access (e.g., through indexes of interviews and side-by-side comparisons). Some of them became the basis for textual displays (e.g., the document I made up to analyze the discourse-based interviews was the basis for Figures 8.5–8.8).

Naturally, my interpretations were not built just from research data. As I was collecting data on Moira's case, I happened to read a new book by Wertsch (1991) that discussed Bakhtin and Vygotsky in ways that added much to my reading of their works. I found Wertsch's discussion of authoritative and internally persuasive discourse quite clear and this led me back into Bakhtin (1981) to reexamine the passages that discussed these notions. The research log I kept from this time indicates that I was applying this notion to my own communication patterns at home as well as to Moira's reactions to West's responses. To some extent, reading Wertsch (1991) and Bakhtin (1981) triggered my decision to modify the discourse-based interview procedure as described earlier, a decision that produced the central data in my analysis of Moira's case (chap. 8).

I engage in several kinds of informal and formal writing. As I read, I mark passages in books and articles and write questions, summaries, and evaluations in margins or elsewhere. For formal writing, I produce multiple drafts, dozens of them in fact. I write into the computer, print out text, and then edit it and write new text on hard copy. My most productive periods have involved concentrated writing in which I produce some text one day, get up early the next day and edit–compose on the hard copy, then write in revisions onto the computer (often composing new text as I do so), print it out, get up the next morning to read–edit–compose–read, and so on. My wife and others often read drafts, and I talk with Julie about my ideas at length.

To motivate my writing, I have intentionally structured intermediate presentations. Thus, as I was conducting the research, I responded to an invitation to submit a chapter for a book (Belcher & Braine, 1995). I indicated that the chapter would overview the research. I have also routinely submitted proposals to conferences that related to projects I planned to be working on at that time. In addition to motivating my work, these papers also pushed me to consider and eventually discover what audiences might be interested in, what I would need to be able to present to others to communicate my interpretations.

Putting these kinds of practices together for research that has covered over eight years would involve another book (at least) the length of this one, so I will present one early example that evokes the blending of these the interpretive practices. (Chap. 10 describes some later examples.) In December 1992, I attended the MLA Conference in San Francisco to interview for faculty positions. One day, I was in a diner across from my hotel reading Vygotsky's (1978) *Mind in Society*. I had mentioned my interest in Vygotsky in my letters of application and then began to think that people might expect that I had read *Mind in Society*, something I had been intending to do, but had not yet done. I came across a passage where Vygotsky argued that children do not engage in imaginative play before the age of three. I immediately thought about my daughter, Nora. Starting at 18 months (after about two months in daycare), Nora had begun to turn our living room into her version of naptime at the daycare. I recalled the living room, the curtains pulled and a lullaby tape playing, with Nora (the teacher) murmuring to and rubbing the backs of her "children" (stuffed animals and dolls) spread out across the floor on their "cots" (pillows). I wondered if Vygotsky was depending on dated, inadequate research, but then began to recall conversations with my wife about how children often seem to display less advanced skills in clinical test settings than they apparently do at home. I wondered about this difference and then started connecting it to our daughter more. I began to speculate that the home environment itself was a kind of supportive scaffolding environment, a familiar, comfortable matrix in which our daughter's attention could be directed to new paths more easily. Then I asked myself whether this had anything to do with composition instruction, a question I anticipated being asked in job interviews. I thought of composition workshops, which reminded me of identity negotiations, which I had been reading about in Brooke (1990). That thought then connected back to Vygotsky's argument that higher psychological functions were first seen in assisted social interaction and then became increasingly internalized and truncated until they disappeared into automaticity. As what I was thinking about now amounted to an issue of identity, I began to consider the possibility of seeing identities as psychological tools. I found this thought interesting and wrote it down in the back of my copy of *Mind in Society*. It eventually made its way into a presentation at the CCC Conference in Cincinnati three months later. Much later I connected it to Lave and Wenger's (1991) notion that learning is the historical production of people and to Leont'ev's (1981a) quote (see chap. 1) that internalization is a process by which consciousness is formed. The point of this example is that it evokes the blend of circumstances, anticipated audiences, reading, internalized dialogues, imagery (our living room), and writing as activities that characterize interpretive practice. Much as I have analyzed students' and professors' literate activity in the chapters of this book, I believe that methodological accounts of interpretive practice should focus on the situated, laminated, practical activities of research more than on epistemological positioning or allusions to canonical idealized designs.

Appendix B

Conventions of Data Representation

The following transcription symbols are used in this book:

(1) =   latching of speech, that is, no perceptible pause across a turn
(2) / He /
    /No /   overtalk (i.e., simultaneous talk)
(3) ( )   unintelligible
(4) (yes)   uncertain transcription
(5) -   abrupt self-interruption
(6) [ ]   explanatory note
(7) [1 s]   note indicates a pause of over 1/2 second, estimated in half-second intervals
(8) "Go ahead"   quotation marks indicate constructed dialogue
(9) …   material deleted from transcript
(10) *Italics*   Emphatic or special utterances (In the figures of chap. 8, italics are added to interview comments to highlight points for analysis.)

Different levels of transcription are represented in this book. In transcribing interviews for *Language Research* (chaps. 2 and 4), I removed false starts and repetitions. For the other seminars, closer transcription was done for classroom interactions than for interviews. For the interviews, backchannel talk ("umhm") has been deleted to save space. Capitalization, punctuation, and line breaks are included to aid in reading the text. In chapter 6, I include pause times in the transcripts of Park's presentation because pauses seemed quite a marked feature of that talk. Finally, I should note that names of people, places, and institutions have been routinely changed to pseudonyms in the transcripts.

Texts from the seminars are reproduced in varied ways in the figures and text. All such texts have been retyped and all handwritten comments from professors have been recopied (in my hand). Texts have not been edited to correct errors or to standardize style. Ellipses mark material deleted from the texts. Italics, bold print, underlining, boxes, and other devices have been added at various points to highlight specific points for analysis (specific conventions are explained in each case). Names of local persons, places, and institutions have been changed in the texts to limit identifiability of the research participants.

References

Amann, K., & Knorr-Cetina, K. (1990). The fixation of (visual) evidence. In M. Lynch & S. Woolgar (Eds.), *Representation in scientific practice* (pp. 85–122). Cambridge, MA: MIT Press.

Anson, C. M. (1988). Toward a multidimensional model of writing in the academic disciplines. In D.A. Jolliffe (Ed.), *Advances in writing research volume 2: Writing in academic disciplines* (pp. 1–33). Norwood, NJ: Ablex.

Aristotle. (1932). *The rhetoric of Aristotle* (L. Cooper, Trans.). Englewood Cliffs, NJ: Prentice-Hall.

Bakhtin, M. M. (1981). *The dialogic imagination: Four essays by M. M. Bakhtin.* (C. Emerson & M. Holquist, Trans.; M. Holquist, Ed.). Austin: University of Texas Press.

Bakhtin, M. M (1986). *Speech genres and other late essays.* (V.W. McGee, Trans; C. Emerson & M. Holquist, Eds.). Austin: University of Texas Press.

Bakhtin, M. M., & Medvedev, P. (1978). *The formal method in literary scholarship.* (A. Wehrle, Trans.). Baltimore: The John Hopkins University Press.

Bakhurst, D. (1991). *Consciousness and revolution in Soviet philosophy: From the Bolsheviks to Evald Ilyenkov.* Cambridge, England: Cambridge University Press.

Ball, C., Dice, L., & Bartholomae, D. (1990). Telling secrets: Student readers and disciplinary authorities. In R. Beach & S. Hynds (Eds.), *Developing discourse practices in adolescence and adulthood* (pp. 337–357). Norwood, NJ: Ablex.

Bartholomae, D. (1985). Inventing the university. In M. Rose (Ed.), *When a writer can't write* (pp. 134–165). New York: Guilford.

Bartlett, F. (1932). *Remembering: A study in experimental and social psychology.* Cambridge, England: Cambridge University Press.

Bateson, G. (1972). *Steps to an ecology of mind.* New York: Chandler.

Bauman, R. (1992). Contextualization, tradition, and the dialogue of genres: Icelandic legends of the *kraftaskald.* In A. Duranti & C. Goodwin (Eds.), *Rethinking context: Language as an interactive phenomenon* (pp. 125–146). Cambridge, England: Cambridge University Press.

Bazerman, C. (1988). *Shaping written knowledge: The genre and activity of the experimental article in science.* Madison: University of Wisconsin Press.

Bazerman, C. (1991). How natural philosophers can cooperate: The literary technology of coordinated investigation in Joseph Priestley's *History and Present State of Electricity* (1767). In C. Bazerman & J. Paradis (Eds.), *Textual dynamics of the professions: Historical and contemporary studies of writing in professional communities.* (pp. 13–44). Madison: University of Wisconsin Press.

Bazerman, C. (1994a). *Constructing experience.* Carbondale: Southern Illinois University Press.

Bazerman, C. (1994b). Systems of genres and the enactment of social intentions. In A. Freedman & P. Medway (Eds.), *Genre and the new rhetoric* (pp. 79–101). London: Taylor & Francis.

Bazerman, C. (in press). *The languages of Edison's light.* Cambridge, MA: MIT Press.

Beach, R., & Bridwell, L. S. (1984). Introduction. In R. Beach & L.S. Bridwell (Eds.), *New directions in composition research* (pp. 1–14). New York: Guilford.

Beason, L. (1993). Feedback and revision in writing across the curriculum classes. *Research in the Teaching of English, 27,* 395–422.

Becher, T. (1989). *Academic tribes and territories: Intellectual enquiry and the cultures of disciplines.* Stony Stratford, England: Society for Research into Higher Education and Open University Press.

Becker, A.L. (1988). Language in particular: A lecture. In D. Tannen (Ed.), *Linguistics in context: Connecting observation and understanding* (pp. 17–35). Norwood, NJ: Ablex.

Becker, H. (1982). *Art worlds.* Berkeley: University of California Press.

Becker, H., Greer, B., Hughes, E., & Strauss, A. (1961). *Boys in white: Student culture in medical school.* Chicago: University of Chicago Press.

Belcher, D. (1994). The apprenticeship approach to advanced academic literacy: Graduate students and their mentors. *English for Specific Purposes, 13,* 23–34.

Belcher, D., & Braine, G. (Eds.). (1995). *Academic writing in a second language: Essays on research and pedagogy.* Norwood, NJ: Ablex.

Berkenkotter, C., & Huckin, T. (1995). *Genre knowledge in disciplinary communication: Cognition/culture/power.* Mahwah, NJ: Lawrence Erlbaum Associates.

Berkenkotter, C., Huckin, T.N., & Ackerman, J. (1988). Conventions, conversations, and the writer: Case study of a student in a rhetoric Ph.D. program. *Research in the Teaching of English, 22,* 9–44.

Berkenkotter, C., Huckin, T.N., & Ackerman, J. (1991). Social context and socially constructed texts: The initiation of a graduate student into a writing research community. In C. Bazerman & J. Paradis (Eds.), *Textual dynamics of the professions* (pp. 191–215). Madison, WI: University of Wisconsin Press.

Birdwhistle, R. (1970). *Kinesics and context: Essays on body motion communication.* Philadelphia: University of Pennsylvania Press.

Bizzell, P. (1982). Cognition, convention, and certainty: What we need to know about writing. *PRE/TEXT, 3,* 213–243.

Blackburn, G. (1974). *The illustrated encyclopedia of woodworking, handtools, instruments, and devices.* New York: Simon & Schuster.

Blakeslee, A. (1992). *Inventing scientific discourse: Dimensions of rhetorical knowledge in physics.* Unpublished doctoral dissertation, Carnegie Melon University.

Blakeslee, A. (1997). Activity, context, interaction, and authority: Learning to write scientific papers in situ. *Journal of Business and Technical Communication, 11,* 125–169.

Bloome, D., Puro, P, & Theodorou, E. (1989). Procedural display and classroom lessons. *Curriculum Inquiry, 19,* 265–291.

Braine, G. (1989). Writing in science and technology: An analysis of assignments from ten undergraduate courses. *English for Specific Purposes, 8,* 3–15.

Brandt, D. (1990). *Literacy as involvement: The acts of writers, readers and texts.* Carbondale: Southern Illinois University Press.

Bridgeman, B., & Carlson, S. (1983). *Survey of academic writing tasks required of graduate and undergraduate foreign students* (Rep. No. 83–18). Princeton, NJ: Educational Testing Service.

Brodkey, L. (1987). *Academic writing as social practice.* Philadelphia: Temple University Press.

Brooke, R. (1990). *Writing and sense of self: Identity negotiation in writing workshops.* Urbana, IL: National Council of Teachers of English.

Bruner, J. (1986). *Actual minds, possible worlds.* Cambridge, MA: Harvard University Press.

Bruner, J. (1990). *Acts of meaning.* Cambridge, MA: Harvard University Press.

Bruner, J. (1994). From joint attention to the meeting of minds: An introduction. In C. Moore & P. Dunham (Eds.), *Joint attention: Its origins and role in development* (pp. 1–14). Hillsdale, NJ: Lawrence Erlbaum Associates.

Bruner, J., & Lucariello, J. (1989). Monologue as narrative recreation of the world. In K. Nelson (Ed.), *Narratives from the crib* (pp. 73–97). Cambridge, MA: Harvard University Press.

Bulmer, M. (1984). *The Chicago school of sociology: Institutionalization, diversity, and the rise of sociological research.* Chicago: University of Chicago Press.

Callon, M. (1996, June). *Representing nature, representing society.* Paper presented at the University of Hong Kong Conference on Knowledge and Discourse, Hong Kong.

Carpenter, M. (1981). *Corporate authorship: Its role in library cataloging.* Westport, CN: Greenwood.

Casanave, C. P. (1992). Cultural diversity and socialization: A case study of a Hispanic woman in a doctoral program in sociology. In D. Murray (Ed.), *Diversity as resource: Redefining cultural literacy* (pp. 148–182). Alexandria, VA: TESOL.

Casanave, C. P. (1995). Local interactions: Constructing contexts for composing in a graduate sociology program. In D. Belcher & G. Braine (Eds.), *Academic writing in a second language: Essays on research and pedagogy* (pp. 83–110) Norwood, NJ: Ablex.

Cazden, C. (1983). Peekaboo as an instructional model: Discourse development at home and school. In B. Bain (Ed.), *The sociogenesis of language and human conduct* (pp. 33–58). New York: Plenum.

Cazden, C. (1992). *Whole language plus: Essays on literacy in the United States and New Zealand.* New York: Teachers College Press.

Cazden, C. B., Michaels, S., & Tabors, P. (1985). Spontaneous repairs in sharing time narratives: The intersection of metalinguistic awareness, speech event, and narrative style. In S. Freedman (Ed.), *The acquisition of written language: Revision and response* (pp. 51–64). Norwood, NJ: Ablex.

Certeau, M. de (1984). *The practice of everyday life*. (S. Rendall, Trans.). Berkeley: University of California Press.

Charney, D. (1984). The validity of using holistic scoring to evaluate writing: A critical overview. *Research in the Teaching of English, 18,* 65–81.

Chin, E. (1994). Redefining "context" in research on writing. *Written Communication, 11,* 445–482.

Chiseri-Strater, E. (1991). *Academic literacies: The public and private discourse of university students.* Portsmouth, NH: Boyton/Cook.

Chomsky, N. (1957). *Syntactic structures.* The Hague, Netherlands: Mouton.

Chomsky, N. (1965). *Aspects of the theory of syntax.* Cambridge, MA: MIT Press.

Cicourel, A. (1981). Three models of discourse analysis: The role of social structure. *Discourse Processes, 3,* 101–132.

Clark, G., & Doheny-Farina, S. (1990). Public discourse and personal expression: A case study of theory–building. *Written Communication, 7,* 456–481.

Clark, H. (1992). *Arenas of language use.* Chicago: University of Chicago Press.

Clark, W. (1989). On the dialectical origins of the research seminar. *History of Science, 27,* 111–154.

Cole, M. (1995). Socio-cultural-historical psychology: Some general remarks and a proposal for a new kind of cultural-genetic methodology. In J. Wertsch, P. del Rio, & A. Alvarez (Eds.), *Sociocultural studies of mind* (pp. 187–214). Cambridge, England: Cambridge University Press.

Cole, M. (1996). *Cultural psychology: A once and future discipline.* Cambridge, MA: Harvard University Press.

Cole, M., & Engestrom, Y. (1993). A cultural-historical approach to distributed cognition. In G. Salomon (Ed.), *Distributed cognitions: Psychological and educational considerations* (pp. 1–46). Cambridge, England: Cambridge University Press.

Cole, S. (1983). The hierarchy of the sciences? *American Journal of Sociology, 89,* 111–139.

Coleman, J. (1967). Research chronicle: The adolescent society. In P. Hammond (Ed.), *Sociologists at work: Essays on the craft of social research* (pp. 213–243). New York: Basic Books.

Collins, H. M. (1985). *Changing order: Replication and induction in scientific practice.* London: Sage.

Cooper, M. M. (1989). Why are we talking about discourse communities? Or, foundationalism rears its ugly head once more. In M. M. Cooper & M. Holzman (Eds.), *Writing as social action* (pp. 202–220). Portsmouth, NH: Boyton/Cook.

Coupland, N., Wieman, J. M., & Giles, H. (1991). Talk as "problem" and communication as "miscommunication": An integrative analysis. In N. Coupland, H. Giles, & J. Wieman (Eds.), *"Miscommunication" and problematic talk* (pp. 1–17). Newbury Park, CA: Sage.

Crane, D. (1972). *Invisible colleges: Diffusion of knowledge in scientific communities.* Chicago: University of Chicago Press.

Cross, G. A. (1994). *Collaboration and conflict: A contextual exploration of group writing and positive emphasis.* Cresskill, NJ: Hampton Press.

del Rio, P., & Alvarez, A. (1995). Tossing, praying, and reasoning: The changing architectures of mind and agency. In J. Wertsch, P. del Rio, & A. Alvarez (Eds.), *Sociocultural studies of mind* (pp. 215–247). Cambridge, England: Cambridge University Press.

Denzin, N. K. (1989). *The research act: A theoretical introduction to sociological methods.* (3rd ed.). Englewood Cliffs, NJ: Prentice-Hall.

Dibble, V. K. (1975). *The legacy of Albion Small.* Chicago: University of Chicago Press.

Diederich, P. (1974). *Measuring growth in English.* Urbana, IL: National Council of Teachers of English.

Doheny-Farina, S. (1989). A case study of one adult writing in academic and nonacademic discourse communities. In C. Matalene (Ed.), *Worlds of writing: Teaching and learning in discourse communities of work* (pp. 17–42). New York: Random House.

Doyle, W. (1983). Academic work. *Review of Educational Research, 53,* 159–199.

Dreyfus, H. (1992). *What computers still can't do: A critique of artificial reason.* Cambridge, MA: MIT Press.

Duin, A., & Hansen, C. (1996). *Nonacademic writing: Social theory and technology.* Mahwah, NJ: Lawrence Erlbaum Associates.

Duranti, A. (1986). Audience as co-author: An introduction. *Text, 6,* 23–47.

Duranti, A. (1993). Intentions, self, and responsibility: An essay in Samoan ethnopragmatics. In J. Hill & J. Irvine (Eds.), *Responsibility and evidence in oral discourse* (pp. 24–47). Cambridge, England: Cambridge University Press.

Durkheim, E. (1982). *The rules of sociological method and selected texts on sociology and its method* (W. D. Halls, Trans.; S. Lukes, Ed.). New York: Free Press.

Dyson, A. (1988). Negotiating among multiple worlds: The space/time dimensions of young children's composing. *Research in the Teaching of English, 22,* 355–390.

Edmondson, R. (1984). *Rhetoric in sociology.* London: MacMillian.

Engestrom, Y. (1987). *Learning by expanding: An activity-theoretical approach to developmental research.* Helsinki, Finland: Orienta-Konsultit.

Engestrom, Y. (1993). Developmental studies of work as a testbench of activity theory: The case of primary care medical practice. In S. Chaiklin & J. Lave (Eds.), *Understanding Practice* (pp. 64–103). Cambridge, England: Cambridge University Press.

Engestrom, Y., & Escalante, V. (1995). Mundane tool or object of affection? The rise and fall of the Postal Buddy. In B. Nardi (Ed.), *Context and consciousness: Activity theory and human-computer interaction* (pp. 335–373). Cambridge, MA: MIT Press.

Erickson, J. (1981). Communication assessment of the bilingual bicultural child. In J. Erickson & D. Omark (Eds.), *Communication assessment of the bilingual and bicultural child: Issues and guidelines* (pp. 1–24). Baltimore: University Park Press.

Faigley, L. (1985). Nonacademic writing: The social perspective. In L. Odell & D. Goswami (Eds.), *Writing in nonacademic settings* (pp. 231–248). New York: Guilford.

Faigley, L., & Hansen, K. (1985). Learning to write in the social sciences. *College Composition and Communication, 36,* 140–149.

Faris, R. (1967). *Chicago sociology 1920–1932.* San Francisco: Chandler.

Fleck, L. (1979). *Genesis and development of a scientific fact.* Chicago: University of Chicago Press.

Flower, L., & Hayes, J. (1981). A cognitive process theory of writing. *College Composition and Communication, 32,* 365–87.

Flower, L., & Hayes, J. (1984). Images, plans, and prose: The representation of meaning in writing. *Written Communication, 1,* 120–160.

Flower, L., Stein, V., Ackerman, J., Kantz, M., McCormick, K., & Peck, W. (1990). *Reading-to-write: Exploring a cognitive and social process.* New York: Oxford University Press.

Foucault, M. (1972). *The archaeology of knowledge and the discourse on language.* (A. Sheridan Smith, Trans.). New York: Pantheon.

Freedman, A., Adams, C., & Smart, G. (1994). Wearing suits to class: Simulating genres and simulations as genre. *Written Communication, 11,* 193–226.

Freedman, A., & Medway, P. (Eds.) (1994). *Genre and the new rhetoric.* London: Taylor & Francis.

Freedman, S. W. (1979). How characteristics of students' essays influence teachers' evaluations. *Journal of Educational Psychology, 71,* 328–338.

Freedman, S. W. (1984). The registers of student and professional expository writing: Influences on teachers' responses. In R. Beach & L. S. Bridwell (Eds.), *New directions in composition research* (pp. 362–380). New York: Guilford.

Freire, P. (1970). *Pedagogy of the oppressed.* (M. Ramos, Trans.). New York: Seabury.

Geertz, C. (1983). *Local knowledge: Further essays in interpretive anthropology.* New York: Basic Books.

Geisler, C. (1991). Toward a sociocognitive model of literacy: Constructing mental models in a philosophical conversation. In C. Bazerman & J. Paradis (Eds.), *Textual dynamics of the professions: Historical and contemporary studies of writing in professional communities.* (pp. 171–190). Madison: University of Wisconsin Press.

Geisler, C. (1994). *Academic literacy and the nature of expertise: Reading, writing, and knowing in academic philosophy.* Hillsdale, NJ: Lawrence Erlbaum Associates.

Gellert, C. (1993). The German model of research and advanced education. In B. Clark (Ed.), *The research foundations of graduate education* (pp. 5–44). Berkeley: University of California Press.

Gere, A. R. (1980). Written composition: Toward a theory of evaluation. *College English, 42,* 44–58.

Gibson, J. (1979). *The ecological approach to visual perception.* Boston: Houghton Mifflin.

Giddens, A. (1984). *The constitution of society: Outline of a theory of structuration.* Berkeley: University of California Press.

Gieryn, T. (1983). Boundary-work and the demarcation of science from non-science: Strains and interests in professional ideologies of scientists. *American Sociological Review, 48*, 781–795.

Gilbert, G.N., & Mulkay, M. (1984). *Opening Pandora's box: A sociological analysis of scientists' discourse.* Cambridge, England: Cambridge University Press.

Giles, H., Coupland, N., & Coupland, K. (1993). *Contexts of accommodation.* Cambridge, England: Cambridge University Press.

Goffman, E. (1981). *Forms of talk.* Philadelphia: University of Pennsylvania Press.

Goodwin, C., & Duranti, A. (1992). Rethinking context: An introduction. In A. Duranti & C. Goodwin (Eds.), *Rethinking context: Language as an interactive phenomenon* (pp. 1–42). Cambridge, England: Cambridge University Press.

Goody, J. (1986). *The logic of writing and the organization of society.* Cambridge, England: Cambridge University Press.

Grice, P. (1989). *Studies in the way of words.* Cambridge, MA: Harvard University Press.

Griffin, P., Belyaeva, A., Soldatova, G., & the Velikov-Hamburg Collective. (1993). Creating and reconstituting contexts for educational interactions, including a computer program. In E. Forman, N. Minick, & C. Stone (Eds.), *Contexts for learning: Sociocultural dynamics in children's development* (pp. 120–152). New York: Oxford University Press.

Gusfield, J. R. (1992). Listening for the silences: The rhetorics of the research field. In R.H. Brown (Ed.), *Writing the social text: Poetics and politics in social science discourse* (pp. 117–134). New York: Aldine de Gruyter.

Gutierrez, K, Rymes, B., & Larson, J. (1995). Script, counterscript, and underlife in the classroom: James Brown vs *Brown v. Board of Education. Harvard Educational Review, 65*, 445–471.

Hanks, W. (1996a). Exorcism and the description of participant roles. In M. Silverstein & G. Urban (Eds.), *Natural histories of discourse* (pp.160–200). Chicago: University of Chicago Press.

Hanks, W. (1996b). *Language and communicative practices.* Boulder, CO: Westview.

Harding, S. (1991). *Whose science? Whose knowledge? Thinking from women's lives.* Ithaca, NY: Cornell University Press.

Harris, J. (1989). The idea of community in the study of writing. *College Composition and Communication, 40*, 11–37.

Harris, W. H. (1977). Teacher response to student writing: A study of the response patterns of high school English teachers to determine the basis for teacher judgment of student writing. *Research in the Teaching of English, 11*, 176–185.

Heath, S. B. (1982). What no bedtime story means. *Language in Society, 11*, 49–76.

Heath, S. B. (1983). *Ways with words: Language, life, and work in communities and classrooms.* Cambridge, England: Cambridge University Press.

Hengst, J. (1995). *Cindy Magic.* Unpublished manuscript.

Hengst, J. (1996) *Collusion in family play.* Unpublished manuscript.

Heritage, J. (1984). *Garfinkel and ethnomethodology.* Cambridge, England: Polity Press.

Herrington, A. (1985). Writing in academic settings: A study of the contexts for writing in two chemical engineering courses. *Research in the Teaching of English, 19*, 331–359.

Herrington, A. (1988). Teaching, writing and learning: A naturalistic study of writing in an undergraduate literature course. In D. A. Jolliffe (Ed.), *Advances in writing research, volume 2: Writing in academic disciplines* (pp. 133–166). Norwood, NJ: Ablex.

Herrington, A. (1992). Composing one's self in a discipline: Students' and teachers' negotiations. In M. Secor & D. Charney (Eds.), *Constructing rhetorical education* (pp. 91–115). Carbondale: Southern Illinois University Press.

Holland, D., & Cole, M. (1995). Between discourse and schema. *Anthropology & Education Quarterly, 26*, 475–489.

Holland, D., & Reeves, J. (1994). Activity theory and the view from somewhere: Team perspectives on the intellectual work of programming. *Mind, Culture, and Activity, 1/2*, 8–24.

Horowitz, D. (1986a). Essay examination prompts and the teaching of academic writing. *English for Specific Purposes, 5*, 107–120.

Horowitz, D. (1986b). What professors actually require: Academic tasks for the ESL classroom. *TESOL Quarterly, 20*, 445–462.

Hoskin, K. (1993). Education and the genesis of disciplinarity: The unexpected reversal. In E. Messer-Davidow, D. Shumway, & D. Sylvan (Eds.), *Knowledges: Historical and critical studies in disciplinarity* (pp. 271–304). Charlottesville: University of Virginia Press.

Hoskin, K., & Macve, R. (1993). Accounting as discipline: The overlooked supplement. In E. Messer-Davidow, D. Shumway, & D. Sylvan (Eds.), *Knowledges: Historical and critical studies in disciplinarity* (pp. 25–53). Charlottesville: University of Virginia Press.

Howe, P. M. (1990). The problem of the problem question in English for academic legal purposes. *English for Specific Purposes, 9*, 215–236.

Hull, G., & Rose, M. (1989). Rethinking remediation: Toward a social-cognitive understanding of problematic reading and writing. *Written Communication, 6*, 139–154.

Hull, G., Rose, M., Fraser, K. L., & Castellano, O. (1991). Remediation as social construct: Perspectives from analysis of classroom discourse. *College Composition and Communication, 42*, 299–329.

Hutchins, E. (1995). *Cognition in the wild*. Cambridge, MA: MIT Press.

Hymes, D. (1971). Competence and performance in linguistic theory. In R. Huxley & E. Ingram (Eds.), *Language acquisition: Models and methods* (pp. 3–28). London: Academic Press.

Hymes, D. (1974). *Foundations in sociolinguistics: An ethnographic approach*. Philadelphia: University of Pennsylvania Press.

Ingram, D. (1985). Assessing proficiency: An overview on some aspects of testing. In K. Hytenstan & M. Piermann (Eds.), *Modelling and assessing second language acquisition* (pp. 215–276). Clevedon, England: Multilingual Matters.

Jacoby, S., & Gonzales, S. (1991). The constitution of expert-novice in scientific discourse. *Issues in Applied Linguistics, 2*, 148–181.

Jarmon, L., & Bogen, D. (1996, March). *Making sense with materials: 'Object-situations' as an emergent order of instruction*. Paper presented at the Annual Conference of the American Association of Applied Linguistics, Chicago.

Johns, A. M. (1981). Necessary English. *TESOL Quarterly, 15*, 51–57.

Johnstone, B. (Ed.). (1994). *Repetition in discourse*. Norwood, NJ: Ablex.

Jolliffe, D. A., & Brier, E. M. (1988). Studying writers' knowledge in academic disciplines. In D. A. Jolliffe (Ed.), *Advances in writing research volume 2: Writing in academic disciplines* (pp. 35–88). Norwood, NJ: Ablex.

Kamberelis, G. (1995). Genre as institutionally informed social practice. *Journal of Contemporary Legal Issues, 6*, 117–171.

Kamberelis, G., & Scott, K.D. (1992). Other people's voices: The coarticulation of texts and subjectivities. *Linguistics and Education, 4*, 359–403.

Kaplan, R. (1966). Cultural thought patterns in intercultural education. *Language Learning, 16*, 1–20.

Kendon, A. (1990). *Conducting interaction: Patterns of behavior in focused encounters*. Cambridge, England: Cambridge University Press.

Kinneavy, J. (1971). *A theory of discourse: The aims of discourse*. Englewood Cliffs, NJ: Prentice-Hall.

Kintsch, W., & Mannes, S. M. (1987). Generating scripts from memory. In E. van der Meer & J. Hoffman (Eds.), *Knowledge aided information processing* (pp. 61–80). North Holland: Elsevier Siemen.

Klein, J. (1990). *Interdisciplinarity: History, theory, and practice*. Detroit, MI: Wayne State University Press.

Knorr-Cetina, K. D. (1981). *The manufacture of knowledge*. Oxford, England: Pergamon.

Knorr-Cetina, K., & Cicourel, A. (1981). *Advances in social theory and methodology: Toward an integration of micro- and macro-sociologies*. Boston: Routledge & Kegan Paul.

Krashen, S. (1981). *Second language acquisition and second language learning*. Oxford: Pergamon Pres.

Landau, M. (1991). *Narratives of human evolution*. New Haven, CT: Yale University Press.

Larson, R. (1984). Classifying discourse: Limitations and alternatives. In R. Connors, L. Ede, & A. Lunsford (Eds.), *Essays on classical rhetoric and modern discourse* (pp. 203–214). Carbondale: Southern Illinois University Press.

Latour, B. (1987). *Science in action: How to follow scientists and engineers through society*. Cambridge, MA: Harvard University Press.

Latour, B. (1988). *The pasteurization of France*. (A. Sheridan & J. Law, Trans.). Cambridge, MA: Harvard University Press.

Latour, B. (1993). *We have never been modern*. Cambridge, MA: Harvard University Press.

Latour, B. (1996). *Aramis, or the love of technology*. (C. Porter, Trans.). Cambridge, MA: Harvard University Press.

Latour, B., & Woolgar, S. (1986). *Laboratory life: The social construction of scientific facts*. Princeton, NJ: Princeton University Press.

Lave, J., & Wenger, E. (1991). *Situated learning: Legitimate peripheral participation.* Cambridge, England: Cambridge University Press.

Law, J. (1987). Technology and heterogeneous engineering: The case of Portuguese expansion. In W. Bijker, T. Hughes, & T. J. Pinch (Eds.), *The social construction of technological systems: New directions in the sociology and history of technology* (pp. 11–134). Cambridge, MA: MIT Press.

Lazarsfeld, P. (1993). *On social research and its language* (R. Boudon, Ed.). Chicago: University of Chicago Press.

LeFevre, K. B. (1987). *Invention as a social act.* Carbondale: University of Illinois Press.

Leont'ev, A. N. (1978). *Activity, consciousness, and personality.* Englewood Cliffs, NJ: Prentice-Hall.

Leont'ev. A. N. (1981a). The problem of activity in psychology. In J. Wertsch (Ed.), *The concept of activity in Soviet psychology* (pp. 37–71). New York: M. E. Sharpe.

Leont'ev, A. N. (1981b). *Problems of the development of the mind.* Moscow: Progress.

Lessing, D. (1992). *African laughter: Four visits to Zimbabwe.* New York: Harper Collins.

Leventhal, R. (1986). The emergence of philological discourse in the German states, 1770–1810. *Isis, 77,* 243–260.

Lindstrom, L. (1992). Context contests: Debatable truth statements on Tanna (Vanuatu). In A. Duranti & C. Goodwin (Eds.), *Rethinking context: Language as an interactive phenomenon* (pp. 101–124). Cambridge, England: Cambridge University Press.

Linell, P. (1992). The embeddedness of decontextualization in the contexts of social practices. In A. Wold (Ed.), *The dialogical alternative: Towards a theory of language and mind* (pp. 253–272). Oslo, Norway: Scandinavian University Press.

Lunsford, A., & Ede, L. (1990). *Singular texts/plural authors: Perspectives on collaborative writing.* Carbondale: Southern Illinois University Press.

Luria, A. (1928). The problem of the cultural development of the child. *Journal of Genetic Psychology, 35,* 493–506.

Luria, A. (1932). *The nature of human conflicts, or emotion, conflict, and will: An objective study of disorganization and control of human behaviour* (W. H. Gantt, Trans. & Ed.). New York: Grove Press.

Luria, A. (1979). *The making of mind.* Cambridge, England: Cambridge University Press.

MacLaughlin, B. (1985). *Second langauge acquisition in childhood: Volume 2, school age children.* (2nd ed.). Hillsdale, NJ: Lawrence Erlbaum Associates.

Mari, I. (1989). The recovery of the generalized use of Catalan in Catalonia. *Catalonia: Culture, 15,* 22–23.

Mason, A. (1983). *Understanding academic lectures.* Englewood Cliffs, NJ: Prentice-Hall.

McCarthy, L. P. (1987). A stranger in strange lands: A college student writing across the curriculum. *Research in the Teaching of English, 21,* 233–265.

McClelland, C. (1980). *State, society, and university in Germany 1700–1914.* Cambridge, England: Cambridge University Press.

McNeil, L.M. (1986). *Contradictions of control: School structure and school knowledge.* New York: Routledge & Kegan Paul.

Mead, G. (1934). *Mind, self, and society.* (C. Morris, Ed.). Chicago: University of Chicago Press.

Mehan, H. (1979). *Learning lessons: Social organization in the classroom.* Cambridge, MA: Harvard University Press.

Messer-Davidow, E., Shumway, D., & Sylvan, D. (Eds.). (1993). *Knowledges: Historical and critical studies in disciplinarity.* Charlottesville: University of Virginia Press.

Michaels, S. (1987). Text and context: A new approach to the study of classroom writing. *Discourse Processes, 10,* 321–346

Miller, C. R. (1984). Genre as social action. *Quarterly Journal of Speech, 70,* 151–67.

Miller, C. R., & Selzer, J. (1985). Special topics of argument in engineering reports. In L. Odell & D. Goswami (Eds.), *Writing in nonacademic settings* (pp. 309–341). New York: Guilford.

Miller, D. (1991). *The handbook of research design and social measurement* (5th ed.). Newbury Park, CA: Sage.

Minick, N. (1993). Teacher's directives. In S. Chaiklin & J. Lave (Eds.), *Understanding Practice* (pp. 343–374). Cambridge, England: Cambridge University Press.

Minick, N., Stone, C. A., & Forman, E. (1993). Introduction: Integration of individual, social, and institutional processes in accounts of children's learning and development. In E. Forman, N. Minick,

& C. A. Stone (Eds.), *Contexts for learning: Sociocultural dynamics in children's development* (pp. 3–18). New York: Oxford University Press.

Moll, L. C., & Greenberg, J. B. (1990). Creating zones of possibilities: Combining social contexts for instruction. In L. Moll (Ed.), *Vygotsky and education: Instructional implications and applications of sociohistorical psychology* (pp. 319–348). Cambridge, England: Cambridge University Press.

Myers, G. (1989). The pragmatics of politeness in scientific articles. *Applied Linguistics, 10,* 1–35.

Myers, G. (1990). *Writing biology: Texts in the social construction of scientific knowledge.* Madison: University of Wisconsin Press.

Nelson, J. (1990). This was an easy assignment: Examining how students interpret academic writing tasks. *Research in the Teaching of English, 24,* 362–396.

Nelson, J., & Hayes, J. (1988). *How the writing context shapes college students' strategies for writing from sources* (Tech. Rep. No. 16). Pittsburgh, PA: Carnegie Mellon University, Center for the Study of Writing.

Newman, D., Griffin, P., & Cole, M. (1989). *The construction zone.* Cambridge, England: Cambridge University Press.

North, S. (1987). *The Nature of knowledge in composition: Portrait of an emerging field.* Portsmouth, NH: Boynton/Cook.

Nystrand, M. (1982). Rhetoric's "audience" and linguistics' "speech community:" Implications for understanding writing, reading, and text. In M. Nystrand (Ed.), *What writers know: The language, process, and structure of written discourse.* New York: Academic Press.

Nystrand, M. (1990). Sharing words: The effects of readers on developing writers. *Written Communication, 7,* 3–24.

Ochs, E. (1988). *Culture and language development: Language acquisition and language socialization in a Samoan village.* Cambridge, England: Cambridge University Press.

Ochs, E. (1990). Misunderstanding children. In N. Coupland, H. Giles, & J. Wieman (Eds.), *"Miscommunication" and problematic talk* (pp. 44–60). Newbury Park, CA: Sage.

Ochs, E., Jacoby, S., & Gonzales, P. (1994). Interpretive journeys: How scientists talk and travel through graphic space. *Configurations, 2,* 151–171.

Ochs, E., Smith, D., & Taylor, C. (1989). Dinner narratives as detective stories. *Cultural Dynamics, 2,* 238–257.

Ochs, E., Taylor, C., Rudolph, D., & Smith, R. (1992) Storytelling as a theory-building activity. *Discourse Processes, 15,* 37–72.

Odell, L., & Goswami, D. (Eds.). (1985). *Writing in nonacademic settings.* New York: Guilford.

Odell, L., Goswami, D., & Herrington, A. (1983). The discourse-based interview: A procedure for exploring the tacit knowledge of writers in non-academic settings. In P. Mosenthal, L. Tamor, & S. Walmsley (Eds.), *Research on writing* (pp. 221–236). New York: Longman.

Olson, D. (1977). From utterance to text: The bias of language in speech and writing. *Harvard Educational Review, 47,* 257–281.

Ong, W. (1982). *Orality and literacy: The technologizing of the word.* London: Methuen.

Onore, C. (1989). The student, the teacher, and the text: Negotiating meanings through response and revision. In C. Anson (Ed.), *Writing and response: Theory, practice, and research* (pp. 231–260). Urbana, IL: National Council of Teachers of English.

Ostler, S. E. (1980). A survey of academic needs for advanced ESL. *TESOL Quarterly, 14,* 489–502.

Packer, M. (1993). Away from internalization. In E. Forman, N. Minick, & C. A. Stone (Eds.), *Contexts for learning: Sociocultural dynamics in children's development* (pp. 254–265). New York: Oxford University Press.

Perelman, C. (1982). *The Realm of Rhetoric.* (William Kluback, Trans.) Notre Dame, IN: University of Notre Dame Press.

Phelps, L. (1990). Audience and authorship: The disappearing boundary. In G. Kirsch & D. Roen (Eds.), *A sense of audience in written communication* (pp. 153–174). Newbury Park: Sage.

Pickering, A. (1993). Anti-discipline or narratives of illusion. In E. Messer-Davidow, D. Shumway, & D. Sylvan (Eds.), *Knowledges: Historical and critical studies in disciplinarity* (pp. 103–122). Charlottesville: University of Virginia Press.

Pickering, A. (1995). *The mangle of practice: Time, agency, and science.* Chicago: University of Chicago Press.

Pinker, S. (1994). *The language instinct: How the mind creates language.* New York: Harper Perrenial.

Pratt, M.L. (1986). Fieldwork in common places. In J. Clifford & G.E. Marcus (Eds.), *Writing culture: The poetics and politics of ethongraphy*. (pp. 27–50). Berkeley: University of California Press.

Prior, P. (1991). Contextualizing writing and response in a graduate seminar. *Written Communication, 8*, 267–310.

Prior, P. (1994). Response, revision, disciplinarity: A microhistory of a dissertation prospectus in sociology. *Written Communication, 11*, 483–533.

Prior, P. (1997) Literate activity and disciplinarity: The heterogeneous (re)production of American Studies around a graduate seminar. *Mind, Culture, and Activity, 4*, 275–295.

Rafoth, B., & Rubin, D. (1984). The impact of content and mechanics on judgments of writing quality. *Written Communication, 1*, 446–459.

Reddy, M. (1979). The conduit metaphor: A case of frame conflict in our language about language. In A. Orotony (Ed.), *Metaphor and thought* (pp. 284–324). Cambridge, England: Cambridge University Press.

Reinu i Tresserras, M. (1989). The linguistic normalization of Catalan. *Catalonia: Culture, 15*, 20–21.

Richards, I. (1929). *Practical criticism*. New York: Harcourt Brace.

Ricouer, P. (1974). *The conflict of interpretations: Essays in hermeneutics*. (D. Ihde, Ed.). Evanston, IL: Northwestern University Press.

Rommetveit, R. (1985). Language acquisition as increasing linguistic structuring of experience and symbolic behavior control. In J. Wertsch (Ed.), *Culture, communication, and cognition: Vygotskyan perspectives* (pp. 183–204). Cambridge, England: Cambridge University Press.

Rommetveit, R. (1988). On literacy and the myth of literal meaning. In R. Saljo (Ed.), *The written world* (pp. 13–40). Heidelberg, Germany: Springer-Verlag.

Rommetveit, R. (1992). Outlines of a dialogically based social-cognitive approach to human cognition and communication. In A. Wold (Ed.), *The dialogical alternative: Towards a theory of language and mind* (pp. 19–44). Oslo, Norway: Scandinavian University Press

Rosch, E., & Lloyd, B. (Eds.). (1978). *Cognition and categorization: A historical view*. Hillsdale, NJ: Lawrence Erlbaum Associates.

Rose, M. (1983). Remedial writing courses: A critique and proposal. *College English, 45*, 109–128.

Rymer, J. (1988). Scientific composing processes: How eminent scientists write journal articles. In D. A. Jolliffe (Ed.), *Advances in writing research volume 2: Writing in academic disciplines* (pp. 211–250). Norwood, NJ: Ablex.

Sacks, H., Schegeloff, E., & Jefferson, G. (1974). A simplest systematics for the organization of turn taking for conversation. *Language, 50*, 696–735.

Santos, T. (1988). Professors' reactions to the academic writing of nonnative-speaking students. *TESOL Quarterly, 22*, 69–90.

Saussure, F. de (1959). *Course in general linguistics*. (C. Bally, A. Sechehaye, & A. Riedlinger, Eds.; W. Baskin, Trans.). New York: McGraw-Hill.

Schank, R. (1982). *Dynamic memory*. London: Cambridge University Press.

Schank, R., & Abelson, R. (1977). *Scripts, plans, goals, and understanding: An inquiry into human knowledge structures*. Hillsdale, NJ: Lawrence Erlbaum Associates.

Schutz, A., & Luckmann, T. (1973). *The structures of the life-world*. (R. Zaner & H. Engelhardt, Trans.). Evanston, IL: Northwestern University Press.

Scollon, R. (1995). Plagiarism and ideology: Identity in intercultural discourse. *Language in Society, 24*, 1–28.

Scribner, S. (1985). Vygotsky's uses of history. In J. Wertsch (Ed.), *Culture, communication, and cognition: Vygotskyan perspectives* (pp. 119–145). Cambridge, England: Cambridge University Press.

Scribner, S., & Cole, M. (1981). *The psychology of literacy*. Cambridge, MA: Harvard University Press.

Singer, C., Holmyard, E., & Hall, A. (1954). *A history of technology: Volume I, from early times to fall of ancient empires*. Oxford, England: Clarendon Press.

Singer, C., Holmyard, E., Hall, A., & Williams, T. (1957). *A history of technology: Volume III, from the renaissance to the industrial revolution*. Oxford, England: Clarendon Press.

Smagorinsky, P., & Coppock, J. (1994). Cultural tools and the classroom context: An exploration of an artistic response to literature. *Written Communication, 11*, 283–310.

Small, A., & Vincent, G. (1894). *An introduction to the study of society*. New York: American Book Co.

Sorenson, K. (1985). Modifying an ESP course syllabus and materials through a teacher-planned needs assessment. *MinneTESOL Journal, 5*, 53–74.

Spender, D. (1989). *The writing or the sex? Or why you don't have to read women's writing to know it's no good.* New York: Pergamon.

Sperling, M., & Freedman, S.W. (1987). A good girl writes like a good girl: Written response to student writing. *Written Communication, 4*, 343–369.

Spilka, R. (Ed.). (1993). *Writing in the workplace.* Carbondale: Southern Illinois University Press.

Spiro, R., Vispoel, W., Schmitz, J., Samarapungavan, A., & Boerger, A. (1987). Knowledge acquisition for application. In B. Britton & S. Glynn (Eds.), *Executive control processes in reading* (pp. 177–194). Hillsdale, NJ: Lawrence Erlbaum Associates.

Starr, S. L. (1991). Power, technologies, and the phenomenology of conventions: On being allergic to onions. In J. Law (Ed.), *A sociology of monsters: Essays on power, technology, and domination* (pp. 26–56). London: Routledge.

Sternglass, M.S. (1989). *The presences of thought: Introspective accounts of reading and writing.* Norwood, NJ: Ablex.

Sternglass, M.S., & Pugh, S.L. (1986). Retrospective accounts of language and learning processes. *Written Communication, 3*, 297–323.

Stone, C. A. (1993). What is missing in the metaphor of scaffolding. In E. Forman, N. Minick, & C. A. Stone (Eds.), *Contexts for learning: Sociocultural dynamics in children's development* (pp. 169–183). New York: Oxford University Press.

Swales, J.M. (1990). *Genre analysis: English in academic and research settings.* Cambridge, England: Cambridge University Press.

Swales, J., & Najjar, H. (1987). The writing of research article introductions. *Written Communication, 4*, 175–191.

Tannen, D. (1989). *Talking voices: Repetition, dialogue, and imagery in conversational discourse.* Cambridge: Cambridge University Press.

Tarone, E., Dwyer, S., Gillette, S., & Icke, E. (1981). On the use of the passive in two astrophysics journal papers. *The ESP Journal, 1*, 123–140.

Taylor, C. (1985). *Human agency and language. Vol. 1.* Cambridge, England: Cambridge University Press.

Taylor, C. (1989). *Sources of the self: The making of modern identity.* Cambridge, England: Cambridge University Press.

Taylor, T. (1992). *Mutual misunderstanding: Skepticism and the theorizing of language and interpretation.* Durham, NC: Duke University Press.

Toulmin, S. (1958). *The uses of argument.* Cambridge, England: Cambridge University Press.

Tracy, K. (1991). Introduction: Linking communicator goals with discourse. In K. Tracy (Ed.), *Understanding face-to-face interaction: Issues linking goals and discourse* (pp. 1–17). Hillsdale, NJ: Lawrence Erlbaum Associates.

Turner, S. & Turner, J. (1990). *The impossible science: An institutional analysis of American sociology.* Newbury Park, CA: Sage.

van Dijk, T.A., & Kintsch, W. (1983). *Strategies of discourse comprehension.* New York: Academic Press.

van Mannen, J., & Schein, E. (1979). Toward a theory of organizational socialization. In B. Straw (Ed.), *Research in organizational behavior.* Greenwood, CT: JAI Press.

Van Nostrand, A. D. (1997). *Fundable knowledge: The marketing of defense technology.* Mahwah, NJ: Lawrence Erlbaum Associates.

Voloshinov, V.N. (1973). *Marxism and the philosophy of language.* (L. Matejka & I.R. Titunik, Trans.). Cambridge, MA: Harvard University Press.

Vygotsky, L. (1929). The problem of the cultural development of the child, II. *Journal of genetic psychology, 36*, 414–434.

Vygotsky, L. (1978). *Mind in society: The development of higher psychological processes.* (M. Cole, V. John-Steiner, S. Scribner, & E. Souberman, Eds.). Cambridge, MA: Harvard University Press.

Vygotsky, L. (1987). *Thinking and speech.* (N. Minick, Ed. & Trans.). New York: Plenum.

Vygotsky, L. (1997). *Problems of the theory and history of psychology.* (R. van der Veer, Trans.). New York: Plenum.

Walvoord, B., & McCarthy, L. (1990). *Thinking and writing in college: A naturalistic study of students in four disciplines.* Urbana, IL: National Council of Teachers of English.

Wertsch. J. (1985). *Vygotsky and the social formation of mind.* Cambridge, MA: Harvard University Press.

Wertsch, J. (1990). The voice of rationality in a sociocultural approach to mind. In L. Moll (Ed.), *Vygotsky and education* (pp. 111–126). Cambridge, England: Cambridge University Press.

Wertsch, J. (1991). *Voices of the mind: A sociocultural approach to mediated action.* Cambridge, MA: Harvard University Press.

Wertsch, J. (1995). The need for action in sociocultural research. In J. Wertsch, P. del Rio, & A. Alvarez (Eds.), *Sociocultural studies of mind* (pp. 56–74). Cambridge, England: Cambridge University Press.

Wertsch, J., & Minick, N. (1990). Negotiating sense in the zone of proximal development. In M. Schwebel, C. Maher, & N. Fagley (Eds.), *Promoting cognitive growth over the life span.* (pp. 71–88). Hillsdale, NJ: Lawrence Erlbaum Associates.

Wertsch, J., Tulviste, P., & Hagstrom, F. (1993). A sociocultural approach to agency. In E. Forman, N. Minick, & C. Stone (Eds.), *Contexts for learning: Sociocultural dynamics in children's development* (pp. 336–356). Oxford, England: Oxford University Press.

Winsor, D. (1996). *Writing like an engineer: A rhetorical education.* Mahwah, NJ: Lawrence Erlbaum Associates.

Wittgenstein, L. (1958). *Philosophical investigations.* (G.E.M. Anscombe, Trans.). Oxford, England: Basil Blackwell.

Witte, S. (1985). Revision, composing theory, and research design. In S. Freedman (Ed.), *The acquisition of written language: Revision and response* (pp. 250–284). Norwood, NJ: Ablex.

Witte, S. (1992). Context, text, intertext: Toward a constructivist semiotic of writing. *Written Communication, 9,* 237–308.

Woolard, K. (1989). *Double talk: Bilingualism and the politics of ethnicity in Catalonia.* Stanford, CA: Stanford University Press.

Zinchenko, V. P. (1985). Vygotsky's ideas about units for the analysis of mind. In J. Wertsch (Ed.), *Culture, communication, and cognition: Vygotskyan perspectives* (pp. 94–118). Cambridge, England: Cambridge University Press.

Ziv, N. (1984). The effect of teacher comments on the writing of four college freshman. In R. Beach & L. Bridwell (Eds.), *New directions in composition research* (pp. 362–380). New York: Guilford.

Author Index

Subject Index